Contents

～ v ～

Acknowledgments

*Lately it occurs to me what a lo-o-o-n-ng,
strange trip it's been.*—The Grateful Dead,
"Truckin'"

Every poem, essay, or book is part of a writer's journey, incorporating elements of the writer's life. Confronted by an unfamiliar fact or idea, the writer may have to wrestle it, detour around, or adopt it. Sometimes, to mix metaphors, I have slipped my arms eagerly into a fresh concept later abandoned beside the trail for being too tight across the shoulders or failure to keep me dry in a rainstorm. I am indebted to many people for helping develop the notions I encountered while writing *Land Circle*, though I alone should be held responsible for the weird twist some of them have taken. Our word "travel" from the French *travailler*, originally meant "suffering," but all journeys offer treasures along with their hazards; among mine are extraordinary friends. I am especially grateful to the following:

> as always, to George, who continues to remind me when to say "no"; to stimulate me to work at what I love, and to remind me in unmistakable ways not to get "too poetic";
> to Margaret, who often helps me comprehend life over tea or the telephone wires, and who provides me with a shining example of strength;
> to Tom, Jerry, Bryan, Cathy, whose understanding, patience, and love help me hold on;
> to Lawrence, Master Hyperbole Detector, consultant on natural, and sometimes unnatural, events;

to Deb and the Technical Information Project, Inc., information brokers for the Great Plains;

to The Patron, whose gift of healing, manifested through the lively, tick-infested body of Frodo, set me straight at a crucial time;

to Gina and Liz of Vallecitos Retreat, and to Grete, Olga, and Jean, who shared it with me for the first time, as I completed an important revision of these essays;

and to all the friends, including those I know only through letters, sympathy cards, and telephone calls, who reminded me to believe in myself and the land when I lost George.

Thanks to Sally Antrobus, who performed her editorial work with the meticulousness one hopes for from an editor, charged with keeping readers from finding out how careless writers can be, and with tact and good humor that made our mutual struggle enjoyable. Michael Melius took precious time from his own book, *True*, to help me at a crucial time. And I'm grateful to Ernest Grafe for helping me choose and adopt my new computer. Can it be mere coincidence that the computer is a Falcon? Her name is Alice, meaning "unable to lie" in Greek.

Some readers may be familiar with my previous work, *Windbreak*, a journal of a year of ranch life published by Barn Owl Books in 1987, and *Going Over East*, published by Fulcrum the same year, or my two volumes of poetry, *Caught By One Wing* (San Francisco: Holcomb, 1984) and *Roadkill* (Peoria, Ill.: Spoon River Poetry Press, 1987). A few essays in the present volume were written before those books, and some of the poems and essays here were previously published there or in magazines as indicated below.

"Night in the Country," "Heat Wave on the Highway," "Red Glow in the Western Sky," excerpts from "What's Black and White and Odorous?," "O Holy Night on the Prairie," and "Ignoring the Wind Chill Factor" were all first published in "The Home Forum," *The Christian Science Monitor*, as was "Red Glow in the Western Sky," also syndicated by the *Los Angeles Times*. "Night in the Country" appeared in *A Home Forum Reader*, edited by

Frederic Hunter and published by *The Christian Science Monitor*, a longer version was published in *As Far As I Can See* (Lincoln, Nebr.: Windflower Press, 1989).

"Falcon Dreaming," "Vultures," and an excerpt from "Spring Weather" all appeared in *Northern Lights*. "Thunder Butte: High, Solemn and Holy," "To Build a House," and "Rendezvous!" were first published in *Black Hills Monthly Magazine*. An excerpt from "Rendezvous!" appeared in *High Country News*, where "Aurora Borealis and Bells" and an excerpt from "Why One Peaceful Woman Carries a Pistol" were also first published; an excerpt from the latter was reprinted by *Utne Reader*.

An excerpt from "Lettuce Bouquets for a Dry Country" was first published by *Iowa Woman*. "The Land Circle: Lessons" was first published in *North American Review*, and "Addicted to Work" has been accepted for publication by *NAR* at this writing. "The Part-Time Professional Stepmother" was first published by *Working Parents*.

"The Teenagers and the Spine-Porker" was accepted by *Snowy Egret* for Spring 1991. At this writing, "Setting Up a Headstone" has been accepted by *Nebraska Territory* for Summer 1991, "Rock Lover" has been accepted by *Whole Earth Review*, "Going to the Post Office" has been tentatively accepted by *High Country News*, and an excerpt from "Finding Buffalo Berries" has been accepted by *South Dakota Magazine*.

For poems reprinted in this volume, acknowledgment is made to the following periodicals: *North Dakota Quarterly; Elkhorn Review; Juxtapose*, a publication of the Vermillion Literary Project; *Prairie Winds* at Dakota Wesleyan University, Mitchell; *Northwoods Journal; Green Bowl Review*, Black Hills State College, Spearfish; *Passages North; Caprice; Nebraska Territory; Plainswoman; Swamp Root; Dakota Arts Quarterly; Latuca; High Country News; Midwest Quarterly; Haight Ashbury Literary Journal; Life* magazine; and the following anthologies: *The Decade Dance* (Weatherford, Okla.: Sandhills Press, 1991); *A Change in Weather: Midwest Women Poets* (Eau Claire, Wis.: Rhiannon Press, 1978); *A Windflower Home Almanac of Poetry* (Lincoln, Nebr.: Windflower Press, 1979); and *Men & Women: Together & Alone* (Iowa City: The Spirit That Moves Us Press, 1988).

Introduction:
Fighting for the Chicken Neck

Some readers got acquainted with the country I write about and with my family and neighbors in *Windbreak: A Woman Rancher on the Northern Plains* and *Going Over East: Reflections of a Woman Rancher*. The subtitles of both books made my situation and location abundantly clear. But all of us must look beyond immediate concerns, and this volume allows me to explore other aspects of being a woman and a rancher concerned for the future of the land and culture around me. It also seems appropriate, now that I am a widow in the middle of a normal lifespan, to look at the paths that led me here.

Women through the ages have tried to understand why certain plants grew where they did, have cultivated wild vegetation to feed their families and treat their illnesses, and have mourned the lives they could not save. Millions of women have gone into the darkness caused by the death of those we love, to struggle with pain as grief cut the flesh from our bones. The losses borne by these women, their pain, their bones, were and are mine. I dream my husband's death over and over; his death becomes that of every other human who has died. I enact the rituals of grief enacted by every other woman who has found a man she could live a century with, and watched him die young, watched helplessly through hours of frustrated rage and love. I walked into a cave filled with those who have faced death, and emerged with new lines in my face, more gray in my hair, and more understanding of what life means to all of us. Primitive knowledge and rituals as old as time tie me to women who have been dust for generations, and probably to those who will arrive when I have been dust for more generations still—if we don't destroy humanity first.

Most of us who ranch today realize that while we may operate in physical isolation on the arid plains, alone in our hardships, our solitude is only the appearance. In reality, the cash in our pockets and the cows in our pastures are connected by invisible umbilical cords to cows and businesses all over the world. The ranch that is the viewpoint from which these essays was written is located in the arid grasslands of western South Dakota, near the Black Hills, an area that was once buffalo range. In *Going Over East*, I wrote:

> Today public opinion has shifted again, and populous areas seem to regard the plains as an "empty quarter," fit only for the disposal of garbage, as if it were the country's back alley. Within the past five years, we've entertained proposals for the placement here of: uranium mines and mills, a national hazardous waste disposal site, a national radioactive waste disposal site, a processing and disposal site for sewage ash, several strip mining and heap leach processing operations, a superconducting supercollider, a site for incineration and/or landfilling of PCBs, a sulfide mine, and several sites for the building, testing and disposal of ammunition and other explosive devices. A bill to give a considerable amount of federal forest and grassland back to the Lakota (Sioux) Indians is being seriously debated in Congress. Low population, a crippled agricultural industry, a body of potential employees who used to be farmers, and a lack of factory industry apparently make the area a target for promoters of such plans. A number of hazardous substances have been spilled, and local and state agencies have demonstrated alarming inabilities and ignorance in cleanup.

The trend I saw then goes on. South Dakota Disposal Systems, which despite its name was established in Golden, Colorado, plans to dump up to a million tons of the nation's garbage in a landfill near Edgemont, South Dakota, every year; I chair an organization which is challenging the plan. The state may become a national hazardous waste disposal site. A few years ago a slick operator talked the town of Edgemont into importing 270,000 tons of sewage ash from Minnesota, convincing local citizens the precious metals extracted from the stuff would make them rich. The company defaulted, and the state ended up burying all the ash that hadn't already been blown around the landscape. One member of the state's Board of Minerals and Environment made promotion history, in an eccentric way, when she used some of the sewage ash as a pottery glaze. The advertising and sales potential of glazing pottery with sewage ash staggers the imagination. In an editorial, the *Rapid City Journal* said South Dakota risked being called "Trash Can for the Nation."

After a two-year moratorium on new mining, heap-leach mining is proceeding at a brisk pace in the Black Hills. Several companies plan to incinerate or landfill PCBs. Water has always been scarce, but in some areas the shortage is becoming critical. Gambling, which some citizens consider another variety of pollution, has been legalized in the Old West town of Deadwood, and citizens are now learning about gambling addictions; that's about all they can learn, because a number of businesses including two car dealerships, a funeral parlor, grocery stores, drugstores, and clothing stores have all disappeared to make way for gambling emporiums. Two New Jersey researchers have made headlines by asserting that the plains states will eventually be depopulated, and might as well be returned to wildlife and grass, a vast park they call the "Buffalo Commons." The West's economy has always been bolstered by military contracts, government aid to farmers, Native American tribes, and other special interest groups; much of its so-called "public land" is owned and managed by federal agencies, and it has a steadily declining population. Many western historians insist we are a victimized colony for the rest of the nation. Meanwhile, the states surrounding the plains have gained population, riches, and more votes in Congress. Already, metropolitan regions demand we give up energy resources protected by wilderness, and take the waste products that are too dangerous to store near cities. We are vulnerable to pressure from the government, a primary employer. The West's residents could gradually be forced out to make way for wildlife, waste, and energy production.

Still, South Dakota has some of the purest air left on the planet; we're 46th in toxic air emissions, dumping only 2.4 million pounds[1] into the air each year. Even though our teachers' salaries consistently rank between forty-third and forty-eighth in the nation, and we are about forty-third in the level of per capita funding for education, South Dakota students do well in national tests; they recently ranked third highest in the country on the Scholastic Aptitude Test, fifth among the twenty-eight states that administer the American College Testing program, and twelfth in high school graduations.[2] The former legislative research assistant who compiled those figures said the state excels in "the things money can't buy." Its schools, she notes, "are small and are centers of community life" where "old-fashioned values such as hard work, responsibility and self-discipline" still dominate. Fortunately, our teachers apparently don't consider money the most important thing in their lives; instead of going elsewhere for better pay, they stay here.

One winter I taught a class called "American West: Fact and Fiction" for a local business college. Because the text was a collection of writings from various epochs of western history, with no historical framework, I dug out an old textbook to refresh my memory of the unifying elements. My lectures were concise explanations of how the historical periods connected; my students heard them with open eyes and mouths, and pencils that never moved. Secretaries, they apparently thought, have no need for history.

But I was reminded of Frederick Jackson Turner's thesis that the first frontier of the West, the fighting-Indians-subduing-wild-animals part, ended about 1890. I find that date particularly significant since it was also the date of the Wounded Knee massacre, when inexperienced white soldiers managing the surrender of Big Foot's band of Oglala slaughtered men, women, and children on the frozen plains not far from my home. Public officials and citizens, white and red, still argue about whether the term "massacre" is appropriate, and Indian leaders call for the return of the Congressional Medals of Honor given to soldiers who manned the Hotchkiss guns and pursued and bayonetted fleeing women with babies. The act was inexcusable, but it was also a result of forces they could not control and did not understand. On those frozen plains the nomadic ways of the Indians, who lived lightly on the land, died; the "civilized" ways of the whites triumphed. The land has been in agony ever since.

Ranchers already grazed cattle everywhere, and for a few years they ruled the plains; their cowboys and cattle were nearly as nomadic as the tribes they replaced. Then came the "farmers' frontier," devoted to settlement and farming, as pioneers tore up the land to plant crops adapted to deep soil and more rain than the plains offered. Early cattlemen fought the trend, and sometimes fought the farmers who had been advised to plow the native grass to grow something "better." The farmers were convinced by the agricultural experts of their day that "rain follows the plow" and if they just plowed up enough land, they'd live in a fertile paradise. They won, just as the soldiers won, and with similar results. The industrialization and pollution of the old, pristine West is well underway; land and residents are both suffering.

It is my opinion that we now face the West's third frontier. This time the lines will not be so clearly drawn. Poised on both coasts are masses of people of varying national origins, religions, and political systems; many are hungry, jobless, and angry, and more interested in having a better life than in any theory of politics or ecology. Near them, but not in any sense with them, are more millions of folks who dream of an independent life raising goats or bees or maybe even children on their own little acreage in the country. Land prices are too high near their corporate jobs; they look to the center of the continent for their Shangri-La. When they have time and money for vacations, they wander through the Rockies, staring at the clean lines of the mountains, skiing the pure snow, dreaming of a paradise where they can find some of the same things the old fur traders and mountain men and Indians sought and found—and lost. Centered on the coasts also are dozens of corporations, devoted to profit-making, looking for new resources to exploit and efficient workers. Business and government officials in my state, and many others in this region, have cynically told these corporations that workers here are well-trained, docile, stay-at-homes, willing to work for low wages and trained to obey by heritage and habit.

Here, in the center of the continent, are miles of virtually empty land held by cattle and sheep ranchers, farmers, grizzly bears, coyotes, and other independent types who like space and freedom. The human ones are patriotic and they want to support their country, but they're uneasy about new developments: sprawling, polluted cities, snowmobiles, interstate highways, nuclear and toxic waste. They realize their mineral wealth is valuable, and could bring jobs, but they're not sure they want the increased population such development could bring. Residents know their mineral wealth is sometimes hidden under beautiful mountains, trout streams, pasture land, or just simply "purty country," and they're not convinced it's beneficial to send it all to the city, and get waste dumps and federal aid in return.

To further confuse the issue, land values are so low that the plains have attracted thousands of new residents, people who have no ancestral ties to the land, but are deeply interested in protecting the environment, so that they can continue to ski, hunt, fish, or otherwise recreate themselves. Many of these folks have jobs not tied to any traditional economy, like agriculture or mining, and might be willing to dismantle those industries in order to protect the scenery. Often they can't see that the natives consider the new industries as destructive as the old. Unused to our ways, newcomers sometimes assume everyone who doesn't agree with them is ignorant, stupid, or evil; they often fight to destroy us and our way of life, rather than working to become part of a community so that they can negotiate change.

The terms *monkey-wrenching* and *ecological sabotage* or simply *ecotage* have joined the native vocabulary, and some environmentalists advocate civil disobedience in a cause they consider at least equal to the American Revolution in seriousness. Companies have invested millions in resource development; some of those companies—no longer welcome anywhere else, and desperate for profit—fight ecotage with increasing sophistication and determination. Edward Abbey, who before his untimely death was acknowledged as the loudest and best-armed environmentalist, advocated shooting cattle that grazed on public lands. I don't know how many people have taken his advice, but I know ranchers who would retaliate.

The economy in much of the West is delicately poised; the collapse that has emptied some towns could affect many others. Westerners are learning about homelessness, bankruptcy, drugs. Suddenly there is no more wilderness where your name is no one's business. Some of the people who retreated here from more structured societies are stockpiling arms and paranoia.

The third frontier could become a battleground, with a money-rich, resource-poor urban society pitted against the center of the nation, traditionally the Breadbasket. The Great Plains now hold the best food-growing land left; the plains and mountains of the West are also home to the last grizzly, the last mine, the last well, the last free land, and possibly the last gun.

When my husband George was a child, he lived with his grandparents. They operated a cherry orchard in Michigan, and money was always a little tight. He told me once, only half in jest, that they tried to convince him the neck was the best part of the chicken. Because he was trusting, then, he believed them at first; while other members of the family grabbed for a leg or breast at Sunday dinner, he insisted on the neck. How he built such a large frame on a diet of chicken necks is a mystery.

Perhaps that early training had something to do with the way he could accept whatever came his way later in life; perhaps it had something to do with his patience, his calm, his determination to make the best of his life, and of his death. I see the same attitude in many South Dakotans; a large part of the rest of the world thinks our state is nearly worthless, an arid expanse fit for garbage and exploitation and nothing else. During late 1989, *Newsweek* called five states, including South Dakota, the "outback" of the nation, and the Rand-McNally company left the state out of its new edition of road maps entirely, explaining that no one would want to come here.

But we like it here; we like the country a little bit empty, so we have space for our thoughts. We're used to conserving our resources; most of us were brought up to "waste not, want not," and consider conservation no hardship. When we retire, we visit California, and take pictures of ourselves lying on the beach in Florida, but we come home, and when we speak of those places, there is a trace of pity in our voices. Too many people make us nervous and testy, and cause us to snarl at traffic jams and clean our rifles.

South Dakota and the Great Plains may look like a chicken neck to the rest of the world, but we've made it a filling meal, and we'll fight for it.

PART I

*Where Neighbor
Is a Verb*

Rancher: 1864–1928

I

A broad-shouldered man with a mustache and serious eyes,
he poses beside his wife seated on the porch.

Their first pregnancy bulges
despite the bulky dress and the hot day.

Her first three children are seated
steplike at his left,

with a collection of nieces and nephews behind him,
as if the entire pyramid of flesh

rested
upon his shoulders.

He kept a ledger, with the horses' names in front.
He was fond of his horses, especially

the Belgian stallion Pershing,
and anyway they were necessary to ranching, to

the business of raising food for the family
which never seemed to end. In the summer

his blue shirts turned sweat-dark in back,
and his battered hands played the lines and held in

Fannie and Queen and Betts and Beauty, Min, Alkili,
Katy, Martha and Ester and Mary and May and Dolly.

II

The bills were piled on the kitchen table
where in June 1928

after he shook down the grate and used fine pitch
splinters to start the fire, whistling "Red Wing,"

after the coffee had boiled and his first cup steamed
beside him, while his wife woke in the hall bedroom,

he put on his glasses, carefully curving the gold wires
around his sunburned ears, took up his pencil, sharpened it

with the knife he'd brought from Sweden (gift
of a brother whose name we will never know)

rubbed his left hand across the barked knuckles
and wrote:

Money paid out in 1928:			*Produce Sold in 1928:*		
June 7	*gas 5 g, groceries*	*2.35*	*June 14*	*one can cream 5 g*	*9.54*
9	*drygoods, underwear*	*4.85*	*14*	*3 doz. eggs*	*6.90*

There were a lot of groceries for eight
of his own and several visiting nieces and nephews when
their dad was out of work in the mine.

June 31	*cuff buttons, John*	*7.50*	*June 26*	*45 doz. eggs*	*11.25*
31	*shoes, Anna*	*7.50*	*29*	*one can cream*	*8.50*

Anna later went to school and became a teacher; she added
in careful purple ink under his heading for July 1928:

July 14	*Reeves Merc., hat*	*8.50*	*July 2*	*45 doz. eggs*	*11.25*
14	*Mort Crockett's*	*5.45*	*12*	*12 doz. eggs*	*4.50*

Crockett's was a men's wear store; one of the boys
needed shoes or a shirt for the funeral.

And then:

July 14	*hospital*	*92.40*	*July 11*	*45 doz. eggs*	*12.15*
14	*dress*	*9.75*	*11*	*cream, 8 g*	*12.65*
18	*Behrens Funeral*				
	Parlor	*226.60*	*16*	*5 g cream*	*8.56*

because he'd been cut down (like the only tree in the yard;
it grew into the well and he asked the boys to cut it while
he went to town). Harold, older than Anna and my father, John,
probably wrote the check to the man who buried their father,

gnarled hands still. He'd made them dig a hole for May
the week before: "Don't want her to just lay out there
for the coyotes, boys. She done a lot of work for us."
Perhaps John got to wear his new cuff buttons (he said, "I got
them for graduation, to impress some girl") to the funeral.
The selling of eggs and cream by their mother, Ida, went on.

And then:

July 18	*Dr. Minty*	*200.*	*July 18*	*27 doz. eggs*	*3.24*

Although all he really did, my father said years later, was
to operate and then operate again and kill him because
"Dad was too weak to take another cutting."

And then Anna wrote:

July 23	*5 g gas*	*1.05*	*July 23*	*15 doz. eggs*	*4.50*
28	*groceries*	*1.05*	*23*	*5 g cream*	*7.70*
28	*Sears, stockings*	*1.05*	*28*	*5 g cream*	*7.01*
30	*Hermosa telephone*	*5.35*			
31	*hospital, balance*	*6.00*			
31	*Dodge (car cleaned)*	*7.75*			

Birth

The barn is dark, except for sunlight that slants through the vertical bars of the gate. Outside, meadowlarks and redwing blackbirds sing in branches bare of everything but snow. The lariat is snug around a cow's neck, wrapped twice around a post. The rope isn't tied, because the cow might fall and strangle before I could untie or cut it. Instead I'm holding the end, braced in case she throws her head, but ready to turn her loose if she stops breathing. My father is behind the cow, arm thrust deep inside her. Her eyes are glazed; she's calm from exhaustion. She started trying to have this calf sometime during the night. This morning she's given up.

When a cow is having a calf normally, we see front feet emerge, then a tongue and the calf's nose before the water breaks. This time we saw nothing. But the cow's exhaustion, her straining sides and labored breathing and the ragged ground around her feet told us she had been working hard. If my father can get two front feet pointed at the exit, we may be able to pull the calf. If it's dead, we may still save the cow. Even two hind feet would give us something to fasten the calf puller to. If we can't get hold of any part of the calf's body solid enough to pull on, we'll call the veterinarian to do a Caesarian.

Bent over and breathing hard, my father pushes his hand down the birth channel, wet silk over bone, into the universe beyond, the world before birth. He can trace the shape of the calf's body, feel damp hair waiting to be licked clean by the rough mother tongue. He finds one foot. I hand him the smooth chains I took from the nail where they hang all year; they are still warm from being dipped in the bucket of hot water, so the frost of the night won't burn tender flesh, cow's or man's. My father puts his arm inside the other world again, loops chain over the calf's ankle, and reaches in, searching for the other leg.

My father has gone back, retreated into that unknown silence before birth, our shadowy history—narrow and dark as a grave, warm and wet as an ancient sea. From warm oblivion we're squeezed into life; the door to death is narrow and uninviting. Egyptians pulled the brain out through the nostrils. The calf is dead. Suddenly my father is reaching ahead, into the other wonder—the time that baffles us all our lives. He searches, grasps, tries to pull the calf through to life. He's spent his days doing this work. It is only in my mind that he's close to death, because he's eighty-three and I'm forty-seven. He's begun to remark on the deaths of men and women younger than he, but yesterday he pitched two loads of hay off the wagon to his cows.

"Which vet shall we call?" He can't get the other leg; he knows the cow will die if we don't get help. Time is over for the calf, ended before it began. My father comes back to the living, and goes to call the vet, who takes the calf out of the cow's side, explaining uterine torsion to us. For two days, because we are busy with the living, the dead calf lies shrinking in the lee of the barn, sticky with birth fluids that seem to shrivel his skin. His eyes never opened; his tongue was never sucked back behind his teeth. His mother never bawls for him; perhaps the struggle was too much, perhaps she knew he was dead. Later we skin the calf, tie the skin loosely over a calf whose mother isn't feeding him enough. After several days, the cow whose calf died in her womb accepts the new calf as hers, licks the hide of her dead baby clean. She has forgotten; only the great scar in her side reminds us of my father's reaching into life, reaching into death.

Late March Blizzard

Ankle deep in mud that wants
to suck us down before our time,
we plod through the corral, pitch
hay, fight to get birthing cows
into the barn, drag dead calves
outside. Snow falls so thick
it's hard to recognize familiar cows,
each other's blurred faces.
We are tired and cranky, mud and blood
up to our knees. Our minds squeeze down to
a fire, coffee, dry clothes.

                              A cry
raises our eyes. Two blue herons
circle.   Like a Chinese painting.
Their angled breasts prow
against the snow, lifting with each beat
of the mighty wings.

We sail into the falling snow,
twin graceful shapes who know mud—and more.
Our fragile feet are not stuck in clay;
we pose in a cottonwood,
then lift,
            disappear into time.

Spring Weather

On the telephone, my nearest neighbor—the one who lives across the road, whom I used to join for tea more often—asks quietly, "How are you handling all this?"

She means how am I handling my husband being hospitalized four hundred miles away for two months, while my father and I struggle through spring blizzards and calving. She means how am I handling the news that doctors removed most of a malignant tumor from near George's spine, and that he has permanently lost the use of one arm. What will we do if the tumor paralyzes him completely? She means how will I handle the biopsy scheduled for a part of my own aging body next week. Because she knows me very well, she means how do I handle this without the comfort that she finds in prayer.

My mind is blank. We've talked of her daughter's acceptance as an exchange student to Austria, of her new method for mulching trees, of the Bradley bill proposing return of the Black Hills to the Lakota, and the racism reappearing in our community, of where she should take her visitors from Germany later this month. For a few moments I thought of her joys, not my problems.

I hear myself say, "I saw a pair of curlews courting yesterday. They'll be nesting soon, and next spring they'll nest again, and the grass will get green, and the sego lilies will bloom. I know I can count on those things."

I don't know what else to say, but she seems to know what I mean.

At midnight, I unfold myself from the blankets and pillows on the couch, pull on mud-caked overshoes, coveralls, jacket, and stocking cap, and start down the hill from our house to the corral. Rain is pouring down, the first moisture the skies have given us for months.

Winter was so dry that we watched for prairie fires when the trains passed, and spring has brought only dust storms when the neighbors plow, and more prairie fires. Tonight, with the thermometer at thirty-five degrees, my breath disappears into clouds that barely clear the tops of fenceposts, and the steady drizzle sounds like ice crystals pattering into the tall grass. Puddles have formed on the drought-caked earth, and rivulets of mud run down the road. The night seems to wrap around my tiny flashlight.

When I open the gate, and my footsteps stop reverberating across the prairie, I realize how still the night is. The usual night chorus of birds and coyotes is in shelter. Five two-year-old heifers lie on a mound of gravel near a windbreak fence in the corral, waiting to calve. My greeting makes them stretch, sigh, and stand up so I can peer at the calving orifices to decide if I have to come down in two hours.

A new calf lies tucked against one heifer's side, almost sheltered from the cold rain. I coax the other heifers into the next corral where a rack of hay waits. We've been trying this method of timing their calves for daylight hours, and it seems to work; apparently cows can only do one thing at a time, and if they're eating, they don't calve.

I open the barn door and try to drive the pair inside. The cow balks, not liking the darkness, the smells. I drive her around the corral four more times, shouting. Finally she turns so sharply from the door that she knocks the flashlight from my hand; her shoulder knocks me backward into the mud. Sitting still in the dark, watching the flashlight's glow sinking, I remember my father's saying, "It helps to be smarter than the cow." I wallow to my feet, grab the calf by a hind leg, and drag him into the barn; he bawls frantically and his mother trots after him, murmuring and nuzzling. I stumble around them, shut the barn door, and trudge back up the hill, knowing I've probably saved the calf's life; lying in mud with cold rain falling on his hide would have killed him.

With the flashlight off, I'm suddenly aware of how much light glows through the clouds; somewhere up there is a full moon. By its luminescence I see grass sparkling with rain, stones gleaming like stars, fenceposts turned to shining warriors in chain mail, barbed wire glittering like a necklace of diamonds. I no longer feel the mud seeping through the hole in my boot, or the rain running down my back. I remember many years when we have worried through a dry winter, only to have the rains begin at the most inconvenient time: when we're calving. Each year, I grow depressed in December when the weather is warm and dry, and each year I discover my spirits lifting when my feet are stuck in the mud at calving time. I cannot know what will happen to George, but I know I can make it up this hill in the dark, hang my clothes up to dry, go to sleep so I can get up at dawn to check the heifers again. I can mail another cheery card to George, tell him again that I love him, and will love him in next spring's mud as well.

Carolyn, Miranda, and Me

—for Carolyn

Carolyn comes from the city in March,
bringing a transfusion of bagels and lox,
espresso for breakfast;
helps load bales and feed my cows
instead of feeding her children,
worrying about teaching, and her husband's business.
Her questions remind me why I'm here.
We talk poetry, politics, women's rights,
while we tend cows and sneeze hay dust.
Her teenage son wants to help humanity.
We discuss that, sitting on upturned buckets
in the barn at midnight, waiting for a cow
Carolyn calls Miranda to have her first calf.

Under a pile of planks,
a skunk waits
for us to discover him,
or leave so he can hunt.
Carolyn's son is acting in commercials,
making more money than either of us;
we discuss that too, watching the cow's sides heave
as she pushes the calf out.

The skunk washes his whiskers with clawed paws.
I reach inside the cow,

realize the calf is too big.
We dip chrome chains in warm water,
hang them on the gate, rope the cow.
I tie her with a bowline knot
so she won't choke.
She's pushed for three hours;
head hanging, feet braced,
she's too exhausted to kick me
when I loop chains
over the hind feet of the calf inside her.
The bottoms of his hoofs point up; he's coming backward.
If we pull him fast enough, he won't smother.
I crank until I'm gasping;
Carolyn finishes the job. The cow bawls
and staggers as the hips jerk free,
then the shoulders.
With a waterfall of blood and fluids,
the calf's head hits the floor, bounces.
Carolyn drops the calf-puller—on my toe—
leaps to clear his throat, shoving his tongue
back inside his swollen mouth,
shouts "Breathe, dammit!"
I clear his nostrils. She lowers his head
to drain fluid out of his lungs,
says, "This is just what I did
with Joshua when he got pneumonia."
She dries the calf with a sack;
I bully Miranda to stand.
We watch as she licks her son,
murmuring acceptance.

Wiping my hands, I see the skunk.
He backs away.
We name the calf Jesse Jackson.
Walking home uphill, we talk about stars,
birth, children going their own ways.

The skunk, brave again, marches
toward the compost pile.
Miranda begins eating afterbirth.
Carolyn has hot cocoa;
I put a shot of whiskey in mine,
wonder if I should have had a child.

What's Black and White
and Odorous?

Skunks have been on my mind this spring as my father and I
fed baled hay to our cows. First we noticed a large hole in the side
of the stack—gnawed out of the square regularity of the bales. I
stuck the pitchfork handle into it, and nearly lost it, so the hole was
longer than five feet.

During the days that followed, we got closer to breaking open
the mysterious cavity. One day the pitchfork disclosed the skunks'
restroom, a separate chamber well inside the original contours of the
stack. I was impressed by the neatness and organization this implied,
and the discovery sent me to several books on the habits of mammals
to brush up on my skunk lore. I discovered that only the striped
skunk, the variety we normally see here, makes such latrines. Other
varieties may leave scat, the technical name for manure, in the trails
made by humans and other animals. I assume they choose to
defecate there for the same reason people in the woods like a log with
a good view; in a vulnerable position, they're harder to surprise, and
are able to meditate in comfort. If you're a close inspector of scat,
as I am, you'll often note insects in that left by a skunk; they
frequently dig out hibernating insects.

The United States and Canada are home to five species of
skunks in three genera: spotted, hog-nosed, and striped and hooded
skunks. All of the species may dig a burrow with clawed feet
especially evolved for the job, but usually move into one already dug

by other animals. They also nest in the walls and basements of houses and other structures where they may not be particularly welcome. Culverts under roads often provide a cozy dwelling, particularly in areas where running water is unusual enough to allow them to raise their babies in dry comfort. In colder regions, skunks may actually sleep through cold snaps, becoming torpid as their temperature and heartrate drop.

The scent I was following into the haystack seemed to grow stronger every day, though I was sure our activity must have driven the resident away. As I pitched each load of hay off the rack, I had to hold my breath not only to keep from breathing dust, but to keep from inhaling the odor that seemed to have permeated the hay itself. It even hung around the area where we fed, although it didn't seem to bother the cows to whom the hay was fed.

Striped skunks defend themselves with two musk glands located at the base of their tails. With this equipment, they can spray facing a tormentor, tail raised, with hind feet firmly on the ground. In that position, a skunk squeezes the powerful muscles around its glands, depositing musk onto its tail hairs, then flicks its tail forward, dispersing the droplets in a fine mist. The alternative is to turn and raise its tail for a direct shot from the glands through its handy spray nozzle, aimed at the assailant. Several quick contractions will spray fifteen feet. Even with their smelly armament, skunks are vulnerable to people with weapons. But I've always admired their nerve.

A mother skunk denned up under a tool shed not twenty feet from the house one winter, and when her babies were big enough, would parade all four of them daily from the tool shed to the compost pile a hundred yards away. The dog, three barn cats, my parents, my husband, and I would sometimes stand in a solemn row watching this performance. Mother skunk didn't deign to look at us, unless the dog happened to growl or one of the cats strolled too close. Then she would merely glance our way, perhaps flick her tail suggestively, and continue on her route. I don't know how she kept from laughing at us.

My friend Cynthia once told me of seeing a mother skunk walking a narrow ridge along a country road, followed by five babies.

The parade proceeded peaceably until the last tiny skunk lost its footing and tumbled down the incline to the road. Mother turned as if to admonish the rest to stay where they were, scrambled down the slope, caught the nape of the fallen baby's neck in her teeth, hauled it back to the top, and deposited it at the end of the line. She resumed her place, and the solemn procession went on—until the rear baby fell again. Again she retrieved it and the little parade went on. Again it fell. The third time she cuffed it soundly on the head twice before returning to the head of the line. Until they were out of sight, the little skunk didn't fall again— tribute to discipline in the animal world.

Skunks visit my compost pile; since it's supposed to be decomposing, I assume it won't be damaged by going through a skunk first. Sometimes I "accidentally" leave tasty morsels some distance from the house to minimize the chances that the dog will encounter the skunk, to our mutual discomfort. One night when I was out on the deck enjoying the stars, I heard a rustling directly below me, shone the flashlight down there—and startled a baby skunk who was busily digging next to the foundation of the house. We stared at each other for a minute, while I considered how the odor would rise if I shot the intruder, then both retired from the scene.

One day, as I waited for my father to load the hayrack, I found a collection of deer bones nestled in the hay about twenty feet from the stack. I assume the skunks found a dead deer in the vicinity, and slowly hauled the remains back closer to their den for snacking. I separated a couple of shoulder bones, several slender leg bones, part of a jaw, and hooves, all splintered and gnawed. Skunks can be beneficial because they are omnivores; they'll eat almost anything. Their diet may include insects, carrion, rodents, small rabbits, frogs, crayfish, lizards, and fruit. Some types eat insects and grubs.

But they can also cause trouble if they deviate from their normal habits. Often they displease us when they tear open sack after sack of expensive cattle feed, eat a little, and scatter and defecate on the rest. We constantly struggle to plug skunk-sized holes in our old barn, but we aren't always successful. One winter day I saw an especially fat skunk waddle out of the barn and pursued it across the garden. I thought if I followed far enough I might make it move away. That skunk would let me get within ten feet, then turn, face me squarely, and stomp its front paws repeatedly on the ground, then turn again, wave its tail, look over a shoulder, and proceed. I was so entertained by this procedure that I followed for a couple of miles. I liked that air of confidence. I've seldom seen a skunk scurry, or slink, or in any way seem ashamed. Their lifestyle is relaxed; they walk sedately and erratically, wandering toward whatever interests them, behaving as if their dress-for-success immaculate white and black gives them confidence—when it's really their cologne.

I have shot skunks, because sometimes they stubbornly leave me no choice. For example, we habitually feed our barn cats in an outbuilding in the winter, to encourage them to take up residence and catch mice in their off hours. One fall, when mice should have been abundant, the cats seemed always hungry, and we discovered that as soon as they began to eat, a large skunk emerged from the wall and drove them off, then ate their food.

George and I discussed the situation, and decided to test the theory that shooting a skunk in the spine will keep him from spraying. After the skunk dove headfirst into the cat food, George placed a shot directly behind the skull, but it was no use. As George leapt from the open door, he was enveloped in skunk mist which he later swore was green. I held my nose as he stripped off his clothes outside the back door. We fed the cats outside that night. The next day I entered the building to see if the smell had dissipated enough for the corpse to be removed. As I bent to scoop it up, the corpse moved—and a second skunk raised its head; it had been eating beside its dead den mate. I shot that one, and George held his nose while I stripped. It was a long time before we entered that building without holding our breath.

When we loaded the last batch of bales from the haystack, I was pitching the hay as usual, musing on the way my coveralls had begun to retain the odor, when my fork struck a hollow and I fell forward. Gasping, I lifted aside the last shreds of hay. A few wisps of black and white fur clung to the den's rounded contours. Nearly buried in hay on one side was the crumpled skin and bones of a skunk. Perhaps the weight of snow shifted a bale and crushed it, but skunks are equipped to dig free of such mishaps. Perhaps it died of old age. Anyway, it was dead; holding my breath, I pitched the carcass out onto the prairie and bade it goodbye, knowing the breed survived and thrived.

Chant for the Rain

Sometimes a mild winter
is followed by a hot dry spring
and there is no rain.
Temperatures hit the nineties in April,
drying the new leaves,
and there is no rain.

Temperatures reach a hundred in June
and the ground cracks deep,
and there is no rain.
Day after day blue hot sky hangs;
the thermometer says one hundred ten
and there is no rain.
The alfalfa sprouts slowly, pauses,
withers underfoot, crackling;
dust balloons behind the truck for miles,
and there is no rain.

Haying equipment stands,
the leaves hang,
and there is no rain.
The train whistle explodes in the dry land
and the ranchers, stiff with heat,
get up from the dinner table or stop fencing,
leave off grimly cleaning the barn,
go outside to watch the train pass,
and there is no rain.

They watch for the smoke that hangs,
rises, moves away from the tracks
faster than the train.
And there is no rain.

"I'm dry clear to the bone,"
ranchers say.
"Dry clear to the bone."

Finding Buffalo Berries

Nature is not sentimental; some of her ways are harsh, even while they're fair. In fairness, she compensates in mysterious and surprising ways; if you see her exclusively as an innocent, dewy-eyed maiden gamboling through meadow flowers, or a vindictive slut hurling mountains and vomiting floods, you will miss the subtleties of her character.

During the hottest, driest summer in years, temperatures hung in the neighborhood of one hundred and ten degrees as I mowed and raked hay and George stacked. Dust rolled up behind the tractors, rose above us like a threat, settled down on our faces, slid down our necks. It stung as we moved our eyes, grinding deep into the sockets; it itched in our armpits, burned our cheeks. At midafternoon a coyote began following my mower, catching mice when their protective cover was slashed away. Occasionally he'd trot purposefully to the overflowing well for a drink, then resume following me. George wet his black silk neckscarf, draped it over his head, and held it in place with his hat; droplets of water mingled with the dust and made black streaks on his forehead and cheeks.

On the gray-brown hills, cattle stood with their heads down, or plodded toward the water holes with dust puffing up beneath their feet. Grouse crouched under alfalfa plants panting; meadow-larks stood with wings outspread in the thin shade of fenceposts.

Grass crackled underfoot, breaking off to lie burning on the ground. Buzzards circled continually overhead, eyeing all of us.

Every other day we took a break from haying to drive to our summer pasture over east through air that burned as it went into our lungs and left grit in our mouths. On one trip, we decided to look at the buffalo berry bushes that grow in a limestone crevice beside the trail. Sometimes rain water collects in pools in the rock and stays; like soup stock, it grows thicker and more vibrant with life all summer. We didn't expect to find water, but thought the time spent looking might take our minds off the heat.

The spot can't really be called a canyon; it's a tiny slit in the prairie floor, lined with the gray limestone that sometimes outcrops, but mostly underlies much of this region. We curse the limestone when we dig a posthole, but gently, because it's our secret ally. That layer of limestone often holds pockets of water creating surface springs, or—if we drill in the right spot—wells we can use cautiously for a few cattle; the technical name for these little miracles is "perched aquifer." Where the limestone outcrops, it's as ugly as a city's ruins; it most resembles old concrete, gray and pocked with water-washed holes. Patches of pale green or black lichen crawl across its face, and some surfaces look rusty.

At the edges of plateaus, wind and water erosion often cut into the limestone to create small canyons, little habitats less arid than the surrounding plains, biological marvels: the Hanging Gardens of Dakota. Several kinds of bushes and trees, besides buffalo berry, favor this habitat: plum, currant, chokecherry, and sumac flourish under a few stunted cedar. All of them collect tumbleweeds, until they build an impenetrable tangle of natural refuse which rustles as we approach, as porcupines burrow more deeply into the underbrush. Perhaps the porkies live here because their predators cannot dig them out from under the limestone. When I've told experienced porcupine hunters about this population, they raise their eyebrows in skepticism, since most believe the rodents need considerably more impressive stands of trees than a limestone slit can support.

As we walked toward the spot, we began to see rust-colored clusters at the top of the head-high bushes: berries! Technically, the buffalo berry is *Shepherdia argentia,* a perennial member of the oleaster family, which includes the Eurasian tree called Russian olive. The shrub is seldom more than six feet tall, though one source says it can grow to twenty-five feet. I've never seen any that tall, even on the north slopes they favor, but perhaps with more water they would do better. The leaves are modestly silver on one side, gray and scaly on the other, and the dull brownish flowers appear in May and June. I have often thought the buffalo berry was designed with greedy people in mind. You know the ones: they associate size and glitter with quality. It's not love that counts with them; they look at the size of the diamond. They don't care how a car runs; their eyes shine when they see spoke wheels, shiny red paint, a large price tag. These folks won't notice the boring buffalo berry bush, even when it's covered with berries that range from golden to a deep, brownish red.

Some of the branches were bent nearly double with berries. Since George's son Michael had never tasted buffalo berries, we gave him an example of our postgraduate training in trust: we assured him they made the most wonderful jelly ever to cross a tongue. He learned early, thanks to us, to listen carefully; his trained instincts told him there was something wrong with that statement. But he couldn't quite detect what it was. Stalling for time, he asked us to compare the flavor to something—Pepsi? Root beer? We said the flavor could not be compared with that of any cheap commercial product, but was incomparably wild and unique. Early pioneers, I lectured, crushed the fruit in water to make a refreshing drink; privately, I reflected on how desperately thirsty and worn out those people must have been. Indians dried the berries, adding them to pemmican—dried, pulverized buffalo meat, a staple travel food. Buffalo hunters made buffalo berry sauce for fresh steaks, and once I made sauce from the berries I found in the crops of several grouse I had shot.

Michael stared at each of us in turn, but we have long practice in remaining straight-faced. At last he reached out, plucked a generous handful of berries from a basket of thorns, and thrust them all into his mouth. I've found one can almost always count on greed when setting traps like this, especially when dealing with teenagers; greed and haste.

Fortunately, we also trained Mike to have goo
had chewed the berries only twice before he was spitting
trying to peel away the top layer of his tongue, and mumbling abou
betrayal. We certainly didn't deceive him; the flavor is incomparable.
Upon reflection, I could say it most closely resembles alum, a
cooking ingredient probably no longer to be found in most kitchen
cupboards since most folks don't make pickles. Trust me; it's not a
flavor you'll relish, but it's memorable. One quarter-teaspoon of
alum, or a handful of buffalo berries, makes your mouth feel as if you
are eating Death Valley. The secret of buffalo berries is this: it's
impossible to eat them from the bush, because they pucker the
mouth the way a slug shrivels when salted. They are the ideal harvest
berry, because you get what you pick; you are not tempted to
consume the crop before you get home.

Their hidden weapons make buffalo berries the elite among
wild fruit. The thorns can be up to six inches long, all scientifically
placed so that you cannot pick a single berry without puncturing
naked hands. Even leather gloves don't save you from injury. Some
experts say buffalo berry pickers should wait until the first frost
loosens the berries, then spread a white sheet on the ground under
the bushes, and shake the branches vigorously to dislodge the fruit.
When I've tried that method, I've returned to the bushes after the
first frost to find them bare. The ground under them was decorated
with a few shriveled berries and millions of grouse footprints.
Occasionally, I swear I have heard miniature belches deep in the
underbrush, and the distant thunder of the flock waddling away,
stuffed to the ear slits. That's the time to shoot a grouse, if you can
see the little masters of camouflage. Then gently slit the crop, rinse
the berries inside, and stuff them in the bird's belly; roast it for an
hour, and enjoy the succulent flesh with buffalo berry sauce.

The only really effective way to pick buffalo berries is to put
on elbow-length leather gloves, a long-sleeved denim jacket over a
long-sleeved shirt, and tuck the bottoms of your pants firmly into
your boots to keep some of the ticks from crawling up your legs.
Then grit your teeth, because the worst is yet to come. The berries
are firmly stuck to the branches, so you have to jerk them off. On the

other hand, they hang in clusters; each determined jerk should give you about ten berries. Then all you have to do is get them into the bucket without dropping the whole bunch.

On this hot day, we picked two thirty-pound buckets in about a half-hour; we paused once to staunch the blood pouring from a scratch on Mike's arm. We left a large number of berries for the grouse: all those hidden in the tumbleweeds where we didn't want to reach for fear of rattlesnakes, all the berries higher than George could reach, and a good number in between. Each of us paid a blood price.

But here the compensation sets in. Unlike plums, buffalo berries don't have to be laboriously separated from their seeds, or peeled, or prepared in any time-consuming way. I simply fill the bucket with water, and float the leaves and debris, scooping them off the surface, a cooling job. I don't bother to get it all, because I strain the juice later. Then I drain off the excess water and dump the berries into a large cooking pot with a little water. Those who prefer the security of a recipe should use the sour cherry jelly recipe on a popular brand of fruit pectin, and substitute apple juice for one-third to one-half of the water. I use half the amount of sugar prescribed or less, because I appreciate the berries' tartness. When the juice has been boiled away from the seeds, I strain it before adding sugar for the second cooking.

The jelly is a tawny peach color, and the flavor is hard to describe. I might compare it to apple pie with lemon: sweet, extra tangy. But another element lurks in the flavor that I can't compare to anything else. I think it's the essence of wildness, clean prairie air made solid. It contains the deer that nibbled the leaves in winter, the brush of a grouse's wing as it picked berries from the ground, the blundering invulnerability of a porcupine living under the ledge. It's the taste of blinding white drifts slowly being built and smoothed into glittering sculpture outside the house as you make morning toast, slathering it with butter and buffalo berry jelly. The jelly brings the flavor of summer heat to your tongue, a sheen of sweat to your shoulders; even as you watch the blizzard, it reminds you of spring fragrance and the cool nights of fall.

And there's something more. Buffalo berries are symbolic, to me, of the answer to the question all plains people are eventually asked. "Why?" the questioner will ask, looking around just before getting back onto the plane to return to some metropolis, and smiling a little disdainfully. "Why do you stay here? You could be anywhere; you could make more money, have all the advantages. I know it's beautiful, but." The questioner will shrug, wait a few seconds for an answer that doesn't come, and turn to climb the steps to the seats between the mighty engines which may or may not fall off during the flight.

I want to say, "Because of the buffalo berries." These tart little berries on hidden, thorny bushes are what the modern people of the plains have become. We're not easy to find, and we tend to be a little prickly if we've been here long. Hardship and freedom breed stoicism, and don't leave us with much patience for such questions. But when you get to know us, when you understand a little of the plains, we're rare and tasty.

Although it's difficult to transfer hot jelly from a large pan into a tiny glass, I use my smallest containers for buffalo berry jelly. Almost none of it leaves the ranch. The people I give it to can be counted on the fingers of one hand bloodied with picking berries, and include the best people I know. A few years ago I published in one of my books a map of our ranch; I included specific directions that made my family a bit nervous, and a lot of detail: where the horse stepped on me, where my favorite horse is buried, the dam where the coyotes hunt. I've paid for my candor every time someone uses the map to drive into my yard and ask for a "tour of the ranch." But even while being so forthright, I didn't put in the ravines where buffalo berries grow, and it's no use asking me. Find your own. Like Mother Nature, I can be harsh; like her, I've given you fair clues.

Coffee Cup Cafe

Soon as the morning chores are done,
cows milked, pigs fed, kids packed
off to school, it's down to the cafe
for more coffee and some soothing
conversation.

"If it don't rain pretty soon, I'm
just gonna dry up and blow away."

"Dry? This ain't dry. You don't know
how bad it can get. Why, in the Thirties
it didn't rain any more than this for
(breathless pause)   six years."

"I heard Johnson's lost ninety head of calves
in that spring snowstorm. They
were calving and heading for home
at the same time and they just walked
away from them."

"Yeah and when the cows
got home, half of them died
of pneumonia."

"I ain't had any hay on me since that hail
last summer; wiped out my hay crop, all
my winter pasture, and then the drouth
this spring. Don't know what I'll do."

"Yeah, but this is nothing yet.
Why in the Thirties the grasshoppers came
like hail and left nothing green on the ground.
They ate fenceposts, even. And the dust, why
it was deep as last winter's snow drifts,
piled against the houses. It ain't bad here yet,
and when it does come, there won't be so many of us
having coffee."

So for an hour they cheer each other, each story
worse than the last, each face longer. You'd think
they'd throw themselves under their tractors
when they leave, but they're bouncy as a new calf,
caps tilted fiercely into the sun.

They feel better, now they know
somebody's having a harder time
and that men like them
can take it.

Red Glow in the Western Sky

I worked hard in the garden that July afternoon, pulling
weeds and moving hoses on the parched vegetables. Occasionally
I'd straighten my aching back and look west, toward the sullen
clouds hanging over the Black Hills, hoping for rain, but not
expecting any.

After a hurried lunch with my husband and son, I drove the
pickup down toward the garden, glancing west out of habit, then
swung in a tight, dusty arc and roared back, honking. The column
of smoke wasn't thick; it rose straight up and mingled with the
clouds, but we hadn't had rain for months, and I knew the woods
were flammable as gasoline.

The fire looked close. I called a foothills neighbor to ask if he'd heard anything on his police scanner radio. He was casual, digesting lunch; no, he hadn't, and where did it look like it was? I told him to look behind his house, and hung up.

"Watch this," I said, leading my family to the porch, where we could see our neighbor's house and the black smoke exploding behind it. Aloud, I counted to five, and suddenly the red pickup by his back door roared backward, spun around, and raced down the ranch road toward the fire.

The column of smoke was building like a thunderhead, bubbling like a pot of water. It's always difficult to tell precisely where a fire is, but it was too close. The top of the column began to flow toward us as a west wind caught it.

A fire in trees is a dangerous place for inexperienced fire fighters, and our ranch was surrounded by acres of parched, crisp grass that could be ignited by a spark. We spent the afternoon filling the three-hundred-gallon water tank on the back of one truck, moving sprinklers in great circles around the house, and calling neighbors for news.

Breathing smoke as hot darkness came, we sat on the deck and joked about watching a live drama, better than television. Ash floated down, gentle as snowflakes. Often, summer nights are still, but when the wind began, it switched direction every few minutes, as if a thunderstorm was close. I knew I couldn't sleep, so I sent my family to bed and stayed on the deck.

About 10:30 P.M. I saw car lights on the driveway to my closest neighbors' house; they'd been gone all day, entertaining visitors from Germany. The car's brake lights flashed briefly as it topped the hill; I knew they were staring at the boiling red cloud.

Country neighbors never call each other after ten at night; too many of us get up early. I waited five minutes by the phone, and picked it up on the first ring.

"Where is the fire?" asked Margaret. I told her all I knew, and that I was staying up all night; she promised to call me when she got up at five.

All night I worked at my computer in the cool basement, and made trips every fifteen minutes to the deck. Sometimes the red glow seemed to cover the whole western sky; at other times it flickered and dimmed. I listened with growing disbelief to the strange world of call-in talk shows, where people discussed with great solemnity whether or not Elvis lived.

About midnight, a brief news flash reported Mount Rushmore threatened by a forest fire. I could tell flames weren't close to the Shrine of Democracy, but for a New York reporter, I suppose ten miles was close enough. Later, a talk-show caller said, "I hope the forest fire blackens Lincoln's face on Mount Rushmore because he'd be so shocked at what's happening in South Africa today." Trying to figure out that logic kept me alert for an hour.

Several highways had been closed by fire fighters, and some residents were desperate for news amid rumors ranch buildings had burned. I answered calls, but could tell them little. Margaret sleepily called at five, and I went to bed.

By late afternoon, gray ash was falling on the deck, and we took our water truck up to Margaret's yard. Her husband and brother were still on the fire line, and she and her sister-in-law were discussing moving their cattle and buffalo out of the pastures closest to the fire. But the job would be dangerous in the smoke, and the animals might get out on the highway.

All day slurry bombers lumbered overhead; we could tell when they dropped slurry—the engine sound changed.

The wind died during the night, the smoke moved east, and we woke to a landscape that looked foggy. The sun was only a red glow, and we couldn't see fences fifty feet away. It was impossible to tell if our own pastures were burning, and the steady drone of the slurry bombers overhead was gone. No one could be sure what the fire was doing; all flights were grounded.

On the fourth day, with the fire surrounded but not contained, I went into the hills to teach a writers' conference. At midmorning, a sudden rain squall struck so hard that we had to hold down the conference tents, and were laughingly drenched. The squall paused directly over the fire, dropping so much rain that fire fighters' trucks were mired and sliding into trees. My neighbors, exhausted, having spent four days away from their families and their work, came home.

They fought the fire, but they never controlled it; fire fighters say no equipment exists to stop a fire of that intensity once it has begun. The conditions that brought this one small fire in the West's summer of flame still exist. Even if we get snow and rain, they will continue to exist. Our forests contain too much fuel; years of work by environmentalists to stop logging in wilderness areas have resulted in a buildup of brush and crowded trees that need only one spark to ignite. The danger is particularly severe where disease or drought has left dead trees standing. We will lose our wilderness forests to wildfire if we do not learn to manage them more safely by removing some trees.

The joke among local fire fighters was that God looked down and said, "You fellahs aren't managing your forest very well; you've got too much fuel buildup down there," and sent a lightning storm to start a fire. Five days later he looked down and said, "You guys don't fight fire very well, either," and sent a rainstorm.

The Lost Legend of the Ground Hog

—for Sue and Brigid

My children, gather around the fire and hear me.
Long have I been your shaman.
During the bright blue-sky mornings
I have taught your daughters
to be strong women for the tribe.

During the long sunny afternoons
I have taught your sons
the magic they must know for hunting.

During the long starry nights
I have taught all my children
the legends of the tribe, the tribe's memory,
the ways we recall our ancestors.

I have told you legends about bears, crows, deer,
wolves, and birds. I have told you
dozens of legends about coyotes.

But I have never told you
the legend of the ground hog.

Now I am growing old; my sight is dim.
Tomorrow I will go up to the mountain,
and lie down on the good earth. I will go

to enter ground hog's world under the grass.
Tonight I can tell the legend
I have kept secret all my life.

Ground hog's legend can be told only once
in a lifetime, because he is too important
to be only entertainment.

Ground Hog Speaks to the Sun

Chubby dweller-underground,
he has short legs and big square teeth.
But do not laugh. He lives in the earth
mother. He lives with the roots,
with tangled streams of water,
ancient, cold stone
born the first day of the world.

No other animal is so powerful.
All the others wanted to call the sun,
but they were arrogant.

The bear boasted
of his great claws,
to pull the sun from the sky.

The lion screamed
about his great leaps,
to drag the sun to earth.

The stag thought he could
catch the sun in his antlers,
like a fish in a net.

Only the ground hog said nothing,
smiled a secret smile,
thought of the warm, dark earth.

For this he was chosen.
Ground hog speaks to the sun,
and the sun listens.
All year he travels
the underground,
whispering to roots,
singing with water,
listening to the slow
murmur of stones.

Once in the year, ground hog
climbs the ladder of time.
He looks out, and what he does
means everything.

Ground hog can call the sun,
or he can send it away.

He stands beside his burrow,
blinking, and calls the sun
to warm the earth.

If he is frightened,
if he is mocked,
if anyone is spying on him,
he goes back down without calling.
The sun does not come back.
The snow falls, and covers
the earth.

Without ground hog
the snow might stay
forever.

Rendezvous!

Rendezvous! Random House's "an agreement to meet at a certain time and place" is a watered-down excuse for a meaning. Rendezvous was the annual trappers' meeting during the fur trade days; a few days in summer when trappers brought in their pelts, were paid, and bought their year's supplies. They also bragged, fought, and caroused enough to last them through the next long, silent, dangerous year in the mountains. In one sense, the tradition of rendezvous ended in 1840; in another, it has never ended.

The actual rendezvous period lasted just sixteen years; from 1824 through 1840 the mountain men met fifteen times. Trade goods were packed from St. Louis to a designated meeting spot and there traded to Indians and trappers for beaver pelts and castoreum, the scent glands of the beaver. Summer rendezvous was the "big doin's" for the mountain man, where legends were repeated—and sometimes made.

The muzzle-loading weapons of that age, either cap and ball or flintlock, are still intriguing, and often called "front stuffers" to distinguish them from weapons in which ammunition is inserted from the side or rear. In modern times, people interested in the weapons have extended that interest to the way of life of the mountain man, and instituted dozens of such rendezvous in the United States, Canada, Germany, and other countries. Those in attendance are of every age—from infants to octogenarians. Why should people with comfortable homes containing waterbeds and microwave ovens put on long dresses or hot buckskin pants and sit in the dirt beside a smoky fire cooking their food in an iron pot? Partly it's the escape; it's also the quiet; it's the history.

Participants are expected to dress and live in the manner of the 1824–40 period; incredible attention to detail sometimes results. Some enthusiasts create a character who might have existed, and research historical accounts until they can make up a life history, then adhere to its details while in camp. Such a man might tell you that his name is Adam Jones, that he was born in Boston in 1800, ran away from home, and worked for a freighter in St. Louis until he came west with Ashley's first brigade in 1823. Everyone's objective is to reproduce, as nearly as possible, the look and feeling of a rendezvous camp of the period. A place is set aside for the primitive camp, with running water and firewood. Those who have authentic clothing but modern camping gear must camp in a spot reserved for modern tents and tin tipis: campers. "Pilgrims," inexperienced participants or visitors, are sometimes allowed in camp if they make a serious attempt at dressing in period style.

The insistence on authentic attire and accoutrements is not mere whim; the camp's primitive look enhances photographs, paintings, and research, and adds to the enjoyment of people who truly live the period. The mood would be ruined by seeing someone in blue jeans, scorned by modern mountain men because Levi Strauss didn't start making them until 1851. The rule keeps away folks who aren't seriously interested; those who are will be treated with friendliness, and almost any buckskinner will take time to help a newcomer learn how to participate. When you put on buckskins or a long dress, you put on a different mood; I feel serene in a long skirt, though life in the 1840s was sometimes far from serene. Ever try to walk in a long dress and moccasins? You must walk slowly, with grace. The whole tempo of the world changes. That's one of the first things I learned when I married a buckskinner. Some of us are buckskinners at heart long before we hear the word.

Rendezvous: the sun peeps through the open smoke flaps of the tipi, slides down the golden poles, and wakens the sleepers under the buffalo robe. I get up, pull a long cotton dress out of the cedar-lined clothes chest, find my moccasins, and step out to a camp just waking up. I put a few shavings on last night's coals, fill the pot with fresh water—only a pilgrim would wash a coffeepot—and hang it over the fire. While waiting for it to boil, I like to lean against the lodge in the sun and brush my hair, listening to the birds and watching for deer in the high meadows. If we're high enough—several national rendezvous have been held at almost ten thousand feet—I put on my capote, the blanket coat favored by mountain men, before I break the ice in the water bucket. As smoke begins to lift blue from cook fires around camp, I feel I've stepped out of the twentieth century for a while, away from telephones, television, and the other noisy jargon of our lives, back to a simpler time.

When the water's boiling, George gets up in time to dump a double handful of fresh coffee into the pot and settle the grounds with a bit of cold water. I pour the first cup, and morning has begun. A buckskinner wanders over with a cup hanging from his belt. Soon we're talking of guns, or how nice the woods are in the morning. Mountain folk may be lawyers, doctors, housewives, ranch hands, oil field workers, secretaries, but at rendezvous no one asks, and profession is seldom mentioned. Mountain names like Whiskey Lady or Crazy Wolf are used in camp, and you may know someone for years without ever knowing the name he or she answers to in the outside world; camp names are often expressions of character, or of the person's fantasy life. When my stepson Mike was small, he named me Sunflower; I enjoyed being simply George's wife Sunflower, or Linda, in camp; few buckskinners knew that my last name differed from George's, or that I was a writer. Those who did sometimes feared I was collecting material, which diluted my enjoyment, and theirs.

Rendezvous: men stroll past, talking, wearing fringed buckskin pants and shirts, carrying rifles, with tomahawks tucked into broad belts. Many look as if they've been in the mountains since 1840. Women jingle past in buckskin dresses or cotton prints decorated with bells or tin cones, going to the creek for water. Kids run by in breechclouts. Everyone wears sheathed knives, yet this is a peaceful camp. Most of the weapons are authentic reproductions, used sometimes in contests, or to make a fire, but seldom drawn in anger. Much as the pacifist part of my soul hates to admit it, the abundance of weapons seems to help insure peace. In the old days, fights that are still legend sometimes broke out, and even in the early days of modern buckskinning, someone occasionally "acquired an extra belly button." But now most men bring families, and violence is rare. A kind of restraint seems to insure that even when the liquor jugs have made the rounds, no one resorts to weapons.

As added protection, the "booshway"—slang for *bourgeois*,

the organizer and boss of the rendezvous—appoints assistants, called dog soldiers after the Indian term. They help with rendezvous plans, find a doctor in case of accident, dig privies, organize a fire watch that often lasts all night, and generally act as camp police, just as they did in Indian camps. Trouble of any kind brings them in a hurry. A few years ago, I was pleased to be among the first women to serve as dog soldiers at a national rendezvous. Given the nature of the pastime and its male participants, feminism is not generally obvious in camp. The women heard a few references to "squaw soldiers" and female dogs at first. But the day we had a forest and tipi fire, women worked beside men digging fire lines and cutting brush and trees; we stopped the fire before the Forest Service could react. When the emergency was over, so was all debate about whether or not women would be dog soldiers in the future.

Rendezvous: a baby wearing a breechclout over his diaper crawls past. Someone gently directs him away from the cook fire, and he crawls busily on. People wander up to the fire, talk, drift off. It's quiet, except for a horse or mule, a meadowlark, the murmur of a stream or a distant boom as someone fires a gun on the shooting range. Crazy Bear may organize a shinny game for the kids, a kind of hockey played with a ball and sticks the kids carve themselves. They hit someone else's shins oftener than the ball; hence, I suppose, the name.

A rendezvous camp is a small community, though "small" may be a misleading term. At one national rendezvous I attended, a flat fee was charged for each of 850 camp fires; organizers estimated that five thousand people were in attendance, since families or groups of men sometimes camp together to share equipment and supplies. Even in the country or small towns, we're too busy these days for random visiting. But in camp, people visit. Because everyone has at least one interest in common, we often discover others. Even if we share nothing else, we rediscover the joy of casual talk. People take time to lean on the lodge and soak up the sunshine, to wander around to the trade blankets, looking at articles authentic to the period for sale or trade. Traders often follow rendezvous for their livelihood, but they love the life, and they love to haggle; you might be able to trade something you don't need for something you want.

People who crowd dozens of activities and thousands of miles into their so-called vacations always ask, "But what do you *do* at a rendezvous?" Well, this is it; we drink coffee, visit, relax, and enjoy the look of our surroundings.

A modern lodge may be ten to twenty-six feet in diameter, supported by poles twenty-five feet long.[3] Tipi poles are usually lodgepole pine—that's how it was named—because they're straight. The poles are peeled by hand with drawknives, a miserable job. In our Cheyenne-style tipi, three poles are tied together and set up in a tripod, and the other poles laid against them in particular order, then bound into place with a rope. For extra stability, the rope is tied down in the center of the lodge, just behind the fire pit. Two more poles are placed in pockets in the smoke flaps, which regulate air flow and keep the fire in the center of the lodge drawing, instead of smoking. Because a tipi can act like a giant chimney, fires inside a lodge must be kept small, and sparks watched closely. George learned the hard way that a lodge burns to the ground in about thirty seconds; he barely escaped. He reentered the tipi to find his friend Jerry as the poles collapsed, burning, over him. Meanwhile, Jerry crawled out the back of the flaming lodge; George rolled him in snow to put out the flames, but Jerry's hands were severely burned.

The lodge is as unlike an ordinary tent as you can imagine. For one thing, ours, at eighteen feet in diameter, is almost that high at the peak. I love backpacking, but hate putting on my jeans while lying flat on my back inside a sleeping bag with a tent two feet above my nose. In the lodge, I can turn cartwheels while dressing. There may be foam rubber and sleeping bags inside, justified by the often-heard refrain, "If they'd had it, they'd have used it," but once the lodge door is open, modern goods are neatly hidden. Hides or blankets are thrown over coolers; wooden chests hold clothes, food, and cooking utensils. Some folks have rawhide chests (*parfleches*) like the Indians used, painted in the traditional manner.

The liner of the lodge, tied to the poles about five feet up, helps draw cool air inside; if we want more breeze, we can roll up the lodge cover a bit. In cold weather, the liner acts as a dead air space, helping to insulate, and as a privacy shield. Without it, if the lodge is lit, you project your actions on a big canvas screen for a fascinated audience. The lodge seems incredibly light and spacious, and the feeling of the circular shape, with the cone above and the gold poles meeting at the smoke hole, is so mystical that many lodges have bits of the sage sacred to the Indians, or other traditional ceremonial objects, hung somewhere inside. Some rendezvous participants live in a lodge in the Indian way, using accoutrements a Sioux, Blackfoot, or Cheyenne would recognize, and treating Indian culture with knowledge and respect. Most people work out a compromise between 1840 and the 1990s, using modern food and some conveniences.

Despite its canvas walls, the tipi is also a private place. When the door flap is down, no one would think of entering a lodge without permission. To ask entrance in the Indian manner, scratch on the canvas and say, "Hello the lodge." If no one hollers, "Come in," you do not enter. Even when we were visiting a friend's lodge in seventy-five-mile-an-hour winds and snow in Cody, Wyoming in mid-May one year, one friend followed the formula, then stuck his head in and said, "George, your lodge is down." We thought he was indulging in macabre humor; he wasn't. Lodges can stand winds that high if properly staked, but the ground was wet from several days of rain, and the stakes did not hold. In desperation, sacrificing authenticity because we didn't want everything wet, we tied several tipis to trucks to keep them up; the outside poles moved in on the wind side as much as two feet, and bent a lot, but the lodges stood, humming and singing like great canvas drums. Later, the same friend announced a feather shoot. You had to shoot fast; the feathers kept going to Mexico. And as we watched, a square canvas tent was snatched away in an eyeblink, leaving its two residents seated, just raising coffee cups to their lips.

There are no locks, but a lodge with the doorflap closed is inviolate. No real buckskinner would consider entering an empty lodge. Failure to grasp this simple rule is one reason pilgrims are seldom allowed to visit camp. A sign posted outside a national rendezvous a few years ago advised that thieves "would be castrated with a dull rock." At one camp near our home, day visitors were allowed in; that night one of them came back and stole some rifles while the camp slept. The sheriff came to get a list of the stolen items, and said, "If you catch him first, turn the remains over to me when you get done with him."

At some point in the morning, I usually walk through camp, admiring the finery, called "foofaraw" of the men and women. Various historical periods are represented, from Revolutionary days—with the men in knee-breeches and tricorn hats, carrying flintlock rifles—to the true mountain man era, with buckskins and hats of coyote, bobcat, or other fur.[4] There are Indians, real and imaginary, and Scotsmen in kilts with the traditional knives, *sgian dubhs*, in their stockings. Some outfits—they are never called costumes—are antiques; one regular participant wears an eighteenth century priest's habit on cool days, and Iron Woman wears a nun's habit of similar vintage. She usually wears it after playing pranks like sewing lodge doors shut, hoping its age and fragility, and a pious face, will protect her from reprisals.

When it's hot, many men wear breechclouts. An abrupt change from trousers to a breechclout can result in terrible thigh sunburns at the first rendezvous of the season. Although many historical paintings show the breechclout, little has been written about it, and there are no instruction manuals for its use. It's simply a long, narrow strip of cloth which is drawn between the legs. The ends are allowed to hang over the belt fore and aft; if the wearer keeps the belt fairly snug, the garment will remain in place, though sitting crosslegged with modesty takes a little practice. We once saw a gentleman who thought a breechclout was two separate short pieces of cloth. A crowd of chuckling folks noticed his error when he bent over to look at some trade plunder; I presume a kindly buckskinner educated him, because he disappeared shortly thereafter. Once when we hosted a visitor, seven-year-old Mike volunteered to loan him a spare breechclout and show him how to wear it; I heard him say, "I keep this brown spot in back."

Rendezvous: "Hi there, Tanglefoot. I heard you callin' buffalo last night. Too much Bent's Fort?"

"Well, now, it warn't so much the Bent's Fort as it was the rattlesnake juice and peppermint schnapps and blackberry brandy."

Bent's Fort is just one of the things buckskinners drink. They drink beer, too, but since you can't carry the can around camp—it's not pre-1840—you have to put it in a cup, and unless you have a powerful big cup, you have to keep running back to the lodge for refills. Also, cold beer requires ice, and a cooler, and that's extra trouble. So most people get jugs and fill them with hard liquor, or make a mixture. Various recipes exist, such as combinations of whiskey and apple juice; some of these are awful, but no worse than the concoctions the actual trappers drank. Many traders of the 1800s made the whiskey stretch a long way by adding water, then tossed in ingredients guaranteed to give it flavor: rattlesnakes, hot pepper, and tobacco. The assumption was that after a day or two of cramming a year's worth of fun into a few days, the trappers wouldn't notice if the whiskey tasted funny—nor would the Indians, who had never tasted the stuff before. No one is willing to be quite that authentic today. Too much Bent's Fort or other mixture brings on an activity known as calling buffalo, which allegedly brings on a buffalo stampede through camp and results in everyone having headaches the next morning. If you prefer not to indulge, it's easy to avoid a passed jug; there are plenty of people in camp who don't drink. The buckskinner's unspoken code is independence, and what you do in your lodge is your business, and what you do outside it is also your business, unless it interferes with someone else's business.

If you need a bath—and after about three days, everyone needs a bath—you can take the pilgrim's way out and pay for a shower at a campground in town where folks will stare at you. Or you can be authentic and find the pools dammed up in the creek by the dog soldiers. The water can be cold enough to make your back teeth hurt when it's only up to your ankles, a practical demonstration of the reason mountain men only bathed once a year. Biodegradable soap and shampoo are recommended, but not everyone listens. A woman washed her baby's diapers in the creek at a national rendezvous a few years ago, and some of the folks camped below her, who prided themselves on never boiling the creek water, got so sick they had to go home early. Even in remote camps, most folks boil the water these days because of pollution and giardia, a water-borne affliction that can make you sick for months.

Real buckskinners are similarly careful with their fires. Sod is saved when fire pits are dug; when camp breaks up, stones used to circle the pit are scattered, and the sod carefully replaced. Extra firewood is returned to the woods, and children get prizes for picking up litter. When several thousand people leave camp, it can look very much as though no one has ever camped there. Recent dry years have made this difficult, since the sheer volume of vehicle and foot traffic leaves deep, dusty trails.

The privies are often authentic, too: two logs—one to sit on, one to lean on—tied between two trees, with a pit dug underneath and canvas around the outside. One year, after six days in a crowded camp, a friend said to George, "If you're going to the john, take your knife."

George paused, scanning the woods suspiciously, wondering what threat he'd missed. "Why?"

"So if the log breaks, you can cut your throat before you hit."

Such unpleasantness is an unfortunate and hardly authentic result of the crowds; the real mountain men dug isolated holes, and covered them with care to help prevent the discovery of a camp by hostile Indians, and they didn't use toilet paper.

Many buckskinners who thoroughly enjoy themselves never uncase their rifles, but participants usually schedule shooting competitions. Contests include the Seneca run: a series of tests such as shooting at silhouette targets, setting a trap in the water, climbing trees with your rifle, hawk (tomahawk) throws, starting a fire with flint and steel, and other primitive skills. Traders donate prizes, or the club sponsoring the shoot buys or makes them. Smaller scale contests are always arranged for the children.

Sometimes several people will get up a blanket shoot, betting whatever they put on the blanket on their prowess. And although men may seem to dominate buckskinning, the women shoot and join in the hawk throws as well. I'm one of a few female buckskinners who admits to being liberated—my powder horn came from a *female* buffalo—but the fire of independence burns high in any woman who can outshoot a man with a flintlock rifle at one hundred yards, or stick a hawk blade at thirty. At some rendezvous, husbands have been observed washing dishes even when their wives are in camp; a few years ago, they would have drawn a chortling crowd of other buckskinners.

Early in the afternoon, I put the main meal of the day on to cook: meat seared in the black pot over the fire, with vegetables added later. Or I use home-canned cow to avoid having to leave camp for ice to keep fresh meat. The pot bubbles until everyone's hungry, and then anyone in the neighborhood grabs a plate, or the cup from the belt, and eats.

Around dusk, the finery comes out and everyone dresses up for evening; both men and women put on clean clothes, often deerhide decorated with quillwork, much too fine for daylight wear when there's cooking to be done and wood to be hauled. There may be a council fire for announcements and entertainment in the center of camp, and sometimes a communal meal. But even if there isn't a camp-wide gathering, folks will congregate at various fires to listen to harmonicas, banjos, guitars, mouth harps, or bagpipes. Tempos vary, but somewhere during the evening you might hear traditional mountain man songs like "Jim Bridger" or "Ashley's Men," a cowboy ballad like "The Night Rider's Lament," or traditional bluegrass or folk. You definitely will not hear electric guitars or amplification. Jugs are passed in a neighborly way around the fire, and people move in and out as their temperatures vary. Children play around the outskirts until they grow tired or cold, then crawl into someone's lap and doze with the warmth of the fire, closely packed bodies, and companionable singing to make them feel safe.

Sometimes a liar's contest keeps things lively, with applause or boos determining the winners. Or a rousing game of Snort, invented by the Yellowstone Mountain Men of Cody, and certainly in the finest tradition of the breed. Two people sit crosslegged on the ground, with the challenger's hat between them. Each plants a knife at one side of the hat—not as a threat, but merely to indicate the limits of the playing field. Then a small, barbell-shaped piece of wood, called a "snort stick," is placed in the preferred nostril and decorously—and loudly—exhaled. The object is to fire it into the center of the hat, for five points. A rim shot is worth only two points; the first player to collect ten points wins, and must drink from the jug. Both men and women play the game, though I retired after Michael showed his schoolmates at home how to play it, and insisted he had learned it from his stepmother.

When you leave the fire to walk back to your lodge through the quiet camp, your way is lit by a candle lantern, and by the glowing cones of tipis with fires or lanterns inside. The horses are quiet, the children asleep. No sound of motors intrudes; no sight reminds you of the century. Someone may be singing softly or raucously in camp; somewhere a harmonica plays a sad tune, or a drum a lively one, but it all fits. You stroll moccasin-soft through camp to crawl into the buffalo robes and drift off to sleep in utter peace until a frost-crackling morning.

And when camp is breaking up, you can hear the mountain man's traditional goodbye when keeping your scalp was chancy: "Watch your topknot!"

"Watch yourn!"

The Wild and Woolly West

I

Those were the days, boys, when the West was wild,
when Jesse James rode a night-black horse
into a hail of gunfire to take money from a bank
and give it to the poor nesters outside of town,
while protecting them from the gunfighters hired
by the big ranchers who wanted the water.

Those were the days, when Yellow Hair Custer came
to the West Montana plains with West Point ideas.
He thought he'd ride his white horse to the White House
on a pavement of Indian corpses, fitted together
like parquet or the flattened bodies in an Aztec mural.
Meanwhile, Calamity Jane and Wild Bill Hickok loved
each other in the golden streets of Deadwood.

Those were the days, boys,
when the white man
civilized
the West.

II

My grandfather, coming West from Sweden,
saw a wagon full of cow guts, Indian kids

sitting on the sides eating with both hands.
He thought it was funny;
didn't know they had nothing else to eat.
Custer didn't ride far after he met Crazy Horse.
Wild Bill never cared for Jane,
and he was married anyway.
Calamity
died broke.

The Cowboy and the Ride

Broken, snow-scoured peaks poking twelve thousand feet into the sky loom at the end of the dusty gravel road. My husband George, son Mike, and I follow the gravel along the South Fork of the Shoshone River until the road simply ends in a rocky turnaround on the banks of the river. There we wait for the rest of our group: buckskinners who plan to ride to the site of a national rendezvous near Dubois, Wyoming, nearly seventy-five miles away. The Yellowstone Mountain Men have arranged to ride as a group guided by outfitter B. Joe Coy. We're riding at special rates because we provide and cook our food; outfitters usually provide everything but the energy to mount your horse in the morning.

As the sun sets, we perch on skimpy bedrolls beside a sagebrush fire, talking with other riders and looking over our supplies. We have brought pemmican we made from homemade jerky, using organic beef from our own cattle. We ground the dried meat with nuts and bound the mass with chopped dates, then hand-shaped servings into rolls weighing perhaps a quarter-pound each. For variety, we have a little coffee, dried fruit, and commercially made bars of grain, fruit, and nuts. We carry a coffee pot, one change of clothing, and both moccasins and riding boots because we are nervous about riding unknown, rented horses; the two packs containing gear and food for all three of us weigh thirty-five pounds.

I lie awake, wondering if this was a foolish idea. Raised on a South Dakota ranch, I've ridden all my life, but never seventy-five miles of mountain trails in three days. I'm terrified of heights, and will be riding a rented horse I did not train and do not know. Our flatland horses have never been on high trails, or seen a moose or grizzly bear, so we dared not bring them. But I've heard stories about the dangers of riding horses that have been ridden by too many novices. I suffer frequent migraines; one knee doesn't work very well since I chipped a bone in a riding accident. A year ago, another horse walked the length of that leg, tearing ligaments loose, so the whole thing is unreliable and often painful. Will it stand the punishment of the ride? George regards horses as treacherous, with good reason, since he has a permanent back injury from being thrown. I worry about his breathing since his trachea is partially closed by cartilage growth caused by radiation to treat his Hodgkin's disease. He feels well, but is not as strong as he looks. Our son hasn't ridden much, and daydreams a lot.

In the morning more people arrive, and packs blossom on the backs of reluctant mules. A horse bucks its load into confusion, and kicks the man who tries to catch it, gashing his arm. Volunteers quickly bandage it; he wasn't planning to ride, so he can get medical treatment in town. Two men loading a mule named Henry softly mutter threats into his long ears while he quivers and twists under a pack. Henry is tiny as a six-month-old colt, but his brown eyes are old and gleam with wicked intelligence; I have a feeling I'll be getting to know Henry better.

B. Joe, the outfitter, warns me about the dapple-gray Morgan mare named Ginger that I'll be riding; she prefers to stay close to her brother, Ringo, and she doesn't like to stop. When I ride her around camp and experimentally pull on the reins, she rears and paws the air. George is riding Ringo, who doesn't like anything much, and dances in circles until the rest of the riders are ready. Mike's horse, Chief, dozes off as soon as the saddle hits his back.

Even the first day, the Cowboy captures my attention. Hired by B. Joe as a wrangler, he stays at the rear, and helps stragglers with details like how to tie packs so they won't slide under the mules' bellies or catch on trees. He's dressed like B. Joe—western hat and shirt, black silk neckscarf, jeans, boots. But even from a distance his hero-sized handlebar mustache is distinctive; it is thick and dark, and the ends dangle below his chin where he absently twists them to points as he rides. He leads two pack horses of his own, and rides a gray gelding that is lean and stringy as a wolf.

By nightfall, we've all noticed something else: the Cowboy never gets off his horse. At one point, B. Joe dismounts to lead his horse down a steep, slippery, shale-covered mountainside, and orders the rest of us to do the same to save the horses. The Cowboy stays in the saddle, riding easily. B. Joe glares, but says nothing. We begin covertly trying to catch the Cowboy dismounted. Some of the men remark that he *must* get off the horse sometime, for chores that can't be done on a horse. But no one sees him. Whenever I glance over my shoulder he is at the end of the file of riders; sometimes he is helping retie a pack, or almost lost in the shadow of the trees, teeth showing white under the hat.

The trail crosses the Shoshone River—called by Indians the "Stinking Water" because of the sulphurous hot springs along its route—and winds up into the trees. Except for the three white women in our group, and quick lens flashes as everyone takes pictures, we look like trappers headed for the annual celebration to sell furs, buy supplies, and drink all the whiskey in the mountains. We wear wool or leather pants, loose shirts, and moccasins; some carry muzzle-loading rifles, with powder horns slung across their shoulders and tucked under an arm; each of us wears a belt knife. We look tough and competent and authentic, and when we pull off the trail to let a group of modern riders move past, their faces tell us they aren't entirely sure we're not ghosts.

Paintings and fiction often feature trappers riding alertly through a clearing. But such openings are rare in the Rockies, and the woods are a tangled mass of blown-down timber. Boulder-rolling, tree-smashing avalanches have torn great gashes in the mountains' flanks. If he didn't follow Indian trails, a mountain man might have struggled for weeks on the route we propose to cover in three days. If we had to find our own route instead of following trails maintained by National Forest workers, we might ride higher, above timberline. We meet a man and wife on horseback whose summer job is maintaining trails; in this wilderness, they must use handsaws to cut hundreds of trees blown down in a season; motorized chainsaws are prohibited by wilderness rules.

When the trail switchbacks, I see that B. Joe's reins are dangling and he's grinning back at us from under his western hat, eating canned beans from a plastic spoon. He's under no obligation to dress or behave like a mountain man, and I see amusement in his eyes. He's dragged a lot of dudes through the woods, and we'll have to prove we know what we're doing before he believes we're anything more than a bunch of folks playing dress-up.

When we stop to water the horses, Henry the mule jerks his lead rope loose from the tail of the horse ahead and slips into the trees. B. Joe utters his strongest profanity: "Son of a buck" (shortened under stress to "Somebuck"), and spurs his horse. In a moment the mule appears, dashing around obstructions without snagging his pack, and into a clearing. The Cowboy appears, swinging a blackened lasso, and *almost* ropes the mule. Shouting, riders encircle the beast, but he breaks out of the circle and heads straight for George. Ringo dances on his hind hoofs, and George's face is tense as he holds the reins with one hand and reaches. He looks a little surprised when he catches the lead rope, but hauls the little mule to a stop with one powerful arm.

"Henry don't buck though," B. Joe says as he reties the rope to a pack horse's tail. "The somebuck causes all kinds of grief, but he don't buck." I assume this is a compliment.

Some historians believe the route we ride is the way John Colter came in the winter of 1807–1808 when he was sent to convince the Crows to trade furs to the whites. Arguments about the route may never be settled, since Colter left no notes. Riding the route in summer makes me wonder if it could be walked, much less ridden, in winter; folks familiar with the terrain are sure Colter spent the winter snuggled up in a Blackfoot lodge, asking intelligent questions.

Somewhere along the south side of the river, we may pass a salt cave once worked by the Spaniards. Burton Harris in *John Colter: His Years in the Rocky Mountains*, says the Indians told Colter that fourteen days' walk from the forks of Stinking Water would bring him to the salt cave above the mouth of a "considerable river" entering from the south. No one has found the cave. I watch several considerable streams entering on the south side, wishing I had time for exploration.

One minute the path is tree-edged and broad. The next minute my horse steps around a cliff edge and we are on a narrow trail across a boulder-strewn slope hundreds of feet above the river. The trail is almost two feet wide. George, ahead of me, discovers first that when a horse turns a corner on a high trail, its head hangs out over the dropoff a lo-o-o-ong way.

He mumbles, "No wonder B. Joe was grinning at us, the somebuck."

Even thinking of a certain trail in Zion National Park makes my hands sweat, ten years after I tottered up it. I stare between the horse's ears and lean toward the mountain, mentally rehearsing a leap out of the saddle. Rocks click and bounce below us; the sound seems to go on forever. My horse stumbles and lurches toward the edge. I look.

The river looks narrow as my finger although I know it is several hundred yards wide. Henry the pack mule's tiny hoofprints are on the edge of the chasm, where—B. Joe explains later—the walking is easier. Below us the slope resembles a huge gravel pile: steep, slippery-looking talus with nothing to slow a slide, then an abrupt cliff at the edge of the river.

I always thought "trust your horse" meant she knew what she was doing, but I repeat it anyway. She's been over this trail before. I'd be glad to lead her, but there isn't room to dismount, and no one else is walking. Maybe they're not nervous, but I hear words stronger than "somebuck" when a horse stumbles against the pack horse ahead; a few rocks roll off the edge of the trail and clatter down the slope. Later we hear that a rider in a group ahead of us stayed on his horse when it went over the edge here. When they untangled themselves at the bottom, the horse immediately began struggling back up the slope, and the bruised rider just hung onto its tail until it got to the top. Then he started feeling a little battered.

"Aren't the horses afraid?" I ask B. Joe.

"They don't know it's that high, or they'd never go up there in the first place."

As I ride, I test Ginger. Indeed she likes to stay close to her brother Ringo. If she can't see him, she fidgets and trots until he comes into view, no matter how rocky the trail; if I try to stop her while Ringo moves on, she rears and threatens to buck. She seems sensible in other ways, but I'm never certain what she will do. At midmorning we cross a swift river bordered by slick rocks. I'd like a picture of George crossing the river behind me, and think a smart horse won't buck among rocks where she might break a leg; since she's ahead of Ringo, she should be pleased to wait for him. I stop the mare, turn in the saddle, and focus. The horse explodes.

Off balance, I'm nearly split in half by the cantle, and the camera hits me in the teeth. The jolt throws me onto Ginger's rump, headed for the rocks; I know I am going down. I have a quick picture of myself with a broken back or concussion, twenty miles from the gravel road that leads to the highway that leads to the hospital. I catch the saddle horn and try to haul myself back to the saddle as Ginger bucks for a quarter-mile through the trees. Only the strength in my thighs and arms keeps me in contact with the saddle; I don't get my feet back in the stirrups until she has stopped. George catches up, and we talk about how lucky I am while the two horses blow air into each other's nostrils. Several passing riders nod approvingly as I check my cinch and wipe blood off my lip, but mountain men aren't big on compliments. After I catch my breath, I begin to wish someone had photographed the whole thing, to help me figure out how I redeemed myself, but no one has.

For the rest of the day, the slightest pull on the reins causes Ginger to buck. I hold on to the saddle horn, which any experienced rider hates to do in public, and ride out her fits until she decides she's stuck with me.

At noon we loosen cinches and fall into shade for lunch, pemmican for us and sandwiches squashed in saddlebags since morning for the others. Wyoming natives drink from canteens filled at tiny springs along the way. We flatlanders, fearing giardia, doggedly add purification tablets. Resting, we stare at the sunlit mountains around us, the clearing in the trees; we've already used up all the adjectives we know. George smiles at me with a look of intense contentment that I know mirrors my own, and says it's good to see scenery, because he hasn't opened his eyes all morning. I ask B. Joe how many more high trails we face.

"Not far now," B. Joe says cheerfully. "One little place we call the Catwalk."

Why didn't he tell us the names of the terrifying trails we crossed this morning?

"None of 'em had names."

Assuming only the worst spans have names, if none of those were named, what is the Catwalk like?

B. Joe tugs at his black hat; by morning we'll recognize this as a signal he's about to tell a story. "I rode out of here once November tenth in the snow. Drifts were so deep you couldn't tell where the trail was. I was leading pack mules, and had to ride across bad places twice to break a trail through the drifts." He grins, making light of what must have been a freezing ordeal. Inspired, he talks for a half-hour about his experiences hunting these mountains for twenty-five years. He not only looks like the old-time cowboy, with his black hat, black silk neckscarf, and drooping black mustache; he's lived the life. He's casual about awful trails, bear attacks, avalanches, snow slides, bucking horses, runaway mules. He grins wickedly as he remembers bringing a hunter to this spot in the dark. "When we rode back out of here in daylight, and he saw the trail we'd come over, he turned white as a sheet."

"How far to the end of the trail?" someone calls as we mount.

"Not far now," B. Joe says, his smile waggling his mustache. We soon learn that "not far now" is the outfitter's favorite phrase.

"We never tell anybody how far it is," B. Joe admits on the last day, "or they'd never make it. And we never tell them about the high trails, either." He gives me a level look from under his hat brim. "Would you have come up here if you'd known about that?" He jerks a thumb over his shoulder.

He's right; if I'd known, fear might have talked me out of it. A year and a half later, George died. One of the men who convinced us we could make the ride said to me, "George has just gone ahead with a good horse and pack string; he's waiting for us in a green meadow." I wouldn't have believed it if I hadn't made the ride with him; I wouldn't have these memories.

We reach Bliss Creek Meadows just at dark, and tumble sleeping bags and panniers hastily into chosen camp sites. I am abruptly reminded where we are when B. Joe hangs the food chests in a tree in the middle of camp, too high for a grizzly bear to reach.

"We're camped right on a black bear trail," he mutters to George as they tie off the ropes.

We mount up to ride two more miles to a fishing camp where we're expected for supper. One rider, crossing the creek, whoops and points to grizzly tracks deep in the mud. Fresh grizzly tracks. Riders who have been strung out in a long line as darkness falls casually ease closer together; some check their powder. Since most of us carry muzzle-loaders, which take from thirty seconds to two minutes to load—depending on the state of your nerves and powder—we ride with them loaded. I notice several folks checking the .357 magnums tucked inconspicuously under their shirts or inside a pouch; the mountain men didn't have such advantages, but if we meet a grizzly, no one will quibble about authenticity.

At the fishing camp, a semipermanent complex of tents where food is always kept on a platform high in the trees, we're treated to stories about the resident grizzly. He's shy; he may turn over a few horse-sized rocks near camp, but he won't bother us. "He just wanders around up on the ridge. Not like those garbage bears over in the [Yellowstone] park," one guide says with a smile that's supposed to be reassuring.

We sit wearily down to eat roast turkey with dressing, mashed potatoes and gravy, and even dessert, though most of us are too tired to appreciate it. As soon as supper is over, we head back to our own camp through a valley suddenly infested with bear-shaped rocks and stumps. The air is nippy, and the soft drumming of our horses' hoofs, quiet talk along the line of riders, the jingle of gear, are the only sounds. The meadow grass shimmers with moisture and moonlight.

We exchange a few medical supplies: salve for human muscles and horses' cinch sores, aspirin. A man riding with a sore back swallows "bute."[5] Another, who hasn't been on a horse in eight years, is walking as if trying to keep his leather pants from touching his thighs; it's funny to see, but I know how it feels and take him some painkilling lotion. B. Joe hobbles some horses and bells others, and the camp is quiet in minutes.

Our bedding consists of blankets inside old army bedrolls, laid on the thinnest of pads, another attempt to be true to the mountain man's experience. We put our brightly colored plastic tarps down first and cover them quickly, embarrassed by the discordant note they strike in this camp. We couldn't afford canvas ground cloths, and hadn't yet discovered that we could make them cheaply by waterproofing painters' drop cloths.

We sleep deeply and well; we are becoming calm, centered, unafraid of the real or imagined hazards of this last bit of true wilderness. We are learning that bruises and minor scrapes can't take our minds off the wonders around us. We are well fed, filled with energy, fresh air, and exercise. Even Michael, whose idea of heaven is riding a Harley through a room filled with VCRs, rock bands, and beautiful girls, seems happy.

I'm awakened by a scream that sounds like a panther. I nudge George, who mumbles, "I hope if there's a grizzly around, he eats me before I have to get back on that horse," and sleeps.

I listen tensely, but the night is too beautiful for fear. Wind walks the knife-edge peaks, horses snort and jingle and munch. Sleeping riders are widely scattered around the clearing; city dwellers might be inclined to sleep close together out of nervousness, but these folks trust themselves. If an old trapper left behind in 1840 were scouting our camp, he'd find it familiar: no lanterns, no shiny plastic tents or flashlights, just sleepers rolled in blankets and tarps, heads resting on saddles.

At breakfast, mist still rises from the grass as we back up to the fire; most of us are surprised we don't hurt more. Three deer graze among the horses in the meadow; a moose and calf cautiously cross the creek nearby. Someone mentions being awakened by bells.

"I only wake up when the bells stop," mutters B. Joe. Silence means the bell mare is gone, and has probably taken the whole pack string with her.

"What was that shriek right after we went to bed?" I ask with false casualness.

"Henry. You oughta hear the somebuck scream when he sees a grizzly; makes that sound like singing. That's one reason I put up with the somebuck's tricks; when he hollers 'grizzly,' I reach for the rifle." B. Joe shakes his head. "Fellah I bought that mule from, he told me Henry got away from him once in a little patch of timber in the middle of a meadow. He knew the mule was in there, but he couldn't find him. Finally he started walking in circles, looking behind every tree, and the patch was so small he got to the center pretty quick. There was Henry, behind a tree, and as the guy walked around it, Henry kept the tree between them, so if he hadn't heard a little noise from the pack, he mighta looked for that somebuck all day."

Warming his hands around a tin cup of coffee, B. Joe tells us about Sam Bliss, the horse thief who blocked trails into this natural corral and filled it with stolen horses—until federal officers tracked him down. They knew his reputation, so they didn't bother to parley; when he stepped out of his outhouse, they shot him and buried him in the meadow. A year later one of the men found the corpse dug up by bears, and buried it again. Bliss's bones certainly aren't alone.

B. Joe gazes across the meadow and tells about the 350-pound black bear he killed here after it attacked his camp. He's good enough at his profession that he can admit he was nervous: fired the first time with an unloaded gun. He reloaded on a galloping horse and didn't miss the next time. The environmentalist inside me shudders at casual bear-killing, but B. Joe was protecting his hunters.

This is isolation enough to satisfy most folks, but the trail we came over is nothing compared to the trail to B. Joe's hunting cabin—a switchback monster so steep that several pack mules have tumbled backwards when they forgot to lean into it while resting. The first day, he seemed to say mostly what he had to; now he talks warmly about the loveliness of the vast plateau above us, and adds seriously, "You oughta go up there some time, just to see it."

Just to see it. That's the spirit of the mountain men, the first and best tourists. They were ostensibly after beaver pelts, but much of the time they were just looking around, enjoying what they saw.

They trapped beaver for profit, of course, but they ate a lot of the meat so it wouldn't go to waste. When they hunted, they didn't kill more than they needed. When the demand for beaver ended—someone invented the silk top hat—most of the trappers stayed in the mountains. They loved the wilderness, but they combined their love with knowledge of survival and a clear-eyed practicality that is missing from all sides of land-use debates today. Unfortunately, modern folks tend to picture the trappers as bloodthirsty land-rapers, and their modern heirs as worse. But around our breakfast fire, many of the buckskinners get misty-eyed thinking of "just living up here, you know, never having to go back" to the world of cars and jobs.

Then a woman shrills to her husband, "Pack my makeup kit on top," and I am brought back to modern reality. She uses it twice a day, but I am happy to wash my face in a stream so cold it freezes my wrinkles. After the first morning, I no longer think about my hair. In the photos, I'm smiling, which is the best a face can look anyway. After a day, the men smell like men, not some manufacturer's idea of male musk. The women smell like men, too, a natural odor of human bodies well exercised; sadly, advertising techniques have convinced us it's unpleasant. We all smell of clean air, sweaty horses, and wood smoke, scents so magical and meaningful that nothing chemists have concocted is a worthy substitute. It can't be done, folks; nothing smells like the original.

The Cowboy has discarded his western boots and jeans for the greasiest, blackest, most disreputable-looking pair of buckskin pants I've ever seen. Rendezvous pride requires one's buckskin clothes to look old, as a gauge of one's experience in the mountains. Most buckskinners wipe greasy fingers on them, and layers of dirt and soot accumulate in camps where chairs are not allowed; the wife who washes this fine patina from a set of leathers has made a serious error. The Cowboy still wears his hat and western shirt, but his pants declare him one of us. A huge Bowie knife hangs from his belt. He volunteers to teach George a quick knot for securing a horse to a tree; I take this as a sign of approval. Watching, I see that a thin black scar begins near one eye and switchbacks down the side of his nose almost to his mouth.

As we pack up, the natives exchange stories of mules and horses toppling off these cliffs and having to be shot. No one mentions the survival rate of humans. The subject of Colter arises again; natives doubt that he could have ascended the valley in winter, over drifts that may be forty feet deep. If he stayed beside the river, he'd have been "rimrocked," hemmed in by vertical walls, just below the divide we'll reach today. The slender trail that winds up the wall of stone is often impassable except in July and August. I'm astonished to find myself just as terrified as I was yesterday, even before I see grizzly claw marks in the dust of the trail, going our way.

Soon after we begin moving up an increasingly narrow, high trail, Ginger begins shaking her head dizzily, turning to nip at the cinch. She still hates to be far behind Ringo, but she seems to have a hard time traveling in a straight line. Distance grows between riders as we move cautiously across a shale slide three hundred feet above the river, which foams and rattles over the rocks. The mare twitches, clearly nervous as Ringo moves away, then breaks into a staggering gallop. I pull gently on the reins, to try to slow her without inspiring her to buck. She slows to a trot, then steps off the edge. In panic, I haul on the reins, literally pulling her back on the trail. She stops, and I dismount on the cliff side to loosen the cinch, trying to give her some relief.

Other riders edge carefully past me, and I remount, letting the horse set her own pace. Suddenly I'm alone, with no other rider in sight, a feeling at once so terrifying and wonderful that I inadvertently pull on the reins to stop and enjoy it. The poor mare is almost too sick to buck, but she manages to slam the cantle against my kidneys, and I continue my meditating on the move.

At the next rest stop, the Cowboy stops his horse next to mine; I realize that since this morning, he's discarded his western shirt for a black leather one.

"I'll show you a knot so if that horse goes down, you can jerk your saddle off with you when you fall off," he murmurs around the mustache. His eyes look almost kind. So he noticed.

"I'm not very good at knots."

He shoves my leg out of the way and deftly secures the cinch.

"This way you won't have to crawl all the way down there and get it off her if the fall kills her," he says cheerfully. Pause, while he shifts a chew of tobacco the size of a ground hog inside his cheek. "The fall don't usually kill 'em." Pause. Spit. "Don't hardly ever kill the rider either," he adds smiling.

I hear a faint shout, "Moose!" and see a solitary bull only a few yards away, sunlight glinting off his horns, his body disguised in the trees. Moose may be more dangerous than grizzlies, but I'm too busy nursing the horse along to be afraid. Along a creek I notice prehistoric joint grass, literally older than the mountains. Hundreds of wildflowers shiver in the chill wind from glaciers above us. Waterfalls hang like spiderwebs against colossal rock walls. A rider stops to pick up a cigarette paper, the first scrap of trash I've seen.

We eat lunch at ninety-eight hundred feet on top of Shoshone Pass, and stand astride the trickle that will become the South Fork of the Shoshone River. Most of the afternoon we're walking downhill, to ease the horses; Ginger and I are last in line, followed by the watchful Cowboy. Once I hear the clink of a bottle and catch a flash of sunlight on glass. "Trail-shortener," the Cowboy explains, offering me a swig. My taste buds identify it as Yukon Jack, but by then it's too late; it's already hit the back of my throat. I breathe fire the rest of the afternoon, wondering if I should give some to my horse.

As sunset blazes on the mountains above us I hear a voice call, "How far is it?"

"Not far now," comes the faint reply from a mile ahead.

At dusk we reach Dundee Meadows on Dunoir Creek. Here, only about fifteen miles from a highway, the wilderness is giving way to the ugly tinges of civilization: hikers have failed to bury their personal wastes and one must walk carefully in the woods. The smell of excrement mingles with the scent of flowers.

While we cook and eat supper, we watch my horse, clearly in pain. Finally she lies down. I pull and coax while Jeff, one of the ride's leaders, shoves until she gets up. Fearing she has colic, we walk her back and forth, dose her with most of the dish soap in camp, an old colic remedy. Men and women shove the horse along, talking to her, suggesting remedies, for more than an hour. Then, in mid-stagger,

Ginger stiffens and drops. We all stand still, sweating and breathing hard, staring down at the mare as the tension leaves the muscles under the glossy gray hide. Someone swears. B. Joe leans down to close her staring eye. Ashamed to cry in public, I go off in the trees; George finds me and wraps his big arms around me until I stop sobbing.

Later, as we sit around the fire, B. Joe hopes aloud that a bear won't claim the dead horse as its territory during the night; the other horses are too worn out to move the corpse. Someone plays a guitar that has ridden a pack for sixty miles and soon we're all singing softly. B. Joe demonstrates the cowboy sense of humor by suggesting "The Old Gray Mare." Some one, certainly not B. Joe, whispers that he has only borrowed the horse from another outfitter; that she's worth several hundred dollars. I wonder if he—or I—will have to pay for her. After the ride, several veterinarians told us the mare could have hurt herself bucking and bled internally, or died an unusually quick colic death after changing from dry hay to the wet meadow grass. The long, tough trail after an easy summer of hauling greenhorns over shorter trails may have worn her out. All assured us I wasn't to blame.

In the morning, three men tie ropes from the horse to their saddlehorns and drag her away from the campground. Horses that die in Yellowstone Park are blown to bits with dynamite to prevent grizzlies from gathering to menace tourists; once we get out and notify rangers, this may be Ginger's fate.

B. Joe readjusts packs and upends my saddle on a mule; a real mountain man would have walked the rest of the way to rendezvous carrying his gear, and might have balanced a horse haunch on his shoulder to gnaw on the way. Holding to the tail of a pack horse, I'm towed to the top of Bonneville Pass; it's easier than walking, but I'm gasping in the thin air when I climb on behind Jeff to cross a soggy meadow.

We meet a thin, tired backpacker who gazes in admiration at the string of horses and says, "That looks like the way to go."

Without a pause, one rider says, "There's a good horse down in the meadow you can have if you can get her up." The backpacker looks interested, and trots away, a victim of mountain man humor.

Several riders trade off with me, walking while I ride.

"How far is it?" rings a voice from behind.

"Not far now," says B. Joe from somewhere ahead. I distinctly hear John Colter's ghost chuckle. Before long we see several hundred tipis shining on a hillside under heavy, fast-dropping clouds.

We lead our horses down a steep ridge covered with slick rock, being careful to leave distance between us in case a horse above loses its footing.

I am nearly down when the woman ahead of me gasps and points up. Without pausing the Cowboy gallops out on the knife-edge ridge and plunges down, his pack horses thundering behind. Rocks roll; dust billows. The Cowboy's expression is calm. No one says a word, but I hear a lot of exhaling when he reaches level ground. I drop back for my last conversation with the Cowboy, hoping he'll offer me a little trail-shortener to ease the chilling effects of the coming rain. We proceed in silence, common politeness among folks who spend a lot of time in the wilderness. Talk isn't welcome unless it's necessary. Finally he says, "That ridge wasn't nothing much. I was just showin' off."

"You must have ridden country like this a lot." This is as close to a question as I feel it is safe to come; westerners don't pry into personal matters. He's just quit his last job, he says, after spending five years working for the government's wild horse roundup program. A long meditative pause.

"You know what they do with them horses? Horses that run wild all their lives?" I shake my head; his mustache and expression are ferocious, his voice almost shrill.

"They lock 'em up in corrals and feed 'em hay. For the rest of their lives." His expression could shrivel cactus. "I'd rather have my throat cut," he says savagely.

I break another western rule; I want to know the name of a man who could cut through the wild horse controversy with the one thing no one has explained to me: why it's a kindness to put wild horses in a cage. And he tells me his name.

We ride across a highway lined with impatient tourists headed for Yellowstone, most of whom don't even glance at us; history riding by on a horse doesn't interest them. We'd planned to don our best clothes for a triumphant arrival in camp, but instead break out slickers and blankets as the skies burst like a water balloon. By the time we've passed thirty or forty lodges, I'm tired of explaining why I'm walking to folks who break into disbelieving laughter. I almost wish I was carrying Ginger's haunch as proof. My friend Mimi waves a whiskey jug from the sidelines and I drop out of the march, hugging her and the jug alternately as we watch the riders disappear into the rain.

"How long has it been raining?" I ask.

"Eight days," she growls. "Around here we don't use the R word."

She leads me to her nearly dry tipi, where I tell the story of my dead horse, and am promptly given a new mountain name: Horse-Killer. George and Mike stagger through the doorway and sit down beside me on a wooden chest. B. Joe and the Cowboy have left camp with the horses and pack mules. As water pours out of his hatbrim onto his soggy buckskins, George tells me our gear, including saddles and sleeping bags, is under a tarp at the other end of camp.

"Where's our tipi?" I ask innocently.

Our van is stuck in the parking lot; the road is so muddy we can't get it into camp, or out to a dry motel. We haven't got room beside the van to put up our lodge, even if we wanted to. Before dark, we must carry our gear, on our backs, a half-mile uphill to the van.

"Other than that," someone asks, "what was it like?"

Soon all the relatively dry people—well away from us on the other side of the lodge—are pointing and laughing, and we wrap wet, muddy arms around each other and laugh until we slide to the soggy ground.

"Next year," I gasp, "we want to ride for a week."

After the Storm

Shaky, I climb the ladder to see if the wind
tore off more shingles, or hail pounded holes.
From the roof I can see clear
to the next ranch, the Badlands—and no farther.
I can't tell how the Supreme Court will rule,
if the famine will get worse,
the war go on.

Birds glare suspiciously. I can't hear the telephone
ring. The car and its engine trouble are tiny
and far. The garden isn't crops and weeds,
only a green rustle of corn, a swirl of squash vines,
orange bulge of pumpkins. The air is pure, the wind fresh,
filled with strange voices.

A bird swoops past, chuckling.
Dinner time, but who can cook on a roof?
I can't pay bills or vacuum the living room.
There is nothing
I should do
that I can do
on the roof.

Addicted to Work

> *I once knew an educated lady, banded by*
> *Phi Beta Kappa, who told me that she had never*
> *heard or seen the geese that twice a year proclaim*
> *the revolving seasons to her well-insulated roof. Is*
> *education possibly a process of trading awareness*
> *for things of lesser worth? The goose who trades*
> *his is soon a pile of feathers.*—Aldo Leopold, *A*
> *Sand County Almanac*

Virtually all of my friends have at one time or another suggested that I get away from the ranch, give up the physical labor it requires, and pursue some respectable occupation like teaching. Why, they ask, should I waste my education and strain my muscles pitching hay to cows? Neighboring ranchers say, "Isn't it too bad you wasted all that time in college when you were just going to come back here and work anyway?" Neither group understands why I laugh instead of answering.

In our admirable desire to educate ourselves, we have begun to believe that an education should keep you from having to work. Many ranchers still urge their children to get college educations, "so you won't have to work as hard as I did." People who try to buy the country place of their dreams discover that they can't afford it; land is so costly that it is often accessible only to big, destructive corporations. Ironically, the ranchers' educated kids—lawyers, doctors, engineers—might be able to afford land, but they've lost the desire to labor on it, and the ability to appreciate intangible rewards. They're sure that agriculture won't provide them with "enough" money; their desire for instant and immense gratification in the form of electronic gadgets, a bigger car, a designer home has forced them to live in towns where they can earn more. More important, they have lost the knowledge essential to making a living on the land.

Many ranchers say that one thing wrong with ranching today is the desire of rural people, encouraged by television's portrayal of some hypothetical "good life," to buy everything town folks buy.

Instead of taking pride in a different lifestyle and a unique culture, rural people have adopted urban goals that force them to depend on urban markets, urban machinery and technology. Stan Steiner, in *The Ranchers,* recorded interviews with ranchers, including Ann Charter, who said: "When the ranchers have to live up to their city neighbors and have all the conveniences they are not going to make it. Life on a ranch has been urbanized; it is no longer a rural way of life. The rancher, he is plugged into the electricity from the city."[6]

Many non-ranchers, such as urban professionals, politicians, and academics, also imply that anyone who *enjoys* physical labor must be too dumb to get an education, or appreciate it. Even today, when farming requires the economic skills of an investment banker, and the scientific knowledge of a chemical engineer to keep from poisoning yourself, some people regard "dumb farmers" as a single word, and are unable to distinguish between the very different occupations, attitudes, and viewpoints of ranchers and farmers.

Most Americans regard work and play as completely separate activities, the former an unpleasant thing you do to get money so you can afford to play in style. I have heard teenagers deny that a lifework should be something one loves to do; they tell me with cold eyes that they're going to be computer programmers or stockbrokers because "that's where the money is." At the age of eighteen, they plan to make all the money they can as soon as possible, so they can retire—and then "enjoy life."

I've tried to suggest to them that nothing in life is guaranteed; what if they do not live long enough to enjoy the deferred pleasures?

I occasionally teach college classes, part-time, but only because I enjoy teaching; I know easier ways to make money legally. I must be wary and vigilant to maintain my present lifestyle. I could write happily for eight hours a day if someone would feed me occasionally, but I can't write when I'm using the same creative energy to teach. If I taught full-time, I couldn't write at all. So I prefer ranching, which blends physical exercise with mental, and allows me some variety in choosing what to do each day. The drawback is that sometimes the ranch work takes twelve hours out of my day, and I'm too tired or sore to write.

If my primary goal in life were to make money, I probably would not live in rural South Dakota; I'd have accepted that offer from a slick magazine in New York. Money isn't my goal, but sometimes my attitude is considered inappropriate in our society. At an engineering college where I taught, for example, students were skeptical when I insisted that anyone with a college degree should be able to communicate clearly, not only out loud, but on paper. They judged success by income, and many of them would be making thirty thousand dollars a year the minute they graduated; consequently, they had little respect for advice from someone making less than an eighth of that for teaching two classes in freshman English. If I were smart, their eyes and their tongues said, I'd be doing something that paid more. These engineering students were interested in hard cash and in technical subjects. They expected to do poorly in English, and they did; by contrast, they assumed that I would be unable to understand even simple chemistry problems, because my master's degree is in English. They had neatly pigeonholed the world in their minds: technical knowledge = technical brilliance, and lots of money; liberal arts = vague stupidity, and poverty. The two types of knowledge, according to their thinking, could not coexist in the same individual.

"Education, I fear, is learning to see one thing by going blind to another," said Aldo Leopold.[7] While writing this essay, I went out into a cold, wet wind and stacked green wood for twenty minutes. When I came back to the computer, my ears were freezing, my back hurt, my blood was racing, my heart pounding, and I was delighted to be struggling with words. When words temporarily defeat me, I can check the cows, or carry wood inside, or pile rocks around my trees. I'm often tired, but never bored. When I'm confronted with a job I detest, six other jobs I prefer can delay it another day.

The variety of work keeps me from becoming blind in the sense I believe Aldo Leopold meant, my vision narrowed until I can see only words, or only physical labor. I believe that for a human being to see, literally or figuratively, he or she must look both near and far off; in the same way, labor should be both physical and mental in order to keep all circuits healthy. A Yale law graduate who took his ailing brother West for his health in 1889 apparently agreed with me. He started Thatcher School in Ojai, California, which still requires students to pitch hay and shovel horse manure before breakfast, on the theory that a connection exists between "caring for a horse and conquering calculus."[8] "There's something about the outside of a horse," Thatcher said, "that's good for the inside of a boy." I can forgive Thatcher for the sexist phrasing of his era, because of the results of his experiment. The school is now modern, admits both male and female students from diverse ethnic backgrounds, and sends graduates to colleges all over the country.

It's popular, and in some cases correct, to call any obsessive behavior "addiction," and view it as a disease to be treated, to be recovered from. We now include work among addictions, and our leisure reading is filled with articles advising workaholics on how to relax. By those standards, since I am not happy when I'm not writing regularly, I am addicted to writing. Agriculture is also a twenty-four-hour-a-day, 365-day-a-year job. I have seen solemn articles suggesting that ranchers and farmers are all workaholics and Type A personalities who don't know how to relax and have fun. If I am to believe what I read, I am addicted both to writing and to ranch work, and in dire need of treatment. There's truth in that accusation.

But our society is selective about what we choose to label as addiction. We use the word when a problem is out of control, when we are unwilling to face difficult solutions; we want the problem to be called a disease so that government money will be available to help science develop a pill to cure it—instantly. I think this tendency to call each problem a disease, with its own set of drugs to "cure" it, is one reason we have had such poor success talking our children out of drug use. Most of us use tobacco and alcohol to help us counter the "disease" we call stress; we pay taxes to subsidize tobacco, at the same time as we pay to label it dangerous. Naturally confused, the young ask tough questions. Have we begun the "war on drugs" to distract them? While real crime rages through the nation, we have to listen to harangues about flag-burning; I'm considerably more worried about several dozen serious threats to our liberty from corrupt, inefficient, and greedy government than

I am about a couple of folks who burn a flag for the television cameras. How can we teach logical thinking in schools when some of our most respected political leaders are featured on the nightly news spouting illogical reasons for prohibiting abortion, or fighting in the Persian Gulf?

Yet we *expect* men and women to spend twenty-four hours a day, 365 days a year, loving their families, and we don't call that addiction. Christian churches expect all of us to live religion full-time; we don't call the doctor to help nuns and priests recover from a religious addiction. Television evangelists may bilk poor people of thousands of dollars, but we do not take action that would stop them. "*Caveat emptor*," we mutter as we shrug and turn away. We seem to apply different standards to activities that we agree are an acceptable part of our lives. Yet some of the stories I have read from escaped priests and nuns sound suspiciously like the experiences of youths brainwashed by charismatic cult leaders, then "saved" after parents have paid for their forcible removal from cult surroundings. Working in relays around the clock, parents, ministers, and therapists often keep the cult member, who may be an adult, awake until cult beliefs are renounced. Apparently, brainwashing techniques are justified in one case but not the other.

Country people generally realize that our families are not divisible from our land; our beliefs about both family and land grow out of everyday practices, rather than theory. Some of us never get around to marrying and raising children because we substitute land for family. Those who have families seem to love them and the land as if they were the same—and they are. The crustiest, most conservative, most anti-environment ranchers will say, with an oddly gentle note, "I *love* this country." Others say, "If you take care of the land, it will take care of you." Or, "We don't really own this land. We're just taking care of it for the next generation."

During summer's dry heat, I have heard: "I ain't had no rain on me since May. There ain't enough grass on me to feed a bird." And, "If I don't get rain on me pretty soon, I'm going to blow away." These ranchers referred to their land in the most intimate terms possible. Plenty of ranchers I know say they could make more money by selling the ranch, putting the money on deposit, and sitting on the porch. But most of them go on to say: "I'll quit when they carry me off the place feet first." And they all know a rancher whose wife persuaded him to retire and move to town. "You know," they say, shaking their heads, "he only lived six months. He quit working and it killed him." They never talk about whether he enjoyed his life that six months; they know he didn't, if he wasn't working.

Rancher Ellen Cotton told author Stan Steiner:

> This place is nothing. It is so small. And I'm a small rancher. But it symbolizes something to me, something I would die for. Money just isn't the thing in my life. That's not why I ranch. No rancher is in ranching just for the money; if he was he'd be in another business. If you wanted to make money on this place you'd have to be a hard-nosed person. And we'd have no room for anything else, the dollar sign would be your God.[9]

Dozens of ranchers would echo her words, if they found it easy to speak of such a complex emotion as love; probably they'd just nod and look away so that an observer couldn't see tears in their eyes. A joke that has made the rounds in cattle country for years made it to the *Congressional Record* in 1989. "What would you do," the city slicker asked the farmer, "if you had a million dollars?" The farmer replied, "I guess I'd just farm until it was all gone."[10]

When a farm couple from the tiny town Dallas, South Dakota, bought a lottery ticket worth $12.5 million in a Lotto America jackpot in the spring of 1991, the wife said, "We've wanted to buy a farm and raise our kids on it." Her husband spoke of buying some pigs and livestock. And Elmer Kelton, a writer of the true West, said in *The Good Old Boys*, "A man could starve to death in a year on a hundred and sixty acres. On four sections it took longer."[11]

Not long ago I visited my bee-keeping neighbors, and talk turned to their recent trip to Germany. Bill is a quiet man who thinks and listens before he arrives at an opinion, and feels no need to force everyone else to share it, or even listen to it. But his enthusiasm was obvious as he showed me a souvenir, an intricately constructed carrying case with everything needed to start and transport a colony of bees. The contraption was fitted with special doors to enable one to transfer a lot of bees to it very quickly, or to create a queen by the delicate manipulation of royal jelly and a tiny royal suite. Minute mesh-covered openings let the colony breathe without escaping. A carved depression enabled the bees to feed on sugar water, and a wee fence kept them from drowning. The whole device was only slightly larger than a roll of toilet paper, and about the same weight, but it was a marvel of engineering. Bill didn't buy it because he needed it— he usually transports bee colonies by truck—but because he admired the workmanship. Later he showed me two pieces of an old beehive, and explained the construction, much superior to that of modern hives. From plans he'd found in an old bee-keeping book, he wants to build one; he doesn't need that, either, but he wants to show visitors how the old boxes were made.

I was enthralled as he talked, though only two things about bees really interest me. First, I love honey. Second, when a swarm settles in a tree over the corral, I want to know where Bill is so he can come and capture them. Like many ranchers of forty or older, Bill was raised to do everything as well as possible, and believes any work done with pride is enjoyable. I consider his kind a vanishing species in an America that used to teem with pride in all its labors, and found enjoyment in that pride, and that work.

I have been speaking of work in general, work as an attitude of mind as well as an exercise of body. I also think not working, in the sense of avoiding physical labor, is literally killing a lot of us. We buy expensive exercise clothing and equipment to eliminate the side effects—obesity, heart disease, stress, lung cancer—of being so well educated we never use a muscle. But no amount of artificial exercise can replace real labor, and the satisfactions that accompany it. Older ranchers were raised with the philosophy that people should not expect to get more than they can make or grow with their own hands and sweat, an idea scorned in our consumer society. Many of them understand that the world in which honest hard work automatically meant respect and a living no longer exists; they know they live in a world where their own government pretends to function even though it's a trillion dollars in debt. Even while they admit to support of the Gulf War, they are uneasy about the speed with which it pushed the savings and loans scandal off the front pages; they know that after every war is over, those forgotten problems will be waiting. But they don't believe a country can function under these economic conditions, and they count on their old-fashioned values to come in handy when the whole shaky mess tumbles down.

Country people are directly responsible for our own lives in ways most people aren't. If I lived in the city and got dangerously cold, someone might call an ambulance. But when I go outside alone at thirty below zero to feed cattle, one mistake could kill me. If someone is breaking into my house, dialing 911 will get me a telephone charge, and a connection to a police dispatcher twenty-five miles away who will explain that I'm outside the police jurisdiction. The sheriff is thirty-five miles away on a winding road. I must deal with the burglar alone. Country people learn self-reliance as a necessity, and sometimes overdo it. I was so busy being a stoic child when I cracked my wrist in a horse accident, for example, that my parents didn't take me to a doctor for three days. They were not neglectful; they simply didn't realize that I thought by gritting my teeth on the pain I would master it. An eighty-year-old rancher who has run his ranch, hired men, built a house and barns, and paid all his debts, has turned self-reliance into success, but you won't see him getting recognition as Businessman of the Year.

My second stepson lived in a small Minnesota town until he graduated from high school. His responsibilities there were simple: he had to get out of bed in the morning, get dressed, go to school, study, maybe take out the garbage or babysit, go to his job as a stock boy in a grocery store. His parents expected him to stay sober and get good grades; his school expected him to learn from books how to be a responsible citizen and to believe in the high morality of politicians, even though the news rang with examples of their corruption.

Instead, he got low grades and felt helpless, unimportant, frustrated. I don't approve of his confusion or its results, but I think

I understand it. Except for the babysitting, none of his jobs was important. He knew the world was full of problems; he was full of energy and youth and confidence, but he was unable to see how anything he did could improve his world. His mother complained that he lost his jacket, couldn't remember where he put his books or his English paper.

When he came to the ranch, if he forgot to feed his horse, she didn't eat. If he neglected to fix the fence, the cows got out and several people and horses had to work hard for a day in the hot sun getting them back in. All of them felt free to explain their frustration to him. If he didn't turn the water on the garden, the sun fried the food we were planning to eat this winter. If he lighted a fire and forgot to watch it, he might start a prairie fire that burned the winter grass of a dozen ranches.

What he did, and didn't do, *mattered*.

People who manipulate papers all day long, or tap the keys of a computer, or buy and sell over telephone lines, go home at the end of the day without evidence that they have accomplished anything. Their muscles don't ache from piling up a stack of hay they can walk around with pride. An executive may be responsible for spending large sums of money, or making the deal that will send bulldozers out to excavate for a housing development, but if he or she cannot see the consequences of that action, it is easy to forget how that work affects the natural world, and easy to forget the chain of responsibility which links us all.

As real concern for the earth increases worldwide, some yuppies are taking a shortcut to the natural look. Men's fashion designers, announcing that burliness, honesty, and integrity are "in," are selling clothes inspired by workers' coveralls. But those old-fashioned traits can't be acquired by wearing plaid shirts and lumberjack pants.[12]

Even ranch families have changed; ranch children are being trained to avoid work. Families used to be large; kids raised chickens and sold eggs for allowances, and contributed to the family support; they were important to the whole family's survival. Now, along with their mothers and fathers, they get jobs in town, and their parents buy them a car; the well-defined connection between work and its rewards becomes indistinct.

The comparison can be pushed back into history; before ranchers occupied this land, it was held by nature, animals, and Indian tribes, all of whom resisted the explorers and trappers who ventured here. If those men misjudged the swiftness of a river, they drowned; if they weren't fair in their dealings with the Native Americans, they risked death. What they did, and didn't do, mattered. They were not all good men, and a little later, they weren't all good women; but they were all tough, because they had to be to survive. Most of the stupid ones didn't live to pass on their genes, a fact we ought to give some thought to now that we try to save every child. Not until they had learned how to live in this land, not until they had removed the most ferocious challenges, was the land available for settlement. Their wealthy descendants, having removed most of the real daily risks, now pay to be subjected to dangerous thrills, but they must realize in some ancestral niche in their minds that what they are doing is only diversion.

Historians sometimes say the pioneers "civilized" the country, but I disagree; they polished it, removed a lot of its dangers, set a precedent of killing anything that hampered them. But they wiped out the natural civilizations of the Native Americans, who had adapted to the country instead of altering it to suit themselves. The animals, who had a complex social structure that kept the ecology flourishing, were slaughtered for daring to inconvenience the new inhabitants. Later settlers, who followed the same patterns of killing, were plenty tough, especially by modern standards, but they didn't have to be nearly as smart or clever to survive. Great Plains civilization has been on a downhill slide since the first white man set foot here.

Certainly, many things are easier these days, but the jury is still out on whether easier is healthier for us, mentally or physically. Among people who study such things, the suspicion is growing that we made a serious error some time back. Researchers on the origin of man believe that physically, we are almost identical to the people who lived in Europe, Africa, and Asia thirty thousand years ago: "Our culture has evolved so far and so fast that there would seem to be no connection between us, but physical evolution is a much slower business. Despite all our electronics and jet aircraft, symphonic music and deconstructionism, we are they."[13] If we are physically the same people that our ancestors were, we may have a clue about why many of us are a lot sicker. If the human body evolved over hundreds of thousands of years to fit a lifestyle that no longer exists, that lifestyle would still be appropriate to us.

What are we losing, physically, by eliminating the work our bodies evolved to do? Anthropologists suggest that for a hundred thousand generations we were hunters and gatherers, while we have been agriculturalists for only five hundred generations, industrialized for a mere ten, and computerized for only one. They believe that the contradiction between our long yesterdays and our brief today is the cause of the chronic diseases that cause seventy-five percent of the deaths in industrial societies. The Paleolithic diet probably consisted of red meat with a lower fat content than feedlot beef, plenty of wild fruits and vegetables, and little fat, salt, or sugar. On that diet, our average ancestors were probably as strong as today's professional athlete. Each day, they faced challenges that kept their muscles strong and quick and their brains active. Admittedly their life expectancy was shorter than ours, but that in turn benefitted the species: anyone who couldn't outrun or outsmart a mastodon was removed from the gene pool. Physicians once saw degenerative diseases such as diabetes, obesity, and lung disease as natural byproducts of aging; now they suspect that they are really "diseases of civilization," consequences of our less active lives rather than the inevitable result of human biology.[14]

We take a body with that history, prop it upright for eight hours while the fingers lightly punch buttons, then seat it in a car where moderate foot pressure and a few arm movements take it home. It hugs the other members of its small tribe, then slumps down on a cushiony surface and aims its eyes at a lighted screen for two to six hours, and lies down on another soft surface until it's time to get up and do it all again. No wonder we're sick.

Even in historical times, we could have learned a great deal from the original human denizens of North America if we'd been less intent on having things our own way. Each step we've taken to make life easier, to turn it into a "lifestyle" instead of a living, has taken away some of the challenge and left us feeling as if what we do is less important. That's why some men go off to war, and others join secret organizations with strange handshakes, or climb mountains or icefalls; that's why some women join the army and others learn martial arts or join the Peace Corps or try sky-diving. People whose lives are a challenge are healthier in every way; by taking the difficulties, the tests, out of life, we've turned it into oatmeal. You can survive on it, and get energy to fuel the furnace, but who cares?

Work has become routine and predictable as a consequence of our striving for efficiency. Studies show that workers who perform the same tasks over and over again grow ill and irritable; efficiency suffers, and some workers turn to vandalism to relieve boredom. The experts who promised that simplifying jobs and creating assembly lines would increase production are now beginning to admit that the human mind does not thrive on sameness, that workers cannot be treated like machines.

Ranchers have always known that; among the unspoken advantages of ranch work are its variety, and the fact that it still involves life and death decisions and challenges. Although ranchers are often pictured as humble, stolid sons and daughters of the soil, they are secret adventurers; they don't like doing the same thing every day, and don't respond well to orders. In another era, some might have been riverboat gamblers. Every purchase of land or equipment, every new bull brought into the herd, is speculation. A rancher buying winter feed is gambling that the feed will last as long as the bad weather. Turning his cattle out to summer pasture ten miles from home is a gamble that rain will help the grass grow until the calves are ready for market. My mother was singing the chorus of a Kenny Rogers song one day: "You gotta know when to hold 'em, know when to fold 'em, know when to walk away, know when to run." My father chuckled. "That sounds like it's about ranching."

Wendell Berry has observed that "farmers do not *go* to work; a good farmer is *at* work even when at rest."[15] By contrast, company directors or factory workers *go* to work, then go home to the people and objects they love; the distance between their labor and their loves is considerable, and they have no trouble making a distinction. A farmer or rancher *lives* at work, where everything valued is in close touch with everything else. Trying to hurry the job and rush on to something else, something more profitable or productive, means losing the careful comprehension demanded of someone who works the land. Yet the thinking that governs a modern economy, and which is accepted by the majority as the "right" way to think about all jobs, requires that we do all work as quickly and with as much efficiency as possible. We never live in or very near the workplace; our great cities with their gleaming high-rise buildings are empty at night of everyone but the feral, the lost, the desperate. This way of thinking leaves no time for considering a job as part of a process, for looking at the consequences. Berry sums up the contrasts:

> Finally, the economy of industry is inimical to the economy of agriculture. The economy of industry is, typically, an extractive economy: It takes, makes, uses, and discards; it progresses, that is, from exhaustion to pollution. Agriculture, on the other hand, rightly belongs to a replenishing economy, which takes, makes, uses and *returns.* It involves the return to the source, not just of fertility or of so-called wastes, but also of care and affection. Otherwise, the topsoil is used exactly as a minable fuel and is destroyed in use. Thus, in agriculture, the methods of the factory give us the life expectancy of the factory—long enough for us, perhaps, but not long enough for our children and grandchildren.[16]

A similar perversion infects those who consider writing as just another job. People often ask me why I bother writing essays about ranching and the environment, when the "real money" is in popular fiction. If I answer that I don't like most popular fiction, and have no idea how to write it, my interrogator has an answer: "Well, read a bunch of it; it's not hard to figure out." True, but why study something that's easy to grasp? When I suggest that I don't want to write just for money, they look at me as if I have lost my mind. Friends suggest schemes for making ranch work easier and less time-consuming, for making it possible for me to sit at my computer all day long and churn out best-selling books. When I wail at an increasing volume that I don't want to write best-sellers, that I need to work outside to keep my brain from being fried in front of the computer, they stare in disbelief.

The same thinking pervades the nation's attitude toward wilderness. Wildlife must be "marketed"; get people out there, make them pay for seeing it, charge extra for their campers and dogs, and put in some entertainment for their kids. To these folks, simply designating a wilderness with a fence around it and leaving it be while the flora and fauna go about their business, with or without visitors, is a "waste of resources."

The same mentality affects business planners who say we "can't afford" to do things by hand, or selectively. They say we can't afford to log a forest selectively; all we can afford to do is clearcut. We can't afford to leave hay on steep hills or along fences for wildlife; big machinery requires wide spaces created when we tear out fences and plow the steepest hills. Those business advisors would explain to ranchers—slowly so we could grasp it—that we can't afford to keep a cow that didn't calve this year, even though her last four calves were fat, healthy, profitable critters, and she will no doubt have another one next year; they would sell her instead of allowing her a vacation from profit this year. Yet when their companies don't make a profit, and the shareholders don't get dividends, the bosses get a raise; after all, the company is an ongoing business, and requires good management, and good managers don't come cheap.

According to industrial thinking, we can't afford to farm without big machinery, can't afford the hand labor that kept one-family farms and ranches going; we educate our children so that they won't have to work with their hands. We've created labor-saving devices, most of them requiring fuel we must buy outside our region, to save us from awful hand labor. Yet in our leisure time, we may prowl the antique and gift shops for symbols of that labor, for handcrafted furniture, for hand-made pottery, hand-woven rugs. We may plant a few seeds in pots or window boxes, desperately seeking symbolic dirt under our fingernails, but we consider planting large fields by hand beneath our dignity, and until recently thought such work suitable only for uneducated people with dark skins.

My neighbor Margaret once asked if, in spite of the growing national passion for antiques, I'd ever seen an antique wastebasket. After the silence on the telephone line had lasted quite awhile, she said softly, "Our ancestors never threw anything away; they didn't have anything to waste."

I once spent an afternoon watching craftsmen and women from several New Mexico pueblos seated on a porch in Santa Fe, bargaining with tourists eager for their pottery and jewelry. The Indian people leaned against an adobe wall which bore hand prints from the women who had patted the mud into place and whitewashed it. The artists, technically at work, relaxed in comfort in the warm sun, smoked, nibbled piñon nuts, exchanged low-voiced comments the tourists couldn't understand, smiled, and enjoyed themselves.

The vacationing tourists were edgy, unsure how much they should haggle, arguing shrilly over which pot would look best on that shelf above the fireplace; they reached eagerly for their money as soon as an agreement had been reached. They looked exhausted and haggard when they left, clutching their prizes; the Indians packed up slowly at day's end to go back to their mesa where, in an unhurried way centuries old, they would make more jewelry and pots for sale.

Obesity, flabbiness, and lack of muscle tone have become prime concerns of workers who sit behind a desk, as well as factory workers, housewives, and the public in general. We have become so concerned about our lack of physical fitness that we have made dieting and mechanical exercise huge industries. At the same time, the nation has thousands of former workers whose jobs have been destroyed by mechanization, or because the business for which they worked couldn't make enough profit to compete with the industry giants. So while thousands of people pay for exercise, thousands more need jobs. Somewhere in the middle are farmers and ranchers who are unable to hire help since they can't compete with wages paid by big industry. The farmers are forced to buy machines, which provides employment for the workers who build them, but demands more cash. Farms and ranches go broke when the kids move to town because a farmer can't afford to hire labor, or can't find anyone who knows how to do agricultural work.

We're all familiar with the scenario, because it's been the immediate cause of many farmers losing their land. Couldn't those problems be combined?

Millions of people sit idly collecting welfare in cities. Some might be glad to raise their children in clean air, while doing physical labor on a farm or ranch. Why not offer some of the unemployed work that would improve their bodies and keep their kids a long way from crack? With a little guidance they could support themselves by gardening and raising pigs, perhaps on a little leased acreage in the country where they'd have a chance to kick the habits of the cities. Such a program, if government-sponsored, could cost no more than one B-1 bomber or a couple of missiles, and might actually get some people off welfare permanently. A trained pool of agricultural workers might go a long way toward saving the family farm, and give farmers a sense of pride as they helped their new neighbors learn country ways. Most thoughtful farm commentators now agree that the machines and chemicals that have streamlined farm labor are creating some of our problems with pollution, but many people would still resist the idea that doing work by hand is a step forward, because we associate strong, work-hardened hands with a lack of education.

I can hear the Washington economists snickering at my simple, naive plan. Where are the studies by economists? What about cost projections? If they took my basic idea and ran it through a couple of think tanks and a couple of million-dollar federal studies, added some machinery, some fuel, some experts, a few chemicals (so big corporations could benefit), they'd like it better, and more profit could be siphoned from the rural areas into city pockets. But can we "afford" to continue as we are?

Absent farmers are replaced by machinery, which requires money, as do petroleum, chemicals, and other purchases which should not be part of a healthy farm economy. In fact, these replacements are actually dangerous to our productive power, part of the cancer that is destroying us even as we buy more. We recently went to war in large part because we refused to heed a warning twenty years ago to conserve fuel and develop alternative energy sources. Thanks to years of believing "bigger is better," and the practice of making profit our criterion for success, agricultural people are the worst polluters; our newspapers tell us so daily. Country people who love the land are suddenly its worst enemies.

When white people occupied this country in large numbers, we believed this abundant land could be exploited wildly without being destroyed, but we were wrong. We do not have the right to destroy; our current behavior toward the earth, influenced by our attitude toward work and profit, has led us to the edge of disaster. And it is silly to place blame only on big business. We are all to blame; each of us who eats, drives a car, wears clothing, and buys vegetables in a supermarket rather than growing them at home, is contributing to the earth's pollution. The solution is up to us. Production tends to move from the country to the city, and profits are taken in the city, where the majority of voters live. Country dwellers are few, with less representation in government, so we have to be noisier.

Frequently, when two ancient ranchers meet, their conversation goes like this:

"How are you?"

"If I felt any better I'd have a runaway."

I don't know if they are talking about their health, or being optimistic, but I do know folks like that can wait out a lot of social change before they feel the need to alter their behavior.

I think time is on the side of the hard-working country dweller. Armed with the strengthening effects of fresh air and exercise, and saved from the mental problems created by urban stress and overcrowding, country people who regularly do physical labor are healthier and saner than anyone in the city, and we'll outlive and outsmart our critics. Then folks who like to sit down can open clinics to teach other former city dwellers how to love physical labor, and give seminars on Adult Children of Yuppies: How to Learn to Work for a Living.

And we'll start the cycle all over again.

Thanksgiving Prayer

Behind me, the black shadow of a church
reaches out from every height in Scotland.
Through chaotic centuries, their stone hymns
drown screams, the whine of sword blades.
Conflicting legends paint their floors
with the thick, red blood of martyrs;
smoke from human flesh sketches
separate creeds against blue sky.
From their aisles blows a chill Christian wind
driving men and women to their knees
in the blood of their own ancestors,
their own children.

Surrounded by ancient churches—
with the opulent liquor of entreaty, hymns
and Christian sanctity oozing from their stones—
I pray on the beach.
Empty my pockets of stones
and shells from the stormy coasts,
place them in a circle around sage from home.
Earth lies quiet under my feet; air sweeps past
in storm clouds; rain runs down my face;
warmth from my heart and fingers
stands for the fourth element, fire.

The salt stings my throat, scorched raw
by years of bawling adoration

into empty stone vaults and naves,
of begging stone-eared saints
to turn their sleek smiles on me.
My eyes burn with tears
for love I'll never know again.
Sharp-tongued Cuillin Hills chant ferocious love
from heather heights to lakes filled with tears.
Today he walked beside me.
Inside his coat, I crawled down the tunnel
to the burial crypt.
I did not lie down.

Now I stand facing sea wind.
White foam sweeps away the lighter stones,
the sagebrush and tobacco.
I ask only to come back here;
salt spray eases the pain in my throat.
The hand inside my pocket clutches heather
dug between the standing stones.
When I get home, I will plant it
on my husband's grave.

Rock Lover

—for Margaret

I bend my knees and set my feet solidly, fit my hands around
the rock, and lift. I'm picking up the ancient earth piece by piece,
carrying rocks to pile around trees I have planted in a steep prairie
hillside.

This is not good terrain for growing trees, this rocky northern
slope covered with tangled prairie grasses, high above a gulch in
which water may flow briefly this spring when the snow melts, and
after a hail this summer that destroys half our grass.

I persist in planting trees here because a few years ago I noticed two tiny pine trees which had rooted themselves on an even steeper slope above a stock dam. At first I thought they were yucca; its green, spiked foliage can look like a pine tree at a distance. I looked at the green patches sticking out of the snow with binoculars, but couldn't be sure. Yucca can also look remarkably like a lost or dead calf, whichever a rancher is expecting to find. One warm day in spring, I slowly climbed the hill, clinging to tufts of grass and rocks to keep my balance; the rocks were so numerous and the grass so thick that I saw no bare ground at all. When I reached the middle of the slope, I was astonished to realize that what I'd seen really were pine trees. Cattle had not broken them off because the trees had emerged among the rocks. I reasoned that they know what they are doing, and piled up a few more rocks while catching my breath. If possible, cattle will avoid stepping on rocks, or anything that might make their footing insecure. Also, rocks will help catch snow in winter, and keep the ground cooler in summer so that natural moisture will evaporate more slowly. These trees weren't going to get any help on their water supply from me; if I could hardly haul myself up the slope, I certainly wasn't going to climb it carrying buckets of water.

A few days later, as if seeing the first two trees had opened my eyes to another dimension, I saw two green spots on the slope of the big hill directly south of my house. I scanned them with the binoculars—more pine trees. Suddenly I felt like a spy in enemy territory; the armies of the forest were invading! Without any human assistance, after two of the driest years in this century, pine trees were springing up on the prairie.

Next, riding my horse along a limestone cliff in the bottom of a gully, I glanced up. Just above my head, a scrawny cedar tree was growing out of a limestone shelf no bigger than a dinner plate. Some of the tree's roots were visible below the shelf, exposed to sun and wind, and the tree above them was partially brown. But it was alive. I sat and stared at it for a moment, but other than breaking up the shelf with a pick and planting the tree somewhere else, I could think of no way to help. It is safe from damage by the cattle, at least, since no cow can or will climb up the cliff to walk on it. My horse Oliver has been known to eat the tops out of newly planted pine trees, but while I pondered, he reached up as high as he could and wasn't even close to being able to chew on this one. I wished the tree well, and rode on.

Not long afterward, I read about a researcher who smashes rocks to create fertilizer. Ward Chesworth, a geologist at the University of Guelph in Ontario, is one of a group of experts reviving agrogeology, the process of harnessing the natural fertilization that takes place when weathering breaks rocks into their constituent elements. The researchers visualize farmers, particularly in African countries with humid conditions and worn-out soil, covering their fields with crushed volcanic stone rich in potassium, phosphorus, and other nutrients, key ingredients in commercial fertilizers.[17] The idea appeals to me for several reasons. If it caught on, some of the big fertilizer companies might go out of business, and I wouldn't have to watch their advertisements on television, knowing that they are killing the soil while promising to protect crops. Moreover, some of our pastures are carpeted in rocks; if I took to thinking of profits instead of all these philosophical ideas that clutter my brain, I might become a rock export magnate. My neighbor Margaret, who has planted many more trees than I, confirmed that she had tried rock mulching. A deep pile of rocks can retard weed growth around trees which cannot be mechanically cultivated. The rocks can hold down magazines and mail-order catalogs, which will smother weeds close to the trees, and hold moisture in the soil. I take fiendish delight in never complaining about the large numbers of catalogs I receive; the marketing and mailing geniuses who send me duplicate copies and put my name on new mailing lists don't know they are helping my trees.

As I drove through the pastures that fall and winter, feeding cattle, I carried a pry bar. When I came to a rock that jolted my teeth every time I bounced over it, I laughed nastily, stopped the truck, pried it up, and put it in the pickup. I didn't confine myself to small rocks; I took anything I could lift. Thus I sometimes found myself temporarily unable to breathe, and while I leaned on the truck and gulped large volumes of oxygen, I saw things I might otherwise have missed: an antelope barely peeking over the rim of a gully nearby, or a thirteen-lined ground squirrel sitting at the entrance to its hole. My actions completely puzzled the cows, which hung around staring at me, and occasionally wandered up to lick the rocks. Generally, the arrival of the pickup means someone is bringing them feed, and they couldn't understand what I was doing.

I began to take a deep interest in the rocks I moved. Often I would begin to pry at a rock, only to discover that, like an iceberg, the greater part of it hid well below the surface. Once I refused to be defeated by a rock's size, and by the time I'd dug, hacked, and pried it out of the earth, the resulting hole shook the pickup much worse than the rock ever had. I was forced to gather smaller rocks and pile them in the hole to save other drivers from breaking their necks.

Speaking not as a geologist, but as a rock-carrier, I've found three types of rocks. The limestone that underlies much of the area is light, rough-surfaced, often covered with a pale green lichen. Rain and wind carve spider-sized caves in it; I did intricate little dances when I was lifting a forty-pound rock and saw a ten-pound wolf spider racing up my arm. I didn't want to drop the rock on my toe, but wolf spiders look as threatening as their name, and I don't want one inside my shirt. Sometimes I'd lift a slab of limestone and find an entire mouse community hidden underneath, displayed like a diorama. Although mice are hardly scarce, I always gently replace the roof and leave them alone. Limestone is so fascinating that I often picked up more than I needed, and began building a path between the house and garage. A solid chunk of limestone makes a good "deadman." When a fence crosses a gully, the bottom wire is usually high enough to enable an agile cow or calf to crawl under it and escape. The solution is to attach a weight to hold the wire down; a large enough rock can't be shoved aside. If the gully runs with floodwater, however, the rock will catch debris, and may contribute to pulling the fence down in that spot, so the trick is to select a deadman that will move with the water, allowing trash to wash away.

The most numerous rocks are a different type, smooth on the surface and fine-grained inside, a form of granite, hard and heavy. These can vary from the size of my fist to half the size of a pickup box. It embarrasses me to say that they are known by long-time residents as "niggerheads." I have never known any other name for them, and cannot account for the term, since people of African ancestry have always been scarce here. I'm not saying we're not prejudiced; in recent years, as African-Americans have become a larger part of the population, racism has reared its predictable head, but the name preceded their arrival. In all sizes and shapes, these rocks found many uses before I started mulching trees; the lower story of a cabin near my home is built of them.

White and pink quartz chunks are arresting on the dun-colored prairie. I can't help picking them up, but reserve them for a special use: decorating the graves of cats that were good mousers, or the grave of Cuchulain, the West Highland White terrier buried near my house. When we were away from home, he always stood at a particular spot on the hill to wait for us; we'd see his square little white body in the flicker of our headlights. We buried him on that spot, and now the white quartz catches my eye from a distance, day or night.

Intermingled with the quartz on these graves, and set as a border around the few flower beds I keep free of grass, are bones: cow and horse skulls, ribs, leg bones, t-bones, single vertebrae graduated in size from as large as my fist to as small as a fingertip. I began by collecting Frodo's gnawed, unburied leftovers from a desire for tidiness, whimsically putting them on Cuchulain's grave. I have always liked the shapes and textures of bones, and began as a child picking them up in the pasture or boneyard for the pleasure of looking at and touching them. When my collection outgrew my study walls and bookshelves, I used it to mark the sites of special plants, and to create bone borders for particular planting beds.

Bone borders: there's a symbolism in those words. In each epoch of any land, the borders of the known world have been strewn with the bones of those who tried to penetrate the wilderness, the explorers who dared more. Although we make a fetish of erecting monuments to the admired few among our heroes, the breadth of these plains was seeded with the bones of those courageous ones whose names we have forgotten, but whose paths we follow still, literally and figuratively. "Bury me deep," pleaded a dying child on the pioneer trail to Oregon, "so the wolves will not dig me up." But no matter how deeply in the flesh of her mother earth they buried her, she remained alive in her living mother's heart, and her bones could not escape their fate. Bones decay, dissolve back into the richness of the earth. It pleases me to watch them weather through the seasons, to contemplate the length of time these bones will last, in comparison to the fragility of human bones, and in contrast to the the rocks I move.

When I'm checking the cattle, which means not necessarily driving on trails that benefit from rock removal, I collect them anyway. This morning I drive the old buggy trail on top of the high ridge south of my house, created during homesteading days by someone who chose it as his route to town. The high ridge is level, blows clear of snow, and is too rocky to get muddy, so it is almost always passable. In order to make the path more pleasant for his horses, and later his automobile, the man—and probably his wife and children—walked along beside the vehicle, picked rocks out of the trail, and piled them to mark the edges. He probably hated rocks, but I hope sometimes he stopped, as I do, simply to look. In the far distance, the Cheyenne River winds through low hills, looking a little vague, as though mist is rising from it. Beyond it are the rough pink and blue ridges of the Badlands. To the west are the ragged slopes of the Black Hills, a haven of trees which mocks my efforts to grow them here. And just below me is my house, looking small and abrupt; some of my trees are barely visible above the tall, ungrazed grass.

This rock-picking has become a habit, an addiction; when I'm not picking up rocks to put around my trees, I collect them to put in mudholes, so that hitting these with the trucks won't make them deeper. I collect rocks to pile around corner posts of fences, so the cows won't stand around gossiping and stomping down the soil, which will eventually make the corner posts fall down and give me a bigger job of fencing to do. I've begun to dream about rocks, as I lie in bed aching, but I've lost weight, trimmed and solidified flabby muscles. I dreamed last night of making a weight loss video for country folks: How To Lift Rocks for Health. Anyone can do it—no special machines or clothing are required. Simply adjust the size of the rocks to fit your age and condition. For widows, there is an additional benefit:

it is impossible to cry while moving rocks. Crying blinds you and you only drop a rock on your toe once before you are cured.

Another spring has come. I've spent a warm morning in sun and melting snow wandering along the pasture trails, prying rocks out of the chilled earth and loading them into my truck. I've dawdled, in the finest sense of the word; I took time to sit on the tailgate and drink coffee, and throw snowballs for Frodo, the Westy who goes everywhere with me now. When the truck box sagged alarmingly, and the motor growled more than it ought to, I drove slowly back to my belt of trees, feeling a satisfying ache in my muscles. One by one I chose the stones, lifting them out, piling them on top of a layer of magazines and catalogs around the little juniper trees that don't yet reach my knees. We've had two earthquakes in three years, neither strong enough to do more than rattle dishes and light fixtures, but I fit each stone against its neighbor as if these plains rocked every day, unsteady on the earth's broad lap. I make joints between the stones fit as well as I can, moving a stone until it settles comfortably into the earth, nestled tight against its neighbor so that no grass will grow up between them.

When I pick up a piece of limestone, I turn the crisp, pale green lichen up to face the sun, careful not to flake it off, hoping it will continue to grow. I position pink and white quartz chunks big as my fist to catch the eye, interrupt the tawny prairie colors, so that even if every tree has disappeared, anyone walking through the deep grass on the hillside will see these piles of stones, and know another person worked here.

I am part of a species which seems to thrive on change, a species which bulldozes grass to make parking lots, cuts trees to build houses, blasts holes in the earth to create glittering jewelry, and dams valleys to create lakes where we can roar noisily, mindlessly about in speedboats. But I love these rocks because I can do almost nothing to them. I might make them smaller if I went back to the garage for the forty-pound maul, and pounded at them all afternoon. I can move them from the spot where geology dropped them. But I can't change them. I can only pile them around my trees to kill the weeds, to mark the spot where I labored to help these trees grow.

There they will provide hiding places for small plains animals the tourist brochures don't mention: thirteen-lined ground squirrels, gophers, mice, and all kinds of snakes, from blue racers to bull snakes to rattlesnakes. They are all welcome in my little wilderness.

Forty years in the future, my body will be turning into earth that will blend with yellow clay and become nourishment for grass and weeds. As I worked, I pictured the rocks I piled today remaining here, though the trees may have been killed by drought. The sprawling city is twenty miles north of me; I have always thought that distance enough to save my little monuments, but lately there is serious talk of building a new four-lane highway to "improve business" by connecting that mid-size city with the Brown Cloud, Denver. If it's built where logic and flat ground dictates, the Western Expressway would be less than one quarter-mile from my bed, making my house uninhabitable even if construction didn't destroy my hillside and my trees.

A "task force" has been appointed and a million dollars appropriated to study the idea of constructing the highway; many of the small towns along the route have contributed a hundred dollars each to the study, in the innocent belief that the highway will make them grow, and that growth will improve each of them. I know that once that kind of money is spent and a project is named, it's hard to stop.

Most of my neighbors sincerely believe the highway will be safer. Many tractor-trailer rigs drive faster than the fifty-five-mile-an-hour speed limit on the present two-lane highway; people seem to believe that since the speeding can't be stopped, they need more room to dodge. To my mind, this logic is unsettling, as if we reasoned that we couldn't do anything about the earth's destruction, so we might as well speed it up. I think a highway of this type will be like a vast river, sucking the lifeblood from small communities along its route to feed the larger ones. The large communities here in the middle of the plains, in turn, see themselves as mere satellites to the Pacific and Atlantic coasts. The leveling goes on in many ways, and gradually the country becomes only a blood donor for the megalopolis, an empty place to send garbage.

When I mention my objections to my neighbors, most suggest that I sell my house and land for as much as I can get, and move somewhere else. But I have not viewed my home as an investment, to be turned into cash the minute it doesn't satisfy me. To "invest," in medieval Latin, was to clothe in vestments, robes of state or priestly garments. This land has invested me with its personality, its spare beauty and harshness, and I have invested it with my love and care. The bones of Phred and Cuchulain lie here, and their friendly presences accompany me on my walks as surely as Frodo sniffs along behind me. Here I have built fires scented with sage, and prayed in my own way. My small monuments stand between earth and sky here, places where I feel close to my husband's spirit, and to the spirit of the land and air. I cannot claim age-old traditions for this particular piece of land, nor do I rate my occupancy of a few years more sacred than the occupancy of gophers and spiders, deer and cattle. I cannot point to ancestral ruins or artifacts, but my investment in this land involves much more than money, and there is no compensation for what I will lose if a highway passes over it, or so near as to make silence impossible.

But I am forty-seven years old, and fighting a project of that size would take vast amounts of time, energy, and cash. If a majority of my neighbors are in favor of it, I may not fight this time. I may simply do what I can to preserve my own small spot, and gradually spend less time here. After all, I'm getting what I want out of this experience.

I build a monument to each tree. I mark this windbreak I've planted during my temporary life, creating shelter for the temporary grouse and mice that share this place with me, all of us gone before these stones. If the stones disappear under asphalt, the spirits of the land will still be here.

At the Balloon Races in Custer, South Dakota

In this green and granite canyon Horatio Ross found gold;
Yellow Hair wrote dispatches while the miners met.
In this green and granite canyon
we find sunrise and balloons.

Coffee steams as balloonists talk
to ranchers; breath explodes in still air;
three women in shorts jostle in a patch of sunlight.
Seven baskets lie beside seven fans,
chill air swells silk pockets bigger than the bank,
the blue and white one looms over the courthouse,
twice as high as the sheriff's office.

Patchwork colors shimmer, as if
christening dresses and ball gowns
were sacrificed and stitched
into flight.
                No man can steer a balloon;
wind is its only master.

Seven balloons inhale flame;
Bags of air high as mountains
bob like boats on a bowl of air.
Like fat men in bright nightgowns
bumping bellies, the balloons quiver.

A burner blazes. There is no signal.
A balloon rises. No one cheers.
The man below the burner waves;
we all wave back.
                    Seven balloons lift
over the broad green valley where the ghost
of Custer rides. Eight hundred spectral men
pick pale flowers to garland spirit horses.

Custer nods, waves, smiles to see
they sent balloons to meet him;
his worth is recognized; now
he can send the gold dispatches,
begin wresting this land
from the savages
who don't appreciate him either.

Thunder Butte: High, Solemn, and Holy

> *Hugh worried a little that Thunder Butte*
> *behind him didn't get any smaller. In almost*
> *two days of crawling south away from it the dull*
> *redstone butte still seemed to loom over him as*
> *lofty as ever ... as holy, solemn and high as*
> *ever.*—Frederick Manfred, *Lord Grizzly*

One October weekend George and I went hunting the wily sharp-tailed grouse, and ended our hunt by climbing Thunder Butte, one of the state's least known and most impressive heights.

Thunder Butte stands on private land in the plains near Glad Valley. Should you want to visit, stop at the Glad Valley General Store (which stocks everything from plastic pipe to thumbtacks, from dime novels to beaver traps) and ask the name of the current owner, and directions, so that you can ask permission to make the dangerous climb. If you're looking on a map of South Dakota, Glad Valley is a long way straight north of Philip, in a land of strange names: Usta, Firesteel, Twilight Road.

We thought of the butte before we saw it, going north. Fred Manfred had written: "The sun was setting upon it and gold light limned all its silhouette, while red and then rust deepened the shadow on its near side. The butte looked like a huge mammary sliced off at the top exactly at the nipple."[18]

The butte apparently derived its name from the frequency of lightning strikes, and the Lakota belief that the Thunder Horses, creators of storms, lived there. "The Sioux spoke of it as the pulpit of the Great Spirit Wakantanka. The butte was also used as an aerie by golden eagles. Around it on all sides—east, west, north, south— the long tan sloping bluffs and hills lay stretched out like languorous mountain lions," wrote Manfred.[19] *Lord Grizzly* is his saga of Hugh Glass. In 1823, Glass was wounded by a grizzly north of the butte and left for dead, but recovered and crawled most of the two hundred miles to Fort Kiowa, near Chamberlain. He no doubt crawled directly through the present site of Glad Valley.

For two days we tramped through the brushy valleys and soil bank acreages, stumbled through the plowed lands of shelterbelts, and shot grouse. Unless one has lived thus, intimately with the prairie, it is a universe difficult to understand, to feel. In appearance, northwestern South Dakota is wide open, bare. To quote Manfred again, "It was shortgrass country: good soil, little or no cactus, very few stones; a minimum of wild salt. It lacked only rain and rain at the right time, to become the Garden of Eden at last, the wild lily of the valley of men's dreams."[20] Only by hunting and walking—or crawling—through it do you discover it to be full of wildlife, with some of the best game bird hunting in the world, and abundant surface water. As we hunted grouse, antelope season ended, and hundreds of antelope lined the roadsides, as if making themselves easy targets for disappointed hunters.

When we had shot our limits of grouse, we abandoned most of the weaponry for a climb up the mighty butte, which had haunted us through the days. "The whole jagged tossing country seemed pegged down and held in place by the massive redstone butte," said Manfred.[21] Though the butte is visible for miles, the vastness of the prairie conceals how high it really is—2,755 feet above sea level. Once the traveler decides to approach it, the trip seems to take hours. John G. Neihardt noted, in *A Cycle of the West*, that even when Hugh Glass had crawled past it, the butte haunted him: "The butte, outstripped at eventide, now seemed intent to follow. Every now and then the crawler paused to calculate again what dear-bought yawn of distance dwarfed the hill. Close in the rear it soared, a Titan still, whose hand-in-pocket saunter kept the pace."[22]

We began the climb cautiously; ranchers had shot more than sixty rattlesnakes on one recent day. We poked every bush, looked carefully under every rock—and saw nothing but a carpet of shell casings from snake hunters. As we neared the top and exhaustion, we began to relax. At one point the dog—which was supposed to have stayed in the car—was nosing under a rock while we rested. There was a buzz; the dog did a backflip and landed twenty feet away as we danced nimbly about, waving our pistols in the air. We shot five rattlers that day, and as George said on another day along the Bad River, we only killed the ones that attacked us.

The most obvious impression of the butte from the northwest is that it has been hand-laid because the limestone blocks of which it is composed are stacked so neatly, so horizontally. The second impression, as one seeks handholds to climb this bricked-up surface, is that it was certainly laid a long time ago. In spots the rock crumbles away at the lightest touch, adding to the hazards of the climb.

The weathered top of the butte lies naked and gray as primeval earth. Exposed to the full strength of the elements—the sun's heat, the wash and pound of rain, hail, and the thunder horses; the sweep of wind and snow—it endures. Let No Name, Manfred's vision-questing youth in *Conquering Horse*, describe it: "He found that the whole top was about as large and as round as their village circle. Most of it was covered with frost-shivered shale and eroding gray rock, with here and there some clumps of grayish sage, and the pale green tufts of new buffalo grass. There were innumerable ant mounds."[23] So it is today.

Although our climb was late October, comfort was impossible; we were too hot in the sun, too chilly in the shade. Yet for four days the Lakota boys on vision quests lay here, at each of the four sacred directions, fasting and seeking a vision to guide their lives and make them men. Here on this butte top, the enduring target of the elements, the spiritual world would surely wax, and material concerns wane.

To make the agony worse, anyone on top of the butte would look down on the south side to a circle of boulders laced with plum bushes, green and cool. Here the moisture from the butte drains off through a gap "at least ten horses wide and four deep" and here the Indian youths staked their horses while awaiting their vision.[24]

From above, we saw a fox, dead before the mouth of his lair—poisoned or shot elsewhere perhaps, and trying to get home when he died. We found evidence, in great white stains below crevices in the rock, that many owls and eagles live there, no doubt feeding on and with the snakes. Despite the great snake-kill of a few days before, we saw not a single carcass.

Entering the ten-horse-wide, crumbling gap in the south side, we looked out over the valley of Thunder Butte Creek, and realized how very high we were, how utterly separated from the prairie. Everyone who sees the photographs taken that day believes we are on a cliff high above the sea. Here, in the shelter of the butte, we found many hieroglyphs from earlier tourists. The prehistoric visitor left only hand prints; the modern tourist seems compelled to leave details of love lives as well.

Sitting in the opening, we looked down at the cluster of rose and chokecherry bushes and fallen rock from the rim of the butte, and remembered the history that has washed over this land, from the moccasined steps of the Lakota, trapper, and mountain man, to the booted feet of the military and the leather shoes of the farmer. (An early-day sod house still stands, a few miles away.) Before those travelers, the prairie was disturbed by underground heaving, the march of dinosaurs. Through all of it, Thunder Butte has stood. "Again, at sunset, the wind died away. It became very still. The sun sank, a yellow ball falling out of a light blue sky into a yellow-blue horizon. ... Night raced out of the east. Stars lowered into sight. The high rock cooled."[25]

Like Conquering Horse—as No Name was called after his vision quest—we were revived by the evening's cool, and descended from the butte in the last light just when Hugh Glass would have awakened and begun crawling in the night to avoid Indians and heat. "A great round moon followed. ... In it the rusty tips of the dead bunch grass resembled yellow day lilies. In it the dull red rock of Thunder Butte resembled a sunflower. The great round moon filled the silver valleys with rivers of milk. He made up his mind not to look back at Thunder Butte for awhile."[26]

Miles away, when we, like Hugh, looked back:

> The capricious flare
> Reveals the butte-top tall and
> lonely there
> Like some gray prophet
> contemplating doom.[27]

Driving to Red Scaffold

The Belle Fourche River is muddy and galloping.
I just hit a meadowlark; he struck
at the top of the windshield, leaving feathers.
I think of going back, but let myself off easy.
I know how he'll look; if he's not dead,
I'd have to kill him.
Bear Butte is blue behind me;
and here's an empty house,
a dam running over, broken corrals.
In the house peak
a triangular window, high under the eaves,
where a child stared at the butte, the horizon.
Now there's only a red-tailed
hawk, hanging on the wind, hunting;
a poet passing by.

An old frame house
with a foundation of dry unmortared stone
glares across the road at a missile silo.
No gas station, but four pickups are parked
in front of a trailer labeled "Enning School."
At White Owl, a white deserted school and outhouse
precede a farm and cemetery—
the necessities of life and death.
At Plainview, two silos stand beside a garage
surrounded by thirty-five old cars
and a pile of gravel visible for five miles.

Just beyond is a church
under one coat of white paint,
a cemetery with a red wooden cross,
fewer than twenty graves.

Howes has a post office, liquor,
outdoor bathrooms.
The door is off the men's side;
a stiff breeze blows up the hole in the women's.
As usual, visitors have brought their pens,
left their creativity at home.
What could I write?
The plains are a cemetery for the mind.

Going to the Post Office

Going to the post office is a social occasion as well as a major undertaking on the South Dakota plains. I live only six miles from my symbol of the federal government's attempt to guarantee mail delivery, but it's still not a trip one makes in house slippers and bathrobe. In winter I often go in the coveralls in which I've just fed cattle—splashed with some of the less pleasant by-products, noisy in my five-buckle overshoes, with my stocking cap pulled down to meet my muffler. I always hope no one will recognize me, an absurd idea, since every neighbor for twenty miles knows my pickup, my walk, and the coveralls I've been wearing for the last eight years, except in periods of major weight gain, when I wear a size larger with no stripes.

The first stop is at the mailbox itself, located at the end of our half-mile ranch road, leaning gently against three other mailboxes. My parents' box is perched on the axle from a 1920s vintage car, set in concrete badly chipped when the road grader hit it one winter. My mailbox is larger, newer, with a patched bullet hole, and several dents caused when our second-nearest neighbors took the corner a little short with a stack of hay. They considerately set the box upright and repaired it; neighbors in the country are like that. We speak of "neighboring" with nearby ranchers, as in, "Do you know the Smiths?" "Yes, we neighbor with them." That doesn't simply mean that our land lies next to theirs, but that we help each other out in times of trouble, physical or mental.

Next is the box shared by that neighbor and his son, who has helped us in several major crises; this is a large box topped by the silhouette of a buffalo. The buffalo disappears every now and then, and we speculate on who has taken considerable risk, given ranchers' reputations for being quick on the draw, to saw through the heavy metal legs for the privilege of displaying this art object. Next to that box is the whitewashed one belonging to my closest neighbor and friend Margaret, who first pointed out to me that the word "neighbor" is a verb, and her husband Bill. She is the sister of the man who patiently makes the buffalo, and thus daughter of our second-nearest neighbor.

Today I tuck a Christmas gift in the back, hoping this week's carrier will leave it there. Last time I left magazines for her, tightly banded and labeled, the carrier carefully unwrapped them, read the address, and placed them in my box. People who live fifty miles from postal service used to conduct business through their mailboxes. They'd leave unstamped mail and several dollars when they were out of stamps, or a note requesting the carrier to bring a loaf of bread and milk the next day. Some postal carriers delivered medicine, tractor parts, or anything else they were asked to carry. In today's world of specialization, where the postal carrier is no longer a neighbor but the lowest bidder for the route and maybe a stickler for regulations, such friendly help is rare.

As I top the hill on the highway, headed toward the little town where the post office is, I note that our neighbor to the north has taken his cattle home. He left them longer than usual this year, because we've had no snow, and grass is everywhere scarce. But now he'll have to feed hay, and this pasture is too far from his home ranch to do it conveniently. In the next few days, he'll bring his bulls down, and they'll lean through our fences all winter, making eyes at the too-young female calves in our corral. The little pine tree Margaret and I watch has scarcely grown this year, and the cows have rubbed it ragged; I hope it will survive.

A derelict car is parked in the next turnoff; I slow to look, but no one is visible. For three days, I've debated looking inside for an injured or frozen driver, but I don't have the nerve, and the Highway Patrol surely has. I note a new pile of beer cans and a mattress in the ditch; this turnout is especially wide, and seems to have become a favorite dumping spot. To be fair, it also serves as a parking place for joggers who leave nothing but a little sweat.

Out of habit, I watch the tops of fenceposts and electric poles for the teardrop silhouette of a hawk or eagle; as they migrate south, we often see non-native species, including snowy and barn owls, peregrine falcons, and whooping cranes. Once a tiny merlin shot between me and an approaching car to snatch a meadowlark out of the air. The driver of the other car didn't react, but I nearly drove into the ditch, shocked at the swift ferocity of the strike.

The next neighbor is out in his yard, leaning against the door of a pickup with its engine idling, the preferred visiting method in all weather but a blizzard. He's ready for winter: haystacks are neatly aligned next to the barn, not too close together in case one of them catches fire; the tractor stands in front of the garage where he's been checking oil and antifreeze.

Just up the road, a pickup is parked next to a pile of broken railroad ties. Two men are pitching chunks into the pickup box, presumably for firewood—a dangerous practice, because ties are soaked in creosote, which builds up inside chimneys. But we're due for snow any day, and fire danger was so high in the woods during most of the summer that use of chainsaws was prohibited; if they can't afford to buy wood, this may be the next best alternative. The railroad has piled the ties in readiness for winter, when a crew will spend days pouring gasoline over them and setting them afire; columns of black smoke will rise a hundred feet straight up as all that wood turns to ash. I can't stand the waste; I pick up all I can lift and turn them into snow-catching fences. Our hilltop now looks like a fortified redoubt; I only half-jokingly call it Fort Snell, in honor of

George. He likes to live high up, his view unobscured by trees and with, as he puts it, "a good field of fire." He denies being paranoid; "it's not paranoia if they really are after you," he says.

At the next place, a cow is licking a newborn calf, while others look on with what appears to be approval. Calving in December is a calculated risk; if the calves get a month of good weather, they'll be four to five months larger than calves born in spring, and probably bring more money at sale time. But if we have snow tonight or tomorrow, this calf, and others, may die.

The next house intrigues me; it was built on a single high sidehill acre at the edge of a rancher's land. The single-story, shed-roofed house came first, then a greenhouse nearly as large. Because winter was upon them, they erected a sheep barn out of bales of hay, supported inside by a meager framework of two-by-fours. By spring, the sheep had eaten nearly through the inside walls; they polished off the structure during lambing. That summer, the father and three sons built a wood barn, while the wife planted a huge garden, for which she won prizes at the county fair. Together, they planted several rows of sheltering trees, now head-high to a tall cowboy—on a horse. From a bare hillside and three years of sustained work that family made a home, just as pioneers did a hundred years ago. Overhead, rolling clouds indicate those trees may be catching snow by nightfall; water is scarce on their hilltop, and the snow will percolate down and reduce the amount of irrigating needed next summer.

The cemetery is cold and barren today, the wind whipping fragments of plastic flowers into the lilac bushes, scouring the old headstones. The county's history is here, from the victims of the diphtheria epidemic and the women who nursed them to the newer graves of youngsters lost to speed and alcohol since the highway became a major truck route. Just below the hill of the dead is the store, surrounded by pickups as folks stop by for groceries, a newspaper, or other items they suddenly need before a storm rolls in. I've always been comfortable there, even with the small amount of its history that I know.

I'm not the only one in coveralls in the post office. We wait for our mail, steaming gently, our faces red from the wind, noses dripping discreetly into red cotton handkerchiefs, silk neckscarves twisted around our bare throats. We talk about who's in the hospital, who's gone south, the likelihood of a storm, how much we need moisture but that we'd just as soon get it as rain in the spring. One by one we collect our letters, discard the junk folders in the trash, clomp back to our pickups. I wipe the windshield with a greasy glove, and head for home and more feeding. We feel a little more in touch with the world now that we've used our voices in friendly greetings to our neighbors, maybe for the first time in several days. The precious rolls of mail we carry will keep us busy for hours later tonight—after the outside work is finished—as we warm the chill out of our joints, and perhaps stare at the square screen where we never will see lives like ours. The post office is our real link to other worlds.

Wolves

I know your pirate face,
your eagle nose, scarred throat,
at any time of day,
any mood or season.
I know all of you
in the dark, your cough,
your mountain scent
in a sweating crowd.
Every inch of me
would know any inch of you.

Now I know your swollen grave
by smoking red sunset,
by ice-white moonlight,
by snow drifted into deer tracks
between the rocks.
I've seen an eagle spiral up
at sunset over your mound.

In the wolf hour
I've heard you howling on my scent,
tasted your touch,
seen your wolf soul.
You find me constant,
staring into the dark.

Night in the Country

At midnight in midwinter the sky is a deep blue-black, lit only by a few cold stars and shards of ice in the deepest ruts. The temperature reached nearly fifty today, and the scent from the deep golden grasses on the rolling hills south of the house hangs in the air, tangy and sweet, mixed with the sharper odor of manure from the corrals, and the heavy scent of burning wood. Moonlight gives a faint silver sheen to tall bronze bluestem, tawny foxtail, brown alfalfa.

I turn slowly, enjoying a skyline molded to the smooth shapes of hills; no straight-sided buildings break that gentle arch, no trees slash upward. This is the prairie, during the annual warm spell between the first snow and the spring storms that strike when our cows begin calving in March. To the north, a glow marks the nearest town, twenty miles away. If I lean forward over the porch railing, I can see my neighbor's yard light a mile away.

As a city child, I lived in terror of the dark. Even now, on brief city visits, I lock doors and look wistfully out of high windows at night, awakened by sirens and inexplicable shrieks. Out here, where strange sounds in the night may mean a prairie fire or someone stealing cows, I can't avoid the responsibility of investigating. But here the night is more than peaceful; it is inviting, an opportunity not to be missed. Often, I get up and prowl outside in my nightgown just for the pleasure of it.

On a moonless night when I was a teenager, I found myself on a tired horse far from home after dark. Coyotes howled; a booming rush overhead told me the nighthawks were hunting insects. In my fear, I complained to my horse. She blew her warm breath on my face and reminded me that a good horse will take a rider home even in a blizzard. I mounted, loosened the reins, and waited. She raised her head and began trotting confidently straight into smothering blackness, as if a sack had dropped over my head. But I trusted her. Soon the nighthawks swirling around me became benevolent night spirits; the coyotes sounded happy to be alive. Grass swished against my horse's legs just as it did in daylight; my saddle squeaked. After a while, I could see the birds, and the grass seemed to glow faintly, as if lit from within. Before I'd seen enough, I was home. My fear was gone.

A coyote howls from the east, near the carcass of a cow that died of old age yesterday. In the distance a series of puppy-like yips and yaps begin, and I can trace the young coyotes' high-spirited progress through the gully toward the dead cow by their cheerful arguing. If I wanted to leave the porch and walk a half-mile to the hilltop, I could hear them growling over the old cow's thin ribs.

Directly below me, tall weeds around a waterhole rattle briefly—a coyote hunting mice, or a skunk headed for the compost, or the seven deer come for water. A yearling calf bawls, one of the bunch of twenty-six heifers we're raising for replacement breeding cows. They've been fed together since they were weaned and always move—like teenagers—in a compact and usually raucous bunch. Faintly I can see black shapes lying close together a half-mile away, and a light-colored blotch moving toward them from a gully. Perhaps they left her while she dozed, and she woke alone, frightened as a child.

I breathe deeply, glad the blizzard roared over our heads two days ago. We could almost inhale snow from the heavy gray clouds, and the winds left a fifteen-foot hole in the plank corral, plastic flapping on barbed wire, hamburger cartons jammed under tumbleweeds in fence corners. The next blizzard is on its way, and we may not get off so lightly next time. When snow is piled deep on the plains, so that even normal sounds are muffled, I put on my sheepskin moccasins before my midnight trips. But I still go.

If I'm patient, on some night when the thermometer reads ten or fifteen degrees below zero, I will hear the grouse calling. First a single note, like the mellow tone of a monastery bell, will ring from the top of a haystack, and be answered from the shelter of the willows down the gully. I'll try to get outside without making a sound. If I shut a door too hard, or speak, or even shiver, they stop and may not start again that night.

But if I am quiet enough, I might listen to them ringing back and forth across the prairie for an hour. Finally, with a thoroughly undignified squawk, the first one will launch itself awkwardly and fly toward the others. Then they will all take off, floundering in the air like flying turtles, clucking and muttering, until they bury themselves under a rosebush to peck after seeds and gossip for the rest of the night.

Then I move, take a step and hear the snow squeal with cold underfoot. Each step seems to reverberate until I can hear nothing else. The world shrinks to the sound of my footsteps—painfully symbolic—until I stop, and wait for the natural sounds to reassert themselves.

The neighbor's dog barks, a high, frantic yelping. The spell of the moonlight is broken. I'll come back another night, after the snow, to hear the grouse. Now it's time to go back to bed, the warm tangle of husband, dog, and cat, to drift back to sleep among faint coyote howls.

Driving Home
from Rockyford School

A gray highway lies light on the winter-bleached land
blue shadows climb pink spires that break against the sky.
A green car is smashed and rusted in a gully;
leaves like shards of light lie under a naked tree.
Another rusted car lies on its top. Someone
told me a sniper hid here once, shot out tires, gas
tanks, burned the wrecks. I feel him (on that peak, maybe—
a glint of sun on a rifle barrel, menace
in that shadow).
                 I left a third grade girl crying,
her hair the color of the moon in November's
storm sky. Maybe she's the sniper. Eight red and white
cows, tails to the wind, face the black south, all chewing.
The land sings in color under a pale cold sky.

I'm told that somewhere in these buttes, visible
only from the air, is a prehistoric turtle shape, made
of wrecked cars. The ancient dweller in these seas
crawls the land again, to watch or warn.

Ignoring the
Wind Chill Factor

"Wind chill is seventy to ninety below zero." I shrugged as I snapped off the radio. I moved cattle on horseback one day when the wind chill was sixty below. Once it's that cold, what difference can a few degrees make?

But let a national newscaster say "wind chill factor" and drop his voice to whisper "ninety degrees below zero," and my phone starts to ring. I sometimes say I got an answering machine so I'd have time to throw wood in the fire and eat between calls. Friends call from California, Texas, and Florida, to ask how we keep warm when the wind rises and the wind chill drops. I tell them cold weather is nothing new for us.

But a ninety-below wind chill makes new demands. As soon as I go outside, my often-frostbitten hands begin to ache and don't stop until hours later. Exposed flesh freezes in well under a minute. When I open a gate, which takes about as long as reading this sentence, the naked skin behind my glasses begins to sting. The scarf over my face slips as I hack at six inches of ice on the cattle tank, and the tip of my nose is bone white when I get back into the pickup. My lungs ache, though I breathe shallowly. My eyes will burn for several days, and my face feels sandpapered.

I follow all the well-known rules for living through cold weather. I keep a little water running, flush the toilet frequently, check the sewer vent pipe for frost, haul in an armload of wood every time I go outside, plug in the truck heaters. If there's no one else home, I call a neighbor before I go out to do chores, and report in when I get back safely. If I don't call within fifteen minutes of the time I expect to return, one of them will come looking for me, or call someone who will.

The first rule of keeping warm in cold country should be: "Never listen to weather reports." Think about it. We know winter is coming. We stock up on firewood and propane. We have heated cars, miracle fabrics, and warm pets. But every time the sun goes behind a cloud, news photographers dash out to get footage of people shivering and complaining loudly. Do they ever talk to cows? Horses? Sheep? Those animals are out there in their nature suits— only a little thicker and hairier than ours—and no one hears them complain. They survive not because they're stupid, but because no one has ever told them about the wind chill factor. If they ever heard how cold it is, they'd stampede south every fall like geese. Public officials frequently debate citizens' "need to know," usually when politicians have something to hide; we certainly don't need to know the wind chill factor. I'm not sure I believe it anyway. A North Dakota climatologist has said that wind chill does not really measure coldness, but the rate at which naked human flesh would cool; that figure is then expressed in simplified form as a temperature that would cool bare flesh at the same rate in windless conditions. But most people have never been outside naked when it was fifty-one degrees below zero, so the figure really has no meaning, especially to folks well insulated against the chill.

I often ignore weather reports because they're usually wrong. If weather broadcasters scream, "The blizzard is coming," for three days running, I can relax. But when the chimney smoke drops down off the roof and crawls across the ground shivering, I get in more wood.

My second rule for keeping warm is to throw away my razor; I never shave anything after October first. Men know hairy chins are warmer, even icicle-covered, than naked ones. And once the hair on my legs becomes entangled with my long johns, I'm warm all day. Provided I don't give in to some passing fad for miniskirts, no one needs to know. On May Day I perform my annual spring rite: shave my legs. The year it snowed on June 2, I declared spring June 15. Once I went wild under a full moon and shaved during the January thaw; I regretted my impulsiveness all through March calving.

Third, I hoard wool. I've been colder in a sweat-soaked down jacket than in anything except a mountain stream with snow on its banks. Feet can freeze solid in socks containing polyester. When I went to the mailbox the other day, three cars filled with "cool" teenagers in t-shirts and tennis shoes honked. I heard raucous laughter and possibly the words "bag lady." My feelings were injured, since I was wearing the ranch woman's dress-for-success look: two wool stocking caps in contrasting colors, a long red scarf wound three times around my head, two pairs of mittens, an army jacket with a fur-lined hood, my husband's coveralls, and fleece-lined boots two sizes too large. Under all that was a sweater, wool German army trousers, wool socks, and a pair of red long underwear. The long handles aren't sewn on, as they were in the old days; I wear another pair while sleeping. Power dressing in a Dakota winter is stylish: lots of layers. I had enough clothes on to dress every one of those teenagers, and if their car had broken down, they'd have envied me. Out here, cool is cold; cold may be dead.

One doesn't have to ignore style when dressing for winter. When I was in New York recently, I noticed that black was "in"; there it's a practical choice, since it doesn't show the stuff that falls out of the sky. Out here, we wear black to soak up sun rays. In the morning, a black cow on a hillside is up curling her eyelashes while a white cow is still frozen down. It is impossible, however, to find a hairstyle that looks good after four hours under a stocking cap. I don't take my cap off until I get a hair appointment in May, but I still have both ears. Which reminds me, I always remove the earrings from my pierced ears for the winter. Frostbitten hands are only slightly more painful than ripping off a stocking cap and removing an earring—out the side of your ear lobe.

Even in a blizzard, one never enters a plains house without knocking, not because it's impolite, but because we hang old blankets over doors, and pile rugs at the sills to keep out the brisk wind. Anyone trying to get inside without help may need the fire department's extrication maneuvers to escape.

If I'm suddenly warm, and the pickup isn't on fire, I know I'm experiencing one of the first signs of hypothermia. The best solution is to get inside. If I can't do that, I fight off a desire to sleep, and keep moving until false warmth is replaced by the real thing. Any exposed skin is at risk when the wind chill is below zero, including lungs. I hate wearing a scarf over my face, because my breath condenses and forms icicles, but inhaling through a scarf warms the air. Breathing carefully also requires one to pace the work; deep, gasping breaths can be unhealthy. This means I work slowly, which is better for me anyway.

Diet is important; I can't walk far in knee-deep snow on lettuce and carrots; I require meat and potatoes, preferably with gravy. This principle is the same as that behind the simple lamps our ancestors made with a wick in a dish of fat. In order to have energy, you must have something to burn.

I also like to cultivate international understanding in winter. Nothing starts a cold day like *huevos rancheros*—eggs and chili peppers. Chinese mustard warms the coldest sandwich, and Cantonese hot and sour soup can cure colds, 'flu, and most sinus conditions. *Chili con carne*, especially the traditional Texas red, has been responsible for unexplained Dakota thaws in December, when the jet stream was visiting Oklahoma. When the brief winter day is nearly over, and shadows turn blue behind snowdrifts, the perfect warmup is English Breakfast tea, preferably with buttery Scottish shortbread, and with the sound of bagpipes in the background. Or a shot of Scotch whiskey.

As usual, I digress. But I also survive. And that amazes me. I go outside often, though the radio announcers advise people not to, because I have work to do. I carry fifty-pound sacks of cake to the cows, chop ice, duck behind a windbreak when I can, put my free hand inside my shirt when it hurts too much, and drive back to the house more often to warm up after the pickup heaters stop working in December. Sometimes I go out just to look at everything with new eyes: to see how the animals are staying alive. Grouse cluck at me from bushy branches of a cedar, an owl drops silently out of a broken barn window. Some of the cows have gone over a hill to a gully on a south slope and don't reappear until two days later. Their eyelashes are frosty, but their month-old calves are fine. I resist hunting for them in the deadliest weather, remembering my father's rule: "A cow can stand more cold than you can."

That's what amazes me: that humans survive at all. We are so dependent on our machinery and our miracle fabrics, so overconfident about our often-wrong interpretations of nature, that I don't understand how we've lasted this long. News reports constantly confirm my suspicions: in Montana, a freight train barrels out of control into a town because the air brakes didn't work; anyone who has heard her own giant footsteps on a thirty-below morning knows cold air is thinner. In Pennsylvania, misguided folks feed starving deer and chase them away from hunters, thinking to help. They don't realize that when deer are starving, their population has outgrown the available grazing. Chasing away the hunters means that instead of the deer dying quickly, they will starve slowly to death, or be smashed on the highway.

Our lives are so nearly automated that a problem requiring thought can kill us—because we are not used to thinking. We're accustomed to relying on our fallible machinery. But if you're not thinking when the wind chill is ninety below zero, you can be dead. Muttering angrily at silly people who don't think, I reach above my head to pull a bale of hay into the pickup. Two bales, averaging seventy-five pounds each, drop from the stack and strike my chest, knocking me backward. Instinct makes me go limp and roll over the side of the pickup. I kneel in the snow for a minute, cursing my inattention and thinking of the possibilities. Heavier bales might have knocked the wind out of me, broken a bone, made me fall on my head. I can think of a half-dozen ways I might have been badly hurt. Ten minutes of lying in the snow would have killed me. When I pull down the next bale, I don't stand below it.

For the Last Time

They came to the oldest ranch in the Badlands, parked
their pickups by the house, ankled through the gumbo
dust past the cook wagon, looking at the horses
snorting in the corral, sank down to chairs, coffee
and cake in the kitchen. He'd called them here, to brand
the old rope-swinging way for the last time. He smoked
his pipe and laid it out: no pickups, no modern
gas-fed fires. Only one camera, for the record.

The bawling cows and calves hung dust for fifty miles,
stringing into camp in front of curses, swinging ropes, hats.
The men came for friendship, all hardened and easy
to their work, moving steady through the heat and sweat,
rolled cigarettes dangling from a lower lip, Skoal
bulging pocket or cheek. The camera eyed it all,
hung the moments out for anyone to see,
showed each crease in sun-browned skin, hat brim rolls, smoke,
spurts of blood; caught four men, each one
ten years older than the last. They stopped, stared,
at once aware of the man, the outsider
behind the camera, catching the stories
of their lives in the lines on their faces.

Choosing the Boneyard

The cow was at least twenty years old, maybe more. When I was twenty years old, a junior in college—before I'd met my first husband (seven years) or my second (nine years and counting); before I knew I'd never have children of my own and fell in love with my four stepchildren (by two fathers); before I graduated from college; before any of my writing I still respect had been published; before I learned any of the lessons I've won by pain and love—she had been born.

Her birth night was no doubt a cold one in March. Her mother probably lay in the scant shelter of a low prairie hill that created a little windbreak; if a storm was brewing, she was shut in the corral with the other cows, and had her calf in a sheltered corner. But probably she was in the pasture, where snow sifted into a drift behind each clump of grass. Once the calf slid out, steaming among its birth fluids in the icy air, the cow stood—a little shaky, perhaps—and began licking the new calf vigorously.

Her rough tongue lifted the wet, skinny flanks clear of the frozen ground as she licked, forcing the blood to flow beneath the tender hide. Occasionally the cow raised her head into the wind and sniffed, and listened to the coyotes circling around, afraid to come too near even though the calf and the smells of blood and tissue were tempting.

The cow licked the calf all over, from her pathetically thin tail along her spine and the fresh umbilical wound in her belly to her slick black head and drooping ears. By the time the cow's motherly chore was finished, the calf's ears were almost dry, pink-tinged inside; the calf's eyelashes were separated and beautiful around the white-rimmed black eyes; the soft yellow hoofs had begun to harden as the calf scrabbled to stand up on ground slippery with fluid, grass, ice and fresh snow. While the cow tiredly chewed afterbirth, the calf struggled to stand, collapsing frequently, until at last the cow finished her strength-giving meal and began to murmur encouragement.

Finally the calf was more or less upright, legs spraddled ridiculously, tongue reaching out. She found a teat, and sucked her first milk, the rich, warm colostrum, packed with extra nutrients for her first few days. By morning, when my father came in the warm pickup to check the cattle, the cow lay with her back to the storm, the calf tucked into a hollow by her belly, blinking at him in the dawn light. Coyote tracks in the snow led away, as the coyotes hunted mice and birds, having given up on fresh calf.

But tonight they have her, after waiting twenty, maybe twenty-five years. While I finished college and married, and learned about pain and loss and death and hatred and stepchildren, the coyotes waited. They raised their pups on mice and crickets and gnawed the bones of cattle we hauled to the boneyard in winter, and fat steers that ate too much wet alfalfa and died of bloat. Maybe coyotes prefer beef, but their main strength is their adaptability, and they'll eat anything, including snakes and fruit. Ninety percent of their diet is meat, and most of that was dead before they got there.

The calf born that night was branded and earmarked and vaccinated for disease two months later, in May, and learned her first lessons about pain. She was turned out with her mother to summer grass in June, and grew fat and beautiful, in a young cow's way, until my father brought her to the corrals in September. He put all the young steers in one corral and the young heifers in another, and slowly looked the heifers over. Most he put into the pen with the steers, to be sold. He kept twenty or twenty-five heifers that year because they looked as if they would grow into good cows capable of raising healthy calves and feeding them well. He judged by a number of qualities—straight back, ample udder, good lines, and some indefinable quality that a good rancher instinctively recognizes. (Some modern ranchers have to keep elaborate bloodline records because they don't have the instinct, or don't trust it.) She was one of the ones kept, turned out for the winter to be fed with the grown cows. A female bovine is called a "heifer" and usually kept separate from older cows; she is bred to a bull chosen for his small head, to make birth of her first calf easier. Even then, she may require a rancher's help in birth. After that, she is known as a cow, and is expected to calve without help. During calving season, we observe older cows, but usually don't help with birth unless the calf is too large, or incorrectly positioned in the womb.

She went with other heifers and an Angus bull to a private pasture for the winter, and in the spring, perhaps with my father's help, she bore her first calf in a dark, chilly barn. She went on having calves every spring, raised them through the summer, went back to the pastures in fall when they were weaned. All we ever did for her was provide grass, water, and a little salt in summer, protein-rich cake and hay in winter. In return she gave us between eighteen and twenty-two calves. We took most of them to the sale ring and sold them; some of her daughters stayed here, to become cows and mothers, and support us with their offspring.

In the spring we discussed how old she was; she wore a tag of a type I swore we hadn't used for twenty-five years; my father insisted she couldn't be that old, but I think he knew she was. By July, she was thinner than usual, and her calf had almost given up trying to suck milk from her shrunken bag. But he was fat; though he'd miss the milk she gave, he was doing well on green summer grass. The cow seemed glad to abandon him; she began to limp, and was always a little behind the other cows when we moved them to new pasture, a little slow to move to water.

Afraid she'd suffer, we began slipping her extra feed. One fall day when we'd hauled the horses to the pasture, I decided to take her home in the trailer so she wouldn't have to walk when we took the other cows home. She'd slow the entire herd down, and she might simply be unable to walk that far. I found her on top of a hill, where the breeze kept flies away and provided relief from the heat. When I approached, she didn't shy away, but raised her head and stared at me. I shouted at her to start her down toward the trailer. Then, when she didn't move, I slapped her on the flank. She turned and took a step—and I heard a grating sound from the region of her hips. Slowly, carefully, like an old lady in a walker, she worked her way down the hill. I followed, my hand on her hip, listening to her old bones grate together. She made no sound, and didn't wince as if she were in pain; I heard only that awful grinding.

We pushed and pulled her into the trailer—she didn't fight us, as a healthy cow would have—and brought her home to the corral. My father fed her oats and cake every day for a month, but she grew no fatter, and the grating sound didn't go away.

"I haven't got the heart to shoot her," he said. "Take her to that good fenced bottom with the running water, and turn her loose. If she lives, we'll sell her in the spring. If she dies ..." He shrugged. "If she doesn't start putting on weight, or if it storms, you'll have to shoot her. Don't let her suffer."

For another three months, through mid-January, we fed her a daily ration of a couple of pounds of cattle cake. She always ate eagerly, shuffling toward us through the belly-deep grass she ate the rest of the time. But when we turned other cows in with her, she avoided them, staying by herself in the shelter of an old barn.

Then one day she was standing where she had never ventured: beside the gate. On the other side was only the field containing the boneyard. George took it as a sign, a cow demonstrating the right to die, and opened the gate.

She shuffled through, hips still grating loudly, and tottered up the slope. The grass is good in the boneyard, fertilized by the bodies and bones of dozens of cows that have died over the years. If they're in the corral, or anywhere near the buildings, we hook a chain to their legs and drag them to the boneyard—far enough away from us so we won't get the smell, and the coyotes can feed without fear.

The cow stared at us a moment, then lowered her head to the tall grass, and began to graze. George placed the pistol near her ear and pulled the trigger. She folded up, dropped, and then her old legs scrambled like a newborn calf's as she tried to flee her fate one more time.

When she was still, we drove away. Six months later, gathering bones, I would notice her pelvis, as full of holes and delicate as lace where age or decay had eaten it away: the source of that grating. The morning after we shot her, only the great pink arch of her ribs rising above the grass showed where the coyotes had fed. They'd waited a long time.

PART II

George:
In Beauty Walk

The Ditch and the Liberated Woman

This week I met a ditch seven hundred feet
from the well to the house.
A man sitting aloof
on a dragline dug it in twenty minutes.
We laid the pipe in one day,
but the dragline man had gone on
to other work.

The men working here have other skills;
I volunteered to fill the ditch.
Standing on the edge, I looked down
a hundred years, past the thin dark line
of good soil to the clay beneath,
a liberated woman with a ditch to fill.

"Write what you know," I tell my students,
and I know that ditch.
Hour after hot hour I work, back hurting,
sun-battered. I know the blast of heat,
brown arms lifting each shovel full,
the rhythm of each throw.

Many poets would add a stanza here
that seems unrelated to ditch-digging,
but which, upon careful reading,
would reveal that the ditch
is a metaphor for the poet's life.

Metaphor or hole in the ground,
all I know is that damn ditch,
hour after hot hour,
third day following second day,
until I can straighten up—slowly—
and say, "I filled that ditch."
No one is listening;
hammers ring in the noon glare,
as the men and the boy build basement walls.

This morning, just as the sun rose,
I found the sod the dragline ripped off first,
set the drying tufts of grass upright,
hoping it will grow to cover the scar
of birth.

To Build a House

Deep in most people's hearts lurks the desire for a home of their own. Women especially seem to long for the security of a nest, and their husbands often insist, "We can't afford it."

My husband, faced with the prospect of marrying me and learning how to run a ranch on the arid plains of western South Dakota, adapted well. He seemed to enjoy the hard work of running a cow-calf operation, and to slip easily into the economies that are so necessary to maintain our way of life.

So when the desire for a home overwhelmed me, I decided we should build it ourselves. After all, Americans are self-sufficient, able to build better mousetraps and steam engines and missiles. Why shouldn't we build a house? When I suggested it, my husband wasn't enthusiastic. I probably mentioned it first on our wedding night, as we snuggled down in our tiny apartment in my parents' ranch home. I may have mentioned it now and then in the two years that followed. He says I mentioned it every fifteen minutes, but I think it was more like once a day. That doesn't seem excessive, does it?

When he moved out of his house and into my apartment, he brought six guns, a ton of equipment for making his own bullets, a full set of unused barbells, furniture, all his back issues of several gun magazines, every check he'd ever written, a blacksmithing forge, and fifty-eight boxes of books. We stuffed some of it into the apartment, but most of it went into the granary, the chickenhouse, and the barn. Finally, my father pointed out that we had filled all the space he normally used for cattle feed, and that if we intended to remain in the cow business, we should build ourselves a house. I smiled.

"Just what I've been suggesting," I said, and went to town to buy magazines with house plans in them, and a carpentry book. The rest of the winter, I ecstatically drew floor plans, and George sat before the fire reading the book. Like the loving couple we were— I mean are—we discussed every detail of our home together. The conversations went something like this:

"Honey"—(this was in the planning stage; later other terms replaced this simple endearment)—"Honey, do you think the kitchen should be next to the bathroom so we can put all the plumbing in one wall?"

"Mmph."

"It says here that's much more efficient."

Silence.

"OK, then, I'll move the sink over to the west wall of the kitchen so that it will back up to the bathroom sink and commode. That means the range will have its back to the dining room. Is that OK?"

"Mmphmph."

This went on for some months. Each time I proudly completed a floor plan and presented it to George, he would look at it for a few moments. Then he'd point out some tiny little flaw, like, "But you don't have a stairway from the basement to the upstairs," and go back to his book. Occasionally, as I was explaining that the large pantry would hold the canned food from our garden, he'd intone, "Linda, did you know that the board that goes around the outside of the rafters is called the *facia*?"

In spite of this cooperation, ground-breaking day finally came. The excavator, an understanding man, listened patiently as I asked him not to drive his machinery around unnecessarily, since I wanted to preserve the buffalo grass.

Then he said, "Take a picture before I take the first bite out of this hillside. It won't ever look like this again."

Wise and philosophical man that he was, he might have added that neither would we. My husband has lost thirty pounds and his jeans are gathered around his waist like a ballerina's tutu. My hands, which weren't exactly delicate and feminine anyway, are now layered with calluses. I have a permanent lump on my head from being in the wrong place at the right time, and I'll match my biceps against those of any weight lifter you can produce. Naturally, we learned a few things.

First, never start building your house without spending time with a house builder. We did not do this, and we goofed. We have the second best thing: a close friend, Jim, a carpenter who visits often. If you have no close friends who are carpenters, try to be related to one. If you aren't already related to one, rearrange your family until you are. I have several times threatened to divorce George and marry a carpenter, a plumber, an electrician, or a concrete salesman—and he has made the same threat. Choosing a spouse of a different sex or the same religion is not nearly as important as having one who can construct things.

Second, buy a good carpentry book, but remember that it won't tell you everything. "You should complete floor framing before backfilling," the book will casually remark. But it doesn't add that if you backfill concrete walls before their tops are braced by upstairs flooring, the walls will fall in. That's why you need both the book and the carpenter handy at all times.

Once you've agreed on a floor plan, remember to stay away from the magazine department of the supermarket. Refuse to look at magazines with floor plans and articles on house design, and those reports on how someone "bumped out" the kitchen to put in a skylight. Decide what you can afford, and then don't ever look back. It's safe to look at articles on interiors; you might find more efficient ways to arrange the cabinets. But never look at anything that might make you dissatisfied with your floor plan, because it's already too late. Instead, go to the medicinal section of the store and stock up on liniment for sore backs.

You can learn many fascinating things if you read the carpentry book while your husband is doing something you can't help with, but I caution you not to read too far ahead. Asking questions about how to put in windows when you've just begun digging the basement tends to confuse novice carpenters. And you might find out, as I did, that he hasn't read that far yet. This tends to diminish one's confidence that a home will ever rise above that ugly hole in the ground.

Try to get some idea of what each step in building will cost before beginning. Talk to contractors, carpenters, lumber yards. We thought we had plenty of money to complete the basement and first floor framing—until we asked for estimates on having the basement poured. At dinner for many nights, we studied estimates, and considered living in a tipi for the rest of our lives. We elected to get a neighbor to bring his concrete forms, which we helped him set up, and which brings me to another rule.

Good neighbors are essential in building; if yours aren't helpful, with garages well stocked with tools, move to a better neighborhood. The next best thing to being related to handy people is having them for neighbors. And preserving good relations with handy neighbors is a lot more important than staying on good terms with your husband's brother in Spokane, or working for peace in the Middle East.

Once the forms were set up, we continued to save money by ordering concrete ourselves. Nothing gave me quite such a feeling of power as calling up the concrete company and ordering eight yards of concrete. When it arrived, the driver would lean nonchalantly against his truck door, watching while George and our neighbor danced nimbly about on top of the forms, pushing long poles down into the gooey mess to prevent air pockets in the walls. I thought a few air pockets would be nice: little grottoes to put things in, like flowers or stone arrangements, but George pointed out rather grimly that they would also make the walls fall down.

Building our basement was a source of great pride for us in many ways, but chiefly because a building slump had hit the area, and the papers were filled with stories of contractors going out of business. We smiled through our tears as we wrote the checks, knowing that while others may talk about doing something for their country, we were doing something—keeping an entire concrete company in business.

Another important aspect of building a house, even in the country, is coping with the building inspector. Our house is on our ranch, six miles from the nearest town. As soon as rumors circulated—as rumors do, in the country—that we were planning to build, we received a call from the county inspector. He lectured me on septic tanks, drainfields, venting the plumbing, and other unsavory topics, all of which I had studied diligently during my planning winter. Having lived in the country since I was a child, I was already far too familiar with the seamier side of life as represented by septic tanks and the ordeals of draining and cleaning them. Finally, the inspector named the amount of the building permit, and said to notify him when we put in the plumbing. I paid the permit fee, and thought that would be the last we'd see of him.

When we scheduled the arrival of a plumber who would help us lay plumbing pipes, I called the inspector's office as required. Several days later we laid the pipes in the basement and poured at least twenty-seven tons of concrete over them. A bulldozer covered the drainfield. We heaved a sigh of relief, and went to town for groceries. The next morning, the phone rang.

"Say," said the building inspector jovially, "I was up there looking at your house yesterday. You done covered up them pipes. You can't do that unless they've been inspected."

"Well," I said, gritting my teeth, "the office said your inspector would be down the day we laid pipe. We hired a plumber to put in those pipes and we couldn't keep him standing around here for three days waiting for you to inspect. Anyway, is it legal for you to come into the house when we're not here?"

"Oh, you bet. I can go anywhere. By the way, you're going to have to dig out that drainfield so I can see what size rock you put in it. We have regulations on that, you know." I explained that since our septic tank was on our land, as was the drainfield, and the entire two-mile valley below it, and since I didn't want to pollute our own land, we had been careful.

"I still got to inspect them rocks, so you got to dig out that drainfield," the inspector said blithely.

By this time, my normally sunny nature had deserted me. I clearly remember telling him that if he wanted to inspect the rock in our drainfield, he should bring his own shovel. I must have dreamed about telling him he'd fit nicely in the oversize septic tank we'd purchased to be sure of enough capacity. After that, my memory fades, but George believes I may have made some remarks that could be considered intemperate. We never saw the inspector again.

My advice about dealing with officials is to find out before you cover anything up who the inspector is, what he wants, and how likely he is to force you to dig out the drainfield to satisfy regulations. Also, keep samples of the drainfield rocks to show the inspector. You may show the rocks to him from whatever distance you choose.

Eventually, despite all this, we reached the point of Raising the Walls. Again, good friends and neighbors are essential to this phase of home building. Our carpenter friend made squiggly pencil marks on boards, threw down a lot of studs in what I presume were the right places, and told us to nail. Suddenly people appeared from everywhere. Men, women, children—all wanted to nail, because that's fun, and makes a lot of noise. Blood and bruises sprouted everywhere, nails twanged and flew through the air, and pretty soon we had a wall lying on the floor. Then our friend directed us all to squat down, grasp the wall, and raise it. Everyone groaned, grunted, strained, and suddenly the wall was up! We were so delighted that we all let go and dashed around taking pictures and clapping each other on the back.

Suddenly Jim, the carpenter, bellowed, "Who's holding the wall?" He pointed out in obscure carpenter's terms—I didn't have time to take notes—that it wouldn't stand up until he braced and nailed it, especially with the brisk wind that was blowing. We all scurried back to our places, much subdued.

In carpentry, one does not use the same language I've been using all my life. Oh no! There's a special language for house-building. There are no instruction books or language tapes, and no dictionaries. You pick it up in the same way you pick up the language if you suddenly move to another country: by listening carefully, making foolish mistakes, and occasionally wandering into the wrong lavatory. A carpentry book may define some terms, but in a spirit of friendliness, I've decided to compile a handy glossary of those that a book won't tell you.

"Stud"—those 2x4 or 2x6 boards that are hidden inside walls where no one ever sees them, but which are vital in keeping walls upright. A 2x4 stud, I'll bet you didn't know, is actually one and a half inches thick by three and a half inches wide. I maintain that it should thus be called a "one-and-a-half-by-three-and-a-half," but George says true carpenters don't have time for all that.

"Tolerance"—this is a term indicating how big a mistake you can make without the house falling on your head. When measuring for studs you usually put them "sixteen inches on center." This means that the center of each stud must be sixteen inches from the center of the next stud. When we built our first wall, George measured its entire length, carefully placing marks for each stud sixteen inches apart. Then he measured individual studs and placed his pencil mark exactly in the center of each stud. When he measured this first wall, he repeated his measurements until everything was correct to 1/32 of an inch—that was his tolerance.

"Close enough"—a very important term. As we measured the third or fourth wall, I could hear George muttering, "One eighth plus one sixteenth is—oh heck, that's close enough." (Your definition of "tolerance" shouldn't allow you to be more than a half inch off, or your house will begin to tilt alarmingly as the years go by.)

"Compensating"—another meaningful term related to measurement. If your husband-builder says he is compensating, that means he measured the window frames wrongly, and he's going to have to put little pieces of plywood on the bottoms to make them high enough to fit in the wall. If he's like George, he'll cut out all the little pieces of plywood and you and the children will nail them on. I mention this because you are supposed to do it without asking why; if you do ask, he will only say he is compensating.

"Hmmmmm"—a familiar expression that takes on new and varied meanings when applied to home carpentry. It may mean anything from "Oh, Lord, this stud is six inches too short" to "I dropped my hammer and it's going to hit you on the head very soon." It has also been known to mean "I forgot to get galvanized nails, so you're going to have to go to town again, dear. I realize this is your third trip today, but I'm thinking of important things like siding and can't think of every little thing like nails." It's vital to study your particular carpenter's facial expression and mood so that you will become familiar with the possibilities of this innocent-seeming term.

"Double hernia"—an expression used when a husband and wife building team unload windows which were loaded by four strapping football players. Hernias can also be caused by the:

"Carpenter's belt"—a massive leather and webbing belt worn by builders and wannabes, containing neat little leather pockets bristling with nails, measuring tapes, nails, dust, a pencil, nails, scraps of paper with strange hieroglyphics on them. George also keeps a tooth in his, knocked out of his smile by a flying nail. Hammers hang from special loops on the belt. Carpenter's belts are very bulky, with sharp objects sticking out all over them, making it painful to hug anyone wearing one. No doubt this is why one seldom sees carpenters embracing at a building site.

"Square"—this is a key concept, because a house that is not square will be twisted, and even a little twist will make it shake, rattle, and eventually roll. When we squared our concrete walls—after they were poured and solid—my husband handed me one end of a fifty-foot tape measure and strolled along the top of the wall along one side. Over his shoulder he said, "Hop up on that other wall and go to the other end." I froze. My hands sweat when I write about heights; you'll notice I don't do it often. Gingerly, I stepped on the plank that slanted up to the wall, helped along by the fact that George was yanking on his end of the tape. Carefully, with both arms out from my sides for balance, I tottered along, trying not to look at the broken earth eight feet below. When I reached the end of the wall, I sat down, clutched it firmly, and refused to move. George had to get a ladder to get me down, and wait until Jim came to finish measuring all the walls to make sure they were the same length and thus square.

Taking notes on details of this kind is an occupation that's necessary when building, but difficult to fit into the scheme of things. Often, Jim would begin giving us instructions when I had nothing handy but a piece of 2x4. That was fine; I became adept at writing on boards. Often, however, before I had a chance to recopy notes, or do what they instructed me to do, the piece of board had been nailed in place. Despite my feeling about heights, I have had to scurry to the rafters and hang upside down to read notes that had suddenly become part of the roof.

Fear of heights brought me closer to George than ever before during the building phase. Jim refused to put up the 2x4 on the south side of the rafters—because he'd have to nail it while clinging to a rickety ladder twenty-five feet off the ground. He advised us to get better ladders and do it ourselves.

"Don't worry," he said to me. "If you fell and lit on that concrete, it wouldn't kill you."

I was somewhat reassured, until the day we were preparing to nail the 2x4, when I asked George if Jim had ever fallen that far and landed on concrete. He hadn't. I thought not.

When the ladders were in place, George told me my job was to climb one ladder, hold the 2x4 out behind me against the rafter, and continue to hold it while he nailed one end, climbed down his ladder, moved it to the other end of the 2x4, and nailed that. Then I could let go.

We gazed up at the rafters, kissed each other, and murmured protestations of love. George opened his heart and revealed to me for the first time that he, too, was afraid of heights. We began crawling up the ladders, holding the 2x4. When we got to the top, we each grasped a rafter firmly with one hand and with the other held the 2x4 in position. Then George paused while he figured out how to hold on to the rafter with one hand, the 2x4 with the other and still hammer nails. I couldn't see him, so I suppose he clutched the rafter with his teeth, since he hasn't got three hands. My arm ached and shook. I spent the time gazing out over the valley below our house for what I firmly believed would be the last time, and crisply informed George that if he ever brought another wife to our home, after my untimely and fatal fall, I would definitely haunt them.

We're not finished with our home yet; when we get into bed at night, I whisper in George's ear, "Molding, molding, countertops, countertops, closet doors," and other hypnotic refrains. But we've learned a whole new set of skills. At parties—we don't go to many, we're too tired—we can absolutely stop conversation with knowing chatter about *soffits* and *cripple studs*. Of course, we soon notice that other guests develop glazed eyes and drift off to the kitchen to replenish their drinks, no doubt lost in rapt contemplation of building their own homes.

White Buffalo

—for Gina and the Spirit Canoe

In the hospital, nurses pad
on rubber-soled feet.
Doors are closed. My husband's
oxygen bubbles in the corner.
"This is a terrible way to die," he says,
"slowly suffocating."

A white buffalo stands
at the hall's end. His mane
brushes the ceiling; frost
glitters on his beard. He stomps
a black hoof, shakes his head.
Ice shards clatter
on marble but no one hears.
His horns punch the ceiling.
His breath chills, blows papers.
He walks; the building rumbles.
"B-1 taking off," says an airman,
blind to buffalo. There are no lights
on the landing field. The buffalo
passes the nurses' station,
picking up speed; gallops
into this room.

George opens deep blue eyes.

The buffalo bellows once,
leaps to the bed;
both of them are gone.

Outside, the shape
of a tall man is drawn
against the stars. He strides
as if he knows where he's going,
glances back over his shoulder.
He winks at me, smiles,
goes.

Hairs on My Chin

Two days after my forty-fifth birthday, while George fished, I sat in the van with my notebook, studying my face in the rear view mirror. "The gray hardly shows," say my friends, meaning my hair was always this mousy color.

Wrinkles are harder to ignore; the vertical one between my eyebrows appeared the first time I encountered fractions in grade school, so I'm used to it. Folds under each eye and at my mouth corners show when I smile, so I like them. The lines framing my chin, however, suggest jowls, so I walk with my head high.

My eyebrows are black and bushy; I hate pain too much to pluck them. My eyes are green, but, no matter what the makers of contact lenses say, they've never made me a temptress. Below my chin is a neck that looks as if it's been twisted daily for forty-five years as I looked back and forth over the prairie. Some folks call these "rednecks," and we ranchers take that as a compliment, especially coming from someone noticeably larger than ourselves.

The rest of my body, exercised regularly, is doing as well as one might expect from a woman who lifts weights, handles 75-pound bales of hay, and rides horses. I have what a friend might call "strong" thighs, if my friends discussed my thighs. None of the decay bothers me unduly, because I've made major physical demands on my body, and it's accomplished a lot.

The hairs bother me. Not the gray ones on my head, but the black and white ones on my chin and upper lip. I always fondly believed (the root word of "fond" means "foolish") that the sun naturally bleached them, until George said, "I'll love you even when your mustache is gray." When I was thirty-five, three black hairs sprouted on my chin. I clipped them off; four grew to replace them. I yanked them out; six appeared. Once my hairdresser, who sees me twice a year, waxed half my eyebrows and all my chin and lip hairs, and ripped them off, telling me about weight-lifters who have their entire bodies waxed. After a day of redness, my face looked cleaner, and I had new respect for weight lifters.

But I'm a poor redneck ranching woman in a dry year; I can't pay to have hairs taken off my chin when all the strong and wonderful old women I know let them grow. These women are the keepers of the community wisdom; they remember our names and heritage; with their age-knotted fingers they make quilts with stitches I can hardly see. They bury our dead and speak our epitaphs. If chin hairs don't bother them, I shouldn't let them bother me.

I wrote about my chin hairs four months ago, sitting in the sun while George fished. He was having trouble casting because of his shrunken arm, and I was having trouble watching him struggle without crying. Today he has been dead nearly three months, and I found the unfinished essay while trying to write because my writing has always saved my sanity in a crisis. I wonder how I could ever have been so concerned about a few hairs. I never feared aging because George said he wouldn't mind my wrinkles; he only asked me never to dye my hair blue.

I must learn, now, how to get old alone, but I won't be altering the natural signs of age: I have sunsets to watch.

George's Poem

required few words.
Even dying, he kept it simple:
"Be happy. Watch the sunsets."

What kind of philosophy is that
to get me through the next forty years?
I have to figure it out by myself—
but that's not new.
He believed I could.

He helped me up if I fell,
but he didn't grab my arm
when I strode ahead.
When I cried and clung to him
on his hospital bed,
he muttered, "Don't get too poetic."

George's poem is one doe
standing knee-deep in Slate Creek.
She scratches an ear
with a shiny-wet hoof.
A man and woman read in sunlight
on a lichen-covered rock
rearing out of autumn snow.
Near a blue tent,
a white dog chases gophers.

Walking at dusk, they hear a fawn
wail in fear and cold.
All night the dog sleeps between them.
At dawn, snow collapses the tent.
Entangled, they all crawl out
laughing, throw snowballs, make
coffee. The fawn's tracks cross
the meadow beside his mother's.

Now he is dead, I remember
how he smiled as he drank coffee.
He was writing a poem with no words.
I cannot read it in a book.

No one else
will ever read it at all.

George R. Snell, 1946–1988

When I met George, after his second recurrence of Hodgkin's disease, he was receiving chemotherapy regularly at Fitzsimons Army Medical Center in Denver. After a treatment, he would drive ferociously north, trying to get to a particular truck stop before the aftereffects made him vomit. After that, he would sometimes be weak enough to let me drive the rest of the way home. Otherwise, he ignored Hodgkin's disease, a form of lymph cancer.

He told me once of standing in an air force office in Germany, looking at a map of America; the center seemed to blur, and he saw a vignette of a smiling blonde woman. He had nearly forgotten it until we met, and he recognized me as the woman he had seen. Early in our relationship, we spent a weekend in a cabin above Buffalo, Wyoming. We strapped on snowshoes and went for a walk in hip-deep snow among the trees and high peaks. Once I stopped, gasping for breath, and watched him moving easily ahead, his red coat the only spot of color in miles of blue-green trees and white snow. "What am I doing following this big lug around in the cold?" I thought, and knew at once that I would follow him anywhere he wanted to go. So, in the maze of our lives, we found each other.

George was a big man, from the toes of his size ten Triple E Red Wing boots to the crown of his seven and three-quarters Stetson. The first time my mother saw him, descending in an open freight elevator, his shoes came into view first. She gasped and whispered, "Look at those feet!" For a time, we were concerned that his son Michael, who clearly had inherited George's feet, hadn't inherited the height to balance them. We teased him, gently, about being like the toys weighted on the bottom so they can't be knocked over; we told him that would be an advantage in a fight, but might result in his staying longer than necessary. George suggested the best fighting weapon was feet: "Put one in front of the other as fast as possible."

When George wrapped his big arms around me, I was enveloped, protected, shielded, and the feeling didn't compromise my independence one bit. Because George wasn't hugged much as a child, he was acutely aware of the need to show love; he hugged me a dozen times a day. I calculate I will lose 360 hugs a month, 4,320 in a year, 129,600 if I live another thirty years. Sometimes his friends asked him why he "let" me go on long trips by myself. He always replied that we trusted each other; then he'd pause thoughtfully, and add, "You try stopping her." Sometimes I pointed out that a woman couldn't do anything a thousand miles away that she couldn't do while she was supposed to be buying groceries. I'm afraid I didn't advance liberation; some of the men looked askance at their wives the rest of the evening.

At that time, George's hair was long and tied with a headband; he'd missed the sixties, stationed with the air force in Germany, and the hair hid long biopsy scars on the right side of his throat from the operations which followed his diagnoses. He liked to tell about the time he was reading a bulletin board in the hallway of a military hospital when an officer strode up. The right side of his head had been shaved for radiation treatments, and he was wearing a hat. The officer bellowed, "Don't you take off your hat in the presence of a superior officer, soldier?" George whirled, jerked off his cowboy hat, and saluted; the scars must have been startling, until the long hair on the other half of his head cascaded down. The officer blushed, saluted, and stalked away. Radiation had damaged George's chin hair, and no matter how hard he tried to grow a bushy beard, it was always sparse on the right side. He experimented with everything from a mustache to a full beard during the time I knew him. Whenever he shaved it all off and cut his hair short, he looked even more than three years younger than I.

Most big men walk into a room heavy-footed, as if they are arrogant, or simply fat. When I was downstairs working and George walked across the floor upstairs, I heard nothing but an occasional floorboard creaking. One of the books he read as a child spoke of Indians walking silently in the woods by putting their toes down first; he practiced until that became his natural walk. One of his greatest joys was walking up on a herd of deer and observing them while they remained bedded down, unalarmed. He seldom shot one, though we both loved venison, because we were never without beef.

Later, he walked into a room as if you shouldn't notice him, but his stillness was louder than a shout. His arms-crossed stance proclaimed a man who stood centered on the earth, sure of death, sure that every minute before it was his to spend. Some men wear belt knives like a shout of defiance that often gets them into more trouble than they can handle. George's knife and sheath were so worn they seemed to blend into his clothing; no one ever noticed. Once when we visited an art museum, he forgot about the knife, and the museum guards didn't notice it until we were on the third floor. Then one approached us, his face white, trying to speak but gesturing silently to the knife, and to the huge Goya painting two feet from us. George immediately surrendered the knife, blushing.

When George put on his fringed leather pants and shirt at a rendezvous, they fit him as if he never took them off. He day-dreamed about being transported back to the 1840s, to the era of the real mountain men. I teased that he would take a fly rod with him, and become so absorbed in trout fishing that the Blackfeet would scalp him before he could reel in.

When I discovered that many mountain men had nicknames like "Crazy Bear," I began thinking that George most resembled a wolf. He had its natural grace and confidence in the outdoors, as well as its loyalty to mate and pack, and protectiveness of its offspring. When I mentioned this to him, he said bashfully that he had always thought of himself as a wolf; later I discovered his middle name, Randolph, was Teutonic for wolf. He enjoyed reading Norse mythology, and was pleased to discover that the wolf was sacred to Odin, Anglo-Saxon god of wisdom, poetry, war and agriculture, and of the dead; Viking warriors often rushed into battle crying, "Odin! Odin!" George, in Greek, means "husbandman," one who conserves or protects; I found that appropriate for a man as caring as he, but he growled at me, because the second definition is "farmer."

At one rendezvous, we both served as dog soldiers, a term and responsibility taken from the Indian practice of camp police. Dog soldiers were entrusted with the orderly advance of the camp in battle, for organizing and timing buffalo hunts, for protecting the women and children. They had no authority but the respect in which their fellow tribesmen held them, and that practice has carried over to rendezvous camps. After that rendezvous, George hung the red arm band that had identified him as a dog soldier on the rear view mirror of his old blue van, and never removed it. I came to see it as a symbol of the man he was, concerned more for others than himself; now it's in my car. He learned as a child that his size made it impossible for him to fight other children; if he did, he was seen as a bully. He seldom allowed himself to be goaded into violence, and he didn't want one particular story told, but I can say that he wasn't afraid to risk his own life to save another's, and he did it more than once.

George adored chocolate and ice cream, and constantly fought weight gain. His jeans and dress pants were hung in categories: the size 38 waists, the 40s, the 42s. He could move back and forth between categories within a month or two, and solemnly insisted that our closet must be damp, because his wool winter pants shrank each summer. When he discovered Devonshire Clotted Cream in Clovelly, I was afraid I'd never get him out of England.

Sometimes people who saw George for the first time were intimidated by his size, the fierceness of his face in repose, perhaps the knife. But once they saw those deep blue eyes, no one ever failed to trust him—or tried to make him mad. When he held a baby or kitten, no one saw the knife, or the earring. They saw instead the lifted eyebrow, ironic smile, gentle hands; they saw that his silence wasn't hostile, but warm, comfort with no need for babble.

He found enjoyment in digging a posthole, if he had to, or in a trip to town for groceries, but he preferred to fish and camp. He made powder horns and knives, built an oak chest lined with cedar, developed and printed photographs; but once he'd mastered a skill, he didn't necessarily keep on doing the same thing. Instead, he tried something new. He ignored attempts to hurry or nag him. Other people slave at jobs they hate because they "have" to, but we were comfortable at an income that is officially listed as poverty, and managed luxuries like a month in Great Britain.

I was born and trained as a workaholic; George taught me to enjoy every day on the assumption that it might be the last, but he was one of the happiest people I ever knew. He worked hard on the family ranch because I love it; often cooked so I had more time to write, and urged me to say no to demands that took me away from my writing. One of my friends wrote after his death: "I think one of the things about George that made him such a powerful person was that he was centered *and* tolerant. Anyone with as much willpower and pure stubbornness that devotes their energies to calmness is gonna get to the center right quick."

When doctors told George that he was free of Hodgkin's disease, they also confessed they weren't sure precisely why. All such patients with military disabilities would be monitored, and their survival rate studied. Some would remain on a maintenance dose of chemotherapy; others would take no medication at all. George chose the latter, and muttered that he'd never take chemotherapy again. The treatments for Hodgkin's caused problems: sterility, cartilage growths in his trachea, a malfunctioning thyroid. When he was forty, he trimmed his hair, sent out job applications, and enrolled in a graduate program to become a high school counselor. He celebrated fifteen years of life after cancer.

The pain started in his left arm and shoulder during October of 1987. He had been cutting firewood with the chainsaw, and for a time believed he had strained a muscle. But the pain intensified, and finally he saw a general practitioner at Ellsworth Air Force Base; she ignored his medical history, gave him a cortisone shot, and advised rest. The pain increased; the doctor was puzzled, but prescribed increasing doses of painkillers.

Months dragged past. I urged George to bypass local doctors and go directly to Fitzsimons. He was reluctant, but never fully explained why. I noticed that he used his right hand to lift his left arm to the steering wheel and the arm of a chair. One night, standing behind him as he brushed his teeth, I saw that his left arm had shrunk; neither of us had realized the extent of the damage. An orthopedic surgeon at Ellsworth sent him at once to Fitzsimons, where he spent most of April, trying to keep up with his graduate studies, bored by long hours of waiting between tests. I drove down to see him whenever I could, but it was a busy time, between calving on the ranch and a part-time teaching job. My first nonfiction book, *Windbreak*, had just been published, and reviewed in the *New York Times Book Review*, then chosen as an alternate for a book club; *Going Over East*, my second, was published in hardback, and my second book of poetry appeared from a small press in Illinois. I was dizzy with the positive responses to my writing, and amazement at having three books in print after years of working unpublished or appearing only in obscure magazines. George was patient, but somber; I grew angry and worried.

By late April, doctors had determined that a tumor caused by the radiation he'd been given for Hodgkin's was growing near his spine; a neurosurgeon made an exploratory incision. What he saw caused him to slap a bandage on the spot and schedule surgery for May. He told George to go home and "settle his affairs." We talked about the ominous phrasing, but believed the tumor was just another side effect that could be endured; doctors told us radiation doses for Hodgkin's treatment have been changed to avoid such tumors. George began to feel first numbness, then tingling in his hands; sometimes he dropped things from fingers with no feeling. Occasionally he stumbled. He carried his left shoulder high, making his torso look twisted. I grew angry at people who stared at his dangling arm, but he ignored them.

Surgery was an ordeal I had grown used to; the doctors estimated four hours, but nearly eight passed while I paced the corridors before the neurosurgeon emerged. Bracing one foot against the wall, he drew a diagram on his surgical greens to show me where the tumor lay, tucked near George's spinal cord. They had avoided sawing through the clavicle, as they'd planned, but part of the tumor was still there. They thought George had been in surgery long enough, and feared injury to the spinal cord. Later, perhaps, they might operate from the back. A sample of the tissue was sent off to a lab for analysis, and George came home with a long incision that gradually turned into a scar. He began physical therapy, and all summer he did exercises, hour after hour, day after day; the arm regained some of its strength. The call we expected, telling us whether the tumor was malignant, never came. One doctor finally told us the tissue so puzzled the first lab that samples had been sent to several others; the tumor was a rare type.

All summer, I nagged George to work on the college classes that had been interrupted by his hospitalization; he didn't refuse, but he ignored me. Yet he encouraged me to buy the new lights I wanted for our house, and spent hours with Mike installing them. As I worked in the basement, I could hear the two of them talking and laughing; during the cold, dark winter that followed, I could still hear their voices around me, and realized how completely George knew what choices he was making that summer.

Early in August, we went to our black powder club rendezvous, high in the Bighorn Mountains above Sheridan, Wyoming. George seemed more relaxed than he had been for months, and spent hours talking with his friends, and with Michael, holding his weak arm inconspicuously. He looked thin, and his friends whispered to me how ill he appeared to be, when I was sure he was improving. Because he was reluctant to take off his shirt in public, a good friend fired up the sweat lodge and the two of them prayed and sweated alone with their sons. Gina, the publisher of *Windbreak*, joined us for several days, meeting George and Mike for the first time after reading about them in the manuscript for three years. On the way home, George said it was the best rendezvous he had ever attended.

I wanted to let Mike fly home to Minnesota, but George wanted us to take him so he'd have two more days with his son. His pain was so intense that he couldn't drive. By the time we left Mike, I was desperate to get George to the hospital; his right foot had begun to tingle. Hour after hour, I drove the old blue van as fast as I dared, and George sat silent, staring at the highway.

When we got home, I called Fitzsimons and told them he was coming. The doctor insisted the hospital had no room, but a doctor at the base made arrangements; on Saturday, August 27, we boarded a Medevac plane. George brought a cane, but refused a nurse's help descending the steps.

The next day, a young doctor took us into an exam room, and watched George struggle to walk, then told us the lab report said the tissue from the tumor was necrotic and malignant; he seemed surprised we knew the meaning of both words. Then he added, "I have no authority to tell you this, but the prognosis is poor."

"What does that mean?" I snapped, tired of medical evasions.

He looked at me. "That it is terminal." He explained that paralysis would come in definite stages: first George's legs and arms would fail, then his bowels and kidneys, and finally he would be unable to breathe because his diaphragm would be paralyzed. I helped George back to the bed, and sat by his side, both of us numb, until the nurses insisted I leave at midnight. Visiting hours were over at ten, but they had sensed our shock.

My journal entry that night is filled with fear about my ability to care for George if he were completely helpless; my mind would not accept the word "terminal." I couldn't imagine him sitting for years, blue eyes empty of hope. Now I realize that in the year's long silences he had already considered his alternatives. I told him the next morning that we'd take it one day at a time, as we always had. I've always feared my ability to cope with an invalid, but I've spent a lot of time in cow manure and urine and blood, and learned to deal with it. His mother, his son Mike, and several other relatives came to the hospital.

Within a few days, George was paralyzed from the waist down, officially pronounced "hopeless," but he never grew angry at clumsy technicians who couldn't draw blood from his battered arms, or at X-ray nurses who asked him to raise them. He quietly explained, again and again. The paralysis had come on so quickly that he still looked strong; the nurses tended to believe their eyes and not his words. He could no longer lift his left arm, but several times a day he'd say, "Hug," and I'd put my arms around him, lift his left hand to my waist, and we'd hold each other. When the technicians needed an X-ray of his chest, they put a vest shield on me, and I raised his arms to my shoulders. Then all the technicians left the room and we hugged each other as the machine hummed its radioactive song.

The doctors ran test after test, until I realized that they were only keeping us busy; they had already said nothing could be done. The neurosurgeon who had been so confident four months before shook his head, smiling. "Nothing we can do, but I guarantee you won't have any pain. You can have all the painkillers you want." He never talked directly with us again, though we saw him swishing through the ward, visiting other patients; I believe he never really looked at us again.

The next day I demanded to take George to the Ellsworth Air Force Base hospital, and I talked with a home care nurse. I still believed he might recover enough to live, and if not, I wanted him to die in the house we had built together. I told him I wanted him any way I could have him. He asked to see an Episcopal priest; he had once been a deacon in the church.

On the flight back, George smiled and winked when I looked his way. I stood by the head of his litter when the medical evacuation crew would let me, reading softly aloud of medical miracles, the power of positive thinking. Once we reached the hospital, air force rules required that visitors receive a pass at the main gate; the gate guards called me for approval of everyone who came to see George. Each call meant I had to leave George and run down the hall to the nurses' station; finally I asked the airman on duty to simply let everyone who asked to see George in without calling me. He apparently didn't realize where I was, but his curiosity had been aroused. When another friend asked for George, the guard asked, "Who's this Snell guy? He having a party or something?"

Our friends gathered at the hospital to offer help and love, and say goodbye in many ways; they told stories, and filled George's room with balloons, children, gifts, music, photographs, and prayers from every organized religion, and a few disorganized ones. Jerry, who had trapped and camped with George, and known both of us as long as we had known each other, came to Ellsworth and stayed. The nurses thought he was George's brother, and he was. George had once dragged Jerry from a burning tipi and gotten him through deep snow to a hospital, but Jerry was not merely repaying a service.

Doctors said George might live for weeks. Once he understood that no treatment could reverse his paralysis, he said, "I'd like to go as quietly and easily as possible," but he smiled and talked to everyone. Even when the morphine dripped constantly, his blue eyes would flicker open when anyone made a sound in the room. Only in oblique ways did he mention his suffering. "It's hard work suffocating slowly to death," he said, and "I wish the doctor could give me something to ease me out." Once he said to Jerry, "This is no fun no more," a brief phrase to carry so much of his humor and his strength. His eyes were watchful and clear, and at the end he said, "I love you," over and over, to me, his mother Bette, his son Mike, and to Jerry.

George died early in the morning of September 7, at what is known as "the wolf hour," when life ebbs. When I realized he had stopped breathing, I automatically looked out of the window. I saw him as a dark shape against the stars, walking jauntily, swinging his arms; he glanced over his shoulder at me, winked, and strode away. The Blackfeet name for the Milky Way is "wolf road." George the Wolf walks it in the night sky.

All kinds of people gathered on the bare hillside at sunset on September 9. The parents of our friend Tom wore yellow, symbolizing the happiness George wanted us to find in the rest of our lives. Members of the Yellowstone Mountain Men came from Cody in fringed and beaded buckskins; they apologized for those who couldn't come because they were fighting the Yellowstone fire. The air was thick with smoke from the inferno five hundred miles west, and the sun was blood red.

Years ago, we had discussed the absurdity of fancy coffins, and George had fantasized about building a Viking ship to bear his body on its burning deck; we both had laughed, picturing a frantic search in the Black Hills for a stream large enough to float a ship. We couldn't quite picture a fiery Viking funeral on one of the man-made lakes; a charred hulk washing up on a dam would be a serious anticlimax. I wished his friends could build a coffin, but there simply wasn't time, so I bought the cheapest one in stock, and covered its gray felt with George's Hudson Bay blanket, white wool striped with red and green. On top, I placed his oldest rendezvous hat with its battered turkey feathers; less than a month before he'd worn it in the camp near Sheridan. Jerry added an arrowhead he'd made, beside a medicine bundle tucked under his pillow at the hospital by Indian friends; its symbols included red, white, and blue because he was a veteran, sage and sweetgrass for purification, and an eagle feather for his courage in living, and in dying. Another friend had created the casket spray of local wildflowers: wild currant and chokecherry, bear grass, moss, pine branches, wild roses, yellow curlycup, asters, brown-eyed Susans, juniper, curly dock, and, for George's heritage and love of Scotland, thistles.

When everyone was gathered, Fred of the Yellowstone Mountain Men fired one round from his .50-caliber muzzle loader. Leonard played "Amazing Grace" on his flute, the notes thin and lovely and lost in the wide sky.

An Episcopal minister read a passage I'd written the day before, mingling quotations from Thoreau and some of George's ideas on life. He ended with "Desiderata," which might have been George's statement of his beliefs if he'd been given to longwinded declarations. We gathered in a circle to recite the Twenty-third Psalm and the Lord's Prayer, in the sonorous King James language.

An honor guard from Ellsworth fired the traditional twenty-one-gun salute, at Mike's request; later a friend who taught English at the base received an essay from one of the young men, who said the funeral had moved him more than any other he'd seen. A bugler played "Taps," and the notes seemed to glow bronze.

The sun dropped to the black rim of mountains, and slowly turned to a single glowing coal. Friends lowered the coffin; Mavis dropped two red roses into the grave, and a neighbor added a bundle of wild grasses. George's cat, Phred, had died the night before, and I thought—too late—that we should have placed him with George, where he'd so often slept.

Women from the community's three churches served supper at the American Legion Hall. I felt a strong sense of continuity; even friends who had never been part of Hermosa seemed to take comfort in the warmth symbolized by the food and sharing. I looked into the eyes of other widows, who conveyed their understanding in simple ways: offering me more coffee, insisting I sample their cake. It would be hard for some of these people to speak words of love, but the room was filled with it.

Later, friends led me to George's van, and took me home. We told stories about George late into the night. Jerry slipped out to the stone cairn George had built on the hillside, drank a toast, said goodbye, and quietly drove away.

I had not slept in our house since I left it with George; a couple who had come from Cody with no sleeping bags slept in our bed, and I took my sleeping bag to the deck with everyone else. At dawn I smelled campfire smoke in my blankets, and for a lovely moment believed it was all a bad dream, and we were all together at rendezvous.

Digging the Bulbs

Dear Wilford,

This afternoon I dug gladioli bulbs.
Autumn sun warmed my back; I lifted
each bulb carefully, whacked off
the stalks with the knife he kept sharp
for me. With naked hands
I sifted dark earth for the baby bulbs.
You taught me to save them each year,
watch them send up tiny leaves
until they were large enough to bloom.
Your hands popped new white bulbs
from shriveled brown husks.

Each year I would think of you and Beth,
laboring together on that dry farm
to produce new plants, save those that might disappear.
When you wrote me last, she was dead.
You sent a photograph of the gladiolus named for her.
You didn't want to live.

My husband planted railroad ties in the earth
as a border for my flowers.
He died a month ago.
I am digging these bulbs for the last time.

Lately I have done many things for the last time.
I'll give these bulbs to a friend.

Each spring I've remembered
the way you smiled at each other,
wrinkles disappearing into love;
each summer when I cut blooms
I saw your faces turned to each other.
When you wrote to tell me she had died,
I did not know what to say.
I cried, did nothing.

Now I know to tell you only
that I care, that I remember.
We have worked in partnership
with the friendly earth for years;
now both our loves lie in the cold dark.
What am I to make of this?
I use the spading fork to lift another clump,
reach deep to raise the knobby bulbs
into the light.

Setting up a Headstone

A week after George died, the first monument salesman called
me; he explained that he'd seen my husband's obituary, and knew
I'd be needing a monument, and that he'd like to be of service. I was
shocked, horrified, and impolite; I believe I mentioned that I'd
never buy a headstone from someone who would telephone a
widow a week after her husband's death. After the third salesman
called, I realized that the monument business—they never mention
gravestones, or refer in any way to death—is highly competitive and
limited. Shocked customers are vulnerable, but also confused and
uncertain. A forceful approach may win a sale. Monuments don't

offer much opportunity for multiple sales, nor will the customer return in a year for a new model. The use of the newspaper's obituary column and telephone must seem like an efficient and reasonable way to do business, but I was filled with resentment of the whole system anyway. Not long afterward, Jerry called to ask if I'd considered finding a headstone in the Black Hills; he offered to come and help me look. I felt my heart open in relief; I had been dreading the procedure because it seemed so impersonal, so standardized.

We found the perfect stone one chilly October afternoon, following the tracks of deer hunters into an isolated canyon. Whenever we spotted a likely slab of rock, but were unsure whether or not it was strong enough to withstand weathering and drilling, we'd upend it and let it roll down a hill. The ones that leapt into the air, dropped gracefully, and shattered when they hit were automatically rejected, and after a while, I heard myself laugh out loud—for the first time since George's death—at the picture we made toiling up hills, apparently just to roll down large hunks of rock. I would also bet we ruined the deer hunting in that neighborhood for a week.

The massive slab of granite we chose lay on wet ground in long pine shadows at the bottom of a deep canyon. Through the trees a quarter-mile away we could see the ghostly glow of an eighty-foot cliff of white and gray quartz glittering with slabs of mica as large as my hand; mica miners had dynamited the cliff, then broken the mica from the rubble at the bottom for sale. The headstone lay slightly above the trail, so with two of us prying and shoving it slid over the wet earth into the pickup, but I wasn't certain we'd ever get it up the steep, corkscrew trail. When we arrived home, we looked at the stone more closely; it was deep black and brown, flecked with tiny sparkling particles of mica. We backed the pickup into my garage, and built a framework of used railroad ties high enough to slide the stone straight out and have it at a height comfortable for carving a niche to hold the bronze plaque George's mother had sent. When the work was finished, we could slide the stone right back into the pickup for transport to the cemetery.

We both bent down, got a good grip, and heaved. The stone didn't move. We breathed deeply, and heaved again. Nothing. The third time, our faces got very red, and the stone twitched a little. After we'd managed to shove, lever, and curse it halfway onto the platform, I decided we needed help, and went into the house to call the neighbors. I later told Jerry this was a plot: I knew that any normal man threatened with calling for help would move the stone alone if it killed him. When I returned, the stone was on the platform, and he was draped artistically over it. Between gasps, he offered his opinion that the stone weighed at least five hundred pounds. We sat on the sides of the pickup and admired it for a while.

"You know," I said thoughtfully, "this was a wonderful idea, and now that we've found a stone this beautiful, I've decided I want one just like it. I know I can count on you to get it for me."

Jerry glanced up from under his hatbrim. "Right. I'll scratch an arrow and 'Linda' on the bottom of this one."

Even lying on a makeshift bench in the garage, the stone had a primitive look. We decided not to change its natural shape, and carefully preserved a patch of green lichen growing along one edge. All winter, whenever I drove into the garage, my headlights struck the stone and I was reminded once again of its mass, literally and figuratively. Each time I walked through the garage, I touched its rough surface. This tombstone was not chosen with the help of a salesman practiced in soft speech and the whims of widows; it was a gift from the earth. It was not represented by a canceled check and a bill; it was living rock, and it came to symbolize George's life, his way of altering the world as little as he could while enjoying it as much as possible. When the plaque was finally bolted in place, it seemed to perch lightly on the stone's face, a scrap of human handiwork on a mountain.

A hundred years ago, people died at home, surrounded by family; each member of the household was part of a death, as they had been part of each other's lives. George had to die in a hospital, with oxygen bubbling in the corner, tubes in every orifice, and nurses who broke into the middle of our last words with one another to take his temperature. They asked me to leave the room while they bathed him, when I'd been bathing with him for years. Their well-meant attentions added to the pain of death the feeling that it was unreal. I think our modern mode of death prolongs our feelings of suffering and helplessness, and postpones acceptance of the secret George discovered too early: that he was going to die. He arranged his priorities from that knowledge, accepting that life *requires* death, is a completely natural component of it. I believe many country people have the same sense: that death gives real meaning to life.

When a man died a few years ago, his body was washed and clothed for burial by people who loved him, who were able to say goodbye while doing a last intimate service. Now we pay professional people to take care of details we consider distasteful; people who never knew the living person are hired to apply cosmetics to conceal death, the central fact of our lives. Strangers who never saw the smiling face attempt to paint on dead flesh a portrait of what he might have been in life. In church, a minister who would not recognize the man recites a list of accomplishments that seems pitifully short, because the pastor cannot speak of what really made the man, but only of what he studied, what jobs he held; he can recite the names of the woman he married, the children he fathered, but not why and how they loved each other as a family. Then, because church audiences are small and restless these days, the minister lectures people who have faced death, perhaps for the first time, about the brevity of life. Cruelly, he distracts us from the reality of loss by promising a fantastic heavenly paradise, implying we will gain it only if we come to a particular church. We hide the body inside an ornate box containing enough wood to build a small house, a box that costs enough to feed a child for a year. We stack fresh flowers around it to conceal further the fact of death and its aftermath: decomposition.

Neighbors used to tell stories about the dead while they dug his grave, knowing others would do the same for them; they might pass a small bottle of whiskey from cold hand to muddy hand if the temperature were below zero. The shovel shifted from one to another in a ritual as old as time, so that everyone who felt the need to help dig a grave was part of the event. Even though the diggers were always men, the ceremonies of death brought a community together in a way that acknowledged death's inevitability, and gave a healthy start to the healing process. Our present methods try to conceal death even from the dead. I had resolved at my grandmother's funeral never to encourage such travesties, and George's was as different from the norm as I could manage at the time.

Early in June, I planned a day to set up the stone. A funeral is public, but to this rite I invited people who had known George long and well. Four men, grunting, moved the stone into a pickup as gently as if they were moving George's body. These were men who barely knew each other, but who had been close to George in assorted ways: a rancher, an artist, a carpenter, and an engineer. As they moved the stone, differences between them were bridged by their companionship with George, as if they were brothers who had been separated a long time. Under a black sky rolling with thunderheads, a solemn procession of cars followed the stone out of our yard and up the highway. Just as we got to Hermosa, a fire engine screamed out of town, dodged the slow-moving cars, and turned north, headed for a fire along the railroad tracks. The volunteer firemen in the procession kept their places.

At the cemetery, the men lowered the pointed end of the stone into a hole dug in the yellow clay, helped unload the cement materials from the truck, and gathered around the wheelbarrow. More helpers had arrived than were strictly necessary, but as I watched, a fascinating dance began. No one gave orders. All seemed to move in and out of the tasks so that there was no hurry, and everyone participated in mixing the concrete as if doing so were part of the ritual. One dumped cement, another added gravel, an artist directed water from the nozzle of the tank George and I used to haul water to our cattle, while a hairdresser steadied the wheelbarrow handle and a musician explained the process to his son. I felt as if it was not my place to do this work, as if this was something the men must share. I stood with the other women, watching.

Somehow the atmosphere was different than the official mourning of a funeral. We were people gathering together to show our respect and love for George by doing this work ourselves, instead of hiring someone to do it. This was no pastel headstone with lettering carved by a machine; this stone seemed to have torn itself from the mountains and plunged into the hillside like a challenge.

When the stone was firmly set and braced, and covered with plastic to prevent the cement from drying so quickly it cracked, we were ready for the ceremony. I had not known how much time to allow for the work, so the bagpiper had not yet arrived. Clusters of people wandered through the cemetery, visited, studied grave markers, and sat on the Civil War–era cannons discussing how much black powder would be required for a truly memorable salute to George. We had comfortable conversations about and above the dead, made them all part of our ceremony of grief. I realized that since many members of my family are in their seventies or eighties, I will have more graves to care for in a few years. A few years after that, no one will be left to care for mine. I carefully drained the water left from mixing the cement onto the native plants on George's grave and adjoining plots.

There were few tears; it seemed we were ready to accept what shock and pain had kept at bay at George's funeral ten months before. When the piper arrived, resplendent in a new kilt, we gathered around the grave for a ceremony that was simple, moving, and intensely private. Then the piper played a lament for the clans who died with Bonnie Prince Charlie's hopes for a Scots kingdom at Culloden in 1746; we had both cried over the single stones marking the mass grave for each clan. After a pause, he played a lament traditional at the funerals of British royalty. The silver on the pipes glowed dully; high, wild notes dissolved into the cloudy sunset. Through it all, Frodo lay at the foot of the grave, staring at the stone. "George Randolph Snell," it read, "1946–1988. Mountain Man. Dear Husband and Beloved Son." The slab of black granite looks like a huge Stone Age dagger driven into the earth.

Old Friends

They came until the halls bulged, the air trembled
with balloons and flowers. Children's drawings clung
to the walls, photographs crowded the table.
The tall man in black, his famous scythe
disguised as a briefcase, had to elbow
through, even with an appointment.
No one tried to stop him,
but no one got out of his way, either.

George made him sit at the end of the bed, listen.
We all told stories; whoever sat beside George
held his right hand; he could still feel that.
Death kept clearing his throat,
pointing to his watch, fingering the catch
on his briefcase. Everyone ignored him.

Finally he caught on, told a joke,
told stories about George, how they'd met before.
He admitted admiration for the man's direct
blue gaze, the way George threw him out.
This time he knew he'd win, but he played
by the rules: none of that grim faceless stuff,
no swinging the wailing scythe, no tears.
He threw back his hood, laughed for
the first time in years.

Campfires flared in the bright room, drinks

were shared, domes shingled, parties planned,
enjoyed, over. Tipis were pitched, struck,
folded; fish were caught; deer were shot at,
missed.

Among the folks at the cemetery, in clothes
as wildly varied as their natures,
Death's outfit didn't turn a head.
He kept his distance from the mountain men
and honor guard.
                                    Someone said
he and George walked off
toward the smoky sunset mountains,
fishing poles over their shoulders.

Rolling up the Hoses

People who mean well have told me that I should feel anger at George for dying and leaving me alone. I cannot be angry at him; he worked hard to live every minute I knew him; if he could have borne more suffering to be with me, he would have. I think it is significant that he died when Michael had nearly reached eighteen, as if he kept a promise made years ago to raise his son, and that was all he could do.

My anger isn't directed toward George. I have been angry at hospitals, which do not allow comfort for the dying and the soon-to-be-bereaved. At the military hospital where we were told George would die, his bed lay in view of fifty others; though we could get some visual privacy with the curtains drawn around it, the next bed was so close that its occupant could hear the slightest whisper. I could not lie down beside George, or hold him while we cried. On the television we could not turn off, because it served several patients, we watched men wearing military uniforms discuss the need for weapons and airplanes costing billions of dollars while my dying husband and the other veterans who lay around him couldn't have privacy. And in an ironic commentary on our priorities, the science capable of devising a bomb that kills people without damaging property has not created a condom catheter that works well enough to protect a man's dignity. During previous hospital stays, George twice lay helpless while a man in the bed beside his died. Technicians were too busy to move George, who had to endure the two terrible deaths before his own. The employees did their jobs well, but they were short of supplies, space, and help.

I have felt angry when I saw wives and husbands screaming at each other, or people abusing their children, or heard people whining about how hard their lives are. I keep gritting my teeth not to say, "Don't waste a minute of this beautiful life!" After George's funeral, an often-suicidal friend came to the house. When I looked at his face, I remembered endless hours his friends had spent talking to him, or taking his car keys away when he drank too much. Instead of thanking him for his sympathy, I snapped, "You son of a bitch. Stop wasting your life. Better men than you are dead who really wanted to live." I felt as if I was being hard, but not necessarily unfair.

I have been angry at the things people say and write, and at people who have said nothing at all. The message on a traditional sympathy card is cruel and jangles the nerves of anyone sensitive to words; we use mass-produced cards to fill the silence of fear. But when I think of what I have said and left unsaid when friends were bereaved, I am filled with shame. Death is something no one can rehearse; no response that does not come from experience and suffering is adequate. In fact, nothing said or done really helps except the knowledge that someone cares about your suffering. Oddly, one of the comments most dear to me came from a woman in the community who has been married several times, with varying results; she said to me, very seriously and very kindly, "The good husbands always die." I was startled, but she had survived both divorce and widowhood, and suddenly I knew that I could, too. I am amazed that anyone can survive this.

There are several things I will never say again to the bereaved, including, "It takes time." We can always count on good old Time.

Blame everything on Time. And what does Time do? Grays your hair, jostles chunks out of your memory, plays nasty tricks like taking away the memory of whole nights you spent crouched by the bedside watching his face, watching his chest move, his lips whisper love. Time makes you remember things you'd like to forget, like how he looked after he stopped breathing, and forget things you have to remember, like how he smiled when I came home after a trip.

I've read everything I've seen about widowhood, and talked to widows and widowers, but still made discoveries no one warned me about. For example, widows must be the most unhugged people on earth, with the possible exception of divorcees. Then there's the clumsiness. Every time I pour hot coffee, I dump it in my lap; fortunately I'm wearing black clothes. When I pick up a pen to sign some official form, it skitters away; when I bend to pick it up, I kick it another twenty feet. A puzzled air force private returns it to me, saying, "Here you are, Ma'am," and I burst into tears, because George was taught to call older women "ma'am." After I broke my favorite cup, I stopped touching things I valued, though I did get rid of several gifts from people whose tastes differ from mine. When I must drive, I signal for blocks ahead of each turn, and check my mirrors three times. I dropped the can opener on the dog's head, my toothbrush in the toilet. My knees are as skinned as they were when I was ten. I burned my hand on the electric coffeepot, and cut myself slicing salami after I stopped cooking because I'd set a pan on fire.

Modern Americans have largely abandoned the outward symbols of death, like wearing black. That's a mistake; the reminder—maybe a red W for widows—might warn people who make tactless, painful remarks, and serve as a warning to every observer that a widow's driving might be erratic. Native American women cut their long hair and gashed their arms as signs of mourning; perhaps the real pain, pain that could be located and observed, helped them cry and heal the inner wounds more quickly. Today we are supposed to believe such actions unnecessary, if not uncivilized, and to quietly seek professional therapy for heartache. I think knife slashes might be preferable to our method of maintaining outward serenity while wounds fester in mind and heart. Someone told me of a survey done of young urban professionals, who were asked how long they thought it might take them to recover from the death of a spouse; thirty days, some said, or maybe as long as six months. It is tradition in Italy for widows to wear black and wail daily at the graves of their husbands for five years; on the morning that begins the sixth year, they are ready to begin their lives again. Perhaps these are two extremes, but I am convinced it is important not to hide the pain, because the infection will remain.

My greatest effort has been toward reconciling two contradictory ideas: that George is dead, buried, and won't be back, and that his spirit is with me. A man told me I'm still in the first stage of death, denial. Later I spoke with a woman friend whose daughter died eight years ago. She snorted in disdain; "If that's what it is, I'm still in the first stage too, because I still don't believe she's dead." To keep my memories alive, I run over a mental list: the look on his face when I said something he disagreed with; the particular dark blue of his eyes; his big feet, the callous on his left big toe; the deformed fourth fingernail on his right hand, broken when a friend stepped on it wearing football spikes in high school; the perpetual blood blister and the long scar behind his right ear. Yet none of these details are really him, and I shouldn't be surprised or angry at myself if someday they disappear from my mind.

I wake often, convinced I have just had my worst nightmare, that it cannot possibly be true. Repeatedly, I have dreamed of being with George, and of telling him, in tears, that I dreamed he was dead. Modern technology gave me an opportunity few widows in history have had, and I destroyed it. In April, when George was in the hospital, he left messages on the answering machine. I kept them the entire time he was gone, until it occurred to me that I was superstitiously afraid to obliterate them. I erased them as a symbol of my belief that he would live; now I would give anything to hear his voice.

When I traveled away from George, I wrote in my journal over and over how much I loved him. When I traveled by plane, I often pictured the plane crashing; I knew a compassionate rescuer would find my journal in the wreckage, and return it to George. As the plane bounced and rattled, I'd be writing furiously, "I love you, George." Now I discover myself writing in the journal as though he will read it. Now I'm in the wreckage alone.

Suddenly everything I've written about the meaning of my life is being tested. Whatever I make of my life without George, whatever his memory means to me, will take work. I talked a good line about doing things for myself, about the necessity to be selfish and single-minded in writing, but he was always there behind me, with that little smile of pride. I knew that no matter what might happen to either of us, we could help each other. I am incredibly lucky to have found him in the maze of our lives.

Twelve days after George's death, walking on the rim of the high cliffs encircling Billings, Montana, where I was to give a reading, I was struck by similarities to the Black Hills: the same hot sandstone and pine needle smell burned my nose; I stumbled on broken beer bottles. Frodo sat down and refused to walk, and I realized we were both just searching for George. I had promised to do the reading, and it was good for me to keep that promise, to realize I could still speak, to get away from the empty house. I had expected to wander the West for a couple of weeks, relaxing from the hospital stay, but I suddenly knew it was also important to go home, to realize he was not waiting for me there.

As I drove the autumn plains toward the Black Hills, the slopes of Inyan Kara, an isolated peak south of Sundance, Wyoming, looked voluptuous and gold as honey in the sunset light. Beehives stood in shadow in the valley. I didn't want to stop driving even when the dog huffed to be let out. I felt that the beauty unrolling past my window might stop, vanish when the road stopped running ahead of me and the sun disappeared over the edge of the world. I had a fantasy of driving fast enough to catch George, and then realized I could only catch him by dying. If he came back, would he know me? In the twenty-four days since George and I had gotten on the plane to fly to Denver, I had hardly touched food or water. I was nearly thirty pounds lighter; my hair was lifeless and almost fully gray.

As I have worked to remember and adopt George's calm, his inner serenity no matter how the whirlwinds howled outside, I've asked myself how many of his particular qualities arose as a result of his cancer. If he'd been completely healthy, would he have been less extraordinary? Thinking along these lines brings me perilously close to the dubious Christian philosophy that God gives burdens to those who can bear them. But why should God want to torture the strongest? What are they supposed to gain by proving over and over again how much they can endure?

When I found a picture of George in his air force uniform, brash and young, his hair cropped short above a broad and somewhat lecherous smile, he said, "You wouldn't have liked me." Paused. Added, "I don't suppose I'd have liked you either."

But he was the only man I ever found willing to live with a compulsive writer, with the savage selfishness I learned the hard way, from seven years of being a good wife to a man who wasn't a good husband. I didn't know George when the Hodgkin's disease struck the first time. That was a box no one should have to open; he took it in his hand, made it part of him; he decided to live, to create a marriage, a son, life from death. Somehow he found the strength not to become too bitter to live or love when he was left alone; he insisted on becoming part of his son's life no matter how difficult that job was made for him.

Staring at old pictures, I wonder what his life would have been without cancer. Was that poison, that killer, the gift that made him love us all so much: his son, his friends, the sunset's light, low laughter at a campfire? Did the gift of death make life worth living? If so, why doesn't it work for all of us? The one thing we are all sure of every second of our lives is that we will die, and yet few of us behave as if we believe it.

George was so intently aware of life that it is impossible to think of him as cold and unaware. One perception of the dead is that they don't have sensations. What if it's the other way around? I smell English Breakfast tea at four each afternoon, whether I'm driving down the highway, or lifting weights, or working at my computer; maybe George is reminding me of the afternoon tea habit we brought back from England. Or perhaps he is having tea, enjoying all his favorite flavors, and only a trace of the sensation slips across to our world; maybe in that world the pleasure is stronger than we can imagine, and we only get the ghost of it. Pain and weakness limited his physical activities for the year before he died, and when he lay in the hospital he didn't even crave chocolate, or ice cream, or tobacco. Maybe now he's eating the finest Swiss chocolates daily with his tea; I hope so. Each time he suggested a Sunday drive, it always ended at the best ice cream store in the state. On good days I imagine he is on an eternal Sunday drive, anticipating ice cream.

For ages, people have conversed with their dead; only in recent times has it become shameful, or cause for therapy, to talk to yourself. Humans are strangely subject to delusions; some believe they are God, some believe they have the right to kill anyone with religious or political views counter to their own, some believe AIDS is God's way of punishing *only* the evil. Surely talking to my beloved dead, hoping he is drinking tea and eating chocolate, is harmless beside these ideas. On a night when the moonlight was so bright that I could write in my journal on the porch, I couldn't believe George wasn't sharing it with me. I tell myself that cold fact indicates he is absent, but I wonder if my crude senses, centuries out of practice, are simply too weak to see and smell and hear him as my ancestors might have.

I seem to need to say and write the words over and over, avoiding the convenient euphemisms that plague our language: George is dead. My husband's death. It's as if repeating the word "death" often enough will bring redemption, or at least release from disbelief.

Most of the official forms have been filled out, the mortuary bill paid. I've done what I needed to about taxes, insurance, death certificates. I've found official papers and keepsakes in safety deposit boxes, closets, drawers, and money he stashed in Skoal cans, jacket linings, and hatbands. I used to tell women who were looking for time to write that I had given up folding clean clothes; they laughed nervously and looked at George, but it was true. Now I've washed and folded his clothes for the final time, except the ones I wear. His photographed smile is everywhere, but in the dark bedroom I reach all night for his hand; sometimes I feel its grip. My cold feet stay cold;

his dog lies on his pillow whimpering in sleep. I lie awake listening for footsteps, repeating it like a chant: he's dead. I hear him chuckle in the night, almost see his lips telling me not to be afraid. Once I dreamed that he was standing at the foot of the bed, looking at the *parfleches* on the shelves there. He was turning toward me as I sat up, calling his name. The telephone rang before I saw his face. After I hung up, I tried to go back to the dream but it eluded me.

Another night I dreamed that several huge shapes made of black marble had invaded the house; one sat in the middle of the living room floor. One lay in the center of the bed, so that I had to cling to the edge to sleep, and was afraid it would crush me in the night. One sat in the dining room, where the table used to be. I felt that one was squatting inside my chest, and another in my brain; in my dream it had smashed the bushes where I picked blooming poems. I couldn't see inside the black shapes, or shift them. They simply crouched, eyeless, soundless, obscenely large. I shattered a maul against one, hoping to break it so I could carry it away. Finally I gave up and simply began to walk around them, to sleep curled around the one in the bed.

When I woke up, I realized the sculptures were George's death, and an answer to the idea that I will "get over" it; that's not how it works. I will learn to live with it; if I marry again, as he told me to, I will not come home to find the black marble shapes have disappeared.

On a later night I woke to hear gentle rain on the roof, trickling down the spouts, after months of drought; my first thought was that it was falling on the yellow clay of the mound over his body, and he could not hear it or feel it. Often when I wake in the morning, a song he used to sing softly in camp is running through my mind:

> Sunrise, bring in the morning;
> Sunrise, bring in the dawning,
> spreading all the light all around.

I don't know its origin, or where he heard it, but I found myself humming it one day in the park in Spearfish, where I'd gone to clear up some details with George's bank. I could see George walking in the park as he used to do, with his two cats—Janet, a gray-striped female, and her son Jacob, a fluffy black giant—and the white poodle Loki, all of them poisoned by some misfit years ago. One morning, I woke to deep purring, and saw Jacob crouched on George's chest; their noses were pressed firmly together. "This is how he tells me he's ready to go out," George mumbled into the cat's whiskers. When a German Shepherd came into the yard, the poodle stood his ground, and the two cats advanced in lock step, hissing and yowling, to his defense. The big dog took one look at the three little animals ranged against him and fled yelping.

Today, my head throbbing from too much gin last night, clutching a cup of coffee, I joined the dog on the deck. The sun baked our backs, and we relaxed in the sun. I thought of all the things that won't happen now. No one will say how much younger than me he looks. When he stands silently by while I autograph books, no one will wonder what I saw in him, or what he saw in me. No one can whisper how healthy—or unhealthy, or fat, or thin—he looks. No one can say "Why doesn't your husband travel with you?" He teased me gently about having no gray hair when mine began to turn; now I'll never see his hair and beard turn gray. No one will hug me in the closet. No one will lick the bowl when I make brownies, if I ever do again. No one will make pineapple pancakes shaped like cats and rabbits for me. I'll never have to stumble over his boots in the dark. No one will rub my back or feet after I've lifted one bale too many, or sat in front of the computer too long. When I tell stories, he won't clear his throat when I finish, and tell what really happened.

Then I noticed the hoses scattered in the frost-covered grass. Every fall I asked George to roll them up; he never did. About mid-October, I'd get angry and do it myself, as I do now. I'd pull each one up over the porch rail to drain, then coil it on the deck where late fall heat will cook it dry inside. In a few days, I'll shoulder each heavy roll, carry it inside the garage to the hangers George built. All winter, my headlights will show them waiting like snakes for spring's green grass, when I'll drag them to the trees we planted together, hook them to the drip irrigation system he put in place to save water. George wanted more cedar and no lilacs, a beech to remind him of Michigan. We took turns digging, cursing when we struck lime-stone. Next spring I'll hook the hoses into the irrigation pipe, hearing his voice telling me how. All through another dry, hot summer the water will coax the trees to live.

Late in the afternoon, after I drape the hoses over the rail, I'll plant the irises my cousin Darlene brought me. She labeled one box "deep blue," and I planted those at the foot of George's grave, and hope they are the color of his eyes. By doing both these mundane jobs, I have made a promise to myself, and to George, that I will be alive in the spring to continue the work I've begun.

Windbreak Now

My book about our life together filled
two hundred thirty-three closely-spaced pages.
The title was what everyone needs on the plains,
and what you meant to me:
a windbreak against the cold,
between my trips into politics,
workshops, blizzards of loneliness.
You always said, "I love you anyway,"
when I got a rejection slip.
You died—not slowly like our trees
for lack of water—
too fast for me to follow.
My life has changed in every way.
I don't save scraps of meat to make soup stock;
canning jars boxed in the garage hold dust;
my complexion brush scrubs mushrooms;
the apples in the freezer won't make pies.

I stand on the deck in starlit dark
and talk to you, feel you close—
but ghosts don't break real wind.
You still stand between me
and a world I love but don't like much.
I see that look when I think revenge,
or say things mean and small.
You're inside me like a second heart,
beating a little out of time with mine.

I feel your breathing
against my chest in the good nights,
slower, longer breaths going deeper.
Outside, at seventy below zero,
I wear your coats and overalls—
my windbreak now.

Notes Written with a Bullet

Falcon Dreaming

The mind heals itself in intricate and surprising ways, and
even during such serious work, demonstrates its sense of humor.
One winter night I dreamed I was walking up the entrance road after
getting the mail, and came upon a pile of clothing. I immediately
recognized it as George's: his worn belt, the big shoes, the circle his
Skoal can left in his shirt pocket. Everything he might have worn on
a normal work day was there; I unfolded each item and looked at it
closely, breathed his clean scent from the wrinkles. Tucked inside,
I found a note; George explained that he was really an explorer of
our world, sent from an advanced, star-traveling race to see if we
were civilized yet. He said he was sorry to go, but he had other
planets to visit; this was his third visit, and when he came back, I
would be long dead, because his kind lives so much longer than ours.

I woke up smiling, and then laughing. George was always
fascinated with space, and would have traded his rifle for a chance to ride
a space shuttle. He loved to read science fiction and speculate on the
possibilities of advanced races. Part of my mind was still not willing to
believe that he is dead; it was comforting to fantasize that a higher duty
took him elsewhere. And I still resented the well-meaning person who
had laundered all the dirty clothes we left behind when we went to the
hospital; only his oldest work coats and his leather buckskinning clothes
still held his scent, and I longed for it enough to put it in my dream.

Another night, later in the winter, I dreamed I was on a pack trip with three other people in terrain that resembled Jackson Hole. We were well equipped, carrying our gear on pack mules and riding good horses. The day was sunny and cold, but we were comfortable in our wool and leather rendezvous clothing, or perhaps it was really 1840. I felt no fear, only a deep freedom and joy to be riding through such country before the white man's greed destroyed it. George wasn't with us, but I felt comfortable with the other riders, though I can't name them. I sensed that George would meet us somewhere ahead. I felt vibrantly alive.

While we rested high above a broad valley a brilliant turquoise falcon with gold wings alighted on my wrist. The other riders simply nodded as if he was expected, and we rode on. I was following the snow-crusted rump of a buffalo, which didn't seem incongruous. Glancing up, I noticed that a large eagle was circling above our group, and accepted it as a sign of George's guidance. I knew the little falcon wouldn't leave me, and put him on my shoulder.

Suddenly the lead rider galloped over a steep wall into a streambed, and the buffalo followed. I was worried about my horse falling, so I dismounted and ran ahead; I heard the horse thrashing behind me. The falcon lifted a little from my shoulder, balancing himself with spread wings. I fell rolled over in a flurry of snow, and stood again, brushed myself off and was ready to mount and ride on. I felt no fear, only assurance.

Almost at once I woke, encouraged by the dream. I knew the eagle was symbolic of George's protection, as the falcon was of my own strength. I'd been doing something I was capable of, with strong friends, in the freedom and magnificence of a mountain wilderness. The white buffalo, sacred to the Lakota, was with us; I had seen him stalk into George's hospital room, heard the rumble of his hooves, which an airman mistook for a B-1 taking off. George and I had often daydreamed about being able to live the old mountain life full-time, and apparently the dream still lived inside me. I was going to survive George's death.

A phrase from the Navajo Beauty Way chant is inscribed inside our wedding rings: "In beauty may I walk." George's ring rests in a parqueted wood box on the dresser; mine is still on my finger.

Signs

The only thing moving in the snowy landscape is a woman getting into a pickup. She wears her husband's faded red coat. It is too large; sometimes she pauses to push the sleeves up. Her movements are slow, and seem incomplete. Each thing she does she used to do with him: chop the ice on the tank and pitch it out onto the ground, lift hay bales to the truck, cut the strings and let them fall to the cattle, fill buckets with cake and scatter it in the tire tracks. In each action, there seems to be a space beside her, a hollow, an echo. Jobs that brought laughter between them are done in silence.

The red coat is visible from a long distance against the stark white of the prairie. Even the pickup is white, and the dog that trots at her heels as she works. The red coat glows like a single coal, a single spot of warmth in an icy landscape. The woman shivers. She pictures her house as a glowing cave of warmth, holding an icy box where she keeps food. Always there is this contrast: the icy box is inside the warm one; the warmth is frozen in the huge cold box of the prairie. Her warm body pulses inside the red coat; inside it lies a heart cold and gray as ash.

There were signs everywhere, but I was slow to see them, slower to understand. All I moved out of our closet at first were your shoes and jeans. I wore the shirts, rolling the sleeves above my elbows. I love the pockets, the comfortable width of the body and sleeves, the way the tails keep my thighs warm. Women's shirts are always tight on my arms, which apparently carry more muscle than a woman should have; the pockets are too small for my notebooks, and the tails too short. Everyone assures me that wearing your shirts is perfectly normal.

Then I stopped reading the papers, and only later remembered that you never read them. You never seemed out of touch with the world of current events, but what took place outside your body and your presence were less and less important to you in the last year.

One night I heard snoring, not the dog; his wheezes are higher, lighter; certainly I couldn't be snoring. Next I lost my taste for breakfast eggs, and craved pancakes. During the blizzards of March, I began gazing west, toward the Rocky Mountains, where I knew the snow still lay deep and impenetrable; still, I saw the slopes covered with flowers. I couldn't imagine going to a rendezvous without you, and putting up the eighteen-foot lodge alone; besides, you'd left it to a friend in your will. I studied the buckskinning catalogs that came in your name, and bought a tent.

I could no longer leave the dog at home with you when I went to poetry readings, so I began taking him with me. He demands his comforts, but growls at strangers as if he could protect me. During the first trip he climbed up on my shoulder, and watched the road; he used to do that when you drove. He wasn't as happy sitting on my thigh next to the door; my thigh isn't as wide as yours, and he had trouble keeping his footing.

The first time I grew angry, I stopped to think, as you did, then answered as though I were six feet tall and had nothing to prove, having proved it all. I forgot to bring a pencil and notebook with me today, and am writing these notes on scraps of paper with a bullet from the pistol; you taught me that.

So that's where you went so suddenly, right into the air beside me, the air inside my lungs.

Pennies for Luck

A heron flaps upstream, the color of fog over the river.
The bridge throbs under my tires.
I roll the window down, throw as hard as I can, listening.
I don't hear a ricochet;
the penny must have sailed past the bridge railings
dropping down, down toward the water.

I've been throwing pennies-for-luck
into the Missouri River for years.
Only today do I wonder what happens
when they fly out beyond the bridge rail heading for water.

Fish may leap for the sparkling lure
and die with pennies in their guts;
seagulls may snatch them in midair;
what kind of luck is that?
A news story I never see may tell of fishermen
mysteriously unconscious. "I don't know,"
he said, "I was fishing under the bridge
alone in my boat and it felt like someone
dropped a rock on my head."

One passenger didn't understand the ritual;
with both hands he scooped parking change from the dashboard
while I laughed helplessly. But he's an environmentalist;
he needed all the help he could get from the river gods.
Once a penny leapt back, spanging against the car door.
I drove with extra care that day.

Today I threw twice, for good fishing
where you are.

These Casual Brutalities

Returning to the Ellsworth Air Force Base hospital one day just before Christmas to fill a prescription, I saw the young airman again; he didn't recognize me, of course, but I stared at him so intently that he broke stride, and a baffled look crossed his face. I turned away, but my teeth were clenched. He had been driving the bus on the airfield when the Medevac plane landed after the long flight from Fitzsimons in Denver. Regulations required that Michael and I wait near the gate until George's litter was loaded on the bus; then, a nurse assured me, the driver would stop for us. When the bus raced toward us, it was clear he had no intention of stopping. I stepped in front of him; his brakes squealed.

"You can't ride in here, lady," the airman yelled through the open window, already shifting to drive on.

I grabbed the rear wing mirror, remembering a woman friend who, while parking cars at a rock concert, ripped one off and smacked a rude driver behind the ear with it. My face had felt like a mask for days; I showed my teeth at him, and said, "Yes, I can. That's my husband in the back."

"Tough. You can't ride in here."

By this time I had the passenger door open and I motioned to Michael to sit in back beside George. "I'm riding in here, kid," I snapped. His face showed that he had realized his only option was to throw me out physically.

"You have to fasten your seatbelt," he said, trying to reestablish his authority.

"Fine." I fastened it, and said nothing else as he drove, too fast, to the hospital. In the back, Mike tried to steady the litter on the corners.

When the young driver reached the emergency entrance to the hospital, he stepped out and walked briskly to the waiting attendants. "Where's this terminal guy go?" he said loudly.

One snowy night, years ago, I drove too fast down the half-mile gravel road that leads to the ranch; I have no excuse, other than being mad, tired, in a hurry. Without warning, a yellow tomcat sprang into the headlights and ran down the narrow passage my truck tires had made in the deep snow. I was gunning the pickup to make it up the steep hill when I saw him. My reflexes were slowed by surprise; I couldn't brake in time. Scrambling frantically ahead of the tires, he made it to the top before I could stop. The pickup skidded just as he paused to look back. I felt the crunch in my foot through the pedal.

By the time I found my flashlight and stumbled back through the snow, he'd dragged himself out of the rut with his front legs. He was crouched in deep snow with his ears back, eyes glaring in pain and fear. He hissed, yowled, and spat at me as I bent down. My hand stopped above him; the blood and the way he lay told me his back and hips were ruined.

I stood by the truck a moment. He wasn't one of our tomcats;

someone from town had dumped him here, or he'd strayed from a neighboring ranch. The longer I tried to decide what to do about him, the more he suffered. He could not recover. I found a wrench. It was hard to strike between his staring eyes but I had no choice. I tried to make it quick.

Sometimes when I come home late at night I have to back down and take the hill twice, because I still see him there, scrabbling at the icy trail. Sometimes when I see a young, brash face, I hear the words, "this terminal guy."

I thought of the cat and the young airman last night, driving home alone on Christmas Eve. I sent no cards. On some of those I receive, friends have written, "I know your Christmas will be terrible." Many friends cope with George's death by not mentioning it, perhaps believing they are being kind. George's mother says sensibly: "Don't be alone on Christmas. If you have to go among people, you'll have to keep up a front, and that's good for you." I follow her advice.

O Holy Night on the Prairie

Folks who are used to bustling, fur-wrapped shoppers and greenery hung with lights would see the wide prairie that stretches in front of me as a bleak place to spend Christmas. The grass is a mountain lion pelt—not one color, but gold, fawn, red, brown, and colors for which no names exist—blended into each other over the rolling hills. A few limestone outcroppings studded with pale green lichen and a scatter of white and granite-gray boulders decorate the scene; there are no trees, no green, cone-shaped evergreens that mean Christmas to many. In the deeper gullies, an occasional bare cottonwood shows a white, lightning-stripped trunk against the grass; buffalo berry and plum bushes stand naked in narrow crevices beside ground-hugging juniper bushes blending green and bronze.

In the eastern distance are the Badlands, pink, gray, and blue spires a finger's width above the horizon, made higher this morning by mirage which is rapidly spreading, to disappear as the sun comes up dull gold. To the west rise the Black Hills, a handsbreadth of tree-covered hills, rising in five distinct ranges and glowing blue in the morning light.

Here, while Christmas songs play on the pickup radio, I see nothing at all to remind me of the season. The grass is short, because we graze these distant pastures in summer, and bring the cattle closer to home in winter. I am making a last survey, picking up salt blocks and fence panels, to be sure gates are closed against the neighbor's buffalo. When I turn homeward today, I will be shutting the door on this part of the ranch until spring, when we'll bring cows and young calves here to graze through the summer.

A coyote slips down a draw, glancing back over his shoulder. Except for his quick movement, a flash of white at his throat and a nearly-black ridge on his spine and tail, he would be invisible against the grass. My eye catches movement again, and I turn to see thirty antelope run over a hill, white rump-patches flashing. One pauses, silhouetted against the sun.

The gray limestone of Silas Lester's house has descended a little more toward the ground this year; the blank windows look like half-shut eyes. The house was never finished; dry years came, and Silas sold his land for two dollars an acre to my grandfather, who took the risk and stayed. The spring Silas found and enlarged still runs gently from the hillside, into a tank George and I dug into the hillside and covered with wood chips to keep the water from freezing. I open the gate to it, so the wild animals can safely drink, and leave a few chips of salt nearby; a really thrifty rancher would take them home to the calves, but I like to think of the antelope and smaller creatures—porcupines, skunks, mice—enjoying the rare treat of salt this winter.

Another year has passed. Some years George and I made this final trip in deep snow, laughing as the pickup plunged into a drift, apprehensive when it dropped too deep and the tires spun. We've shared picnics here under the talking leaves of the cottonwoods in summer, shoveled together when the pickup was stuck in winter. Feeling a little foolish, we shut off the motor and observed a worldwide moment of silence in honor of John Lennon a few years ago, then sang his songs on the way home, and didn't feel foolish at all.

The chores we did together I now do alone. The Christmas songs on the radio mean the solstice is near, when the days will almost imperceptibly begin to lengthen. Now the sun has risen far south; it will make a shallow arc in the southern sky all day, and the moon will shine in the south windows of the bedroom tonight.

We started a tradition a few years ago, when Michael came in a dry summer with a trunkload of fireworks; it was too dry to shoot them then, so we saved them for his winter visit, and fired them on New Year's Eve. Last year, I did it alone; this year, I may invite friends to share the ritual. On Christmas Eve I will join my cousin and his wife and their children, one my godson, in church. I attended the same church when I was five years old, and my mother sang in the choir. It's famous for its massive organ, and as the tones swell into the familiar "Oh Come, All Ye Faithful," I—who have been anything but a faithful churchgoer—will find myself in tears. The organ tones express to me the largeness of the land, rising over the small minds and bodies of the people who live upon it.

Slowly, as Christmas passes, snow falls, grouse mate with bell-like calls in the winter night stillness, the days will grow warmer, and spring will come. If we get spring rains—which have not come for three years—the tawny grass will show a hint of green at the roots in April and by June the hills will be rich with new life.

"I believe in the Israelite," sings a low voice on the radio, backed by the sound of bells, and I wonder. Surely no one who sees the seasons turn as I do, who observes the prairie's stillness in this season of rest, and the inevitable coming of spring life, summer's lushness, the harvests of fall, and the chill of winter again and again, can fail to believe that all is arranged as it should be. That no matter how great are our personal sorrows, the world is proceeding in an orderly fashion. That we are all part of a great cycle, and our job is to help the earth in its turning, to keep it pure and beautiful and clean for those who will surely come after us.

Valentine's Night

You didn't like Valentine's Day,
going to the mall to find a card
among fake flowers.
Surprised, I dried the roses
you brought last year,
saved the pink heart box.
I keep your letters in it;
your grave is six months old.
My mother sent a card.

Moonlight lurks behind clouds;
I stand under a silver ceiling.
Snow falls; coyotes sing of romance.
Wearing your socks,
I shuffle a heart huge on the deck,
scribble promises in frost on the rail.

To Love and Honor

Ten years ago this morning, on March 10, 1979, we got out
of the same bed and dressed nervously. You wore a blousy riverboat
shirt of heavy cotton with a "Made with love by Linda" label in the
back, a suit instead of the jeans I hoped you'd choose. I wore an old
ivory satin blouse under a new ivory lace vest with a small-waisted
maroon wool skirt you liked, high boots hiding peach and silver
socks my friend Kathy had sent. We drove up in the Hills, not yet
green this early in March. Patches of snow hung on hillsides. Your
former wife brought your son, so he could stand with us and a few
close friends while we promised to love each other all we could.

Neither of us was sure marriage would work. I'd bought a car
the day before, as if I could never buy one again, and thought about
driving into the sunset. You kept looking at Michael, and I wondered what you were thinking; much later you confessed to fear of

commitment, fear that you would fail your son, or me.

I had bought a bunch of spring flowers in the supermarket the day before, and Markie and I nervously divided them in half in the bedroom, then took deep breaths and came out to stand with you and her husband Dick before the fireplace. When I'd read a poem at their wedding, right after my ex-husband read one, you smiled and gave me courage.

The minister dispensed with lectures, and left "obey" out of the service at our request. Afterward, he pulled out his harmonica and jigged a little as he played it, then taught seven-year-old Michael to play a simple tune. The ceremony was over so quickly that we lingered awhile, and posed for an old-fashioned picture. You are seated solemnly in a chair, looking at the distance, one arm around Mike, whose head is on your shoulder; I stand submissively behind you with my hand on Mike's shoulder; we are all smiling.

Back home, in our apartment at the side of my parents' house, we ate food our friends had brought, drank home-brewed mead, and watched our cowboy friends meet our hippie friends, while our buckskinning friends watched nervously, backs against the walls. After a few tense minutes, everyone brought out violins and mouth harps, guitars and mandolins, and learned they all played the same music. Someone brought overripe zucchini, so those of us who couldn't play a real musical instrument could use them as drums; when we beat one to a pulp, we tossed it out the door and got another. We even sang—quietly; neither of us could carry a tune— and opened presents from people who knew we had everything we needed. Some of my relatives came, to make our marriage official, but they looked a little uneasy about the whole thing. We had chosen a date when my parents were still in Texas for the winter, to save everyone's nerves; I'd never met your parents, who were no longer married to each other, or your grandparents, who raised you. You told me this omission was intentional, so you'd have my signature on the dotted line before I realized what I'd gotten myself into, but I liked almost all of your family when I met them five years later.

When most of the guests went home, one couple stayed; the next morning I showed the three children still there, including

Mike, how to feed calves. We all sat down on the feed bunks in the corral, and the kids alternately gasped and squealed as the yearling calves tasted their coats, their hair, and their ears. Only Mike had enough patience to move his hand slowly, slowly toward a calf's nose until he succeeded in petting it. Later we built forts of snow and had a snowball fight, your side against mine. The couple who stayed that night were divorced a few years later.

We stayed together, astonished at loving each other more, at trust neither of us had ever known, at the strength that grew between us like a web. When you plucked a strand, I was there. I always wondered if I'd be strong enough to help you die if the cancer came back; I feared nothing more than being weak beside your strength, than letting you down.

This morning I know I didn't. I wouldn't mind doing it all again, though I'd change a few things: times I said things I didn't mean, occasions when I missed the sunset while balancing the checkbook. My blouse and vest are packed away; the skirt was snug last winter; now that I haven't been eating, it hangs on me like a tent. I buried you in the shirt.

Aftershock

Since *Windbreak* was published, an odd dilemma has developed. When George first discovered that the book contained an accurate map to our ranch, he raised a questioning eyebrow, but neither of us really believed anyone, friendly or dangerous, would actually come to our home.

Then readers' letters began arriving. I wrote personal notes the first few months, but soon the mailbox was stuffed with messages from old friends, from people who envied or feared my outdoor life, people who kept diaries, who wanted to move West, people who had lost their land. Many of the letters began: "Dear Linda, After reading a year of your diary, I feel I know you. I have never written to an author." Suddenly hundreds of people knew George, Frodo, our neighbors; they worried about our calves during blizzards, offered advice on where to buy long underwear, wrote poems, sent photographs, shared their lives. A horse breeder sent me a picture of a filly he named Red Feather Dancin', a phrase I'd written about my mare Rebel. Some asked about George's health; after he died, I used a form letter to ease the pain of repeating the news and save time. I was moved and grateful for every letter; some days, I believe they saved my sanity.

In July of 1989, *Life* magazine published "Journal of a Woman Rancher," with photographs of me in manure-splashed coveralls and stocking cap; the daily entries I wrote revealed George's death. In a fresh flood of letters, bereaved readers offered sympathy and assured me that I could survive. An ex-marine, retired from police work, said he was so tough he had not cried over his wife's death until he read the story; he thanked me for showing him the strong could cry. Each time my spirit dropped, a warm letter from a stranger proved that human compassion exists. But some effects of publicity were distressing; in a local café where I used to collect stories, one rancher interrupted his yarn to bellow at me, "Now, I don't want to read this in some (expletive deleted) magazine."

The first visitors who knocked on my door were apologetic, but by the time I had stammered that I really couldn't conduct a tour of the ranch, and given autographs, an hour of writing time was gone. It was unnerving to see a strange car crossing the field while I mowed hay, to look up from branding to see a camera over a corral gate. I led a bus load of German students to a community barbecue, then slipped away, mortified but relieved. The salutation of a letter postmarked in an Asiatic country stunned me: "Dear Auntie." The writer, a well-educated man with a wife and children, wanted me to adopt or hire him, or give him land where he could farm and become an American. Without my husband, he noted, I needed help on the ranch.

Overall, the visitors have been considerate; complaints seem churlish. But while I love to answer letters in odd intervals, most writers' addresses remain secret, with mail forwarded from publishers. In my small prairie community, I am as visible as a single cottonwood; other residents, justifiably proud of South Dakota's reputation for friendliness, give directions to anyone. I bless the people who write to say that they recognized the house from my description, honked, waved, and drove on. Although I come from reticent stock, I can bear to write intimately in isolation, assuming readers will share my thoughts in their own solitude. Often, I discover new ideas by writing, or reveal more on paper than I am comfortable discussing even with close friends, and learn from readers who share my confusion and grief. I feel comfortable enough reading or lecturing on my work to endure meeting strangers and facing cameras, but I don't truly relax until I am home again. If *Windbreak* is reprinted, the map will be altered to encourage readers to enjoy the scenery without finding my home, in an effort to preserve my privacy, and readers' illusions.

Requiem for Thirty Raccoons

When the dog barked last night,
I ran into the dark carrying a gun;
you were eating sweet blue Hopi corn
from the only three stalks I'd planted,
gobbling the ears you missed last week.
My intentions toward you were not kindly.
After the dog chased you to the bank of the dam,
you tried to lure him into swimming after you.
Your intentions were not honorable either, masked raider.
If you'd drowned my dog, I'd be after you still,
unless you were dead in the hayfield, paws over your eyes.

I spent an hour brushing burrs,
trying to explain to the dog
why chasing you is unwise,
though your round body looks slower than his.
I mentioned what your kind does to dogs in water,
though I had no documentation;
atrocity stories may be exaggerated
in these inter-species conflicts.

Today, driving across the state,
I've counted corpses,
your cousins and one red fox,
his quick feet still, ears empty of wind.
Each was caught by the flat blade of light,
spun into darkness by our tires,

crossing from one feast to another in darkness.
Masks flung aside, paws curled, tails rippling,
they look peaceful after the brief violence of death.

None of you deserve to lie still
while speeding trucks
pound your plump carcasses flat and dry.
I'd rather feed you corn—
if you'll leave my dog alone,
and tell your kits to stay out of the barn.
One way or another, our sweets corrupt you.

In Defense of the
Common Sunflower

I grew up, like any well-trained child on the prairie, knowing
sunflowers were my natural enemies, because they were not allowed
in the garden. Hoeing was a job I attacked with vigor because I hated
it: hated the heat, sweat pouring down my face, my glasses steaming
up and sliding down my nose, my straw hat scratching my forehead,
the calluses on my hands. (I changed my attitude when I discovered
girls were supposed to wear dresses, but that calluses and a pocket
knife were my ticket to the boys' mumbletypeg games on the
playground.) Most of all, I hated weeds, including sunflowers.

Weeds were the prison bars between me and a long horseback
ride on the prairie where I could explore every pile of rocks, wade
in every trickle of cool water. The weeds fenced me in under the
watchful eye of my parents; if I destroyed the weeds, I could escape
into the prairie to become an Indian maiden or warrior, a Hun raider
on the steppes, or anything else my imagination could devise.
Unfortunately, the best I do was to clear a row or two, and hope my
parents would let me ride anyway.

Sunflowers were not quite as annoying as buffalobur and

Canada thistle, both of which left stickers in my gloves, jeans, and fingers for weeks. But the tiny sunflowers I missed one day grew like Jack's beanstalk; the next day they would reach my knees. The thick, tough stems couldn't be chopped; they had to be pulled, one by one. Leave them a week, and their hold on the earth was greater than my strength.

We shed many of our childish prejudices as we grow older, particularly if we have children who can be forced to hoe the garden because work is as good for them as it was for us. By the time I planted my own garden, I had modified my views on sunflowers; because they attracted birds, which ate insects when they weren't nibbling sunflower seeds, I left them on the edges of the garden, and among the squash and corn.

When George and I built our house in 1981, construction left the earth bare around it. For a while after native grasses have been destroyed or damaged, unpleasant weeds like fireweed and cheat grass proliferate. A rather predictable and orderly succession of plants, some of which we call weeds, will follow before native grasses return. Instead of planting fragile lawn grass, we walked around the yard using our pocket knives to lift tiny plugs of buffalo grass, no more than a half-inch in diameter, tucking them into bare spots where they would spread. We left the sunflowers, because they were a vivid green in the bare brown earth. They grew tall, blossomed, and began to make seed, attracting goldfinches by the dozens. From our windows, we could watch the birds hanging upside down, digging seeds out of a brown head, sometimes almost invisible among the golden blooms. But in the hot summer of 1990, I came to appreciate sunflowers for a reason I could never have guessed.

Every day seemed hotter and drier than the day before, but rains in June made the grass and hay grow; by the end of the month, everyone was frantically mowing the biggest crop of hay we'd had in five dry years. By July, when no rain had fallen for three weeks, unmown hay and dry pasture grass became a fire danger. My father wanted a record of the tallest brome grass he'd seen in eighty years, so I photographed my Bronco in the hay field: the brome reached to the middle of the windows. I began tying my horse to posts around my house, where he'd alternately graze and trample the grass, creating a bare strip, a fire guard. In spring, I planted only enough new trees to replace the dead ones in my windbreaks. In my father's junk piles I found discarded hoses, used duct tape lavishly to patch the worst holes and longest splits, then fitted them into my existing system, inventing "leak irrigation." In several spots I planted two new trees below older ones, reasoning that water would soak down to them. But the higher trees and the dry heat absorbed every drop of moisture. I taped short pieces of broken hose over leaks to water the lower trees. Friends who walked through the windbreak tried to understand how the system worked, but remained bewildered. Jerry, an engineer for the Wyoming Highway Department, said, "If this mess works, you could get a job in the hydrology department any day."

My trees survived except where I failed to provide shade during their first weeks. When I couldn't write another line, I would walk the winding hoses, carrying duct tape and pieces of hose, patching leaks that weren't watering trees, or that were drawing too much water. Once or twice I wound the tape around myself, the dog, the hose, and the waist-high grass, and had to cut us all loose. Collapsing in helpless laughter didn't stop the leaks, but it did me good.

I had known from the day we buried George that growing flowers on his grave would be difficult. Most of the soil that covers the prairies is only an inch or two deep, light gray because it doesn't collect much humus; the soil raised to the surface when a grave is dug in the cemetery is much worse, a thick yellow clay. When thoroughly soaked, it is as impossible as molasses to scrape off shoes; when it dries, water can only seep through cracks. In the spring after George's death, many plants on his grave were crushed when we set his headstone in concrete. By then, temperatures were reaching nearly one hundred daily, so I planted a few bright flowers for temporary color, and began collecting more permanent plantings from the prairie. Walking through the pastures and the outer edges of the cemetery, I collected native plants, using a belt knife to slice narrow fragments containing roots out of the earth. In this way, I tucked into the grave earth both female and male sage, the latter called "winterfat" by the Lakota because it kept the bison fat against the cold; snakeroot (purple coneflower); buffalo grass, johnny jump ups (Nuttall violets); and other plants that might be tough enough to live there. In late summer, I carried old plastic bags in my pockets every day, collecting wildflower and grass seed to plant on the grave.

By September of 1989, a year after George's death, the only living things on the grave were irises my cousin had grown on a dry ranch in the southern Black Hills, a pincushion cactus from our home hillside, and the tough, prickly weeds and creeping jenny I pulled daily. But tucked into every crack in the yellow earth, and nestled between chunks of sandstone I'd placed at the foot of the grave to slow the rain runoff were dozens of seeds from penstemon, gayfeather, purple prairieclover, rush skeleton-plant, woolly verbena, scarlet gaura, and several varieties of mint. I'd planted a bed of catnip at home for George's cat Phred; he died the day after George did, and I didn't have the presence of mind to tuck his long gray body into the grave with George's. That fall, a sprig of catnip appeared on the grave. Oh, and the onion.

Not long after the soil was heaped over George's coffin, a tiny shoot of green appeared in the bare yellow earth on the north side. I laughed when I first saw it, suspecting what it was. Someone who visited the grave with me stared, and finally asked gingerly, "Did you plant that onion?"—wondering, I'm sure, what obscure symbolism it held. But I had nothing to do with it; I interpreted it as George's ironic comment on the futility of planting flowers on this hillside, and perhaps on why we plant flowers on graves at all. When, rarely, I picked wildflowers for a bouquet, he'd say, "Oh, you killed some flowers." The onion thrived, and I watered it daily, along with the wild garlic a friend had dug at a rendezvous in the Bighorns after I told her about the onion; "for George's grave," she said. She may also have heard George's tale of how he and his friends always got a day off from school when the first wild onions appeared. Children who had eaten a double handful of wild onions exuded fumes unbearable indoors until the odor had worn off.

Still, the weather soon became too hot for the young native

plants to survive without help. No water is available at the cemetery, so I began filling two five-gallon jugs with water and hauling them to the grave each evening. I missed our long evenings together, sitting on the deck to watch the sunset colors drop over the land, coyotes hunting the valley below the house, bats swooping for insects around the eaves. Sometimes we'd sit quietly for more than an hour, perhaps holding hands; the only sound was the clink of ice cubes in gin and tonic. George often said it was his favorite time of day. I'd watch his face as the sun made it glow with golden light, then hid it in shadow; his gaze grew remote, his eyes narrowed as if he were looking a long way. To the mountains, I thought then. Now I think he was looking into a much greater distance.

At first, I dreaded the trips to the cemetery. I spent the day alternately sweating in the heat at ranch work, writing in my cool basement, adjusting the water to my trees, and watching for fire. But I knew the drought would kill all the plants if I didn't help.

The first hot afternoon I hauled water to the cemetery, Frodo ran barking ahead of me as I carried the hose. I remembered the game he and George had played, and turned the water on again. He grabbed the end of the nozzle, trying to bite the rushing water, yelping and ducking away when it shot up his nose, then dashing in again. In moments he was soaking wet and I was laughing. I thought of leaving him behind, but I knew he'd gallop down the road behind me, collecting dirt until he was a mud ball, barking frantically. I put old blankets over the seats, and we started to the cemetery. I always played cheerful music on the drive, and still arrived crying; song lyrics take on new meanings when you sing them on the way to your husband's grave, and it was painful to see that mound of earth settling an inch or two a week.

When I arrived, I'd tuck the car into the lilac bushes so that other cars could pass, and drag each jug up the hill. By mid-June, the irises at the foot of the grave were tall and green, a spot of freshness I could see from the highway. I was looking forward to their blooming, hoping they would be nearly as blue as his eyes. Next, I'd water the Stella D'Oro day lily I'd ordered from a specialist in plants for arid regions; George had once noticed that summer's prairie flowers are often yellow, and its bloom would be a rich gold. An evening primrose would bloom at night, and I'd mulched runners from wild strawberry plants, hoping they'd create a woven mat of green to hold water until grass grew. The red dragon's tongue and silver sedum I planted as ground covers were spreading and adapting well; by the end of the summer, I could break off sprigs to put on other family graves.

One day, after the water was gone, I sat down beside the stone, leaned my shoulders against it, and sobbed. I cried even harder when the dog stuck his nose under my arm, crept into my lap, and licked my cheek. Then I sat up, my shoulder against the rough granite, and looked out over the valley while the hot wind dried my tears. The silhouettes of tombstones, like my own, stretched out before me, turning deep black as the sun dropped behind the cemetery hill. Slowly, they darkened the store, the school, the playground where I'd played tag, the houses, the hayfields where I'd learned to operate a mower. Pickup engines revved as local men pulled up to the store and the bar; a few housewives came for groceries. I thought bitterly that the shadow of the cemetery hung over them all, whether they knew it or not.

Finally, I turned and watched the sun drop behind the Black Hills, and the sky grow gold, then red, then a dark rose. I didn't leave until it was so dark I accidentally put my hand down in the greasy yellow mud. I smeared most of it onto a patch of buffalo grass on my way to the car, but when I opened the door to let the dog in, his feet were wrapped in sticky yellow balls; I realized he'd walked across the grave. By the time I'd scraped most of the mud off him, my hands, shirt, face, and steering wheel were covered with it.

The next night I came to the cemetery a bit later, and when I'd finished watering, I deliberately sat down, my arm across the shoulders of the stone, and watched the sunset. It wasn't quite like sitting on the deck to watch it with George, but it was the best I could do. That may have been the day I first noticed the sunflowers. I'd ruthlessly yanked them out during the first summer, but their tiny leaves were a deep green; in the summer hell it seemed criminal to destroy anything alive. One grew in the precise center of the grave. Michael had named me Sunflower when he noticed that most of the people who went to rendezvous had "mountain names." No one else called me Sunflower, but I liked the name's reminder of mountain sunflowers in Sunlight Basin where we'd loved to camp.

By midsummer, the prairie was brown, dust rolling up in choking clouds behind mowers of ranchers determined to cut anything that might furnish cattle feed next winter. My visits to the cemetery had become the best part of my day, as our evenings on the deck had once been. I'd dig up plants with my Green River knife, watch the sunset, write in my journal, talk to George, or cry while I pulled weeds. Often I'd take a long time to dole out ten gallons of water, watching with satisfaction as it soaked into the yellow earth, waiting for the evening primrose to open.

Sometimes I walked among the other graves, studying different methods of decoration. Covering black plastic with crushed white quartz seems another death to me. As the plastic breaks down, weeds spring up between the white stones, which seem unnatural among the prairie colors. Other people dig up the burial plot every spring, to plant a fresh batch of annual flowers; the blooms are attractive, but by midsummer weeds have smothered the fragile flowers. What will happen when there is no one to replant them?

Many people bring artificial flowers to the cemetery on Memorial Day; they add an air of gaiety for a while. But many people never come back to remove them; as hot summer days pass, the flowers droop, come apart. Plastic roses and daisies blow out into the prairie grass, where they lurk for years, like fragments of some radioactive disaster. Other folks turn the soil each spring, resolutely pulling each plant, so that the grave always looks horribly fresh. In the corner of one family plot is a huge cedar tree; but the caretakers asked me not to plant trees or large bushes that would hamper their mowing or eventually tumble headstones. Some of the graves have not been tended for fifty years or more; slowly the buffalo grass has crowded out the weeds, and wildflowers have seeded themselves. These graves comforted me most, as if the people in them had truly gone back to the earth, and to the nurturing of its best plants.

One evening I found wild irises growing by the hundreds near the cemetery gate, where the caretakers had never mowed. For several evenings, I dug clumps from the center of the crowd and planted each bulb separately on the grave, knowing they would spread. We'd bought four cemetery plots, since my parents had never purchased any for themselves, so I planted irises around the edges of all of them. If I live a normal life span, I will be buried there after I have no family left to tend my grave. With the irises, I defined the outline of the rectangle, hoping holes for my parents and myself can be dug without destroying the flowers. I carried extra dirt to fill in the old, unused road that slants across that part of the hillside. Cemetery officials had planted steel bars to block the path, but ruts remained, and heavy rains washed them deeper.

One day, after an evening rain shower, I went to the grave and was shocked to see deep car tracks across it. No one could have failed to see the grave and the huge headstone in daylight; perhaps teenagers using the hill for nocturnal nature study had simply made a mistake. Still, Jerry brought three more narrow slabs of granite, and buried them nearly four feet in the earth one hot day. "If they drive over those," he remarked quietly, "they'll leave their transmission behind so you'll know who they are."

A few nights later, I arrived to find that the hired caretaker had driven his riding mower along the edges of every grave; at George's, he had neatly chopped off the day lily, nearly ready to bloom. The irises outlining the grave plots had been slashed a half-inch above the earth, and were turning brown in the heat. The next day I drove to a pasture where blocks of sandstone had been piled when a railroad culvert was dismantled, and brought back the largest ones I could lift, tucking them along the sides of the grave.

When the sunflowers on the edges of the grave began to crowd plants I preferred, I cut or pulled some of them, but most remained. Some evenings I was surprised, after the day's heat, to find damp patches of earth; eventually I realized that the huge sunflower leaves provided shade. One evening, as I sat by the tombstone, I saw two tiny toads hopping among the strawberry runners. Their little hides were glistening green; when I was six years old and saw such toads in the garden, I believed they were fairies, who changed shape when a human child *almost* saw them. I wondered if I'd ever told George about that fantasy, and what he would say. He had been a dreamy child, too; perhaps he would have told me some story of his own childish ideas, some tale I will never hear. After that, I nearly always saw the little toads in the evenings.

When I passed the cemetery, as I do every time I go to town, reflex made me glance up at the grave; I could always pick it out, even from a half-mile away, because it was framed in deep sunflower green, stunning in the dusty brown countryside. In the precise center of the mound stood "my" plant, nearly eight feet tall, covered with yellow blooms that swayed in the slightest breeze. The headstone was partially hidden at first; eventually, the stem was bare nearly four feet up from the ground.

I smiled each time I passed, imagining that George would approve of the sunflower's incongruity, see it as a sign of hope, with the onion blooming beside it. Like us: the sunflower and the onion, the pair people thought had nothing in common. Each day we were together our bond grew stronger, and our trust in one another's different strengths increased.

One evening in early fall, as I turned toward the cemetery from the highway, I realized something was missing. Sometimes it takes a while, even in looking at a familiar scene, to find the anomaly, or perhaps my mind refused. I had parked and turned off the ignition when it hit me: the sunflower was gone. All the sunflowers were gone. I could not breathe.

Eventually, I got out of the car and walked closer, carrying the jugs. At the grave's foot the irises were blooming, deep blue heads against the dark granite; they were not the color of George's eyes. Much of the mound was covered with silver and red sedum. At the center was a hole at least eight inches deep. Framing it, one on each side, were two large footprints.

I dropped the jug, inhaled, looked around. The riding power mower had cut all the weeds short; they were burned crisp from the day's sun. Around the grave, sunflower stems stood short and gray. Footprints, knee prints, and jagged holes in the earth showed how difficult it had been to cut and pull the tough stems. Because my watering had created a thick clay cap over the grave, the sunflowers didn't come neatly up from a central hole; each plant's roots tore out a large chunk of earth and all the plants growing in it, plants I'd tended so carefully all summer. The center was the worst; the two big feet had crushed irises, smashed sedum, broken the globe of a nipple cactus that would have bloomed a vivid pink in another day. I'd set small, flat stones on edge to protect two Rocky Mountain columbines; the stones had been knocked away, the fragile stems were broken. Clods of earth were scattered everywhere, with limp plants hanging from them.

I noted grimly that the destroyer hadn't moved the sandstone block; the day lily was blooming in the middle of the destruction. Then I sat down and began picking up the broken clods, tucking them back into the earth and sprinkling a little water on each plant, knowing the day's heat had probably already killed them. I didn't see the tiny toads; perhaps he'd stepped on them, or sprayed them with poison.

The longer I worked, the angrier I got. I could see the rigidity that shielded George's face when he was angry. I wanted to scream profanity over the town, to smash the face of whoever had done this; George never raised his voice, or threatened. But sometimes, to the surprise of those who didn't understand that stillness, he acted swiftly and decisively. As I muttered, the dog gave up his meandering around other tombstones and came to lie at the foot of the grave, staring toward the stone.

The irises around the grave had been cut short again; this time they might not survive. The shells and stones I'd collected on walks by the sea in California and Scotland had been stepped on, ground into powder. While grumbling, I planned a ten-foot-high fence around our grave sites—until I realized such a fence would be ugly, and make tending my plants difficult. I pictured myself roaming the prairie, digging prickly pear cacti by the dozens, but they spread in dry weather or by mowing; I would be condemning the entire cemetery to their intrusion. I thought of putting up a sign: "Do not mow this grave." But I didn't want to disrupt the stone's beauty. I tried to consider the caretaker's point of view; presumably, it was he who had done this. He probably thought I was an elderly widow, too weak to pull the sunflowers, and too dumb to pull them while they were small. Surely he didn't mean to be so destructive, to cause the pain in my heart. But how could I prevent him from doing it again?

A half-hour after dark, when I knew my parents would be worried about my absence, I was calm enough to stop at their house to explain my delay, and to practice what I would say to the caretaker. My father, who never let hired men swear in my presence, grew very still, as George might have, and said, "We'll put up a fence so the son of a bitch can't get in there." I explained why I didn't want a fence; he offered to help me do anything I thought was necessary, but I said I'd handle it, and drove home.

By the time I'd made enough calls to discover who took care of the cemetery, I was crying again, and the woman who had hired the caretaker assured me that she would explain my outrage to him, being certain he understood that I wanted him never, ever, to touch anything on my husband's grave again, no matter what it was. She seemed to understand; she is a widow.

Then I sat down to study my outrage. Sunflowers, after all, are common, even here, even in a drought. The cemetery is a public place; now that volunteers have arranged for regular care, logic dictates that people who use it submit our will to that of the majority. I cannot remove the plastic flowers and quartzite chips that offend me from someone else's graves, nor should I condemn what another thinks beautiful.

We are easily moved to defend the helpless: let a child fall down a well, and we send help, without condemnation, or questions about how the mishap occurred. Let whale or grizzly habitat be threatened, and we expend ink by the gallon to defend it.

But what have we done for weeds lately? If we save only the exotic species, our world will be a vast concrete desert, with a few rarities under hothouse glass, exhibited for a price most of us can't afford to pay. The unique and uncommon draw defenders by the millions; who will defend the insignificant, the plain, the sunflower-strewn prairie used as a passageway by people accelerating toward the splendors of Yellowstone? If we don't save the commons, first there will be no setting for the wondrous; later, there will be no wonder.

It is winter now, ten degrees below zero; George has been dead two years. When I returned recently from a trip to Scotland, I sat on a snowdrift by his grave with my pockets full of slate picked up near a standing stone circle on the north coast, and shells from sea-whipped beaches. As I drew each one out and tucked it into the snow beneath the headstone, I told George about the trip, even though I had felt he accompanied me. A large shell I'd placed earlier held an unlit cigarette, a sign left by a friend who does Lakota prayer rituals here. The snow was drifted more deeply over the native plants and among the broken stems of the sunflowers than anywhere else in the cemetery; they are catching their own moisture for summer. The smooth lines of a white shell exposed by the wind are echoed by the curve of a drift.

Last summer, I collected two dozen canisters of wildflower seeds, including sunflowers; they wait under the stairs. During each warm day this winter, I have lifted another block of stone from some spot where it has fallen out of a wall, or a well curbing, and hauled it to the cemetery. Slowly, week by week, I am laying down a low and subtle wall. Inside it, I will plant wild sunflowers; stone and sunflower shade will protect ordinary prairie plants; the toads can stay; and the weeds will cheerfully renew themselves.

What the Falcon Said

Flat on his back, feathers bloody,
surrounded by drooling cats,
the young falcon hissed,
clacked his beak, clawed air.
His feathers were bloody;
one cat licked a bleeding ear.
Falcon's yellow eyes didn't blink
when I picked him up
like a handful of springs,
like a grenade with the pin pulled.
None of the blood was his.

I put him high in a cedar tree.
He clutched the branch and panted,
glared at me,
then shot straight up like a bullet.
Next day, on my horse, I saw
a redwing blackbird whistling on a post
explode in the middle of a fluid run of song.
The falcon shot away, clutching the corpse.
He screeched once but I heard what he said:

Don't expect pretty lies from me.
I know my job.
You saved me from the cats
so I could live.
I kill to eat.
So do the cats.

So do you.

Vultures

One spring evening, as George and I drove through the calving pasture, we saw a flock of large birds wheeling in the air above us. We got out of the pickup and leaned against it for support, craning our necks to watch the black shapes swoop, playing with the wind currents, diving and rising again without flapping a wing. At first we thought they were crows, or a flock of ravens passing through. But their characteristic ability to move all over the sky without effort, and their increasing size as they loomed closer, convinced us we were watching buzzards. The flock played in the sky awhile, and finally settled, croaking and hissing, into the branches of a huge cottonwood beside my parents' house. We counted them, and looked at each other, tempted to rush back to the house to see if my parents needed assistance. If we had lived a century ago, twenty-three buzzards would have made the oral histories.

This week I've been thinking about buzzards, or vultures, as they are correctly called. I keep these thoughts to myself; a caricature of a buzzard contemplating a roadkill from a fencepost, shoulders hunched under his shining black feather cape, has become a sign of doom and death, filth and horror. Actually, vultures are among the cleanest of creatures, and bathe often. They were once thought to carry anthrax and other diseases resulting from their diet, but we now know these to have been false rumors.

We seem to love inventing horror stories for even the most benevolent of animals; look what we've done to the reputation of the wolf, a gentle, family-loving animal which displays unusual fidelity to its offspring and pack. Because a few cattle and sheep ranchers want to pasture livestock in the mountains to which they are not suited, we may fail to reintroduce the wolf to the Yellowstone Park ecosystem, of which it should be a vital, useful member. We have done the same negative public relations job on several animals; thanks to a couple of spectacularly inaccurate shark movies, many folks are afraid to venture into any body of water larger than a stock pond. I remember a tense moment during the showing of *Jaws* in a theater in Lincoln, Nebraska; when a woman shrieked and tossed her large soft drink in the air, five rows of people screamed in terror. But I'd rather meet a shark in the water any day than a floating mass of medical waste, and I greet vultures as useful members of my own plains community.

I love the symmetrical beauty of a vulture's soaring flight; I often pick up their feathers, as if plumage alone could enable me to float on air waves. Considering the rate at which our flying machines are losing parts and cartwheeling to earth, my imagination will be my only flight for a while. I also welcome the sight of vultures fastidiously picking a dead calf down to its essential bones. Recently, however, a vulture seems to have followed me three hundred miles from the Bighorn Mountains of central Wyoming to western South Dakota, which makes a middle-aged woman with death on her mind nervous.

I first spotted it as I was following a slow horse trailer on the winding road down the east face of the Bighorns above Dayton and Ranchester, Wyoming. As I spiraled down the mountain, the bird rode wind currents, never flapping its wings. First above me, then below, it seemed to meet me around every jagged curve of rock, to appear above every tree, head turning from side to side as it focused first one yellow eye, then the other.

The same wind currents often attract human fliers, hang-gliders who leap from the crest and soar with the vultures until they land several thousand feet below. George and I would often stop to watch them on our way over the Bighorns. Once a young man told us they were flying to commemorate the death of a friend who had been slammed against the mountain by wind gusts the week before. Such hazards to human flight don't seem to affect buzzards.

The day after returning from the Bighorns, I drove along winding streets up a high residential hill to visit a friend from college days. As we sat on her aunt's deck, we spoke of the twenty-eight years we have known one another, and the perfect freedom this affords. We wasted no time on meaningless chit-chat, but went straight to our individual problems: a daughter who has troubles with alcohol, a son who is denying his father's death, our surprise to find ourselves facing life-threatening health problems, the thickening, spreading, sagging, and graying of our bodies and how we are affected when someone of the other sex still finds us attractive. Then her aunt said, "Look—is that an eagle?" I glanced up, and saw the way the big bird's feathers spread like fingers at the wing tips, and the near transparency of the wings; a vulture in flight looks almost fragile, despite its size.

"No, it's a buzzard; it followed me from the Bighorns," I said, shrugging, then yelled, "Forget it! Not today!" and turned back to the conversation. It is a measure of the length and warmth of our friendship that my friend just chortled—and her chortle is my measurement for all others—and we kept talking.

Vultures do useful work for us on the ranch. Sometimes they announce the death of a cow or calf. As I drive toward the pasture, a wheeling speck high in the sky may catch my attention. When I glance up again, I see two specks, wheeling lower, and then three, or six, until I drive over a little hill and see them standing, shoulder tall, heads bent like elderly men on a street corner commenting on the evils of the younger generation. The number of vultures seems to increase with the size of the carrion, though it's hard to figure buzzard mathematics. I once saw eight huge black shapes flap slowly away, and discovered they'd all been lunching on a newborn calf that couldn't have weighed more than seventy-five pounds alive. Only buzzards and kiwis detect their food by scent, a feat rare among birds. Once food is found, some authorities believe, the birds wheel in the air to signal other vultures miles away, since one circling in the sky is soon joined by others. Other sources say vultures land in a way that signals food, and often stay near herds of game or cattle for some time, knowing they may find a meal. They "probably" never attack dying animals, say most authorities; they just find a perch and wait. One of my favorite cartoons features one buzzard saying to another, "Wait, hell! I'm gonna kill something!" Who is to say they always resist the temptation? They leave no living witnesses.

When I mowed hay in our fields, a lone buzzard would often watch from a fencepost until I'd gotten about half the field done, then thump ungracefully to the ground and begin walking the rows of freshly cut alfalfa, occasionally stabbing with its beak for a freshly killed mouse, gopher, or rabbit. The bird looked awkward on the ground, stumbling over the tangled alfalfa stalks, but often stomped around the field for several hours if I avoided it. Once I hit a fawn, which lurched away on three legs, spraying blood from the fourth; the buzzard stalked slowly behind it, then flapped upward to hulk on a branch above deep grass where the fawn had hidden. I cursed myself—although fawns are impossible to miss in deep hay—but I didn't damn the vulture; he was tending to business.

I was a little less pleased when the vultures came for my cow Sweetheart, named by George for a white heart-shaped face marking, and because she ate cattle cake out of his hand. My father had told me she was dead, but when I saw the tall black shape roosting on her swollen carcass, I was shocked. The vulture hopped to her flank, as if sensing my temptation to drive it away. The next day brought a little rain, and when I drove that way again, hauling water to the cattle, two buzzards stood on the cow's broad stomach, backs to the sun and wings spread. I wondered if they were drying their wings; they didn't fly until I'd been sitting nearby, dumping water, for a half-hour. Then they ran a few steps along the cow's body and lurched unsteadily into the air, beating their wings frantically and nearly bellying down to the ground before they gathered enough power to rise. They looked as if they had eaten too much, and indeed buzzards are sometimes confined to the ground until they've digested enough carrion to become airborne again.

A few nights later I woke at two in the morning with the phrase, "Even a cow, even a cow, even a cow can fly," going through my mind. The refrain made little sense as I lay in the dark thinking, until I realized my subconscious might mean that cows can fly when they become part of a vulture's dinner. Before I dreamed the phrase, my friend Tom had begun painting pictures of winged cows gliding over the prairie. I fell asleep smiling at the image of Sweetheart swooping through the clouds with George's spirit, nosing for cake in his pockets.

Americans who speak of vultures, or buzzards, are referring

to a different bird from the one known to Europeans; biologists have discovered differences in skeletons, muscles, and other soft parts, though both types have bare necks and heads, and feed on carrion. Five genera exist in the New World, including the Andean and nearly extinct California condors, and the king, black, and turkey vultures. All feed on fresh or decomposing animal corpses, using their long, hooked beaks to tear open skin and abdominal walls; some also feed on living mammals and birds, though their toes are not suitable for seizing prey. None make nests; they lay their eggs on the ground.

Turkey vultures, called *Cathartes aura* in recognition of their smelling ability, are common from the northern reaches of Canada to the southern tip of South America, and usually hatch two chicks, though only one will survive. The young are fed a predigested "rearing broth" derived from carrion—details I will leave to your imagination. Later the parents regurgitate food from their crops; both crop and gizzard can be expanded to hold a great deal. The chicks need not be fed daily; the species has adapted to periods of feast alternating with famine of a week or more. Vultures may prove to be a hardy species, not easy even for people to exterminate, since they can eat decaying meat which contains poisonous substances fatal to other animals; they secrete digestive juices that break down poisonous products and render them harmless. Even so, we have destroyed the California condor as a free wild creature, no matter how many linger on in cages; eliminated human awe as that glorious creature wheels overhead.

Some animal rights activists are now suggesting that allowing dead cattle to decay in pastures is wrong, and that ranchers should be forced to bury them. Should this idea gain support, vultures and coyotes would be the largest animals whose food supply would be affected, and an important link in nature's chain would be broken. I find a satisfying consummation in knowing a vulture will drop down out of the sky to feed on animals that have been confined to earth all their lives, and by breaking down their bodies, help them return to dust.

I think of vultures as symbolic of the open sky above the plains, and many do prefer open country, but the black vulture may gather by the thousands near large cities, sitting on rooftops and trees, and will eat anything. Perhaps the species will adapt to the metropolis, as coyotes have, and abide cozily with us. Perhaps, since we have so far been unable to find a satisfactory way to dispose of our garbage except by messy and wasteful land burial, we should call on the buzzards to ingest edible portions. As a mark of this useful symbiosis, we could fly a flag bearing a vulture, rampant on a field of garbage.

I once saw a television feature in which Tibetan Buddhist monks took the naked body of one of their number to a graveyard high in the bare, stony mountains. Among multicolored prayer flags rippling in the wind, they placed the body on the ground, and sat reverently in rows facing it. Soon the sky was filled with vultures, which settled, waddled to the corpse, and began feeding. The camera focused on the faces of the monks; the eyes of some of the younger men grew very large as they struggled to maintain the proper reverence. But the old monks sat with chins lifted, slight smiles on their lips, eyes on the vultures or the open sky above them. Obviously, they were at peace with this logical gift of flesh to the sky. Later, they would gather the bones with their thin old hands, wrap them reverently, and bury them in the thin soil beneath flags symbolizing the new spirit's bright, lively freedom. A regional myth says these vultures repay humankind by maintaining an eternal light to guide pilgrims past steep cliffs at night. Hindus and Parsees in parts of India place their dead on the "Towers of Silence," high stone promontories where they believe the spirits will be brought to new life after the bodies have been devoured by vultures.

Many ancient cultures pictured the vulture not as an ugly bird with bad habits, but as the embodiment of immortality, and evidence of the transmigration of souls. In Egyptian temples are found paintings of the long-necked griffon vulture and Egyptian vulture which indicate that these symbolized parental love—perhaps because of their habit of feeding their young with food from their own bodies.

I haven't seen a vulture for several days, so perhaps my shadow went back to the Bighorns, or maybe it's sitting on a rock nearby, waiting. Since I am now a childless widow, and my closest relatives are my parents, I paid for my funeral yesterday under a plan offered by a local mortuary. The amount of my payment guarantees me a certain quality of funeral no matter when I die; in return, the mortuary invests my payment now, and collects interest until my demise. If I die tomorrow, the company will barely break even; if I last another forty years, they'll make a bundle. Like everything else, especially ranching, death is business, and the business is a gamble.

Until I die, I can make changes any time in how I want my funeral conducted, a ritual that may provide me considerable entertainment if I carry out my intention of becoming a crotchety old lady. Changing my will and my funeral arrangements ought to while away a lot of idle hours. After signing the check, I asked the man who drew my contract what he'd do if I died tomorrow, and a close relative insisted on changing my arrangements to include details I had specifically excluded: displaying my painted corpse in an elaborate casket in the funeral home, religious rituals in a church, a choir singing hymns, and tons of flowers. He looked at me intently for a moment. We'd already skirmished when he wanted to "cosmetize" George's face, sure I'd change my mind and want to "view the remains" before the funeral. I have had enough experience with death to know that I didn't want to remember George wearing rouge the rest of my life, and I knew he'd loathe the idea; I threatened to pry the lid off the coffin to be sure they hadn't painted his face, until I realized they'd do nothing I didn't pay for. After that intent look, he shrugged and answered honestly, "We have to deal with the living. But they'd have to pay more." For his honesty, I hope he gets a bonus on my demise, in about forty years, and lives to enjoy it.

But I'd rather be placed naked and unobserved on a high prairie hill and left to the simple, direct attentions of the vultures. Such natural arrangements following death are hardly possible in a modern world that has elevated funerals to a high, if macabre, art. I have often quoted an old Bill Cosby satire on the funeral platitude, "He looks so natural." Cosby said, approximately, "He looks *dead*! Whatta ya mean natural? He looks *dead,* man!"

Recently, I read that a man is making money by freeze-drying pets in lifelike poses. He expected that his customers might be elderly people, facing death and anxious to deny it. Instead, most of his profit comes from young professionals, who greet their stiffened pet with cries of delight, place it in its accustomed place by their chairs, and are pleased at how little it sheds, how little attention it demands. They can simultaneously deny the ugliness of death and decay, and devote more time to the pursuit of money. What a perfect, ironic contradiction.

I classify these folks with the people who eat my beef but don't want to know what its name was before we butchered it; they prefer their nature sanitized and deodorized, tamed so they can scratch it behind the ears without losing an arm. Perhaps all those wonderful television shows featuring the natural lives of animals have conveyed the idea that nature exists in a glass-fronted box, tidily and safely displayed for us to observe when we take a break from the grittier shows featuring cops shooting drug dealers. We can't have nature without manure, blood, pain, unfair deaths, fleas, and a certain amount of confusion and behavior that in humans would be called cruel. If most folks were honest, they might even admit that they don't like *real* nature, just its portrait.

For years, I have enjoyed a copy of a Wyeth painting that shows three buzzards wheeling high over a tiny farmstead set in rolling hills. The viewpoint makes visitors take a second look, because it is that of a fourth buzzard, above the others. It is a dizzying painting; whenever I look at it, I feel a moment of vertigo, before my wings catch the wind and steady me. When I die, I hope a vulture, or ten, will wheel over the prairie grass on transparent wings, a little reminder to us all of our destination in the sky, spiraling my spirit into a prairie sunset.

Had I any way to guarantee that the vultures and coyotes got this body I've enjoyed using, I'd take it. George always said that if he sensed the near approach of death, he'd wall himself up in a certain Black Hills crevice to avoid the rigmarole that goes with the modern funeral; he didn't count on vague promises by doctors and a desire to live which gave him false hope until paralysis prevented escape. We'd discussed cremation, but my shock was such that I missed that option; I would prefer it, but now I choose to be buried beside him.

But if I have my way, I won't lie makeup-covered and stiff in a funeral parlor banked with expensive flowers, while friends file by; I don't wear makeup now, and see no reason to start wearing it after my demise. I wish the coffin could be nailed shut on me about fifteen minutes after death and buried the next morning, but we have made such simple arrangements nearly impossible. I've tried to insure that no one will sing hymns, or use my death as an excuse to berate my friends for not going to church, or offer up a last-ditch prayer in an effort to save me from whatever posthumous fate I've earned. I don't want my friends paying hard-earned dollars for hothouse flowers to hide the business of the day; if it happens to be spring or summer, the prairie I've loved and watered with blood and tears and sweat will provide bouquets enough, along with a reminder that life in an arid country is fragile, and requires death. No modern, hip, "with-it" Bible readings; if anyone wants to quote that noble document, let it be in the old King James version, in honor of my love of the richness of our language. Beyond that, I hope my friends say whatever they have in mind about me, and enjoy themselves; I did.

The Glacier on Crystal Lake

*—The stomach of a mammoth found entombed in
ice contained yellow buttercups from its last meal.*

I've sat in a leaky boat over the blue line
for six months, anchored,
staring at the glacial face
of your life. It's all there: layers of dust,
years of deep snowfall, pictures from
your childhood, frozen.

Last night your grandfather died.
The glacier calved; a chunk of ice
the size of a house rocked
my fragile shell, floats
beside me now, melting,
spinning in cold blue water.
Pieces of your life
are growing smaller as I watch.

Soon I will unship the oars,
row back to the village. Tonight,
by trembling oil lamps
smaller than my cupped hand,
I will tell your stories—
how your grandfather took
you fishing, eating cinnamon rolls
and drinking RC Cola, built an ice boat

to sail Crystal Lake, ran from
the bees through the orchard, down
the hill, up to the barn loft,
into the lake.

Later, when the oil burns low,
I'll tell alone
the stories we told together,
yours and mine.
After the lamps go out,
in the warm, rustling dark,
I will whisper new stories
that will be mine alone.

Far in the ocean,
the color of your eyes,
the glacier will crash and rumble
into the deep.

Aurora Borealis and Bells

On March 13, 1989, seven months after George died, I woke from a dream in which he and I were driving somewhere. As usual, I took a few minutes to realize he wasn't lying beside me, and will never lie beside me again. Often when I can't sleep I read awhile, or walk on the deck looking at the stars and talking to George; under the deep star-filled sky I can believe he is listening. I got up to open the curtains and noticed that the sky was light in the east; I checked the time: one, too early for false dawn, and the moon had set in the west some time before. I couldn't explain the light, but its soft glow made the garage and the van beside it, the woodpile, the whole hillside, completely clear.

Barefoot, in my long flannel nightgown, I went to the frost-covered deck and realized I was seeing the Northern Lights more brilliantly than ever before. Waves of blue and white swept up from the northern horizon to a spot almost directly overhead, to meet in a whirlpool of mingled lights. I got a blanket and put on the moccasins George had made me, lined with sheepskin and faced with buffalo hair. My activity woke the dog and together we returned to the deck. The light began to flow faster, in long streaks of blue and white; each streamer of light seemed to flare more brightly as it moved toward the south, then diminish as it slid back north. All at once the pulses paused, and I began to gather the blanket around me, thinking the show was over.

Then the northern horizon glowed red, and a single shaft of crimson light shot up, to end at the whirlpool above me. Then came another, and another, until the whole sky pulsated like a heart with red veins. I felt like crouching and gibbering, as a primitive woman might have done. Behind the fires in the sky, I could see stars shining calmly in the deep blue.

Once before I had seen red Northern Lights, when George and I were newly married, and lived in a small apartment attached to my parents' house. As we all stood in the yard, my father spoke of watching red lights as a young man. His mother said they foretold war; World War I broke out not long after. I tried to dismiss the idea.

I rose, knowing that I had to call neighbors to share this. When I looked back, I saw two large and two small ovals melted in the frost where the dog and I had sat. Margaret sleepily answered the phone, and looked out of the window even before I hung up, thanking me while she struggled into her robe. Lawrence didn't sound nearly as grateful, but he did say that even in the trees he could see the lights.

Back outside, I walked to the waist-high stone cairn on the hill north of the house; George and Michael had stacked several blocks of sandstone there one hot summer day partly because they were in the way of our house-building crew. Later, as we added other stones, George confessed to wishing he could build a tall stone tower, where he could think and watch the countryside. I love the word "cairn" because of its Scottish origins; George wanted to play bagpipes strutting on this hillside, but his lungs were too weak from radiation. I have a photograph of him wearing the kilt, walking into the sunset. I leaned against the stones, and wrapped the warm wool around me. Frodo explored for a few minutes, then crept into a fold of the blanket and sat staring up, apparently as fascinated as I was.

The lights seemed to streak up the sky faster and faster, changing from red to blue to white to green without pause. Once or twice I craned my neck to look behind me as a single spear of green shot from the vortex of light to the southern horizon. I heard a coyote howl once to the east, a gentle creaking as the wind pushed softly at the snow fence, and the rustle of grass nearby. No cars passed on the highway. No other person was within a mile of me. The wind was gentler than breath.

I thought of the town twenty miles away, where people wasted the night in sleeping while this glory went on overhead. I wanted to wake them all—dial numbers at random, shout, "Northern Lights!" and dial again. But most of their homes are so surrounded by the artificial glare of security lights and streetlamps that they would see nothing; some, fearful of the gadget through which anyone can speak to us at any time of day or night, might call the police to report a crank caller. Later in the spring I would hear Larry Woiwode, a wonderful North Dakota novelist, say that the only difference between North and South Dakota is that southern Dakotans don't see the Aurora. I wanted to tell him this story, but he was surrounded by talkers braver than I am. I kept thinking of people I might call, but I couldn't bring myself to leave the hillside for the house, which suddenly seemed a clumsy way to disfigure a perfectly good grassy hillside.

Then the light wind died completely; all sound ceased. I leaned back against the pile of rocks, expecting thunder, expecting the sky to open and a goddess to descend, expecting a majestic voice. Nothing happened, only the cadences of light continued. I considered drowsing. I felt not only safe, but as if I were in a great cathedral, watching a performance so holy that no harm could even be thought about me. The dog's warmth against my thigh was comforting, but so was the chill stone my husband had set at my back, and the hard ground under me, the roughness of the deer antler on which my left arm rested. I could faintly smell the Scotch several friends had spilled here in an old ritual: pouring some on the stones for ghosts and gods. Other friends, noticing that the cairn was surrounded by antlers I'd found on prairie walks, have begun to leave gifts: beads, lovely bones, feathers, carvings. I've tucked sage, used by the Lakota for purifying a sacred space, into crevices in the rock, and hidden personal treasures from my life with George inside. One massive set of elk antlers given me by a friend arches over the stones, and the cairn feels like an altar or shrine. I think all of us who have contributed think of it as a spot that reminds us of George. I often watch the stars there, or pray.

Then I heard a distant tinkling, like bells. I sat straight, and thought carefully. I might fantasize about a miracle, but this was serious. Rationally, I considered the possibilities. No wind blew. The sound did not resemble any other I had heard that night: the snow fence, the coyote, the breeze. It came again, louder, just as a curtain of green light swept the entire width of the sky from north to south and died overhead at a line that seemed to divide the sky above me. The universe—isn't it odd that there are no synonyms for "sky" when it is the most obvious element of the prairie?—seemed to vibrate with green light. Again and again, the horizon glowed green and the curtain swept, sky-wide, to the center of the bowl over me. Each time green flushed the sky, the bells rang, the sound softening to a gentle tinkle as the light died. I shut my eyes—I could still see a green glow—and waited for an image of what might make that sound. All I could visualize were dozens of tiny glass bells, rung softly by delicate hands somewhere in the darkness.

I pictured the pasture that lay around me: each post, each strand of wire, each tree, the electric pole. I have sat and paced for hours on this hillside, in all weather. Nothing exists here that could make that sound. No one else was near; no cars passed. The sound could not exist, and yet it did.

Finally I remembered reading that arctic explorers insisted they could hear the Northern Lights; they had given no description of the sound, which they declared to be audible only in the far north.

I watched the lights and listened to the bells until three,

drifting into waking dreams in which I thanked George for the lights. Do good souls get to orchestrate the light show? Do several spirits play the lights together, like an orchestra? George could be happy in such company; he had a good sense of rhythm, and a beautiful voice, but he had a hard time staying on the same notes other folks were singing. In a soundless orchestra, his abilities would be apparent.

No one to whom I've told the story can think of a rational explanation for the bells; all but my closest friends look at me with doubt clouding their eyes. I'm satisfied without a logical explanation; some things should remain mysterious.

On July 10 of the same year, reading *Smithsonian*, I learned that sunspots large enough to contain seventy earth-size planets, had come into view on the sun in mid-March. Giant solar flares erupted; the sun threw radiation and billions of tons of matter tens of thousands of miles into space.[28] The earth's upper atmosphere was struck by solar particles carrying electrical currents that created magnetic fields; among the results were interruptions of power and communications, garage doors spontaneously rising up and coming down—and the phenomenon we know as the Northern Lights. One official said all those effects were nothing; a really big solar flare produces enough energy to light a big city for 200 million years.

Not a single scientist mentioned bells.

The Connection Isn't Clear

Last night Robert Evans died.
I can't remember his crime. His death
was nineteen hundred volts of electricity,
according to the newsman's bored voice.
Doctors examined Evans
after the second burst of juice,
and asked for one more.
Fourteen minutes after the first surge,
they pronounced him
officially dead.
His last words were not recorded.

This morning, in a seventh grade class
on a Lakota reservation
far from the prison where Robert Evans was killed,
I talk about writing poems.
I speak to rows of dark faces,
framed in shining black hair;
I say their lives, words, are important.
I say it's time to write.
One girl tears off strip after strip
of clear cellophane tape
and presses it over her mouth.
She will not look at me.
She writes nothing.

I know these two are linked:

the silenced girl,
the electrocuted man.
The sinew that joins their lives
vibrates coldly across the plains.

I read aloud a poem by a Lakota woman.
The girl rips off another strip of tape.

The Teenagers and
the Spine-porker

One day as I drove through the alfalfa field east of my house, I noticed a clump of grass moving. I blinked, looked away, and looked back. That blonde patch of grass wasn't just waving in the wind; it was marching steadily west. I checked its progress against that of the pickup, looked away a few more times, and eventually swung the steering wheel that way, feeling foolish, and resolving to see my eye doctor soon.

The clump of grass proved to be a porcupine. His chubby body was larger than Frodo's chunky terrier frame, even before he erected his golden guard hairs and faced me. I had made a natural mistake, but I was still puzzled. Porkies usually stay near trees; this one was in the middle of an alfalfa field, vulnerable to predators who know how to flip him over, avoid the slapping tail, and sink claws or teeth into his soft belly. He turned a little as I walked around him, trying to keep his tail aimed at me, but mostly defending himself with that intimidating mass of quills that shone like needles in the sun. I advised him that if he continued toward my father's newly planted trees, we would have to kill him; if he spent the winter in shelter there, nibbling tender bark, he could kill all the trees. I suggested that he turn around, and stroll back toward the gully full of willows.

The next morning, when I again headed across the field, I saw the clump of moving grass again. He'd come another half-mile on his stubby legs, and was still headed west. I repeated my speech, perhaps a bit more shrilly, and wondered why he was taking such chances. An eagle could strike him from above; a nervy or experienced coyote could turn him over.

By the third day, I was getting exasperated. The porcupine had made another quarter-mile, and my father had noticed him; he'd live another day unless he turned around. I stopped the truck and marched toward him carrying a shovel, determined to try to force him to change direction. I've shot quite a few porcupines, and consider them little loss; I always salvage the quills for gifts to buckskinners or Indian quillworkers. But I was reluctant to kill this one, perhaps because he had fooled me; humans have more respect for clever and resourceful enemies.

He didn't move as I approached. I prodded him with the shovel, then noticed flies circling his eyes. Dead. Gingerly, I turned him over. His paws, which look so much like the tiny hands of a black child, lay relaxed on his chest. I looked him over carefully, but found no wounds. Perhaps he had literally "gone west" until he died. His long yellow teeth were in good shape; he should have had years of tree-gnawing ahead of him. I left him where he lay, conveniently on his back for wandering coyotes.

For nearly ten years, I have spent three or four days each autumn teaching writing to students and teachers for the Prairie Winds project. The workshop is usually scheduled for November at a rustic camp in the Black Hills. Two months after George died I packed my sleeping bag and went, as usual; I believed it would do me good to keep the commitment I had made, and that encouraging others to write would help me to write as well.

To avoid having to explain George's death frequently, I mentioned it in a lecture to the assembled group. By the second day, I discovered a difficulty I could not have anticipated. Many of these students had experienced the deaths of close friends or family without talking out their feelings. They came to me clutching tear-stained poems about these deaths; I could not refuse to read what they had written. The poems were mostly dreadful, as poetry; many resembled, in a nightmarish way, the sentiments expressed on the sympathy cards with which I had been deluged. I had already discovered how few people are capable of saying something comforting about death by themselves. Most fall back on cliché, on syrupy promises about heaven. I blame no one for this; I had always done it myself, and only the experience of death made me see how much pain I had inadvertently caused. I was gentle with the teenagers' anguish.

By the third day, I could no longer remain inside the class building, sitting with my students in a tidy circle writing about tidy feelings. I warned them to dress for a hard hike, and said we would do our writing outside that day. We would observe nature and anything else we encountered, record what we saw, and sort out later what it might mean.

They groaned and scattered. When the appointed hour came, I realized they had no idea what proper clothing for a November hike meant. Snow lay in low places; the sun would be warm on the heights, but in the shadows under the trees, the wind would be chilly. Steep, rocky trails radiated out from camp. I wore battered leather work boots, jeans, several layers of shirts and sweatshirts, and I'd brought a pair of gloves and a stocking cap.

Most of the students wore unlined denim jackets and artistically ripped blue jeans; under flimsy shoes, only a few wore socks. One student came a little late, tossing her long auburn hair, wearing a sleeveless shirt and hideous plastic shoes: flat, slippery on the bottom, with open webbing on the top. I told her we'd wait five minutes while she changed the shoes and picked up a jacket. She was insulted; she hadn't brought any other shoes, and she didn't need a jacket, she told me sharply.

We stared at each other for a minute, assessing. I saw in her eyes that contempt many young women have for middle-aged ones; she saw my graying hair, the limp I couldn't entirely conceal, my wrinkles. She could not imagine herself so worn, so used. I looked at her fresh face and felt old and awkward. None of these children was over seventeen, all were female, their bodies blooming with health. I was sure I'd be gasping in the thin air before long. It did no good to remember that someday they would feel the same.

We started straight uphill just to get their blood moving, rather than detouring around to the trail. The Plastic Shoe girl literally couldn't get up the slope; she slipped backward each time she took a step. The others good-naturedly formed a human chain and towed her to the top. Then we faced an equally steep downslope, covered with pine needles, to the trail. I went ahead, working my way down sideways and trying to pamper my leg.

When I reached the middle, I turned to check on their progress, and saw the first one as she discovered, in mid-slide, that her shoe soles were slick. She came rocketing and bouncing down the slope like an out-of-control skier, her arms windmilling wildly. I caught her by the hand, swung her into position so that she could catch a tree, and turned to find another one shooting toward me. By the time we reached the trail, all of them were winded and redfaced, their hair disheveled, their clothes awry. I felt invigorated, and made a mental observation that maybe youth wasn't such a great compensation for experience and toughness after all, but I took no satisfaction from it.

I set a slow pace, stopping every time I saw something interesting to deliver a little lecture about it; I knew this would drive them crazy, since they viewed the hike as merely a pleasant stroll in the woods and a chance to visit, but I thought some good writing might come of their frustration. I made them taste pine needles, mentioned their medicinal properties (tea for vitamins and coughs) and the trees' use as support poles for tipis. I intoned that Indians burned cedar branches and inhaled the smoke to cure coughs; already they were exchanging eye-corner glances.

I stopped them before a hole dug into the mountain on the upper side of the trail. A miner had hunted for treasure here, I explained, probably gold since we were above Rockerville, once one of the richest and most unruly mining camps in the nation. The girls couldn't quite grasp that a man had simply sunk a shovel into the mountain here, and dug down to bedrock. He may have pitched a tent in a minuscule flat spot on the slope, and lived beside his hole to guard his claim. They understood the lure of gold well enough; they just couldn't understand digging it out with a shovel. I recited historical facts until their eyes began to glaze, and we went on up the trail to a rocky point overlooking the creek.

The last part of the trail was steep, and the cliff dropped at least a hundred feet, so we cooperated beautifully: holding hands, cautioning each other. Those of us whose palms sweat when they even think of heights—including me—stayed well back from the edge; others perched on it and dangled their feet over the creek far below. We examined the rock, looked at the blue sky and whipping treetops, enjoyed the warmth of the sun, and generally settled down.

There I told them about vision quests, *hanbleceya*, the Lakota tradition of fasting for three or four days on a high place to receive a vision which gave one a name, and a purpose in life. By chance, one of the Indian students was a descendant of Black Elk and had been on such a quest; she quietly told us about her experiences. I reminded them that many cultures and religions had a tradition associating certain places with sacredness, and high places with visions, with clarity of thought. They talked about what high places meant to them; I complimented myself on how well this hastily-contrived teaching experiment was working. Then we were all quiet as we wrote vigorously in our notebooks for fifteen minutes.

Instinct told me that, after the power of that pinnacle, we should lighten the experience with contrast. I started toward the creek, intending to walk along it as we circled back to camp. A few minutes of chatter and silliness as I urged them to sample catnip, spearmint, and cattails would complete the afternoon, and give them a variety of experiences for reflection during their writing time that evening.

Headed downslope, I noticed a pine tree that had been nearly girdled by gnawing teeth. The scar was fresh, probably from the winter before, and about two feet off the ground. I decided to spend five minutes on a test of knowledge that they would surely pass, thus giving them some positive reinforcement. We gathered around the tree, and the girls stared while I asked, innocently, "Who can tell me what animal gnawed on the tree?"

Silence. The girls looked at each other. "Who cares?" said one. It does occasionally occur to me that not everyone is as interested in knowing such things as I am, but resistance only makes me more forceful, probably out of embarrassment.

"You should," I retorted. "You live here. You ought to know who lives here with you, and what's going on in the woods. You might get lost and have to spend the night out here while we get around to looking for you. Wouldn't it be nice to know what's out here with you?" Antagonism only makes teenagers sullen; I've known that for years. But my mind literally did not work normally for at least a year after George died.

Silence. "If you don't know what animal did it, let's figure it out by logic. How high is the mark off the ground, and what does that tell us about what made it?" I expected them to grasp right away that snow would lie deep on this ridge, as several had mentioned skiing. I held my hand at the level of the gnawing, and stared at each face in turn. They all held that look students learn early as a survival technique: earnest desire to learn, thinly masking utter puzzlement.

"OK. We'll go to teaching method number two: the simple question and answer routine." I twisted my voice higher, into a parody of an elderly grade school teacher. "What would be here in the winter, class?"

"Snow!" they chorused happily.

"Good! How deep might it be?"

"About that high!" they responded with glee, noticing where my hand was.

"Then what?"

"Animals could stand on it to chew on the tree!" one nearly shouted.

"Excellent. So does anyone know yet what might have done the chewing?"

One girl said tentatively, "A mountain lion?"

I nearly fell off the hill in astonishment and a struggle not to laugh. I deeply wished I was capable of dropping the whole thing, and tried to think of a way to do so. Somehow, I couldn't find it. "Uh—why do you say that?"

She shrugged, the teenage all-purpose shrug which conveys lack of concern, apathy, and, to me, a trace of boredom that sets my teeth on edge. "Let's think about it," I said, appearing calm. "What do mountain lions eat?" I looked around the circle and saw eight shrugs.

One girl said hesitantly, "Deer?" I nodded, and said "Right!" with more joy than I felt. "Good, so does an animal that eats meat usually eat pine trees?" No one was sure. I digressed again, telling them that skunks will eat almost anything—fruit, dead meat, insects—as will coyotes. Immediately two girls brightened.

"Did a skunk do that?" asked one, as the other said, "A coyote gnawed on the tree!" They'd learned in grade school that a teacher desperately searching for an answer will sometimes offer obvious clues, and if you are silent long enough, shrug often, and listen carefully, you can sometimes get credit for knowing more than you do from a grateful, overworked instructor.

"Sorry. It wasn't a skunk or coyote. Logic again. Do you know what animals live in the Black Hills—or maybe it would be easier to say which ones don't. Are there mountain lions here, this close to Rapid City?" Shrugs. "Let's skip that. I'll tell you mountain lions don't gnaw trees, so we won't be here all day. Use your senses, as we were talking about doing in writing; observe the marks. Mountain lions have pointed teeth, for tearing meat; so do skunks and coyotes, which is one thing that rules them out. What shape were the teeth that made these?"

They actually got down on their knees and looked, and one of them said correctly, "Sort of square."

"That narrows down our choices, doesn't it? What animals with square teeth might eat pine trees?" I was watching them, but also looking at the tops of nearby trees, thinking the One Who Gnawed might be resting above us even as we spoke, and I could point him out and we could get on with our walk.

"Buffalo?" said one girl. I looked around at the steep hills, and took a deep breath. I should have said, "Right," and walked on down the hill. It wasn't my responsibility to teach them natural history, and the sun was starting to set. I knew they were absorbed in their lives, and had their own priorities; because they were interested enough in writing to be here, they would probably be adults I could admire in a few years. I had no right to judge them. I knew my own priorities were jangled; death was the primary subject on my mind. I was looking at everything with the eyes of a person rebuilding her life from a new foundation, since the old one had been taken away in the night.

But something inside me insisted that I could not retreat from this point. Most people once knew intimately their own territory, its animal inhabitants, its food sources, its weather, even its dirt and rocks. As our horizons broadened, we came to know less and less about a broader region; today the most isolated of us has collected quite a lot of general information about the globe, but may not know the name of a single plant or animal that spends its life within fifty feet of us.

Why should we care if we can name plants and animals? I have difficulty, even now, putting this idea into words; it seems to me to be a part of me in a core so deep that it precedes words. But I believe naming things gives us power to understand them, and we must begin at the bottom; before we can name God, we must be able to name a porcupine from its teethmarks, or a flower from its leaves. Knowing a few things intimately makes it possible for us to know larger, more abstract things. I believe that a man could only make a statement like, "God doesn't want women to get abortions," because he does not know anything intimately—not a woman, not a flower, not a bug; without that knowledge, he cannot know God.

Something like this went through my mind in a flicker before I answered. "They do have squarish teeth, so now you need to consider whether a bison would be up on this mountain. Look for other signs—trees they've rubbed their horns on, or manure, or tracks. Use all of your senses to observe this area. See any signs of bison?" They glanced around so quickly that they wouldn't have seen one if it had been climbing a tree by the trail.

"Deer?" said one. Another said, "Antelope," and a third suggested, "Elephant," but I think she was trying to be funny. Obviously, they too had realized that I knew more than they wanted to about who gnawed this tree, and might tell them every bit of it before they got off this mountain. Their lives were passing, they were aging even as I spoke, and this dotty woman wouldn't shut up. They began calling out animal names at random. The list staggered me: bobcat, buzzard, tiger, woodpecker, chipmunk, squirrel, wolverine, lynx, wolf, rabbit, bat, bear, prairie dog, caribou, moose, mouse, woodchuck, fox, cow, horse. They named most living mammals, a few extinct ones, a healthy representation from the bird family, and a reptile or two. Half of the animals named don't exist on the entire continent, let alone in South Dakota, but I consoled myself that they'd been watching the nature programs on television. I kept shaking my head, and staring from one to the other in astonishment.

Finally I heard a soft voice say, "Porcupine?"

I turned to the Indian girl who had told us about the vision quest. "Right. That's why many people hate porcupines, because they gnaw on trees. They move so slowly that they can peel a lot of bark before they get to the next tree, and kill a lot of trees." I took a deep breath while the others looked at her with more liking than they'd shown ten minutes before. She had made it possible for us to leave this tree and go back to camp; maybe now they'd talk to her instead of looking past her at dinner.

Softly I said, "Now be honest: did you say that because you figured it out, or were you just guessing?" I hoped for some revelation; I momentarily fell into the trap that plagues most liberals—of believing that this girl, because she was Indian, felt a kinship with the earth, and had studied its lore. She proved she was a normal teenage girl.

She smiled, looked away, and said softly, "I was just guessing."

I sighed as dramatically as I could, said, "At least you're honest," and looked at all of them. "Why should you care about things like this?"

"That's what we'd like to know," said Plastic Shoes, easing a sore and thorn-bitten foot out of her shoe.

"Isn't it interesting to you?" Blank looks. "Wouldn't it be nicer to walk through the woods and know what you're looking at? Now that you know this was done by a porcupine, look up: he might be napping in one of the tops of these trees." Several of them ducked and squealed. "Look under the trees for porcupine scat."

"What's that?"

"Technical talk for droppings, fecal matter, manure—"

"Oh," said a pretty blonde, brightening, as if at last she knew something I didn't know, "You mean shit!"

I shrugged and walked down the trail; it was all I could do. I didn't tell them that the slow-moving rodent's name originated from the Latin words for pig, *porcus*, and thorn or spine, *spina*, or that the French called him *porc d'espine* or "spine-porker," or mention that the English telescoped this name into *porkepyn*, finally *porcupine*. As I wandered toward the creek I may have talked brokenly of why I like to know things about my surroundings, wherever I am. "Knowledge is power," and knowing the landmarks, vegetation, and residents of any place can keep one from becoming lost, either literally or figuratively. I probably said that knowing a porcupine was in the neighborhood even in July might help one locate him in November, and that the pudgy critter could be killed easily by a resolute and starving person. No doubt I muttered that knowing different plants, and the way streams ran, and what vegetation could safely be eaten might save your life, or save your sanity by giving you something to think about on long winter nights besides death's inevitability.

I'm sure I didn't mention the porcupine I saw in the alfalfa field, or the one we hit with the van one dark night. George slammed on the brakes and swerved violently, but we heard the thump anyway, and backed up, hoping the animal was only stunned and we could hustle it off the highway. The red glow of the taillights illuminated the stubby body: his dark, child-like hands pulled at the road, dragging his hindquarters. His back was broken, and as George bent to place the barrel of the pistol against his skull, the shy animal whimpered like a child. Tears ran down George's face as he took the tiny hand after the shot, and gently pulled the body aside.

"Do you want the quills?" I asked quietly.

"Give them to the earth," he said, and turned away.

When I got to the creek with my students trailing forlornly behind, I nibbled catnip and spearmint and cattails wildly, but couldn't persuade more than three or four of them to join me. Plastic Shoes had been driven to open rebellion, and hobbled back to camp; she didn't tell us that, so I had to retrace our steps looking for her. Two girls sat down on the log bridge beside me and munched spearmint, but I think they felt sorry for me. The others, perhaps puzzled by my sudden collapse from leadership into catatonia, gradually wandered up the trail toward the cabins.

The next day the Lakota girl read an astonishing poem about her vision quest, and presented me with a pen she had covered with intricate beadwork.

PART III

A Woman's Covenant

The Only Place

The only place a woman can go to be alone
is the bathroom.
A woman would like to be wrapped in strong arms
when she cries, without having to explain,
or huddle on the couch wrapped in a blanket and a cat.
But all over America, women crouch instead
on a white, cold monument to wasting water.
We lean against a chilled tile wall,
stare at ourselves in an icy mirror,
flush the toilet to cover howls and curses,
brush our teeth twice to cover the taste of anger.
We lock the door, fill the tub with hot bubbles,
take a long time shaving our legs and armpits,
study the way waves break over bulging stomachs.
We scour the sink and rearrange the bottles under it,
refold towels, throw away old prescriptions,
count bandaids and bottles of suntan lotion.
We turn out the lights, stare into candle flames,
light incense, try to pretend we've taken our troubles
to a glowing temple, placed them in the lap
of a smiling golden Goddess.

Outside, men—who wouldn't know what to do
if a woman curled up in bed and cried—
can relax before bloodless images on TV
and think, "She's only in the bathroom
doing some woman's thing."

Behind a locked door, a woman
spins the empty toilet paper roll
like a Tibetan prayer wheel,
chanting "Help me, help me, help me."

Prairie Relief

Human nature seems to dictate that we destroy what we most revere. For example, a sonorous prayer written by Reinhold Niebuhr of Heath, Massachusetts, for a Congregational church service in 1943 has become so popular it is widely abbreviated and misquoted. Dr. Niebuhr's original words were these: "God, give us grace to accept with serenity the things that cannot be changed, courage to change the things which should be changed, and the wisdom to distinguish the one from the other."[29]

I've tried to be philosophical about differences between men and women—to truly accept what I could not change. For a woman who regularly rides a horse over a mostly treeless prairie, accompanied by males of varying ages and relationships, this demands some special reflection. I am as expert as a coyote in finding concealment where there seems to be none. When I locate any dip in the prairie, I usually stop my horse, leap off, unbutton my jacket, unhook my coveralls, and obtain relief from my full bladder. I'm quick as a coyote, too; given one uninterrupted minute, I can be mounted and mostly re-dressed when the males come into view.

But I confess I am sometimes guilty of envy when I glance ahead of the moving herd of cattle to see a man standing beside the pickup, gazing in apparent rapture at the changing colors of the Badlands in the east. His stance could mean any number of things: that he's looking at smoke in the distance, or cattle, or listening to the odd sound in the engine and diagnosing it. But I know he's not stunned by the magnificence; I know he's not lost in contemplation, forgetting his obligations to the world. I know what he's really doing. If I rode straight toward him at a gallop right now, by the time I got there, he would be smiling, turning toward me, perhaps remarking on the view.

Since I cannot change my own physical construction, I try to cultivate serenity, to see the difference as an advantage. When I am riding, my eyes move constantly, searching for a suitable spot with an absorbing panorama, or a wealth of nearby detail. Once dismounted, I look to nearby minutiae. Electric blue dragonflies with a wingspan no wider than a quarter have perched on my hand; I've used a grass seed to lure ant lions waiting at the bottom of their traps. I have never found an arrowhead, but I return from most rides with a pocket full of seeds, or rocks with fascinating lines and whorls, or strange crystals embedded in their surface. Occasionally I use my belt knife to dig a healthy specimen of an unusual prairie plant, and tuck it in my pocket to be planted on my hillside. I position myself carefully in relation to plants that need extra moisture—an Indian turnip, or bluebell. I once heard of a man so careful of his resources that when he got cow manure on his shoe as he walked across the barnyard, he strode carefully so as not to dislodge it until he came to a bare spot, with only a few scraggly plants. Then he scraped the manure off where it was most needed. That man had the right perspective on his position in the world; he understood sustainable agriculture long before the term was coined. We are fertilizer, literally and symbolically.

Sometimes I regret modern dress codes which dictate that I wear jeans or coveralls instead of a dress while riding horseback. Oh, I know why women adopted pants, and the reasons are sensible; I'm not arguing for a return to crinolines and bustles. But when I'm in a rendezvous camp of black powder enthusiasts I realize the advantages of long dresses. A lady sitting on a log with her skirts spread around her might be communing with nature in any of several ways, and no gentleman would dare intrude. In the woods, I search for a spot that is not only concealed, but has a view, a mood, an ambience. The perfectly positioned log should offer adequate back support, and a rich supply of loose earth and dry leaves.

The prairie has no such equipment, but it does have spectacular scenery. As I gaze at clouds making changing patterns in the sky, or at the rock outcrops behind which I am momentarily concealed, I realize that I am part of a long chain of human—and female—experience. Through millennia, women have felt the same envy, and have been unable to change the facts. We shrug, accept our differences, and transfigure the world in other ways. Perhaps we are the richer sex for the observations we have made while seeking relief. The female is the Earth Mother made flesh, and perhaps her differences should remind us of that. We are closer to the earth, more intimately involved with it than a male can ever be.

Ironing My Husband's Shirts

The iron puffs steam
gently over the damp collar.
Carefully, I iron the shoulder flat.
How satisfying to press around each button,
puff up the tucks in back.
I imagine him sitting,
eyes forward as he takes notes
in his graduate class.
He won't be a middle-aged man
looking for himself,
not in this shirt.
He will look pressed with confidence,
steamed into purpose.
The neatly-buttoned points of the collar frame
his intelligent face,
stripes reflect his eyes' blue.
The professor will sense this man
is at peace with his world,
supported by a dedicated woman.

I hang the shirt,
steam still rising,
between the wrinkled ones in the closet.
It only takes one.

I remember the day I stopped ironing shirts.
I went to college full of hope,

virginal with untested promise,
and met a man.
He took me to parties
to prove his love;
he was a Delt, a good catch.
He promised marriage if I got pregnant.

Each Saturday I ironed his shirts,
laughing with the other women.
One day I set down my iron and thought.
My father fed cows alone so I could study;
I worked at night to join a sorority.
I needed to study, but I was ironing shirts.
I wanted to write, to wait for children
until my first or tenth novel was successful.
But I was ironing shirts.

I was ironing shirts.
He could have bought no-iron shirts;
he preferred starched cotton
with his fraternity blazers,
his perfectly-engineered ties.
I was too young to wear his ring,
but I ironed his shirts.
It meant the same thing.
It meant we would be married
when he graduated.
It meant
I would iron his shirts
for thirty or forty
years.

I set the iron's face
in the center back
of his favorite shirt, turned it on high.
I borrowed a cigarette.

I watched until smoke curled
around the edges of the iron,
someone screamed and pointed.
I unplugged the iron.
One woman nodded.
I left the shirts there.
We all dated Delts; someone would deliver them.

My first husband ironed his own shirts,
after I told him the story.
I unplug the iron, twenty-four years
after setting that final shirt on fire.
"I love you," I tell my second husband.
"Wear a sweater."

The Part-time
Professional Stepmother

—with thanks to
Daniel S. Lusk, Heather (Lusk) Day,
Erin (Lusk) McPherson and George Michael Snell,
my children

For years, during periods of marriage, divorce, and single womanhood, I've replied to the inevitable question, "Do you have children?" by saying, "Yes. I'm a professional stepmother."

This has often led to explanations of my twice-married, twice-turned-into-a-stepmother status. Sometimes I, or my questioner, protested that I wasn't a "real" mother since I hadn't carried my children in my womb. But I've spent twenty-five years involved with the raising of children, and talked with dozens of other women in my position: the second wife with whom the children live part of the year. We're not full-time stepmothers, but we have a lot of influence over the children. Recently I have begun to realize how many of us there are—and that no one has written a Guidebook for the Part-time Stepmother.

Volumes have been written about step-parenting. But those of us who marry a man with a child or children who live with the natural mother most of the time have different problems. These children spend weekends, summers, or other periods of time in the new home we have created with the child's father. They have two sets of "parents" and double the usual number of grandparents, and probably two differing sets of rules for behavior.

First, background: At the time I met my first husband's children, I was young and in love, filled with dreams of being the perfect wife, of having children of my own to mix with his in a glorious tangle of happiness. I believed everything he told me about the reasons his first marriage failed. First mistake; more on this subject later. I've learned a lot, and along the way have become forty-seven, made a conscious decision not to bear children, and then had the possibility snatched away when I married for the second time; my second husband was sterile, but he already had a son.

I soon grew to love my first husband's children, aged only three, four, and five when I met them. He and I were both in graduate school, and I had from one to three other jobs at all times, so I felt no immediate desire for babies of my own. Instead, I threw myself into the Stepmother Gift Program. We were too poor to buy much, and besides, their mother seemed to provide anything they wanted, so I haunted the cheap fabric stores and made clothes. One hectic Christmas I made the boy pajamas and the two girls long flannel nightgowns with matching nightcaps. I no longer have the photos of them, all three bravely trying to pretend they liked their nightwear as well as any game or toy. I immediately forgot all the nights I had sat up late, sewing tiny stitches while my husband slept.

But we muddled along for seven years; they began to call me "Mom," shyly, and I discovered that loving them meant sometimes laying down the law, and sometimes biting my tongue so as not to say that their mother was *wrong wrong wrong* about something, and explaining why we were so poor but still paid for their visits to the doctor. I wouldn't go through it again, but I wouldn't give up the memories. When their father and I were divorced, just before Mother's Day, they sent me presents and notes saying they hoped I'd still love them, and asking if they could still call me "Mom." I stopped the car in the middle of a busy street and cried. The policeman who marched up to my car window took one look at my face and the Mother's Day card I waved at him—I was crying too hard to speak—and drove away.

When I married for the second time, after considerable thought and a five-year relationship during which we discussed, argued, and fought through every conceivable problem of a marriage, I was determined not to love George's child. My heart had too many scars, and I resented the fact that I'd never had children, and never would. My first marriage broke up before it was financially feasible, and in part because my first husband really didn't want any more children. George, my second husband, sired his son after he'd been diagnosed with Hodgkin's disease, and before he started radiation treatments he knew would make him sterile.

But how do you keep from loving a child with his father's wide blue eyes, a child who leads you into his cluttered "summer" room and whispers, "Will you help me make Daddy George a birthday card?" Not possible, not for me. So, with love for him, and undiminished love for the first three—now grown into warm, responsible adults who regard me as friend, mother, and older sister—I have some advice for part-time stepmothers.

First, and perhaps most important—though that's hard to sort out in such a tricky emotional situation—do communicate with the child's mother. This may be extremely difficult. She may hate you for taking away her husband, even if she was finished with him. She may hate you for being younger, newer, or any of a thousand things. But you will need her help, and she yours. You must try to establish communication. Remember—and it's not easy—that the problems she had with the man who is now your husband or lover are not your problems. Yet. You may discover later that they are identical, but that's a different story. You have no right to judge her by what he says, much as you love him. Their relationship is something different, and, apart from your sympathy with their bad times, is really none of your business.

This may involve some juggling. Of course he wants your sympathy and understanding for what he went through; give it to him. Don't take her part, but remember that she has a story, too. You don't need to know it, but remember that it is there. If you had met him first, you might be her. People grow up a lot in a first marriage; that's one reason second marriages often succeed.

If you can arrange to talk to her alone, in surroundings comfortable for her, over coffee or a drink, do so. Try to establish ways in which you are alike. Try to get her to laugh, possibly about his maddening idiosyncrasies.

Why bother? Because you share a job—raising the child or children to be decent adults. Neither of you, husbands and lovers aside, can do it entirely your own way, and both of you will need cooperation from the other to do it at all. You must come as close to friendship as possible. If she's hostile, don't give up. Call her to talk about problems, rather than writing stilted letters. Be honest; point out that you are both concerned with the child, and for his or her good you must talk. Resist the ever-present impulse to shriek at her, to point out her deficiencies.

My second stepson's natural mother (one of the problems about writing on this topic is the shortage of terms for the new relationships created by multiple divorces) seethed for months with resentment after I married George; I could feel her boiling anger from five hundred miles away, despite the circumstances of their divorce, which made it clear George could no longer be married to her, and which also helped her provide for their son. When I finally asked why she was so angry, she had two good reasons: one, Michael had told her that we'd promised he could live with us permanently if he didn't like living with her, and two, he had been leaving her hate notes.

I told her, honestly, that we had made no such promises, and would not; furthermore, that while I felt responsibility toward Michael, and loved him, I didn't want him full-time. As a writer and veteran of living alone, I was having problems enough adjusting to a husband. I certainly didn't want a full-time child demanding my attention. I hastened to add that, if circumstances ever dictated that he live with us, I'd try to be a good mother to him, but that I wasn't plotting to get him. She, I pointed out with some tact, had the hard job of raising him every day; I was in the enviable position of being the "vacation mom." Why should I try to change that? As for the hate notes, they were a ploy, and she shouldn't worry; he spoke of her often, with love, while with us.

My honesty, especially about not really wanting to raise him, broke some kind of barrier between us, and we've been able to talk more freely ever since. I hadn't considered the situation from her point of view: that I might want to take her child. Later, when we both visited her home overnight to collect Michael for the summer, she and I giggled in the kitchen about some of George's idiosyncrasies, while he and her husband, whom George later referred to as his cohusband, talked in the living room.

I didn't talk openly with the mother of my first set of stepchildren, and when I recently got the opportunity to, I apologized. I now realize how much trouble we might have saved, and what an understanding woman she has been. We have more in common now; I understand why she couldn't live with him.

Second, explain to the child as soon as possible and as often as necessary that one of the benefits of divorce and remarriage is extra love. With it comes extra responsibility: your rules will likely be different from her rules. Don't apologize for yours or criticize hers. Make the child understand that you are merely different. Do this even if you know very well you're right. If you are, the child will realize it in time; children are analytical beings, and will compare lifestyles, rules, religions, and somehow make their own choices. By being fair, by admitting the differences and resisting the urge to be "right," you will help to demonstrate that different styles of living work in different ways, and thus to make the child's choices intelligent ones.

Third, make rules and stick to them. Don't try to be the Good Witch in contrast to the mother. So they don't have to pick up their socks at home; they do here. All children will test you, to see what they can get away with. No matter how sunny things seem when you first begin, at some point every child will run a power test. When Mike came to visit us each summer, he almost always tossed a wet bath towel on the floor during the first three days. I reminded him, smiling, of the time I found a bundle of mildewed towels under his bed. I had prepared a washtub filled with soap and bleach, positioned him in the front yard with it, and made him wash the mildewed towels until he got the smell out. After the reminders, he would hang up his towel. He was just checking.

Recognize these little tests of power. Don't let the child get away with them, and don't blame them on the mother, but don't get hysterical about them, either. Once you've established a rule, stick to it—unless by consultation with the child's father you are convinced that it's no longer a valid rule.

George, a child of divorced parents as I am, reminded me that his fondest memories of being raised by his grandparents were the times he spent fishing with his grandfather. Time can't be bought. From these memories came our firmest rule: to show Michael we loved him by being with him, by including him in jobs that we could do together. Gifts can be seen by the child as a reward just for visiting you, or as a bribe to like you best. But time spent together is invaluable. One summer, all three of us worked hard moving a load of cattle feed from the truck to an enclosed bin in the barn. Michael, who was twelve, filled the buckets, and George and I carried and dumped them. It was dirty, dusty work; the temperature was close to a hundred degrees in the barn; we were all hot, irritable, and tired. This was only the last in a whole series of hard, dirty jobs we all worked on during the summer.

But, when he returned home a few days later, Michael said to his mother, "You know, I'm glad to be home, but I think I'm a rancher at heart." That can't be because of the fun; on the ranch he worked hard, and it was years before he got cowboy boots, spurs, or even a hat, let alone his own horse. But he got a lot of time with us, and that, I'm convinced, is the most important thing.

You may find that the mother tries to punish the child by saying, "You won't get to visit your father." The real problem is that this makes the father a "gift" which can be withheld for bad behavior. This is not acceptable; a father has part of the job of parenting, and he can't do it entirely at the other parent's whim. You'll have to be very diplomatic to get this idea across, but we managed it by explaining that it had to work both ways if it was to be used at all; that if Mike's mother could prevent him from seeing his father if he behaved badly, then we could refuse to send him home to her for the school year: the same punishment for the same problem. We had earlier set the stage by good discussions on the fact that not only the once-married couple, but the two step-parents were all part of the four-person parenting team responsible for this child, so his mother saw the logic of our argument.

Try not to compete with the child for your husband's affections, money, or time—difficult as this may be. Spend less time on keeping the house neat and more on activities that can include all of you. Don't become only a cook and laundress. Make sure everyone in the family has jobs, and explain that this is one of the ways you can all enjoy the child's time with you more; the sooner the work is done, the sooner everyone can have fun.

Husbands—there's the catch, in a way. You love him, you love his child. Although she may have a new love, she still loves this child sired by someone she may no longer love, but can't quite put out of her life. The new husband or lover will want to please her, and almost invariably will do so by being indulgent to the child, with varying degrees of damage. This may be one of those topics that will require discussion among the four of you, if that can be managed.

Meanwhile, the child's father will be going through an emotional storm. He loves the child, he loves you, but he feels a little guilty about having you and not the child. He may try to buy affection too, with presents, with indulgences. He may somehow see you as competing for the child's affection.

You must sit down with him and discuss rules, and your views on matters such as money and gifts, all the little stumbling blocks to peaceful existence. The main thing is to be honest, and to keep hold of your own personality and beliefs, not submerge them in what he thinks is best for the child. Yes, it's his child; but it's yours now too, in the sense that you have to behave like a mother while having fewer rights than one. You must have a voice in decisions concerning the child. Otherwise you'll begin to feel as if you are the maid who serves them both; a child can pick up on this quickly, and begin treating you like a servant as well.

Try not to fall into the trap of proving that you're a good mother, and that if you had kids of your own, you'd be perfect. Don't try to be the all-time exemplary mom. Frankly, you don't have to be; at least two other people are helping to raise that child. The responsibility is not yours alone. Not everything you do is a life-or-death matter. Some of your actions will be important to the child—Heather hates peas because she helped me pick and freeze them all one long summer, but I helped her learn embroidery too, and she still does that—while other things will be forgotten. I thought Erin would be permanently traumatized the night I woke to find her sitting at a picnic table, sobbing because the rest of us were so sick we were delirious, and she couldn't find anyone in the campground who would tell her what to do, but she has forgotten the incident. Don't take the job, or yourself, too seriously. Enjoy the child, have fun, give love. You'll see the effects of your work in later years.

Remember that no matter how hard this modern age of complex relationships is on you, it's much harder on a child, much more difficult to understand, more frightening. No matter how young the child was when a marriage unraveled, he or she will recall, even if subconsciously, the breakup of the cozy, familiar world. I have vivid mental pictures of events that probably happened when I was three years old. Any child may retain memories, and fear that the new world you have constructed after one divorce could be shattered again.

When George and I had our first fight in front of Michael, after three years of marriage, he cried as if the world had ended. We both explained to him that normal people fight, even though they love each other. Michael later told me that he knew only one other child of divorce in his small community, and that sometimes this bothered him. You must try to understand that the child fears impermanence; combat the fear by being warm and loving, and by explaining confusing relationships as soon as the child can understand them. Some parents take care never to disagree in front of the child; I think this can make them think any disagreement is world-shattering. But if the child has been given a net of security based on honesty and communication, these minor matters will seem to take care of themselves.

I wrote this essay when my second stepson was twelve years old. As he grew older, George and Michael's mother were both sometimes envious when he confided in me, but I believe he did so because my love was less painful to him. He could feel with his very blood and sinew how they struggled to discipline him through love, and their sorrow when he made dumb mistakes. I believe we became friends as he became an adult, and I could speak to him as one. During his senior year in high school, he watched his father die. During the next year, he careened into nearly every problem that can entangle a normal teenage boy, including some magnificent examples of human greed and selfishness. I had to prove again that I could be tough, but I would never lie to him, and had to demonstrate that lying to me diminishes my trust, but not my love. He is now twenty and married; my communication with his mother ended badly. I remember George's love for his son, but try not to use it as a blunt instrument. I know that George was not, at twenty, the man he was at forty, and hope that Michael will grow to be more like him.

My first three stepchildren are all married. The two women have children; the man does not. None of the three has close ties with their real father, because he was not there when they needed him. Their mother lives near me, and when her children come to see her, they make time for me as well. I am able to enjoy knowing them as adults, without the strain of wishing they would do things a particular way—*my* way, and yet it gives me unutterable pleasure each time one of them says, "I love you," or their children call me "Grandma Linda." I have my reward for the bad times with their father, and every minute of it was worth it for the joy I have in knowing them.

My Last Will and Testament

Being of sound body and mind,
I speak to you who will inherit,
though you were never part of me.

I give you grass roots wound in earth's breast,
coyotes singing in wind,
meadowlarks flashing in the grass,
buffalo shaking the world with his bellow,
plowing with his hooves.
I give you back what our ancestors had.
You earn the land
after your name is on the title.
The sacraments of inheritance
require payment in blood and sweat.
If you only accept, you lose everything.

To hold it, you must fight
the plan to dump sewage in the creek,
fight the scheme to dump nuclear waste,
creating jobs
for people desperate enough to take them.

Fight the silence of the frozen land,
struggle to lift tons of baled hay,
fight for the lives of cows
made stupid by pain;

fight fire in winter grass,
stand helpless as hail booms on the roof.

Even if you are homeless, landless,
beware this bequest;
look this gift in its barbed teeth.
If you've never felt the wind
breathe in your lungs,
earth's blood singing in yours,
think before you accept this freedom,
this prison.

I will be gone.
But I, who have no heir,
speak to you in my blood, and yours.
One day a hawk will fall
through blue air to eye you from a fencepost,
a sego lily will raise its fluted face
beside your path.

Land Circle: Lessons

You have noticed that everything an Indian does is in a circle, and that is because the Power of the World always works in circles, and everything tries to be round. In the old days when we were a strong and happy people, all our power came to us from the sacred hoop of the nation and so long as the hoop was unbroken the people flourished. ... This knowledge came to us from the outer world with our religion. Everything the Power of the World does is done in a circle. The Sky is round and I have heard that the earth is round like a ball and so are all the stars. The Wind, in its greatest power, whirls. Birds make their nests in circles, for theirs is the same religion as ours. The sun comes forth and goes down again in a circle. The moon does the same, and both are round. Even the seasons form a great circle in their changing, and always come back again to where they were. The life of a man is a circle from childhood to childhood and so it is in everything where power moves. Our tipis were round like the nests of birds and these were always set in a circle, the nation's hoop, a nest of many nests where the Great Spirit meant for us to hatch our children.—Hehake Sapa, Black Elk, Oglala Lakota*

I wasn't born on the land; I was reborn here when I moved from a small city to a ranch at the age of nine. I was adopted by the land, and began developing a personal land ethic the first time I looked out on the empty, rolling prairie around my home. Although I have left the ranch where I grew up several times—to go to college, to marry a philosophy student—I have always returned. My second husband, George, joined me in working the ranch with my parents, and now that I am a widow, the land is still most of my family, as well as my spiritual guide.

Most people develop their beliefs about the land in less intimate, less grueling ways: by visiting it on vacations, or by seeing it outside their city or their car windows. I do not insist that living in the land leads automatically to a more profound wisdom, though I suspect it's often true; anyone who lives in the country and pays attention is often exposed to happenings that are not easily explained, and may take time to think about them. I do know that most people in our society look at the land across an ever-widening abyss. I believe that chasm separates us from our best traits. As we become more distant from the land, we begin to regard other animals, including human beings, as if they were warm mechanical playthings. In the process, we are becoming coldly machine-like ourselves. When we lost faith in the old gods and goddesses of the earth, we lost touch with our best traits and capabilities, the best of our own souls. Gary Paul Nabhan believes those who have lost touch with the land are incomplete, not fully developed as humans: "By remaining uninitiated to the power of wilderness, a large percentage of our present human population remains in an arrested, immature stage of development."[30]

To find ourselves in the land, we don't need to buy a farm or pay high prices to so-called Christian priests or New Age priestesses. We are all creatures born to soil and wilderness; the outdoors, not an air-conditioned office or schoolroom with windows that can't be opened, is our natural habitat. Night or day, walk out into the grass or woods alone, sit down, and listen. Dig in the earth; plant something. Walk and watch any living thing except another human. You will find some guidance, some comfort. To find more, to become fully human, you must commit more of yourself to the search. Don't start by backpacking in the Rocky Mountains; start with the closest spot of earth to you right now. Sit outside at midnight and close your eyes; feel the grass, the air, the space. Listen to birds for ten minutes at dawn. Memorize a flower. One benefit that has nothing, and everything, to do with your main purpose is that you cannot overdose on this experience, and it doesn't cause a disease, or require you to seek therapy. You can only benefit.

I have been a student all my years on the ranch; I might have learned the same lessons elsewhere, but I learned well where the tests were life or death for my animals and myself. The lessons of the ranch can be summarized in a way that is almost absurdly simple, yet they cover the larger work of my life as a rancher and a writer, as well as my politics and religion. Succinctly, they give me hope for the simplest and most difficult job I face: survival. The lessons I have learned concern birth, death, and responsibility for the life between.

In 1991, schools in Wisconsin will require that studies of the environment be part of all subjects taught in schools from kindergarten through twelfth grade. Although I can see numerous pitfalls in this approach, by which a poor system or poor teachers could ruin environmental studies much as "creative" writing has often been devastated by being taught, still the theory is correct. The environment is part of everything we live, and it should be part of everything we study.

So I believe the lessons I have learned are relevant for all of us. The environment—the land around us and all the living things on it—is no longer a luxury to which we can retreat for enjoyment when the day's work is over; it is an essential part of our lives; without it we will die, slowly and painfully and without understanding why.

I: *The Road I Took*

It's difficult to understand how an individual arrives at a particular set of beliefs unless you follow the same road, but I know that what I believe is in part *because* of my associations with the land. When I moved to the ranch, I was a typical nine-year-old city kid; the move changed my life drastically and completely.

Ranching I pictured as all white hats and sparkling spurs, prancing horses and green grass, a kind of glorified rodeo played all year long. I didn't know about the work, or the loneliness, and I had no conception of the beauty and rewards.

In the city I was never alone, but protected by a watchful mother and grandmother, surrounded by friends. Sometimes, I suppose, I whined that there was "nothing to do." On the ranch, I rode my horse everywhere, and became absorbed in all the details of the prairie. I raced antelope, but I also sat down and let them approach me, stamping and whistling. My mother and grandmother began to complain that I was growing "unladylike," and tried desperately to get me to care as much about cleaning my room and doing dishes as I cared about my horse. Dear women, they failed; I'd still rather ride a horse than vacuum a carpet. I learned not to complain of nothing to do; when I did, someone handed me a hoe.

Every day, I watched coyotes catch mice, toss them in the air, swallow them at a gulp. I chased them on horseback, laughed as they tripped while looking over their shoulders at me, came to appreciate them as tricksters long before I knew the wealth of Indian myth on the subject.

A great horned owl that ghosted out of a tree when I rode under it taught me to watch for it, because I never heard it. I lay down in the open under a perfectly empty sky and remained still until a buzzard appeared and circled close enough for me to see its head turning, casting first one yellow eye, then the other, on me. I knew what buzzards ate, but it never occurred to me to fear or revile them.

I walked my horse in circles around coiled rattlesnakes to watch them watching me, struggling to stay coiled and in striking position. I learned that their rattle warned me in time to avoid them, if they didn't simply hide, and realized it was seldom really necessary to kill one. Even barefoot in the garden, stepping over a rattler bulging with gophers, or finding my horse with a nose swollen around two fang marks, I respected them and let them escape.

I had no playmates, and no siblings. I learned how to live and play and be happy alone, before I learned how to live with people. Country children didn't visit other children just to play. Our families got together to share work, and enjoyed it if we could, and we learned about sharing responsibility early. We didn't get many toys; our status symbols were work implements: a horse, a saddle, a tractor, a gun, a pickup. We acquired these things when we were adult enough, responsible enough, to use them wisely. We were proud of them; we knew how much they cost, and we knew what they meant: adulthood. Admission to the life of labor our mothers and fathers knew.

I loved the prairie, and became as close to it as to a sister. I started writing at that time—poems, stories, a novel—to entertain myself, and to keep track of all the interesting things I saw and heard. I taught myself to be an environmentalist long before I heard the word. Without my realizing it, Nature became my church as well. Once I chose a secret name for myself, a name linking me to one of the four elements though I didn't know that then, and carved it on a block of sandstone which I hid. Later, I told my secrets to a tree and knew they were safe in the heart of that tall sentry. I found these actions entirely natural in a world where I saw more of trees and rocks than of children my age; I now believe that it is natural for all of us to be children of the earth in this way. Only later, as we learn to stand in straight lines and adhere to the rules, do we learn to give allegiance to patterns outside ourselves, and to value them above our own perfectly correct instincts. Except for the writing, I believe most people who grow up in the country could tell much the same story.

I wrote about my family's relationship with the land in my book, *Going Over East*:

> I realize suddenly that the circle of our world lies within a mile radius. Here lie our homes, the garden whose products supplement our own beef to feed our bodies, the wintering and birthing grounds for our cattle, the hayfields that feed them, the boneyard where they slowly return to earth, the junkyard where dead machinery becomes spare parts, and the garbage dump where we get rid of what we cannot use. All that is missing is a graveyard for the humans; it may not be too late.

> I think of our lives as circular: our work is dedicated not just to profit-making but literally to

feeding ourselves. We are sometimes able to choose work that sustains us mentally, or at least gives us variety, and to plan our own days rather than working to a schedule set up by someone else. But the steady rhythm of night turning to day, spring to summer, birth to death, the progress of the moon and sun, the sweep of wind and rain—those natural cycles determine how we arrange our lives. What does not fit into the smooth circle of our days, into the repeating cycle of the seasons, does not belong here.

When I first conceived the idea of our lives as circular, I had not yet read Black Elk's famous statement, but I knew that work, responsibility, love of the land, respect and affection for both domestic and wild animals, all fit together to keep us fed and clothed and housed and entertained. My parents didn't get a TV until I went to college; I had no idea I was deprived. Television didn't contribute anything to our circle of existence, so I hardly missed it.

In college, I joined a strict, nondancing, nonsmiling church, and when I left it and the boyfriend I'd joined it for, I went to Catholic services for a while, then to a Quaker fellowship that met in a burned-out Methodist church for an hour of blissful silence every Sunday morning. By that time I was married, teaching full-time, studying for a master's degree, living in a city, trying to be a perfect stepmother in the hope that one day I would be a perfect mother. I needed silence more than faith or God, or else I sensed they were linked.

When we Quakers and other war protestors stood in front of the World War II memorial in silent protest against the Viet Nam war, I studied the faces of the young people who screamed epithets at us, and realized that most of them would call themselves Christians. Farm boys with fresh, familiar faces sicced their dogs on us when we sat on the grass on Gentle Thursday. The highway patrolmen who charged out through the front door of the administration building swinging batons and clubbing us to the ground—after the students were killed at Kent State—were good, clean-cut, family men; most of the students were middle-class midwestern youngsters who had gathered on the quadrangle because they were frightened, and didn't understand what was going on.

I taught at an exclusive women's school, Christian College. The girls who cheered and ran laughing through the dormitory when Martin Luther King was murdered were nice, intelligent white girls from Christian families. I was beginning to get a little cynical about Christians and their insistence that they could save the world.

When I was divorced, I retreated to the ranch, the only thing I had left. My parents were there in summer, and in winter I lived alone. I was thirty years old, and everything for which I had prepared myself by going to college and marrying the "right" man and getting an education so I'd have "something to fall back on," had failed me, and disappeared from my life. I didn't trust anyone or anything—but the land.

At that time I wrote a poem called "First Night Alone on the Ranch." The final lines are:

> My family is darkness
> before the flickering fire,
> the cow calving in the barn.

I didn't realize how seriously I meant that for a long time. But suddenly I realized that the things I really valued about South Dakota were its air, its water, its space—and its land. During the next few years I talked more to cows than I did to people, and listened more than I talked. I read a lot about the relationship of people we call "primitive" to the land, and the land healed me, and I began to write seriously and well for the first time. I also started a publishing company, printing the work of Great Plains writers, convinced we had something unique to say to the world that wasn't being heard from anyone else.

When my first book was published in 1987, and received the kind of attention all writers crave—a favorable review in the *New York Times*, selection by a book club as an alternate—it was a journal of a year in my life of seasonal ranch labor. The pages were filled with the beliefs and feelings that accompany my work, taken from the journals I have kept since I was nine years old. After all my searching, all my detours into many modes of thought, I was back where I began, only this time I was armed with some hard-won convictions, and determination. I also had sufficient education to quote Thoreau on my reasons for staying: "I love Nature partly *because* she is not man, but a retreat from him. None of his institutions control or pervade her. There a different kind of right prevails. In her midst I can be glad with an entire gladness. If this world were all man, I could not stretch myself, I should lose all hope. He is constraint, she is freedom to me. He makes me wish for another world. She makes me content with this."[31]

My favorite result from *Windbreak* has been letters I receive from readers. The letters have given me a feeling for the community of farmers and ranchers, their similarities and differences. One day, I received letters from two women—one a farm wife and poet in Minnesota, the other the only woman Episcopal priest in South Dakota. The farm wife wrote: "Much as I loved your book, I do think it's sad that you seem to have turned away from Christianity. With all the TV evangelist scandals, it's especially hard to convert someone right now, and I'm not going to try." The Episcopal priest wrote:

> Though I initially attempted to follow traditional models, I soon discovered that would not work. And so I have embarked on a new road for me. It has taken me into feminist theology, Christian mysticism, native American tradition and culture, the power of myth and story, and a renewed love of the land. I have often thought that I was on that crooked road by myself ... often the journey is lonely. There are few role models in my own neighborhood. Then I read your books ... [and N. Scott Momaday, Frank Waters, John Neihardt, contemporary native American authors] and all that ... catapulted me into a place within my own soul that I knew was there, but was lurking in the corner. And so I bought your books and read them immediately, one right after the other. And I knew that I was on a journey with, at least, another pilgrim ...

The first woman believes I'm a degenerate non-Christian; the Christian priest sees me as a pilgrim like herself. It's not profound, and not enough, to say people find what they look for. When I replied to the farm wife, I suggested that turning away from Christianity didn't necessarily mean turning away from God, but I failed to convince her.

I was gratified by the letter from the Episcopal priest because, while I wasn't really on a pilgrimage to find God, I had certainly been on a parallel road. I was especially struck by her statement that her study of Christian mysticism and Native American tradition and myth had led her to *renewed love of the land*, because that's what happened to me.

By studying unusual subjects—some, like witchcraft, forbidden by religious leaders—and by exploring the histories of people Christian missionaries called "primitive," like Australian aborigines and Plains Indian tribes, I found meaning for my own life, especially as it revolves around the land. I found peace in beliefs about the earth that mingled bits of a dozen different cultures, and knew part of my job is to work for a better understanding of our environment without making futile speeches to legislators who seemed to regard me as an annoyance. When I emerge from my own small circle to catch up with the world, I find that millions of other people are combining their ideas of God with their ideas of worth of the land in ways that make traditional Christians nervous. But if Christians had read and understood their own history, they would know that none of us, no matter how unusual our beliefs, is walking a road that has not been walked before.

I haven't resolved all my questions about Christianity, but I decided to give up church, and spend more time taking care of the land. I decided that if God didn't give me credit for that, He, or She, wasn't the kind of God I wanted to believe in anyway.

I also have come to believe that the only way to save the nation and world from the ecological crisis we've created by our greed and exploitation is for the people who are still in touch with the land to show the rest of us the way out of this mess.

II: *Birth and Death*

> *Appearing with Ronald Reagan at a New York anti-abortion gathering, Peter Grace, chairman of H. R. Grace Co, declared: "Everybody who's for abortion was at one time themselves a feces. And that includes all of you out there. You were once a feces."*[32]

Birth and death are indivisible; because of my ranch experiences, I can't talk about one without talking about the other. They are the most natural of events, yet they are abstract for most people. Most Americans have distanced ourselves from these two most basic events of life. Many of our children are born while we lie drugged in a sterile hospital bed, and we die in the same cold atmosphere, giving up responsibility for both events to so-called "experts." Lately, controversy has boiled around people who have demanded responsibility for the mode and time of their deaths; I find this odd. Surely we should all demand such a responsibility as a part of living on the earth. I signed a living will years ago, and hope that someone will be responsible enough to help me enforce it if I cannot.

When he was eight, my second stepson explained sex to me in terms I didn't learn until I got to college. I hear considerable debate about sex education; I got mine from cows, and my recipe for preventing teen pregnancies is a month on a ranch during calving season—being literally immersed in the messy realities of birth. I get up at three in the morning, step into my pants standing by the bed— they stand because they're stiff with blood and manure and other natural fluids—and shuffle a quarter-mile down to the barn through knee-deep snow, listening to the coyotes and the trucks on the highway. Before long I'm positioned behind a cow with my arm to the shoulder inside her, trying to keep her tail out of my mouth while I decide which leg to pull on to encourage the calf's natural emergence.

When that calf hits the ground I am not thinking of how much money the cow is worth, or what we'll sell the calf for in the fall if it lives. I am aware that I have saved one, and maybe two lives, that would have been lost. I go back to bed with the feeling that I have accomplished something; I have *saved* something.

How many of us can have that feeling? Gandhi said everything you do will be insignificant, but you must do it anyway. I believe most people in towns and cities are frustrated by thinking that when they read about the destruction of the environment, they can't *do* anything. They can send money, but they can't get in there and physically save a life. And we can't all move to the country and raise calves.

Country people live with a continual interweaving of birth and death. We are intimately aware of the death of winter in spring's birth, but we have to kill some of the kittens or we'll be knee deep in starving cats by July. Even if we beggar ourselves to buy cat food, and sterilize the females, we have too many cats. If we keep more than can support themselves on mice, they will kill every songbird, grouse, and rabbit on the ranch. In winter, the warmth of the barn will not be enough, and I will heap their frozen carcasses in the pickup to haul to the pasture. When city people sidestep their responsibilities and drop unwanted dogs at my gate, we must shoot them or they'll grow up wild to chase and kill antelope, deer, rabbits, cattle. We hate to shoot dogs, but we believe we have no choice. In every major city in the nation, thousands of pets are killed at taxpayers' expense each year, abandoned by owners who made promises they are unwilling to keep.

Every year, some of our calves will die, be dragged out of the barn to the hillside to feed litters of coyote pups, and next spring the grass will be greener there. Some of my neighbors shoot antelope each summer to save grass for cows; they'd give the meat to someone who could use it, but shooting antelope without a license is illegal, so they use what they can and let the rest rot or feed coyotes and vultures. Meanwhile other neighbors plow up the native grass, allowing more of the thin topsoil to blow away, to plant crops that burn to death under the sun—because they can receive government payments for planting crops that do not yield. That's not illegal; in some circles it's considered a cleverer way to make money than hard work. More and more of us judge things by legality, and the word "morality" has been so twisted by its narrowest interpreters that thinking adults are uncomfortable with it.

A city friend wrote to me once of her sorrow at having to put her old dog to sleep. "You must get used to it," she said. I wrote rather passionately back to her that we did not *dare* "get used to it," but that getting used to it was different from accepting it, from allowing the knowledge of death to give more meaning to our lives.

Several friends have remarked to me about the courage with which George faced his death; I believe anyone who wants to die as George died, smiling and talking of the love he felt for us, must live as he lived: enjoying what each day gives us, wasting nothing. He truly knew that death could take him at any moment of half his young life; that knowledge gave his days more meaning than most of us ever taste. As Gandhi said, man lives freely only by his readiness to die.

III: Responsibility

> *A powerful class of itinerant professional vandals is now pillaging the country and laying it waste. Their vandalism is not called by that name because of its enormous profitability (to some) and the grandeur of its scale. If one wrecks a private home, that is vandalism. But if, to build a nuclear power plant, one destroys good farmland, disrupts a local community, and jeopardizes lives, homes and properties within an area of several thousand square miles, that is industrial progress.*[33]

The third lesson I have learned from the land, the one that ties the other two together, is responsibility. I believe tribal cultures and most country people are considerably more advanced in their understanding of this significant subject than most modern Americans. Several writers have noted that our society teaches males to think and speak in terms of rights, while females are taught to think of their responsibilities. It is time for all of us to be less concerned about our rights, and take up our responsibilities. This idea will be unpopular, because it threatens our political structure, as well as our sex lives.

Most of us are no longer responsible for providing much of what we need to live—or no longer even understand what is necessary for life, because we are so encumbered with luxuries. The Roper Organization recently asked wealthy people what they couldn't live without; the results were startling. *Fifty-seven percent* said they "couldn't live without" a microwave oven. Forty-nine percent couldn't live without an answering machine, forty-two percent without a home computer, and thirty-six percent without their videotape recorder.

That's how far we've come from understanding survival and necessity. We buy what we want; we don't make or grow it ourselves and we rarely see or know the people who do. We have forgotten where necessities come from, and therefore are out of touch with the consequences of our actions. Most of us don't throw garbage out of car windows along the highways, but we think nothing of driving those cars three blocks for a quart of milk, or of turning the faucet and seeing water come out. We walk across green, water-sucking lawns which we'll have to mow next week before going to the store for vegetables grown in California, when we could grow them all in the front yard and eliminate gas-powered lawn mowers.

We've probably all heard the stories of the child who refused to drink milk after learning that it came from a bag that hangs between the back legs of a cow, or the man who didn't worry when the farmers drove their tractors to Washington, because if they all quit raising cows, he'd just buy his meat at the supermarket like he always did.

Those stories are no longer a joke.

Even many environmentalists have a hazy concept of what really goes on in nature; ecology, says John McPhee, means who is eating whom. When we make impassioned speeches about saving snail darters, dolphins, spotted owls, and grizzlies, we also have to realize we are saving ticks, along with Rocky Mountain fever and Lyme disease. Save wilderness and you save tarantulas, scorpions, and rattlesnakes. You can't have one without the other. But many of us want our wilderness sanitized, safe; we want to see grizzlies, not be eaten by them. It's easy to say the ranchers ought to be willing to lose a few calves so the rest of us can have a wolf population, but no one is willing to sacrifice her child because her neighbor keeps a pit bull. Wilderness isn't something you can look at through a window; if you want wilderness, you have to take your chances. Responsibility requires the same thoughtfulness; we may have to sacrifice some or all cows on public lands in the west in order to have wolves; we may have to sacrifice a hiker now and then for grizzlies. People who want to drink water in Los Angeles may have to give up air conditioning or baths. Responsibility is giving up some things; responsibility requires choices.

I have been lectured sternly about raising beef instead of artichokes or grain, and can recite statistics on how much water and grain a cow can use, and how many people the same foodstuffs would feed. But where the prairie was plowed for grain crops by homesteaders, it has remained nearly barren for sixty years. When several of my cows died of grass tetany in spring, 1991, I discovered that André Voisin, an expert on holistic grazing, believes the disease is caused by grasses that invade where native forage has been plowed up.[34] Any crop that requires plowing this land will ruin it; given that, my job is to select the most efficient grazing animal, use the grass to raise meat, and avoid plowing. It is my job to practice ranching that is sustainable, that will support itself without damaging the land beyond its own inherent power to recover. The animal I choose to utilize the grass may, or may not, be a cow. If it is a cow, then my job is to try to mitigate the damage cows do by their nature—to harvest the land's natural and best product, grass, while doing as little damage as possible. If Wes Jackson develops a perennial grain, as he hopes to do at the Land Institute in Salina, Kansas, established to develop the concept and technology of perennial polycultures, I still must consider whether ripping the native grass out of the soil is a fair exchange for producing grain.[35]

But I sometimes resent the fact that my choices are direct, and clear, and can result in my own immediate poverty. Most people don't realize they are choosing for all of us when they drive a car, or buy a gold necklace. The chain of their responsibility for air pollution and paving the world, for heap-leach mining of gold in the Black Hills, is longer and harder to see. It's easier to notice and criticize ranchers for grazing cattle on dry land.

Last winter, I watched in amazement a television program about animal rights and its implications. While deer died of disease and starvation in the East because of overpopulation, hunting protestors followed deer hunters into the woods, and screamed to scare away the deer. The hunters patiently explained many of the animals they were harvesting would die that winter anyway, and some said they couldn't afford to buy meat; none of them pointed their lethal weapons at their tormentors. In the Black Hills, forest managers have prevented tree-cutting, and some environmentalists say their goal is to stop any cutting of trees here. Now the slopes are so overgrown that streams are drying up, fish dying, water levels dropping, towns rationing water. The forest is choked with dry tinder, and fire danger is immense. During a recent summer an entire subdivision of the state's second largest city might have burned but for the heroic efforts of fire fighters. Neither group stood up to say, "We were wrong. Let's sit down and figure out how to cut *some* trees."

Most of us can cheerfully place responsibility elsewhere— "Call the police!" We dislike the idea of shooting another human being, so we want to ban guns—but we want protection. "That movie offends me, so you shouldn't watch it!" can logically lead to: "That book is offensive; I'll pay somebody to kill the author!" We're in similarly precarious positions environmentally. We move back to the land with our wood-burning stoves, but hate air pollution. We can't escape contradictions in our lives, but we must try to understand the consequences of our actions, and how those consequences relate to our beliefs.

It is a cliché that country kids are different because they grow up already viewing sex and work, birth and death, as natural parts of life, but it's true, and the difference is crucial to our belief systems. And while many people today recognize the difference, they ignore its corollary: that not everything and everyone can live exactly as we please; we have to make hard choices very soon.

Aboriginal mothers in Australia teach their children not to drag a stick behind them, marking the ground; reminded that this is painful to the earth, the children grow up understanding the earth's pain. As reality, this is illogical; we do worse damage backing a car out of the garage, or planting carrots. But as a lesson and a warning to our affluent society, it is powerful; if we regarded each action toward the earth in this light, we might take time to consider all the implications. We cannot afford to lose four tons of topsoil for every ton of grain U.S. farmers produce; to continue justifying such production is to deserve the holocaust that faces us as world populations become ever more hungry, and unable to produce their own food.

IV: Individual Responsibility

> *February 2, 1968*
> *In the dark of the moon, in flying snow, in the*
> *dead of winter,*
> *war spreading, families dying, the world in*
> *danger,*
> *I walk the rocky hillside, sowing clover.*
> —Wendell Berry

Wendell Berry has been writing and speaking about sustainable agriculture and difficult choices for years; I find much of what he has said summarized in that brief poem.[36] Each of us must continue to sow clover on our hillsides, no matter how rocky, and no matter how dark and dismal the world seems to us.

But how can we be responsible, individually, for the health of the universe? How can you, in your small city apartment, join hands with me on the plains of South Dakota, and an angler on the Gallatin River, to save not only the beauty, but the air we breathe and the ground which provides our food?

The first step is to accept responsibility as we should accept death: as a part of our lives, a fact that gives meaning and strength to our daily actions.

Responsible people try to understand the implications of what they do. I cannot know or save the entire world; I would probably love whales if I could hear them singing in the ocean instead of in the box in my living room but I no longer contribute to organizations which work to save them. I know the rain forest is essential, but I spend more time worrying about the tiny Black Hills. Like Thoreau, I can know only a small part of the earth, and I work to protect only a small part of it. I can refuse to buy plastic or styrofoam, because no one knows how to get rid of them. I can refuse to use harmful chemicals on my cows or my weeds. And I can tell everyone who will listen, willingly or not, why I am doing these things; some of those listeners will learn, some will vote, some may make laws. In every case, I can study until I am reasonably sure I have traced an action to its ultimate consequence, and then act so that what I am doing is not simply prolonging the problem, or dumping it in someone else's lap. Working directly for at least some of my food, clothing, and fun, disposing of the waste from my actions, reminds me there's a connection between responsible labor and reward, or even survival. If each of us did so, we would vastly improve our chances of saving the whole. Our society has operated on a delayed payment schedule for a century. If we all begin making payments now, we may avert some of the more devastating forms of interest.

I can grow some of my own food, to make me aware of the health and fragility of this thin skin of fertile earth, and teach others the connections between earth, water, and work, both in providing food and in providing solace for the soul. I don't insist on the religious aspects of this earthly labor, unlike some adherents of specific religions; I won't consign you to hell if you don't do it my way, or appear at your elbow to quote statistics or scream epithets. But every action you take has its consequence; the responsibility is yours.

I know these solutions seem vague; I wish I could give you a neat ten-step program, preferably with a memorable acronym like "STOP WASTE" that would solve all the world's problems. Magazines are filled with articles which do just that, introduced with a little cheery text to make you feel as if you can save the world by separating your garbage. Doing it will make you feel better, and the articles sell a lot of magazines; some are even printed on recycled paper. But anyone who tells you the solution to the pollution crisis is simple is misinformed—at best.

Do South African diamond miners suffer more from poor mining conditions and racism than they benefit from having jobs? If you really believe so, don't buy diamonds. (Not a great sacrifice for most of us.) Does heap-leach mining destroy the earth and pollute water? Don't buy gold jewelry or coins; most gold is mined for decoration or investment, not vital purposes.

The beauty and the threat of human existence on earth is that we have the power to destroy ourselves, and the intelligence not to. Like the fact of our own advancing deaths, this knowledge should make us eager to be responsible and spiritual in ways we can handle. Some people will wander off into fluffy spirituality and spend their lives contemplating their own navels, leaving more work for the rest of us. Responsibility demands consideration of all life.

Barry Commoner, writing in *Greenpeace* in late 1989, noted that Congress began responding to growing concerns about the environment in 1970. Nearly twenty years later he asked, "How far have we progressed toward the goal of restoring the quality of the environment?" The answer was terse: "Apart from a few notable exceptions, environmental quality has improved only slightly, and in some cases has worsened."

But the exceptions clearly show what works and what does not. Every success on the very short list of significant environmental quality improvements reflects the same remedial action: *Production of the pollutant has been stopped.* DDT and PCB levels have dropped because their production and use have been banned. Mercury is much less prevalent because it is no longer used to manufacture chlorine. Lead has been taken out of gasoline. And strontium has decayed to low levels because the United States and the Soviet Union had the good sense to stop the atmospheric nuclear bomb tests that produced it. The lesson is plain: Pollution prevention works; pollution control does not.[37]

The lesson for us is this: compromise doesn't work. We've been good little environmental activists and pacifists, just as we were advised to be in the 1960s; we've compromised, worked within the system, spent our own money and our time talking, talking, talking, trying to convince the public and government that we don't want the earth polluted. That a majority of us, worldwide, are more concerned about the purity of the air, water, and earth than we are with anything else. If we must choose either missiles, bombs, and airplanes devoted to waging war or growing healthy food in countries where children breathe good air and families are self-sufficient, we will choose the latter. It is increasingly clear that our present course has brought us devastation as well as starvation, and despite the downfall of the Berlin Wall, many of the world's fingers are still on a very dangerous trigger. Meanwhile, the polluters have continued to lay waste the earth in the filthy names of Profit and Progress. Only when we have built up anger in enough people and educated voters thoroughly enough to make dangerous activities flatly illegal have we won victories. And even when the profit-merchants have been defeated, some of them have slunk sullenly away to dump waste secretly in our water supplies and on hidden lands. We've made some progress by showing polluters the economic benefits of pollution control, but the big successes have been where we used the power of the law to stop actions that are harmful to the earth.

In some cases, we will have to fight already established law. The 1872 Mining Law, the federal statute that still governs mining almost everywhere, was passed to encourage miners to swarm into the wild West and rip out its treasures; modern miners lobby hard to keep its outmoded rules in effect. "Farming sustainably," as *Mother Jones* recently reported, "is illegal in the United States for most farmers." A farmer operating in the current market is forced to use chemicals to get the maximum yield per acre; most get federal money to subsidize their operations. Lobbyists for chemical companies have influenced government policy, but so have the agricultural colleges, often financed by the same chemical companies. Many banks won't loan money to farmers, and insurance companies won't sell crop insurance, without evidence of chemical use. Banks operate on the same poisonous theory in Third World countries, which don't get loans for anything but the kind of developments that promise fast payback.[38]

Responsible users of the earth must work toward creating a renewable, sustainable economy at all levels; most of the technology exists. Poisonous fuels like oil, coal, gas, and nuclear energy must be phased out in favor of renewable fuels; by 1941 Henry Ford had devised an "all-vegetable car."[39] Where is it? Chemicals that poison the earth must be banned completely, and any mechanism that emits toxic pollution must be shut down if it can't shift to a method of operation that will eliminate pollution. Agriculture, as well as other industries, must take advantage of the knowledge we already have, using organic compounds and encouraging soil conservation instead of waste. Our government, which has handed massive subsidies to the nuclear industry throughout its existence, must end that support, and if possible transfer it to solar and other energy forms which do not destroy.

Compromise has not been enough. There are too many of us, and humanity is too greedy for material goods to rely on individual concern to save the earth. No matter how dire the warnings, we have continued to use beyond the earth's power to regenerate for too long. The bill is due now; we can pay the interest a little longer by radically altering our thinking and our actions, or the punishment for nonpayment will be exacted: loss of everything that has made this the most beautiful of planets. Though the marvelously resilient earth and its plants and animals may survive, it will be unable to sustain human life. We will become the people who murdered ourselves, and did it knowingly.

Cheyenne River Valley at Wasta

Four mares guard four colts,
lying so sprawled they might be dead.
The car swoops at seventy down dry slate hills
pinned together with cedar.

Folded into a hill is a green gully,
edged with plum bushes about to bloom,
cedar for shelter, a thin blade of water.
I know your lodge is there, hidden.
You camped here for the silence of spring,
to read, fish, watch the hills green up.

Everywhere, I see places you might be.
At first I searched them all,
But now I know if you are there,
I'll find no proof.
Sometimes I wave,
or shout my love
on the wind of my speed.

Your body is making grass on a clay hill,
but you are in every pleasant valley;
you stand by each trout stream,
making the line sing over the water.

I have never known these hidden spots
so well as now,

through the eyes of a red-tail hawk
that drops out of the wind
then spins away to some other sky.

Heat Wave on the Highway

Not long ago, I was speeding down highways in a seventy-mile-an-hour crosswind, my hair tangling in my glasses, spitting bugs from my teeth and pulling bee stingers from my bare knees, while radio voices agreed the temperature was 105 degrees. I suddenly realized why people stared as I staggered into the ladies' room at rest stops to scrape bug juice off my glasses. I realized why people looked startled when I stuck my entire head under any faucet I met. I realized why I was seated next to the kitchen door even in truck stops. The door beat a rhythmic tattoo on my shoulder as waitresses dashed in and out. My ears quivered with shouts: "Roast one for three, Mac; hold the mustard on the doggie."

I'm the last one. I'm the zoo specimen, the relic, the survivor who may be captured, dissected, and interviewed. Driving to Devils Lake, North Dakota, I've passed 2,342 cars, trucks, campers, and busses, and several dozen monster tractors growling in roadside fields. I also met eighteen motorcycles with riders peering grimly through windshields decorated with dragonfly wings. Only eighteen of those vehicles didn't have air conditioners.

In fact, I'm not sure some of the motorcycles weren't air-conditioned. The modern machine has radio headphones, tape players, wraparound windshields, and so much other gear that the riders may have weather control, too. Or else those black leather outfits are fiendishly clever refrigerators; how else could they stand the heat?

The air smothered my nostrils with the odor of hot rubber, touched my taste buds with rotting silage and overheated fish; swathed me in fine dust, ashes from a prairie fire, stinging herbicides. I smelled ammoniac cow manure, choking diesel exhaust, the sharp tang of oil wells and aging roadkills, delicious roasted-on-the-stem sunflowers, nourishing vegetable gardens, peppery marigolds, resinous pine trees, bracing sagebrush, newly cut lumber, piny smoke from timber fires in a distant national park, acrid gum weed and goldenrod, sour sweat, cigarette smoke, tarred roofs, brake and radiator fluid.

My unprotected skin felt blasts of hot air from the underside of passing trucks, the chill of a river bottom in arid butte country, and the slimy humidity of a swamp. My face was stung by biting gnats, my arms and knees by bees. My left arm has the distinctive red chevron of folks who drive with an elbow out the window, a once-common badge of honor now rare. Come to think of it, my elbow is probably rare as well, or possibly medium-well.

My nose quivered and sneezed and twitched all day long. My brain was busy sorting, identifying, and cataloging scents—when I wasn't counting cars. I was never bored; I was too busy being alive. But I was alone in sensing that rich tapestry of pasts, presence, and futures. I was the only person to realize a pocket of cold air swept across the highway near Bismarck, making the grass shiver for an instant, causing a horse to turn its nose north and think of winter. I experienced life today more nearly the way animals experience it all the time: as a total sensory experience, washing over my entire body, brushing every nerve, stimulating every inch of skin and each hair follicle, awakening old instincts long before my brain could make sense. All the other drivers sat in gleaming metal boxes that distinctly resemble ornate coffins, and breathed dead air sanitized for their delicate nasal passages.

I'm the last of a noble race of hardy men, women, and children who struggled to reach these plains as pioneers, walked behind a team dragging a plow through the tough soil. They are our ancestors, part of us, but we have consigned their experiences and triumphs to history, and grimace to think of their hardship. Great Plains dwellers once proudly scorned air conditioning in our houses and cars. We sneered at people rolling down highways with windows closed and frost on the dashboard. We pitied them; they were only tourists; they hadn't the strength for our heat. We thrived on it, climbed on clattering tractors that literally boil to gather hay on 110-degree days. We commented that folks with air conditioning can't smell blooming alfalfa, the green tonic of fresh-cut hay, hear meadowlarks and redwing blackbirds trilling from fenceposts. An old plains joke said a real farmer could taste the difference between Texas and South Dakota dust; we proudly compared flavors blowing through open windows wherever we drove. Now only I am left to tell the tale.

I'm no hero; I surrender. Since one can't quickly air-condition one's aging foreign car in the middle of North Dakota, and I couldn't give up my open window, I improvised. I created an air conditioner by filling a plant mister with water. Now I air-condition myself: squirt my hair, blouse, skirt, ankles, and sandaled feet. The hot wind does the rest, changing my personal climate in seconds from tropical to temperate.

My air conditioner has unique advantages; almost anyone can afford it. It's portable—I take it with me when I walk the dog—and cheap to repair or replace. It even has luxuries: I can wash windows, water my dog, and shoot flies buzzing against the windshield. I can soothe an itching foot without taking my attention from the highway, or cool bee stings. Try that with yours. Owners of air conditioning often whimper about cold heads and hot feet; I can independently cool selected portions of my anatomy. I've considered taking revenge on any passersby who burst into hysterical laughter by firing a stream of water to blotch their dusty windows.

Every new invention has disadvantages; I plan stops to avoid strolling into a café dripping water, and one truck driver laughed so hard he nearly drove into the ditch. Like all inventors, I'm sure I can overcome these minor obstacles.

Godmother: For Christopher John on Mother's Day

On Mother's Day
in an old Norwegian church
with dragons crouched on the roof,
I become your godmother.
The church is a reproduction,
but the floor is cold slate,
the backless benches hard,
just like the real ones.

Those dragons aren't just decorations;
one of them snorted fire when I promised
to raise you as a Christian.
Your father almost winked,
sure I wouldn't say "No"
before his parents, and mine.
He knew what I meant
by swearing something else.

I could teach you
how to cheat at solitaire,
how to live if you're lost
in the Hills where you were born,
how to ride a horse—
but your father can teach you
that, and more. He'd rather

I didn't teach you to say "ERA now!"
Your mother will teach you
to be fair to women,
to think before you speak,
to work for what you want.

I could tell you stories
about your dad, your Aunt Sue,
your grandparents; show you
the home ranch—in case they can't.
I'm not entirely sure what my job is,
but know that my mute vow
covered events none of us have weighed.

You cannot say how I might help;
you had no choice, being inarticulate
(though loud). We'll leave the matter open.
If I live, I'll be here
when you are old enough to care.
If I'm not, you have this pledge,
this public statement of my love.
I can't promise all who love you
will see you grow into a man,
or that you'll never have to fight
for your beliefs. I hope you'll love
wolves howling in clean dark air,
moose drinking in a crystal lake.
But I can't promise that.

So I stand before pure water,
between black slate and dragons,
make covenant with earth and fire,
to love you, and your sister,
whatever that may come to mean.

Confessions of a Born-Again Pagan

Going to church doesn't make you a Christian any more than going to a garage makes you an automobile.—"Billy" Sunday

Organized Christianity has probably done more to retard the ideals that were its founder's than any other agency in the world.—Richard Le Gallienne

If Christ were here now there is one thing he would not be—a Christian.—Mark Twain

Forsaken, almost human, he sank beneath your wisdom like a stone.—Judy Collins, "Suzanne"

The majority of Americans now live in cities where any bond with the earth is difficult because few can touch the reality; so much earth is buried under asphalt and concrete. A determined diviner, a dowser for earth if such a person existed, might sense the faint throb of the earth's heartbeat through the sidewalk.

We scurry through our lives, passing the scraps of nature we have saved in cities without noticing them; we seldom sit still to look at nature and listen to what it has to say. Perhaps we see it through colored spectacles, in the form of Sierra Club calendars or nature programs on television, beautifully photographed, but with no smell, no teeth or poison sacs. A lawyer from Washington, D.C., as she made camp on the bank of the Colorado River in the Grand Canyon, said, "I wouldn't take a trip on a river if I knew it was going to be muddy."[40] A New York City concert violinist who moved to the Canadian Rocky Mountain wilderness and lived alone in a tipi for eight months said that at first, "In the stillness of the night and the wilderness my mind started playing back every advertisement and rock song I had ever heard. It took six weeks before the noise quieted down, and then I was left with a profound stillness inside. When I first went to Canada I was afraid of wild animals, afraid of the dark, but I regained communion with nature up there—I reconnected."[41] We have lost the connections that were most basic to us, and we must work hard to find them.

Many people have been hoodwinked by the idea, learned in church or on the playground, that the world can be divided tidily into pure good and pure evil; unfortunately, almost nothing is that simple. Mining executives don't have horns, and Earth First! certainly has no halo. In the last two centuries, we have changed from a nation of self-governing agrarians to urban dwellers struggling under layers of bureaucracy, our every move recorded on a master computer, each act numbered and filed. Evidence suggests we no longer believe in the wholeness of life, or the possibility of changing its chaotic structure. No wonder our early heroes, our childhood ideals, and the philosophies upon which the country was founded, now seem incompatible with modern life; we have exchanged a unified way of living for a plastic "lifestyle." We will not be healed until we can find our way back to the center of the circle from which dozens of ancient and Native American cultures tried to speak to us before our single-minded greed, Christian morality, and superior weapons overwhelmed them.

But hope exists; even in the most crowded, busiest city, people reach for the bond with earth that is our birthright. A tomato plant grows in a pot on the balcony of an apartment building, two stories above a bird feeder; falcons nest on the ledges of high-rise office buildings; a group of neighbors turn a vacant lot into a garden. In some cities it is actually illegal not to water a lawn, or to replace it with plants that require no water. One suburban couple I know is encouraging the growth of wild plants ("weeds" to those who favor lawns), attracting bees to pollinate their fruit trees; they mulch the trees with the neighbors' grass clippings, unobtrusively killing the lawn at the same time. On vacant lots throughout the city, they plant trees, creating miniature parks from emptiness. The man writes to protest my statement that city people have lost touch with nature: "There are other people like myself, wanting to naturalize the urban environments, learning about urban ecology, militantly rejecting lawn services and polluting industries. ... If it were truly impossible for urban dwellers to form bonds with the earth, we would be in worse trouble than we are."[42] Some cities have begun to worry about packing landfills with plastic bags filled with biodegradable trash that cannot rot buried in the earth, and encourage residents to mulch. Recycling and pollution have become part of the nightly television news instead of being covered only by special publications. For example, Greenpeace, the best-known environmental organization worldwide, has a membership of 2.5 million in the United States alone and a budget of $58 million, "more money than they know what to do with," according to a staffer.[43]

In fact, public interest has made the environment big business; new environmental magazines are proliferating, along with products with both real and phony environmental benefits. Television advertisements purchased by big multinational pollution corporations bombard viewers with noble music, lovely color shots, and admirable sentiments about the environment. Shell Oil, for example, dumped oil all over San Francisco Bay's wetlands, and a year and a half later gave the nearest town a bronze statue of John Muir; Du Pont, one of the nation's top polluters, broadcasts a fantasy wherein wildlife applauds the company while Beethoven's "Ode to Joy" plays in the background. Waste Management, Inc. and its subsidiaries (ChemWaste Management and ChemNuclear), together the biggest waste-dumping company in the world, paid between twenty and forty million dollars in environmental fines in the 1980s, but still have the gall to promise jobs and riches to rural regions like eastern Washington and western South Dakota, suffering with low employment, historically low wages, and low populations. All such regions have to do is bury toxic and hazardous waste, and ignore its dangers to groundwater and soil we use to produce food. Waste Management ads show butterflies frolicking over "a scientifically managed sanitary landfill," but fail to mention that toxics from the landfills often leach into the groundwater, and are found in residents' bodies.[44]

Even if urban dwellers never leave the city, they are affected by conditions in distant rural areas, regions that produce our food, cleanse our air, and provide solace for our souls. Many people are asking why we let the condition of our earth deteriorate so far before becoming alarmed; others point cynically to the warnings of the 1970s and search for someone to blame.

I

Christianity bears some of the guilt for detaching us from the land, and from pride in our work as its stewards. Among primitive people living sparely in a desert, the admonition from Genesis 1:28 to "be fruitful, and multiply, and replenish the earth, and subdue it: and have dominion over the fish of the sea, and over the fowl of the air, and over every living thing that moveth upon the earth" was considerably more appropriate than to millions of Christians happily reproducing all over the world. Some industrial-age Christians have extended and twisted that doctrine to mean that we can do anything we like to the earth and other humans, without worry about the consequences, because God's grace will get the elect to heaven anyway. Lynn White wrote in a much-discussed article in *Science*: "Christianity in absolute contrast to ancient paganism . . . not only established a dualism of man and nature but also insisted that it is God's will that man exploit nature for his proper ends. . . . In antiquity every tree, every spring, every stream, every hill had its own *genus loci*, its guardian spirit. . . . By destroying pagan animism, Christianity made it possible to exploit nature in a mood of indifference to the feeling of natural objects."[45]

Because of the ancient connections between acquired wisdom and religious beliefs, when Christians destroyed pagan cultures, they destroyed valuable experience as well. For centuries, as an example, priests serving the goddess Dewi Danu controlled irrigation on the island of Bali, in Polynesia; twice a year, each farmer applied for permission to flood his rice fields from the keepers of the nearest shrine upstream. Ultimately, the priest living in the highest shrine on the island determined the irrigation schedule. A few years ago, the Asian Development Bank started a $25 million scheme to change agriculture by building dams and hiring advisors from Italy and Korea who brought in fertilizers, pesticides, and new strains of rice that could be planted three times a year. Disaster followed; insects, viruses, and rats ravaged the rice; pesticides killed the protein-rich fish, eels, and ducks that lived in the rice paddies, supplementing the farmers' diets while destroying predators. When J. Stephen Lansing, an American anthropologist, developed a computer simulation to discover what had gone wrong, he realized that over the long term, the guidance of the goddess and her priests—clearly based on knowledge of the ecology—grew rice more efficiently and with less damage to the environment than modern agricultural theory. In trying to modernize the ancient system, probably while scoffing at "superstition," the experts had nearly destroyed a complex order perfectly adapted to the island.[46]

Similar examples exist worldwide; despite our elaborate devices for food transportation and storage, only about 150 of the world's 80,000 edible plants are still widely cultivated, a smaller fraction in American diets. "Today's supermarket fruits and vegetables represent about three percent of what was available at the turn of the century."[47] If we have lost simple, practical knowledge about food, what complex concepts from native peoples have we ignored or destroyed?

Ancient pagans were careful with each fragment of nature out of knowledge of the ecosystem, as well as respect for the spirituality of all things. Modern folk *talk* about protecting the earth; it's easy and satisfying to generalize about land stewardship. Churches, environmental groups, even officers of development corporations toss the words "stewardship" and "environmentalism" around with a solemn, pious air, and most folks link stewardship vaguely with religion in their minds. Churches celebrate Stewardship Sunday, inviting local farmers and ranchers to church. The minister says farmers and ranchers are self-sacrificing to feed so many people (seventy-eight per farmer, at last calculation). Everyone politely ignores federal aid to farmers, and the twenty-two million other workers in "agricultural manufacturing and support services ... food processing, transportation, and retailing" who provide farmers with borrowed money, or machines, chemicals, and cheap oil, according to Gene Logsdon.[48] Likewise, no one would be so impolite as to mention that "modern" agricultural methods have destroyed one-third of the nation's topsoil, and polluted our groundwater with farm chemicals. The church ladies stuff everyone with store-bought pie and factory-raised chicken; city business types pat the country folk on the back, and the minister says good-bye, knowing those farmers and ranchers won't be seen in church again until Christmas. Duty, everyone feels, has been done, and isn't it a relief to have it over with for another year?

Gore Vidal sees a pattern linking economics to religion and, incidentally, to sex: "Any sexual or intellectual or recreational or political activity that might decrease the amount of coal mined, the number of pyramids built, the quantity of junk food confected will be proscribed through laws that, in turn, are based on divine revelations handed down by whatever god or gods happen to be in fashion at the moment. Religions are manipulated in order to serve those who govern society and not the other way around."[49]

Since the early church developed in the city, perhaps it's not surprising that religious leaders still aren't deeply involved in rural life. But our world is fraught with tough moral choices: to abort or not, to support pacifist desires with monster missiles or not, to kill people who don't pray as you do or not. You'd think church leaders would recognize the beauty of the stewardship issue. Virtually everyone pays lip service to the idea of preserving the earth that nurtures us; it's about as safe an issue as anyone could hope for, but it's sadly neglected among churches. In my neighborhood, environmentalists are still called "uninformed tree-huggers." If a minister made the same statements, and led followers out to block the bulldozers, critics would be more cautious. No matter how vulgar they are, the public has a hard time believing evil of religious leaders. Despite clear evidence of wrongdoing in several cases involving television evangelists, millions of viewers continued to donate.

Caring for the land must certainly be a godly act, however one conceives of God, and caring for the people on the land, as well as the people who eat its products, can be no less rewarding. As we are coming to realize, we are all in this together. The Lakota people, called Sioux by whites, sum up the relationship neatly in two words: *mitakuye oyasin*, "all my relatives," or "we are all related." Politicians and environmentalists have been saying the same thing in more complicated and less honest ways for years without much effect. We're good at lofty words, not so good at practical reality.

In the 1850s, Chief Seattle, responding to an offer by the government to buy tribal land in the Pacific Northwest, summed up our relationship to the earth:

> This we know: The earth does not belong to man;
> man belongs to the earth.
> This we know: All things are connected like the blood which
> unites one family.
> Whatever befalls earth befalls the sons of earth.
> Man did not weave the web of life;
> he is merely a strand in it.
> Whatever he does to the web, he does to himself.

No one has said it better; Seattle's words are quoted everywhere. If we've been doing to ourselves what we're doing to the earth, we're committing suicide. Perhaps the death of humanity is simply nature operating as it should be; a hundred thousand plant and animal species have become extinct since 1980, worldwide.[50] The earth and its other creatures can live without us, but we can't live if we damage the system too much.

Most of the environmentalists I know are not "religious" in the sense that our parents are; we don't attend an organized church regularly, or contribute to its upkeep. Late at night, we may talk nostalgically about childhood associations with church, but on Sunday morning we're more likely to be hiking than singing hymns off-key. The root of the word "religion" means "to relink," and "to connect." *The American Heritage Dictionary*, one of my favorites, says that the meaning of religion as "sacred rites or practices" is obsolete, and explains that it is ultimately derived from the Latin *religio*, "bond between man and the gods." These days our relationship with the god of our choice seems less often to be a bond than a nonaggression pact, or a contract to pay for services rendered. Many of those whom I see praying most fervently have adopted the idea that if they are good Christians, God will reward them with riches right here on earth, where they can spend wildly. To be fair, I must note that greed is not exclusively Christian; competing believers, such as magicians and New Age theorists, also offer spells and meditations for attracting money.

In fact, it seems to me some Christian groups are trying to be modern in their attitudes toward women and the earth. But, like an aging dancer who unbuttons his red shirt and snaps his fingers to the beat, the transformation isn't convincing; the history of the Christian church, antagonistic to women and the natural earth of which they are a part, makes the new clothes hard to believe.

The minister in St. Louis serving barbecued rabbit to the needy on Easter because he wanted "to shift the focus to the true meaning of the Christian holiday" away from the Easter Bunny, which he termed "nothing more than a pagan icon," worries me considerably more than a satan worshipper. The minister said he "came up with the idea to attract more attention to the original meaning of Easter, a Christian holy day that celebrates the resurrection of Jesus Christ and the promise of everlasting life. ... We like to think of ourselves as a Christian nation, but our focus on a mystical rabbit is really paganistic."[51] A sad, unenlightened view; those subscribing to it would be even more shocked if they realized that many Christian holidays were adopted or perverted from pagan rituals. Reading church history, or the history of our race, would reveal that Christians swiped the Easter holiday from the Old English *eastre* or *eostar*, a festival held at the vernal equinox in March to honor the Teutonic goddess of dawn. Easter is the offspring of thirty-five thousand years of celebrating the Mother Goddess, who represented Earth, her consort, and her divine child, sacrificed and reborn in celebration of spring and the new life of the earth. The fact that Easter is the first Sunday after the full moon, and thus shifts on the modern calendar between March 22 and April 25, is only one clue to Easter's history; its date was not of prime importance, but the date of the full moon was. The idea of the resurrection of a dead god is even older; early Christians were smart enough to choose their symbols from among those already made sacred by history and tradition among the peoples they were trying to convert. The Catholic ritual of making the sign of the cross on the breast is derived from the pentacle sign used by pagan religions, and the dates of eight pagan festivals were adopted by the Catholic church and transformed into days honoring saints. To subvert the "lewd and heathenish" sexual frenzy of the Roman Lupercalia, for example, church fathers invented a St. Valentine, supposed to be the patron of lovers.[52]

Modern Christians, whether they know their own history or not, don't want to be burdened with the guilt of systematic destruction of religious beliefs that have existed since the dawn of humanity's time on earth, or of burning and drowning so-called "witches" to prove they consorted with the devil. Even Christians who do know their history like to say they are not responsible for the errors of the bad old days. But only a knowledge of this history might keep us from repeating it, burning some new group on which we focus our hatred.

If "religion" originally meant "connection," it might refer to any philosophy that recognizes the thick sinews binding humans to the universe. In that sense, religion could cover a wide spectrum of ideas; though most of us have been discouraged from learning, in this nation organized on a principle of religious freedom "under God," how many ways of interpreting God exist. Fundamentalist preachers boast of their personal knowledge of the one true way to heaven, and bellow on radio programs about the necessity to convert "heathen" disciples of Buddhism, Hinduism, and Islam. It is true that almost eighty-seven percent of Americans, about 152 million, identify themselves with Christian denominations.[53] But Buddhism counts 307 million adherents, Hinduism 648 million, and Islam 840 million. In the Middle East, the "cradle of civilization" where many of these religions originated, along with a considerable amount of our history, Christians are today in a minority, perhaps in part because of their cultural bigotry. A church bulletin notes that "bloody battles among Christians help make life in Beirut intolerable," that fewer than "ten thousand Christians remain today" in Jerusalem, and that Christians are fleeing West from the last Arab nation they governed, Lebanon.[54] The Christian philosophy is apparently unappealing to many of the world's citizens.

Plains Indians, like nearly all early cultures, developed religious systems which recognized connections between the earth and sky, between humans, animals, plants, and their origins. Although white settlers who came later to the plains portrayed the natives as ignorant savages, many of them came to connect their own notion of God with the earth; anyone of sensitivity who lives on the plains must feel this link. On the grassland, with its wide horizons and huge sky, it is hard to conceive of a God who can bear to reside in tidy little naves and under fragile shells of roofs the elements can destroy in seconds. Talk to any ranchers long enough and, if you seem an understanding and sensible person, they may allude to a feeling that the earth is a product of an intricate intelligence. That's not really what they mean, and you know it; if you keep listening, they may say, hesitantly, softly, something about a belief that God wants us to take care of the land. The rancher knows the creator has more than a casual or causal connection with earth; God is concerned with its continued health and well-being.

In the Great Plains, where white settlers were primarily Anglo-Saxon and Christian, many people comfortably visualize God as Nordic, with short hair, a natural outdoor tan, and the white forehead of men who wear cowboy hats or caps under the sun. They speak of a God who behaves toward them like a tough but fair boss: he'll fire you (literally) if you make a serious mistake, but he works beside you the rest of the time.

Lately, as people fleeing the megalopolis discover the advantages of living in the country, plains people have been exposed to new ways of looking at practically everything; some of those new views—political, religious, cultural, and sexual—are going to play havoc with old habits. I'm intrigued, for example, by ecofeminism, which defines a belief emphasizing the special connection between women and nature. Ecofeminists point out that Christianity portrayed women as evil, and tossed them out of leadership in a worship that was originally closely tied both to the earth and to the mystery of birth. Europeans in the Paleolithic and Neolithic eras were no doubt matriarchal, living in harmony with nature, worshipping a goddess rather than a god. They learned about life by observing plants and animals, though we don't know if men were as poorly treated in those ages as women have been in our male-dominated generations. In late years, many women have begun exploring the history of the goddess who *is* the earth. Many turn to *wicca*, which literally means "wise"; translated as "witch," the term has been distorted to imply that all practitioners of witchcraft are evil. Like every other religion, *wicca* has many sects: there are classical practitioners of witchcraft, gothic witches, and covens describing themselves as familial, immigrant, ethnic, feminist, and neo-pagan.[55] All make clear distinctions between the practice of good, or "white," and black magic; magic, says one practitioner about his techniques for catching fish with his bare hands, is simply the art of getting results.[56] Much to the shock of plains old-timers, who believe hard work cures all mental illness, some folks even practice what one author calls "the most popular witchcraft religion of our day—psychiatry."[57]

Plains people distrust physicians, too, until they become ill; then they follow every whim or order given by their doctor without question, if they haven't died while waiting too long to seek help. But they have never applied a healthy skepticism to their religion; they believe with steadfast earnestness whatever they are told from the pulpit even if it is dead wrong. Not long ago, I sat openmouthed in a conference of ministers while one pastor asserted that the Bible has to be true because it is the oldest written document on earth. Several Catholic priests laughed so hard they nearly slid from their chairs; the Buddhist, whose ancestors were writing religious documents and building sophisticated irrigation systems while mine were hitting each other over the head with clubs, smiled tolerantly, brown eyes twinkling in his brown face. But we who knew that idea to be ludicrous may be a minority in our society.

II

Despite our constitutional prohibition against mixing church and state, they are inextricably blended since our religious beliefs may affect how we view the earth, and how we act to prevent its destruction or contamination beyond repair. Gore Vidal, among other scholars, has traced this attitude far into our past: "The hatred and fear of women that runs through the Old Testament ... suggests that the patriarchal principle so carefully built into the Jewish notion of God must have been at one time opposed to a powerful and perhaps competitive matriarchal system. Whatever the original reasons for the total subordination of woman to man, the result has been an unusually ugly religion that has caused a good deal of suffering not only in its original form but also through its later heresy, Christianity, which in due, and ironic, course was to spin off yet another heresy, communism."[58] Women have been required to accept a subservient role throughout Christianity's history.

Many women felt left out of both the political activism of the 1960s and the resurgence of religion in the churches in which they grew up. As activists and as church members, women were expected to cook the food for the crowd coming to the meetings, wash the dishes and carry out the trash, raise children for the cause, and be quiet and submissive throughout the ordeal. Women who argued with these rules were sneered at as "feminists," or "castrating females," or "dykes," and effectively eliminated from the community they refused to serve in lock step. Those women didn't just go away; some of them put on a cloak of endurance to cover their anger, and returned to activism or religion; others formed new communities. Many women in both groups now consider themselves liberated politically, and understand the influence women could have in this society if they could unite. If women simply took a day or a week's vacation from religious volunteer work—from arranging flowers for the church, from providing cookies and coffee for meetings, from running rummage sales to buy new pews—their importance to their congregations would be recognized, and their voices might be heard. Instead, many women are leaving the church, believing that the way to peace and spiritual growth is through human and planetary health. Such women look at the world in a way that is either wholly new, or else precisely the way they looked it under the old matriarchal systems; they have turned to the old pagan perception that spiritual means "the power within oneself to create artistically and change one's life."[59] Since their concerns are seldom answered by organized religion, they see no contradiction between their interest in political and social change and their interest in the spiritual and creative.

Many modern women are not satisfied with the old political games, nor with violence and force as problem-solving techniques; they don't vote for a candidate because he's good-looking or won medals in the most recent war. Similarly, ranchers and farmers, some of them women, have noticed that they are unimportant to most politicians between election years, and are moving away from their old voting patterns. New populations moving into the plains are creating new political alliances. The green political movement, which subjugates human interests to environmental concerns, has been powerful in Europe, and is moving to this country. Its platform emphasizes self-reliance, quality of life, harmony with nature, diversity, nonviolence, and the "small is beautiful" concept, all ideas which are gaining strength in the general population of the world. Libertarian candidates have been largely a joke until lately; now their ideas are flourishing. New political groups may be able to attract young idealists who now litter the lower ranks of the two traditional parties, desperately hoping to claw their way to the top through a smothering, rotten mulch of traditional politicians who understand only profit and mutual back-scratching. But many older, educated women have acquired cynicism along with college degrees and second jobs. Although Greenpeace may be the world's most powerful environmental organization, its leadership is largely white, middle-class males, and its errors have been damaging to poor people of color; the famous campaign to end the clubbing deaths of cuddly baby harp seals ruined the seal-pelt market but, according to one activist, "forty native communities in the Arctic had their economies totally devastated by the seal campaign."[60]

Why should we compartmentalize our lives? Why must economics dictate the rest of our beliefs? Fundamentalists often argue that the Bible, every word of which they say is true, dictates that women subjugate themselves to men. As Gore Vidal points out, this is selective reading of the text; Leviticus also prohibits the eating of "rare meat, bacon, shellfish, and the wearing of nylon mixed with wool. If Leviticus were to be obeyed in every instance, the garment trade would collapse."[61] Even the Ten Commandments are impossible for many Christians to keep, not to mention more obscure requirements of their faith. The New Testament is popular with WASP leaders because it was created by a white, male, capitalist power structure specifically to meet their goals. A considerable portion of our society is fascinated with primitive cultures whose world view was similar to that of modern environmentalists and pagans, that all life fit into a circle, a unified whole. Unlike them, we divide our lives, specializing in smaller and smaller fragments of knowledge, and insisting that our work is important only for the cash we earn to buy material goods. Fragmented and confused, with women alienated from men, whites from people of color, rich from poor, we are more easily coerced, controlled, subjugated by our white, male leaders. No wonder we feel divorced from the earth, alienated from all that is important.

III

Women and country people, each existing in informal communities, circles formed around stewardship of the earth, should lead the attempt to rethink our relationship to it. The job is massive, revolutionary; we must overturn the prevailing philosophy of profit as the primary objective of society, and industrialization as the chief method with which we accomplish that goal. We must modify the world's fascination with technology for the sake of gadgetry. But close connections with the earth are part of our heritage, and must be part of our future if we are to survive. We must forget our differences and prejudices and unite around that common goal to destroy the destroyers.

Religion is the one solid link many farmers and women have with society in general. Farmers have been isolated by distance, travel difficulties, work, and their own preference, but most of them go to church once or twice a year, drawn by the load of guilt Christians cultivate. Women have been set apart from society by childrearing, or by overwork as they juggle kids and jobs, as well as by continual debates over the rights they have been "given" by their culture. Militant Christians have used the demands of family life as one way to keep women tied to the hearth; only a skeptic like Vidal would note that "in societies where it is necessary to force great masses of people to do work that they don't want to do (building pyramids, working on the Detroit assembly line), marriage at an early age is encouraged on the sensible ground that if a married man is fired, his wife and children are going to starve, too. That grim knowledge makes for docility. ... A woman who can support herself and her child is a threat to marriage, and marriage is the central institution whereby the owners of the world control those who do the work."[62] Modern people, particularly politicians at election time, speak as though the nuclear family of father, mother, and children is an institution mandated by God at the beginning of time, when it is merely one of the more recent ways humans have chosen to group themselves. The family in such a society, says Vidal, can be kept sacred and central only "by depriving women of equal status not only in the marketplace but also in relation to their own bodies (Thou shalt not abort). That is why the defeat of the Equal Rights Amendment to the Constitution is of great symbolic importance."[63]

Similarly, other disenfranchised groups are controlled by companies that use their land and water and manage their food supplies. Nuclear energy continues to be used worldwide despite the fact that Swedish and West German scientists have said "there is a 70 percent chance of a Chernobyl-scale accident happening somewhere in the world every six years."[64] Since no one has figured out how to store high-level radioactive waste safely for the 250,000 years needed to render it harmless, "experts" have officially labeled one-third of it as low-level waste so it can be dumped in landfills, a solution that could kill up to 250,000 people. Many world leaders have mastered an old trick of control: change the label; divert public attention.

Meanwhile, U.S. farm communities that produce our food are dissolving in crisis, and the economy is heaving with unrest, dislocating both women and farmers from homes and roles they believed to be unchangeable. Both groups may be ready to stand up and fight imbalances in a society that has become twisted by ignoring its origins: women and farmers. We all had mothers, and all of our ancestors at some time were closely tied to the land for survival. In prehistoric times, men hunted the native wildlife the land offered. Women gathered its fruits, and were first to begin cultivating and improving them. It is a "generally accepted theory that women were responsible for the development of agriculture, as an extension of their food-gathering activities."[65] Women likely "invented that most fundamental of all material technologies, without which civilization could not have evolved: the domestication of plants and animals," and in the "primarily horticultural economies of 'developing' tribes and nations ... the cultivation of the soil is to this day primarily in the hands of women."[66] Respected archaeologists suggest as well that "religion was primarily associated with the role of women in the initial development of agriculture," so we have a particular interest in both aspects of our culture.[67]

Agriculture is not inherently destructive; with care and attention to the land's qualities and capabilities, it would be possible to plow and plant some soils without destroying them, as organic farmers do. But agriculture as the production of crops, livestock, or poultry, became agribusiness, the complex of farming with its related industry and business, and profit became its primary aim. Concern for the land became secondary, and then disappeared altogether under the pressure of increased production. As Americans become more resistant to technological fixes and pollution, our companies export our destructive chemicals and machines to starving Third World countries too desperate to notice we are selling them destruction.

By contrast, what we now call witchcraft had its origin in "hearth magic," simple techniques to make housework easier, to heal the sick with herbs; wise women and men worked and lived in concert with nature. Many Great Plains farmers and ranchers who would call witchcraft the work of the devil still plant by the phases of the moon, castrate animals in a waning moon to minimize bleeding, and use herbal or folk remedies on their animals. They prepare for a storm on March 21, knowing that it is the equinox, but they would be surprised to know their knowledge springs from witchcraft. They experience the seasonal cycles in ways that are closely related to rituals held over from ancient times. As a culture, we have adopted, adapted, and corrupted many useful customs; we have turned Halloween from a day when people celebrated the harvest and acknowledged the closeness of death and life to a festival of humor confused with terror. We demolished a beautiful ritual of rebirth in honor of Brigid, goddess of fire and inspiration, and in Ireland triple goddess of poetry, smithcraft, and healing, to turn it into Ground Hog Day, a ludicrous spectacle that demeans an animal with more dignity than those who gather at the burrow to watch it emerge.

The word "pagan" comes from the Latin *paganus*, which means country dweller; "heathen" originally referred to a person who lived on the heaths. As Christianity struggled with the older polytheistic religions, the last people to be converted were often those who lived in relative isolation, the pagans and heathens, and the meanings of those words were distorted to mean nonbelievers, hicks, the godless, "instead of, simply, a member of a different kind of religion."[68] Sloppily, some of us associate paganism with satanism. The fellow mentioned who fills vacant city lots with trees explains that he "felt the sacredness of nature long before I ever recognized that I was a pagan because of it. My early, happy experiences were all in a town. Only later did I learn the joys of hiking and backpacking. One of the most alienating experiences of my childhood was visiting Disneyland. I knew I was supposed to be having fun, but was put off by the complete artificiality of the place. Even the trees were plastic, and the mountain was made from concrete."[69]

I think people who respect nature and deplore narrow modern religion need to declare ourselves pagans and heathens, to emphasize our belief that God did not intend for us to dominate other earthly creatures into destruction. The new pagans are people who realize that all the living beings on earth are in this together, and we must be responsible for all life. I think the time for quiet philosophical debates on environmental ethics and our duty to the earth is almost over; this is an emergency. I propose that women and country people unite, lead the battle to save the earth.

Wendell Berry, the Old Testament prophet of agriculture's New Age, in discussing the admonition of Genesis 1:28 to "subdue" and "have dominion over" the earth, has said: "Such a reading of Genesis 1:28 is contradicted by virtually the rest of the Bible, as many people by now have pointed out. The ecological teaching of the Bible is simply inescapable: God made the world because He wanted it made. He thinks the world is good, and He loves it. It is His world; He has never relinquished title to it. And He has never revoked the conditions bearing upon His gift to us of the use of it, that oblige us to take excellent care of it."[70] Berry, more precise in his writing and speech than most public speakers, has, in my opinion, made an important point missed by most Christians, as well as by environmentalists who have accused Christians of being inherently abusive of our world. The Bible, correctly interpreted, admonishes us to take better care of the world than we have. Unfortunately, many Christians—including James Watt—have misinterpreted or ignored those canons, and chosen to see only a fragment of the original meaning. Real Christians could find justification for their commitment to caring for the earth in their own Bible. The rest of us may not see God as the Christians do, but we could all work together to care for the planet. Unfortunately, "polytheism always includes monotheism. The reverse is not true."[71]

Some ranchers are, without knowing it, high priests and priestesses of a pagan order, the Order of Grass Lovers. They take vows of poverty and obedience to the earth, serve Her all their days with rejoicing; they finally lay down their lives for Her, and go back to the grass they have served so well in an endless, beautiful pagan cycle of renewal. Ellen Cotton, who ranches near Decker, Montana, said to Stan Steiner:

Hereabouts, it's the grass that determines everything.
So our grass out here is like a national historic site.
Some old boy came out here and he said, Do you want
    to lease your land for coal?
And I said, Hell no!
And he said, Would you like to sell your place for good
    money?
And I said, Christ, no!
And he kept on and on and on.
Finally I said, By God! I don't know what's going to
happen. But, by God! I may have to stand with a gun,
a gun in each hand to stop you bastards.
And then he departed in haste.[72]

Her statement, with its biblical rhythms and simple, sonorous words, could be a responsive reading in a church.

I think many country people feel the spirituality of the earth, especially the older generation; many local ranchers, the people I know best, have surprised me with their willingness to talk about God in connection with their work. When a New York City hiker stands on the rim of the Grand Canyon and falls in love, that love is abstract and based on little knowledge of the canyon's realities, though after a hike to the bottom and back up again, that love may be tempered with understanding. Ranchers' love of the land is tested every day. They've gone through hell for their beloved land, sacrificed people they love in some cases—and not for money.

In order to survive and prosper, prairie cattle must be able to graze and get fat, and to have their calves safely. Facilitating grazing is the rancher's job, and it requires making choices. If you keep the cattle in a pasture so long that the good grass gets grazed off and the cattle are beginning to yank it out by the roots, the cattle suffer, as well as the land and the wildlife that shares it. The rancher's first priority isn't wildlife, but many of the conditions that are good for wildlife are also good for cattle; a rancher who knows this cares for both. For example, most ranchers furnish salt licks for cattle. With a little thought, these could be made difficult or frightening for wildlife to use.

But most ranchers don't bother. If asked about it, they'll say, with a self-conscious grin, "The antelope don't eat much." When cattle are moved out of a pasture, the efficient rancher, the "agribusiness" rancher, would remove every scrap of salt. Even then, antelope would lick the ground for months, slurping up every remnant. Most ranchers don't bother; they leave scraps and chunks, sometimes half a block, and if you mention the waste, they'd say, "Oh, heck, I ain't so poor I have to pick up every piece yet." They don't say, "I love to see antelope run, and dive under fences, and to hear them snort and stamp their feet." They don't wax poetic about the place of the pronghorn in the ecological cycle. They mutter, instead, about the damn antelope. Once in a while they shoot one, and say they hope that scares the rest of a large and destructive herd away. If pressed, they say the pronghorns are part of the land, belong here, that it wouldn't seem right not to see them dashing beside the pickup. Their love isn't expressed in words, and isn't always immediately discernible in action, but can be found in what they do not do. Their actions express love.

Environmentalists often don't credit ranchers with sharing a love of the land, or approach land issues in a spirit of compromise. The slogan adopted by some advocates of removing cattle from all public lands, "Grazing Free by '93," is a challenge, and some extremists have advocated shooting cattle on public lands, perhaps in unconscious response to the fact that ranchers carry rifles in their pickups. But not all ranchers are shooting defenseless wildlife, and a few muttered phrases and scraps of salt don't mean all ranchers are equally careful of the earth; most of those I know are. Ranchers have become paranoid about environmentalists; cattle publications are filled with articles warning about the threats they pose to traditional western independence.[73] But ranchers own or control much of the non-federal land left in the West; it can best be preserved with their cooperation.

All of us are sometimes guilty of judging by appearances, a crime we deplore when it's done to us. For example, though I have clearly demonstrated my interest in protecting the regional ecosystem, I have to be careful how I dress to attend public meetings on the subject. When I put on my white blouse and tailored little

Republican suit, environmentalists eye me with suspicion. If I wore jeans and a sweatshirt that said "Greenpeace," the environmentalists would smile and the business people frown. But if I am late for the meeting and haven't had time to change out of my jeans, manure-covered cowboy boots, work shirt, and black neckscarf, the environmentalists don't look at me, and the suited business types grin condescendingly; the local newspaper will quote me, but both environmentalists and business people will ignore every word. All of us have been condemned in the same way, and most of us have made hasty judgments based on appearance. Similarly, if we see a cow on public lands, we automatically assume she and her cohorts are damaging it and don't belong there, whether we've studied the ecology or not.

Duty alone wouldn't keep ranchers at the jobs they have to do to survive, any more than duty alone keeps a woman with her children. Hatred and dislike of the land and its life wouldn't result in the care that these show.

IV

Certain elements appear and reappear in religions separated by generations and continents: the power of a circle, the sun, moon, water, air, earth and fire, the four directions. All are expressions of the natural world, and those who introduced each religion felt a potent and convincing urge to retain some tie to substantial earth while reaching for a supernatural and intangible dimension, a god to believe in, who would set things right.

I have participated in rituals representing many forms of belief, but certain experiences remain particularly clear and meaningful: watching robed monks slip between the tall columns of a dimly lit cathedral; the dawn hymns sung by Benedictines, who devote their lives to prayer for the world's sins; silent meditations among Quakers in a burned-out Methodist church; or Christmas eve hymns throbbing in tall organ pipes. I felt deep awe as I sat on grass within the outlines of a cell at Tintagel where monks lived eight centuries ago; as the sea devoured the Cornish headland, I thought of the cold, the damp, and the faith of those men. Among discarded crutches and fervent prayers in an adobe church I was stunned by the power of belief I could not share.

On one occasion, in brilliant sunshine on the Pine Ridge Indian Reservation, I watched dancers circle the Sun Dance pole, tied to it with thongs through their pectoral muscles; later, I watched the same ritual under thick, damp storm clouds that had just dumped several inches of rain on the region. A participant said, laughing, "The eagles are sitting in a nice dry cave saying, 'What are those Indians doing down there?'" But the eagles came as the prayers continued; four times they dropped out of the clouds to circle directly over the pole and the people praying around it.

I felt the hair rise on the back of my neck under storm clouds over the Bighorn Mountains as a spiritual leader who sells cars during the week passed a sacred pipe to seven of George's friends; later, one of those men spoke of feeling the same power at an ancient stone circle in Ireland.

Seven women who raised a cone of power within a hundred feet of my home vibrated with joyous love and strength, and I fell to my knees at my first sight of Stonehenge—despite having walked through a highway underpass to get there. The Medicine Wheel on a narrow ridge in the Big Horns hums with ageless power, even though it is encircled by a chainlink fence topped with barbed wire. The fence is hung with cloth bags, feathers, and other symbols of prayer left by people who know wire cannot corrupt the spirit existing there. Knee-deep in wet, thorny gorse on a moor in the Scottish highlands, in the center of a ring of standing stones, I felt the warmth of the men and women who erected them, perhaps ten thousand years ago, and of my husband, two years dead. Now I go to a Christian church only rarely, and only as a favor to my mother, who still hopes I can be saved from my heathen ways.

Each spot, each ritual in which I have participated represents a distinctive concept of *religio*, a different idea about the relationship between humankind, the gods, and the earth. The important ingredient was not the specific details of performance, but the recognition of our symbiotic relationship with our world. We choose gods and rituals of worship that help us feel closer to completion, and discover wisdom and joy in understanding our relationship to our world. But whatever our choices, we are linked with the earth as to a Siamese twin—at the head and heart, belly and soul. We cannot find faith without regaining our pagan love and knowledge of earth. Each of us walks alone to whatever faith we find, and ultimately tests that faith against death.

Why are we preoccupied with the beauty of our bodies and the health of our minds while our planet is dying? Why are we concerned about food contamination while subsidizing production of nuclear waste? Why do we build more highways and bigger cars when we can see the end of our oil reserves? Why do we speak of freedom while dropping bombs? Why does our national debt keep rising?

Profiteers dictate our priorities. This new class of tyrant will never act to save the earth unless conservation is more lucrative than destruction. We stop them the same way we should stop rapists— by demanding a high price for the crime, and carrying out the punishment swiftly and ruthlessly.

When we camped in our tipi, I would often see George, out of the corner of my eye, leave a tiny cloth-wrapped offering of tobacco in the crotch of a tree while we were packing up, as Plains Indians did to thank the spirits. He never spoke of it; once when I encountered him while leaving my own offering, he smiled and said, "It was a good camp." I have adopted George's custom of calling out "Thank you!" when a meadowlark sings as I drive by, even though I never knew if he was thanking the meadowlark or God. These are not special rituals for a particular day of the week, requiring words and actions dictated by some authority. The ritual of thanks is part of daily living; like caring for the earth, it requires no decision, it simply is.

Toast to the Cowboy Poet's Wife from the Woman Rancher

After the reading, my bronco (that's a pun, folks)
follows his jeep down gravel roads
where I lose track of turns among the little hills
until he finds a plum-lined drive,
pulls up between the corrals and house.
We haul the pizza to a table on the deck,
where she has beer waiting, chairs in shade.

While we drink and orate, her eyes tally
two blond children, kittens in the grass,
the plump caged rabbit, rhubarb on tart stalks.
Last spring her strong brown hands brushed them all
while I dug holes and she piled earth
around asparagus roots.
She listened to me as carefully,
as if I were one of hers.
I thought of her tan, smiling face
so often in the cold
that I couldn't speak her name when we met again.

My blood is thin and black on paper.
My truths are silhouettes curling
in the flames of her love.
Her blood threads crimson through this earth,
through the child who's not as healthy as she looks.

The poet, and I who count myself his friend,
say, and may believe, that we write truth on paper
where others like us will admire it,
though maybe no one will see at all.
I raise my glass and think a toast,
but envy her so much I cannot speak.
She smiles with us, and never flaunts
what she knows: that her truths walk free;
live, breathe, argue, scatter seed, feed us all,
toss fragrance into the breeze
as if the expense was nothing.

Why One Peaceful Woman Carries a Pistol

I'm a peace-loving woman. I also carry a pistol. For years, I've written about my decision in an effort to help other women make intelligent choices about gun ownership, but editors rejected the articles. Between 1983 and 1986, however, when gun sales to men held steady, gun ownership among women rose fifty-three percent, to more than twelve million.[74] We learned that any female over the age of twelve can expect to be criminally assaulted some time in her life, that women aged thirty have a fifty-fifty chance of being raped, robbed, or attacked, and that many police officials say flatly that they cannot protect citizens from crime. During the same period, the number of women considering gun ownership quadrupled to nearly two million. Manufacturers began showing lightweight weapons with small grips, and purses with built-in holsters.[75] A new magazine is called *Guns and Women*, and more than eight thousand copies of the video *A Woman's Guide to Firearms* were sold by 1988. Experts say female gun buyers are not limited to any particular age group, profession, social class, or area of the country, and most are buying guns to protect themselves. Shooting instructors say women view guns with more caution than do men, and may make better shots.

I decided to buy a handgun for several reasons. During one four-year period, I drove more than a hundred thousand miles alone, giving speeches, readings, and workshops. A woman is advised, usually by men, to protect herself by avoiding bars, by approaching her car like an Indian scout, by locking doors and windows. But these precautions aren't always enough. And the logic angers me: *because* I am female, it is my responsibility to be extra careful.

As a responsible environmentalist, I choose to recycle, avoid chemicals on my land, minimize waste. As an informed woman alone, I choose to be as responsible for my own safety as possible: I keep my car running well, use caution in where I go and what I do. And I learned about self-protection—not an easy or quick decision. I developed a strategy of protection that includes handgun possession. The following incidents, chosen from a larger number because I think they could happen to anyone, helped make up my mind.

When I camped with another woman for several weeks, she didn't want to carry a pistol, and police told us Mace was illegal. We tucked spray deodorant into our sleeping bags, theorizing that any man crawling into our tent at night would be nervous anyway; anything sprayed in his face would slow him down until we could hit him with a frying pan, or escape. We never used our improvised weapon, because we were lucky enough to camp beside people who came to our aid when we needed them. I returned from that trip determined to reconsider.

At that time, I lived alone and taught night classes in town. Along a city street I often traveled, a woman had a flat tire, called for help on her CB, and got a rapist; he didn't fix the tire either. She was afraid to call for help again and stayed in her car until morning. Also, CBs work best along line-of-sight; I ruled them out.

As I drove home one night, a car followed me, lights bright. It passed on a narrow bridge, while a passenger flashed a spotlight in my face, blinding me. I braked sharply. The car stopped, angled across the bridge, and four men jumped out. I realized the locked doors were useless if they broke my car windows. I started forward, hoping to knock their car aside so I could pass. Just then, another car appeared, and the men got back in their car, but continued to follow me, passing and repassing. I dared not go home. I passed no lighted houses. Finally, they pulled to the roadside, and I decided to use their tactic: fear. I roared past them inches away, horn blaring. It worked; they turned off the highway. But it was desperate and foolish, and I was frightened and angry. Even in my vehicle I was too vulnerable.

Other incidents followed. One day I saw a man in the field near my house, carrying a shotgun and heading for a pond full of ducks. I drove to meet him, and politely explained that the land was posted. He stared at me, and the muzzle of his shotgun rose. I realized that if he simply shot me and drove away, I would be a statistic. The moment passed; the man left.

One night, I returned home from class to find deep tire ruts on the lawn, a large gas tank empty, garbage in the driveway. A light shone in the house; I couldn't remember leaving it on. I was too embarrassed to wake the neighbors. An hour of cautious exploration convinced me the house was safe, but once inside, with the doors locked, I was still afraid. I put a .22 rifle by my bed, but I kept thinking of how naked I felt, prowling around my own house in the dark.

It was time to consider self-defense. I took a kung fu class and learned to define the distance to maintain between myself and a stranger. Once someone enters that space without permission, kung fu teaches appropriate evasive or protective action. I learned to move confidently, scanning for possible attack. I learned how to assess danger, and techniques for avoiding it without combat.

I also learned that one must practice several hours every day to be good at kung fu. By that time I had married George; when I practiced with him, I learned how *close* you must be to your attacker to use martial arts, and decided a 120-pound woman dare not let a six-foot, 220-pound attacker get that close unless she is very, very good at self-defense. Some women who are well trained in martial arts have been raped and beaten anyway.

Reluctantly I decided to carry a pistol. George helped me practice with his .357 and .22. I disliked the .357's recoil, though I later became comfortable with it. I bought a .22 at a pawn shop.

A standard .22 bullet, fired at close range, can kill, but news reports tell of attackers advancing with five such bullets in them. I bought magnum shells, with more power, and practiced until I could hit someone close enough to endanger me. Then I bought a license making it legal for me to carry the gun concealed.

George taught me that the most important preparation was mental: convincing myself I could shoot someone. Few of us really wish to hurt or kill another human being. But there is no point in having a gun—in fact, gun possession might increase your danger—unless you know you can use it against another human being. A good training course includes mental preparation, as well as training in safety. As I drive or walk, I often rehearse the conditions which would cause me to shoot. Men grow up handling firearms, and learn controlled violence in contact sports, but women grow up learning to be subservient and vulnerable. To make ourselves comfortable with the idea that we are capable of protecting ourselves requires effort. But it need not turn us into macho, gun-fighting broads. We must simply learn to do as men do from an early age: believe in, and rely on, *ourselves* for protection. The pistol only adds an extra edge, an attention-getter; it is a weapon of last resort.

Because shooting at another person means shooting to kill. It's impossible even for seasoned police officers to be sure of only wounding an assailant. If I shot an attacking man, I would aim at the largest target, the chest. This is not an easy choice, but for me it would be better than rape.

In my car, my pistol is within instant reach. When I enter a deserted rest stop at night, it's in my purse, my hand on the grip. When I walk from a dark parking lot into a motel, it's in my hand, under a coat. When I walk my dog in the deserted lots around most motels, the pistol is in a shoulder holster, and I am always aware of my surroundings. In my motel room, it lies on the bedside table. At home, it's on the headboard.

Just carrying a pistol is not protection. Avoidance is still the best approach to trouble; watch for danger signs, and practice avoiding them. Develop your instinct for danger.

One day while driving to the highway mailbox, I saw a vehicle parked about halfway to the house. Several men were standing in the ditch, relieving themselves. I have no objection to emergency urination; we always need moisture. But they'd also dumped several dozen beer cans, which blow into pastures and can slash a cow's legs or stomach.

As I slowly drove closer, the men zipped their trousers ostentatiously while walking toward me. Four men gathered around my small foreign car, making remarks they wouldn't make to their mothers, and one of them demanded what the hell I wanted.

"This is private land; I'd like you to pick up the beer cans."

"What beer cans?" said the belligerent one, putting both hands on the car door, and leaning in my window. His face was inches from mine, the beer fumes were strong, and he looked angry. The others laughed. One tried the passenger door, locked; another put his foot on the hood and rocked the car. They circled, lightly thumping the roof, discussing my good fortune in meeting them, and the benefits they were likely to bestow upon me. I felt small and trapped; they knew it.

"The ones you just threw out," I said politely.

"I don't see no beer cans. Why don't you get out here and show them to me, honey?" said the belligerent one, reaching for the handle inside my door.

"Right over there," I said, still being polite, "there and over there." I pointed with the pistol, which had been under my thigh. Within one minute the cans and the men were back in the car, and headed down the road.

I believe this small incident illustrates several principles. The men were trespassing and knew it; their judgment may have been impaired by alcohol. Their response to the polite request of a woman alone was to use their size and numbers to inspire fear. The pistol was a response in the same language. Politeness didn't work; I couldn't intimidate them. Out of the car, I'd have been more vulnerable. The pistol just changed the balance of power.

My husband, George, asked one question when I told him. "What would you have done if he'd grabbed for the pistol?"

"I had the car in reverse; I'd have hit the accelerator, and backed up; if he'd kept coming, I'd have fired straight at him." He nodded.

In fact, the sight of the pistol made the man straighten up; he cracked his head on the door frame. He and the two in front of the car stepped backward, catching the attention of the fourth, who joined them. They were all in front of me then, and as the car was still running and in reverse gear, my options had multiplied. If they'd advanced again, I'd have backed away, turning to keep the open window toward them. Given time, I'd have put the first shot into the ground in front of them, the second into the belligerent leader. It might have been better to wait until they were gone, pick up the beer cans, and avoid confrontation, but I believed it was reasonable and my right to make a polite request to strangers littering my property. Showing the pistol worked on another occasion when I was driving in a desolate part of Wyoming. A man played cat-and-mouse with me for thirty miles, ultimately trying to run my car off the road. When his car was only two inches from mine, I pointed my pistol at him, and he disappeared.

I believe that a handgun is like a car; both are tools for specific purposes; both can be lethal if used improperly. Both require a license, training, and alertness. Both require you to be aware of what is happening before and behind you. Driving becomes almost instinctive; so does handgun use. When I've drawn my gun for protection, I simply found it in my hand. Instinct told me a situation was dangerous before my conscious mind reacted; I've felt the same while driving. Most good drivers react to emergencies by instinct.

Knives are another useful tool often misunderstood and misused; some people acquire knives mostly for display, either on a wall or on a belt, and such knives are often so large as to serve no useful purpose. My pocket knives are always razor sharp, because a small, sharp knife will do most jobs. Skinning blades serve for cutting meat and splitting small kindling in camp. A *sgian dubh*, a four-inch flat blade in a wooden sheath, was easily concealed inside a Scotsman's high socks, and slips into my dress or work boots as well. Some buckskinners keep what they call a "grace knife" on a thong around their necks; the name may derive from *coup de grâce*, the welcome throat-slash a wounded knight asked from his closest friend, to keep him from falling alive into the hands of his enemies. I also have a push dagger, with a blade only three inches long, attached to a handle that fits into the fist so well that the knife would be hard to lose even in hand-to-hand combat. When I first showed it, without explanation, to an older woman who would never consider carrying a knife, she took one look and said, "Why, you could push that right into someone's stomach," and demonstrated with a flourish. That's what it's for. I wear it for decoration, because it was handmade by Jerry and fits my hand perfectly, but I am intently aware of its purpose. I like my knives, not because they are weapons, but because they are well designed, and beautiful, and because each is a tool with a specific purpose.

Women didn't always have jobs, or drive cars or heavy equipment, though western women did many of those things almost as soon as they arrived here. Men in authority argued that their attempt to do so would unravel the fabric of society. Women, they said, would become less feminine; they hadn't the intelligence to cope with the mechanics of a car, or the judgment to cope with emergencies. Since these ideas were so wrong, perhaps it is time women brought a new dimension to the wise use of handguns as well.

We can and should educate ourselves in how to travel safely, take self-defense courses, reason, plead, or avoid trouble in other ways. But some men cannot be stopped by those methods; they understand only power. A man who is committing an attack already knows he's breaking laws; he has no concern for someone else's rights. A pistol is a woman's answer to his greater power. It makes her equally frightening. I have thought of revising the old Colt slogan: "God made man, but Sam Colt made them equal" to read "God made men *and women* but Sam Colt made them equal." Recently I have seen an ad for a popular gunmaker with a similar sentiment; perhaps this is an idea whose time has come, though the pacifist inside me will be saddened if the only way women can achieve equality is by carrying a weapon.

As a society, we were shocked in early 1989 when a female jogger in New York's Central Park was beaten and raped savagely and left in a coma. I was even more shocked when reporters interviewed children who lived near the victim and quoted a twelve-year-old as saying, "She had nothing to guard herself; she didn't have no man with her; she didn't have no Mace." And another sixth-grader said, "It is like she committed suicide."[76] Surely this is not a majority opinion, but I think it is not so unusual, either, even in this liberated age. Yet there is no city or county in the nation where law officers can relax because all the criminals are in jail. Some authorities say citizens armed with handguns stop almost as many crimes annually as armed criminals succeed in committing, and that people defending themselves kill three times more attackers and robbers than police do.[77] I don't suggest all criminals should be killed, but some can be stopped only by death or permanent incarceration. Law enforcement officials can't prevent crimes; later punishment may be of little comfort to the victim. A society so controlled that no crime existed would probably be too confined for most of us, and is not likely to exist any time soon. Therefore, many of us should be ready and able to protect ourselves, and the intelligent use of firearms is one way.

We must treat a firearm's power with caution. "Power tends to corrupt, and absolute power corrupts absolutely," as a man (Lord Acton) once said. A pistol is not the only way to avoid being raped or murdered in today's world, but a firearm, intelligently wielded, can shift the balance and provide a measure of safety.

Drought Year

I dreamed I slept alone in a drought year,
and now I do.
I lie in the short grass;
water is a dream.
All day I was fuel for the sun
burning like wildfire over a dry land.
Ghosts of streams slash earth,
water's memory
ripples in sandstone.

I dreamed you died in a drought year,
and you did. Now
I dream water all night long:
hear it laughing in the throat of a cloud,
imagine dry grass brushing the house
is rain. When the killdeer cries
at the edge of the dry pond,
I add my plea to hers
in a voice husky with dust.

I dreamed myself a dry woman,
and I am, the juice gone
out of me. My skin is fragrant
with prairie odors.
I am drying grass, wind-bent.

Long tough roots grapple

deep into baked prairie earth.
Leaves die, but roots dream
in crumbled sod,
wait for rain.

Lettuce Bouquets for
a Dry Country

> *Without rain there is the potential for this to be*
> *a catastrophe.*—The insight of President
> George Bush on the drought.

> *Facts are stupid things*—Former President
> Ronald Reagan[78]

I drifted into sleep about ten-thirty that summer night, trying to believe in a cool breeze through the bedroom windows. A blast of hot air tore the sheet away, waking me; a door slammed, something clattered in the kitchen, papers swished rapidly down the hall. I sat up, confused and frightened; my first breath tasted like burning wood.

When I leapt from the bed, I landed on a stiff cardboard shape, a print of Ranchos de Taos church that shows the ancient structure before the tourist suburbs of Taos engulfed it. I kicked the print aside and glanced at the clock. I don't know why humans want to know the time in the middle of a disaster; ordinarily I don't care. The red numbers glared: 12:42. I looked toward the Black Hills, expecting to see a forest fire. If the fire had smelled like grass, I'd have looked north, toward the railroad and our prevailing winds. The horizon was dark, but the scent was so intense that I thought the house might be on fire.

Slipping on letters, newspapers, photographs, everything that had been hanging on a wall or lying on a table, I checked the horizon in all four directions: darkness. No fire anywhere. I began turning on lights, surveying the confusion, and trying to collect my mind. I couldn't sleep while that hot wind blew; my mind and body twitch at the smell of smoke. Instead, I sat on the deck, and watched the stars and the horizon. The only breeze was a flicker of the air as bats swooped past, inches away from my face. When I calmed down, I realized the smoke was coming from the west, which had to mean it originated with forest fires in the Rocky Mountains, five hundred miles away. My mind drifted to my brief trip to town during the day. Shirtless, hatless boys buzzed past on motorcycles; many people strolled in shorts and halter tops, faces open to the sun's blasting heat. Babies in strollers squinted their eyes; children held tiny hands up to their faces. A hot wind blew dust along the streets, whirling styrofoam wrappers into confetti. I pictured the sun and wind sucking moisture from all of us, drying the skin, blistering, cooking flesh, and starting cancers that people will notice in ten years, or twenty. I go out in such weather only in long-sleeved shirts, jeans, caps or wide-brimmed hats, and still the surface of my entire body often feels desiccated, shriveled. A few years ago, I developed what a dermatologist called an allergic reaction to excessive sun; my entire body broke out in an itching rash when I went outside in summer's daylight.

In fact, the surface of the earth needs the same care, I think, as the surface of our bodies. If we go out unprotected into noon sun, we will be damaged; if we protect our skin, it remains more pliable, healthier. In the same way, ground should not be naked to the sun, but covered with mulch, shade, anything to hold in the moisture and interrupt the baking sun rays. Native grasses have spent centuries developing the ability to survive this dry heat, hiding their strongest resource, their roots, deep in the earth. We have attempted to alter this natural cycle by tearing up native vegetation to plant tender stuff from some other neighborhood.

In town, a sour, hot smell rose from watered lawns, as if the pampered grass was boiling. Sprinklers poured water into the air; I could almost see drops that rose, but did not fall, evaporated in seconds. Precious water ran down the streets; town officials have talked of water restrictions summer after summer and done nothing because "experts" say enough water remains in the reservoirs for "two more years," or "three years," or "one year." So small are the minds of these elected officials and the general public that a year or two sounds like enough time; the grass, downright ancient having occupied the earth for some two hundred million years, would laugh if it could. Meanwhile, dozens of business and civic leaders go on planning increased water use: more houses clustered on the out- skirts of town, more mining that will require the use of water and cyanide to leach ore from earth.

The thermometer had reached 116 degrees that day, and had been above one hundred degrees for ten days; we'd had a half-inch of rain a couple of weeks before, but the ground surface was dry by sunrise the next morning. This hot, dry summer followed a warm, dry winter, when fierce winter winds blew dust more often than they blew snow, preceded by several of the driest years in this century. Faculty members at agricultural colleges in the Great Plains were beginning to compare the three-year drought to the Dust Bowl years of the 1930s; in the next breath they usually assured us that "improved farming practices" and the development of irrigation would reduce its impact.

In western South Dakota, where no sane person irrigates— which means thousands of people irrigate, legally or not—we were seeing the drought naked, not concealed by the machinations of big agriculture. For two summers, we had seen no grass grow in our pastures, no hay in the fields, and the end was not in sight. The Soil Conservation Service figures are alarming, but I am certain they underestimate the real damage. Their records concentrate on farmland, most of which is in the eastern part of the state; second, they assume everyone whose acreage showed damage reported it, which I consider highly unlikely. For example, most of our acreage is not cultivated, so we reported no damage, but even fields with a good cover of alfalfa sent columns of dust into the air on windy days. These fields were full of standing hay; we cut none in the summer of 1989 because the gasoline we'd have bought to do the job was worth more than the hay.

During the day that preceded my hot midnight awakening, the water and mud blend in one of our largest dams had finally become too viscous for the cattle to sip, and adhesive enough to trap them in the mud. Tomorrow—no, today—we would begin hauling water to that bunch. Later we'd move cattle out of a pasture where the dugout had filled with windblown dust to one where a spring piped by a 1920s settler still trickled. Before long, we would have to decide whether to sell cattle, or move them to pastures we normally save for winter.

Drought is no one's fault, unless you want to curse God, Mother Nature, the Goddess, or Whomever Else you worship. But its effects can be worsened or mitigated by our reactions. I think recent droughts on the plains, accompanied by horrible wildfires, dust storms, and heat, are nature's way of saying STOP! Stop tearing native grasses out of the ground, allowing the topsoil to blow away. Stop replacing native flora with vegetation that must be fertilized and cultivated, that does not belong here. Everywhere I see crops that cannot survive without extensive human aid and a massive expenditure of water or other costly medicines—plants like corn, wheat, gladiolus, lawns, spruce trees, and even alfalfa. Cities suck up gallons of underground water yearly in order to water fragile, decorative blossoms, to allow children to swim without getting gravel between their toes, and to provide a lawn where grownups repeatedly strike a small ball until it disappears down a hole a prairie dog didn't dig. Many cities' water rates actually still drop as water use increases. Farmers suck water from rivers to irrigate dainty crops that could not survive without this transfusion; three or four years of drought often kills alfalfa planted at great expense, but native grasses turn green and thrive with rain no matter how long they have been dry.

In answer to the water shortage, the Rapid City municipality is drilling several wells deep into the Madison Aquifer, which underlies and supplies many shallower water sources in the western half of the state. The first well to come in flowed unchecked while exploration went on. In 1980, an environmental impact statement done in Wyoming for the Environmental Transportation Systems, Inc. proposed coal slurry pipeline determined that the drilling of only ten wells into the Madison would severely restrict water supplies in both South Dakota and Wyoming. Meanwhile, the state, which issues permits for drilling, has no idea how many wells have already been bored into the Madison, and cities are not required to adhere to state statutes in such drilling. In short, we not only do not know how much water we have in the midst of this drought, we don't even know how much we're using.

I know only two families who have wells in a deep aquifer; both have had to haul water in summer for several years, and will be forced to deepen their wells in the hope of reaching water adequate for their needs. The cost of deepening the wells will be greater than the amount they paid for their houses and land a few years ago. The U.S. Geological Survey plans a water survey that may give some clue about water availability. Meanwhile, it would make sense for all drilling into the Madison to be stopped, but no government officials are farsighted enough even to restrict water use. Once the study is done—and who knows how long that might be?—it will be time to determine what our priorities really are in water use, and the fight will be on.

I thought of my father. "It's a dry country," he said, leaning on the side of the pickup as the piggyback tank emptied of water we haul daily to cattle. That summed it up. The drought is not particularly unusual, if you look at the weather from the perspective of his eighty years, which include the Dust Bowl period, still referred to as the "dirty thirties." Periods of good rains lull even farmers and ranchers who know better into planting wheat, alfalfa, and other crops that need water, but drought is historically more common to this area than what we call "normal" rainfall.

Studies indicate the last few years of drought are only a hint of what we may be facing; some parts of central North America may have been a desert in the past. The U.S. Geological Survey in South Dakota says the western part of the state, at least, is mathematically due for a drought that could make the 1930s look insignificant. The prediction is based on a 1943 tree-ring investigation in western Nebraska.[79] Harry Weakley looked at old stumps, logs in old pioneer cabins, and trees that had been preserved by drifts of windblown dust for hundreds of years. Investigating rings on these trees, mostly red cedar, helped Weakley determine the climate of western Nebraska as early as 1480. Between 1539 and 1564, many canyons in the region were filled by windblown soil, and probably even native grasses were destroyed. Tree rings for the period from 1480 to 1943 indicated that droughts lasted five to twenty-six years, and averaged 12.85 years. The time between droughts ranged from ten to thirty-seven years, and the average was 20.58 years. Similar tree-ring studies in the Black Hills of South Dakota and the Slim Buttes region in Custer National Forest in the northwestern corner of the state, gave comparable results.

A modern drought might be even more devastating, because since white people arrived on these plains, we've been plowing native grasses; their thick root systems probably held the soil together in past droughts. After the 1930s, the government encouraged shelter belt plantings to protect some land, but modern farmers bulldoze trees to expand grain fields. Carbon dioxide from automobiles and industry may be warming the earth and changing weather patterns.[80]

I can't blame prehistoric droughts on the farmer's lust for plowed soil and dainty crops, but nearly everything we have done since we arrived on these plains could make such a drought much worse. In prehistoric times, most plains ground was protected by native grasses from the worst winds and erosion; now wheat farmers regularly leave fields tilled, naked to scouring winds. Our efforts have steadily destroyed "that dark laboratory we call the soil,"[81] the source of all our food and clothing.

Water here is always scarce. Long ago we should have prohibited its waste. Homeowners who turn the sprinklers on full and let water run down the streets for hours should be arrested; it should be illegal to spray water into superheated noon air, or wash cars. In the summer of 1990, the largest nearby town finally instituted water restrictions when two weeks' worth of water was left in the town reservoir. Many residents thought the restrictions came two years too late, and weren't strong enough. The city itself ran sprinklers continuously on weekends, setting a poor example.

It is not unusual for surface water to be treated casually. South Dakota and other plains states regularly issue permits for commercial companies to pollute groundwater legally; in my opinion, we never could afford that risk, and we certainly cannot afford it now. A state government should not have the power to allow anyone to pollute water that belongs to all of us; neither should a national government. Making pollution legal does not change its power to hurt us now, or in twenty or a hundred years. Groundwater experts sometimes admit that much of their knowledge about how water moves underground is theoretical and will remain so until we devise a way to peek inside deeply buried geological formations. In other words, they don't *know* what's happening down there, and they may find out in the worst possible way: when they discover in future years the effects of pollution legalized today.

Americans frequently debate the question of who makes crucial decisions, and the citizenry regularly demands a voice. I have always believed with Thomas Jefferson that if citizens are furnished with complete and factual information, most of the time they will make decisions that are best for the greatest number. But who decides what facts are correct? How do we know when our knowledge is complete? What about people who vote without studying issues at all? I am considerably more affected by and involved in whether a housewife in town overwaters her useless lawn than in whether or not she bears a baby, but my legislators work to make abortions illegal while they neglect water laws, or restrict individuals while issuing pollution permits to businesses whose officers do not have to live with the damage they do here.

The city is an oasis of false green, busy pretending it is somewhere besides an arid prairie. Just past the last bare earth where a new housing development is being constructed, the landscape changes. The native grasses are brown and shriveled, conserving their strength and moisture in slender leaves and stems, and underground, in roots that may be huge. Aldo Leopold, in *A Sand County Almanac*, wrote of his struggle to preserve a silphium by moving it from a spot where it was endangered to his farm in Wisconsin. It had, he said, roots like "a great vertical sweet-potato. As far as I know, that Silphium root went clear through to bedrock. I got no Silphium, but I learned by what elaborate underground stratagems it contrives to weather the prairie drouths."[82]

Silphium is not found on these plains, more arid than Leopold's Wisconsin, but wild plants have adapted in similar ways. A few years ago my vegetarian cousin read that morning glory root, prized by Native Americans for its ability to hold fire, was edible; she located one and started digging. She dug, and dug, and dug; when she finally lifted her prize out of the earth, it was as big as a human head, and almost as heavy. She tried it boiled, broiled, and steamed. Since she didn't want to waste any of it after all that work, she gave hunks of it away to friends. I preferred it cooked with beef, to give it flavor. But the most surprising thing to me was that this plant, nondescript on the surface, harbored a water storage system of such magnitude. Other prairie plants, such as sage, develop roots that are extraordinary in length, not girth. Buffalo grass saves itself by weaving fine roots into a thick mat below ground; under heavy grazing it sometimes increases production.

Bulldozing native plants to create parking lots and housing developments kills them, and substitutes an entity that requires more water in a week than a native prairie system needs in a lifetime. Modern grazing practices can also kill native species here, just as Leopold noted that they killed silphium: "I saw a farmer turn his cows into a virgin prairie meadow previously used only sporadically for mowing wild hay. The cows cropped the silphium to the ground before any other plant was visibly eaten at all. One can imagine that the buffalo once had the same preference for Silphium, but he brooked no fences to confine his nibblings all summer long to one meadow. In short, the buffalo's pasturing was discontinuous, and therefore tolerable to Silphium."[83] Cattle that stay in one place too long kill native plants, and cause the soil to retain less moisture, which in turn kills more vegetation. The solution to the grazing problem, however, is fairly simple: move the cattle before they damage grass.

But in importing agriculture, we have created a culture antithetical to the natural tendencies of the plains. Vegetation here developed a team principle of species survival, distributing root systems throughout all levels of the soil; what was drawn out by one species was replaced by another. Plowing destroys that well-organized system and substitutes plants which deplete soil reserves without replacing them. Erosion is proceeding at twenty times the rate of replenishment; in 150 years, Iowa—one of the most important food-producing states—has lost one-half of its topsoil. Nationwide, agriculture uses 81 percent of the water supply; cities alone are not to blame for the coming shortages.

Some plains ranchers say native grass ought to be treated the way we treat a national historic site. I agree; by that standard we should treat water as wealth to be revered, conserved, safeguarded, but we have come too far down the road of waste to change easily. Plains dwellers are horrified at the suggestion of two New Jersey professors that the plains will become depopulated, and should be turned into the "buffalo commons." When Frank J. Popper and Deborah Epstein Popper have ventured into the plains to discuss their idea, they have faced angry crowds of residents who behave as though the professors are *causing* the current economic crisis on the plains, rather than predicting it, and suggesting a remedy. The Poppers say: "During the next generation, as a result of the largest, longest-running agricultural and environmental miscalculation in the nation's history, much of the Plains will become almost totally depopulated. The federal government should begin planning to convert vast stretches of the region to a use so old it predates the American presence—a 'Buffalo Commons' of native grass and livestock."[84]

A similar proposal, which would turn fifteen thousand square miles of east central Montana into a wildlife range called the "Big Open" has landed Bob Scott, a former rancher from Hamilton, Montana, in a large kettle of hot water. But Scott and the Poppers are merely realists who have not been blinded by chamber of commerce hype, and the shortsighted greed of plains state governments frantically trying to draw in any industry that promises jobs. This desperation for cash leaves them no time to consider the land itself, or the way it should be related to human existence. The Poppers' error is in believing that as businesses disappear and towns shrink, plains dwellers will move away. Some of us think the place is overpopulated now, and would be pleased to see fewer residents, tourists, and cars, even if the change also meant fewer doctors, grocery stores, and gas stations. I deplore the sameness of the speed strips, home of fast food and fast gas, outside every town I visit. Perhaps a smaller population would cause us to revive our plains adaptability, and more of us would learn to care for our own transportation and illnesses—just as the Native Americans and early white settlers did. If the doctor and grocery store were a hundred miles away, maybe we'd learn to husband our resources.

Plains grazing animals—bison, antelope, deer, cattle—with no interest in proving how tough they are—adapt themselves to the climate instead of the reverse. They lie on hilltops if there is a breeze, or in bottoms where there is shade, water, or greener grass to cool them a bit. During the heat of the day they chew their cud, and rise at night to graze and drink. Judging from the tracks I find at the shrinking pond below my house, smaller mammals and birds follow a similar pattern; grouse, songbirds like meadowlarks and redwing blackbirds, killdeer and curlew, raccoons, skunks, and coyotes, all visit at night.

Where we have not installed sprinklers, but been forced to leave the watering to Mother Nature, vegetation changes. Prickly pear cactus and several varieties of sagebrush have proliferated in the last few years; skeleton plants are numerous. Buffalo grass, western wheatgrass, and other native grasses are a little shorter, a bit browner than usual. But even fireweed (kochia) and creeping jenny (field bindweed) shrivel, droop, and grow stunted in this heat. Spruce trees, though they look so sturdy and beautiful in some regions, cannot survive without frequent infusions of water from human caretakers; a juniper can do well on natural water after its third or fourth year, but before that will die in drought conditions if not watered and shaded. Cottonwoods that establish themselves along intermittent creeks, or in the bottom of gullies where their roots may reach to water, can impart an illusion of cool, lush growth, but must be able to suck water with their deep roots.

Instead of developing new plants that require chemicals, machinery, and abundant water, as scientists funded by profit-seeking companies now do, we need to research plants that love drought. Some naturally occurring plants might become useful resources. Kochia, for example, has produced an average of 1.8 tons of hay per acre on seed trials, and compares favorably with alfalfa in nutritive value and palatability; some sheep selected it in preference to smooth brome and western wheatgrass. While waiting in a doctor's waiting room, I read a farm magazine, and noted a two-page advertisement for an herbicide. On one page were green drawings of thirty-six weeds likely to grow in a soybean field; in the center was the slogan, "When BASF does it ..." The next page was entirely white, representing the complete destruction of all thirty-six weeds, and the confident end of the slogan: "... it's done." Because I had nothing else to read, I studied the weeds named on the first page: foxtail, wild millet, and wild oats are grains used in bread, pudding, and soups. Pigweed and smartweed greens are edible, as are the seeds; the seeds of panicum and sunflowers can be made into flour; lambs quarter, mustard greens, and thistles are still a spring staple in our own South. Ground cherries make tasty jelly, and even the roots of quack grass can be dried and ground, and the meal made into bread. I'll admit that I can't say anything good about field bindweed, known in this area as creeping jenny; it's so pervasive that even folks who prefer not to use chemical poisons often make an exception in its case. In fact, I've challenged vegetarian friends for years to find a recipe for the stuff, theorizing that we might eat it since we can't get rid of it any other way. But nearly every other "weed" pictured has been, or could be, used for nourishing food in our starving world. Yet a farmer who has devoted acreage to soybeans is committed to eradicating all of them; an herbicide named "Landmaster" shows his attitude. Every time I watch television, I have to sit through advertisements that feature a brawny fellow in a hard hat clutching a can of poison and proclaiming how effectively it kills kochia, portrayed as an enemy of America, apple pie, motherhood, and especially the delicate little crops to which we devote our energies. I'd rather see his muscular form clad in the uniform of the Water Police, and hear him threaten to take direct action against anyone who wastes this precious resource, so intimately a part of our lives, and even our bodies.

I grew up in this dry country, but I'll never know all its secrets.

Still, I've learned enough to conserve water. I've resolved not to plant anything around my home that I can't eat. As with all resolutions, this one would be meaningless unless I cheated on it occasionally; I have a peony that belonged to my grandmother, iris bulbs a cousin brought me when I was so depressed that I wasn't sure I'd live until spring, and an evening primrose with bright yellow flowers that open in moonlight. Of course, I can eat petals from the iris and primrose; flowers have become an important part of salads in some sophisticated restaurants.

But generally, the rule guided my planting through another summer of drought. Although I have a 150-foot well that shows no sign of dropping, I believe water is too valuable to waste on inedible or purely decorative plants. That well has to supply my house, and all summer I pumped six hundred gallons of water nearly every day into a tank on the back of my pickup, then hauled it to a pasture for the cows. When the pickup came into view, the cattle would begin to move slowly through the heat waves toward the tank. One yearling steer opened his mouth, clamped his lips around the end of the hose, and got a direct transfusion of water until his sides bulged, oblivious to the cows trying to butt him out of the way.

My young windbreak trees also require large quantities of water at first, but can survive drought once they are established. Some are meant to shelter birds and wildlife—about a hundred juniper and one spruce, along with a hundred bushes, will catch blowing snow; the bushes—buffalo berry, plum, and chokecherry—will also produce fruit for the animals and for me. One winter, I walked my hillside after every light snow, noting where drifts collected behind outcroppings of limestone and native bushes. When spring came, I planted clusters of buffalo berry in several locations where the terrain will help collect snow to water them naturally, and where, in return, they will catch drifts that would block my road. I gave the bushes some protection, and drift-catching help, by building short fences out of railroad ties on their north side; the sturdy fences will also prevent people from driving over the bushes, even if they are buried in snow and a delivery truck has to find a new route to my propane tank. Other bushes will collect drifts to feed a small stockpond below my house that is a haven for ducks, killdeer, redwing blackbirds, coyotes, deer, and antelope. When watering the new plants, I even give a little squirt to two skunkbush sumacs that volunteered at the crest of the ridge, where snow lies naturally. I noticed while walking in winter that these two low bushes, no larger than a sheepdog, catch a south slope drift two feet high and thirty feet long, even in a winter with very little snow. They gave me a lot of water when that drift melted; I can give them a little during a hot, dry summer.

In order to start the shelter belt, we laid out black plastic pipe along each row, punched tiny holes in it, and inserted one-eighth-inch feeder hoses that deliver several drops of water a minute when the hydrant is on. Since the water is fed directly to the earth at the base of each tree, little is wasted, but I usually preserve even more by activating the system at night. Until I could afford to pipe water to my new trees, I filled the tank on the pickup with water every few days, and used the hose to put water near the base of each one. Where I could, I surrounded trees with pits that would hold several gallons of water; in other cases, I cut the bottoms from plastic or glass bottles and buried them neck down beside each tree. After the bottle is filled, it will continue to dribble water to the roots of the tree for a day or more.

Watering trees and bushes, food plants, and cattle would, if I had to choose, take precedence over watering a lawn, if I had a lawn. I don't; I won't water fragile green stuff that I can't eat, and that my cows would ignore for native grass. My house is surrounded by buffalo grass, big and little bluestem, threeawn grass, sideoats, and blue grama. During summer's prairie fire season, beginning at dusk, I water a circle around the house, for a green zone to slow a fire enough so I could hose down my house; otherwise these grasses don't get water unless it falls from the sky.

I no longer plant a garden. George's death reduced my need for fresh vegetables, as well as my desire to do the hard labor alone, and I knew water would be scarce. I wanted to nurture native plants—black-eyed susan, prairie coneflower, columbine, campanula, and tough ground covers like sedum—on his grave. Since the cemetery has no hydrant, I knew I would have to haul water daily to keep those plants alive. I planted a few edible herbs near my house: several varieties of mint, lemon thyme, basil, lovage, sorrel, rocquette lettuce; I thought they might trick me into enthusiasm for eating. Unfortunately, these tasty morsels seem to be as attractive to grasshoppers and other gnawing insects as they are to me. No matter how early in the morning I gather leaves, the insects have nibbled them first, but I don't mind chewing where they already have. I know only mandible marks are on those leaves: no pesticides, herbicides, or other poisons.

Last fall, I dug my gladioli bulbs for the last time, carefully brushed the dirt away, and gave them to a friend with a large garden. Don't misunderstand: I love gladiolus. I have grown them for years, carefully nurturing the tiny bulbs produced yearly like baby wolf spiders clinging to their mothers' backs. After planting all the large bulbs, I would select a spot for the tiny ones, water them faithfully, and dig them up again in the fall, knowing I would do this for several years before they grew large enough to produce blooms. I didn't mind; it was a way of looking toward the future.

And those blooms! Gladiolus have no scent but a clean, liquid fragrance I prefer to the cloying sweetness of many roses, and are infinitely tougher. In the hottest August, the stalks and blooms stand straight, and seem about to whisper a secret to staying cool and lovely no matter how sweaty and blistering the day may be.

No, it wasn't that I didn't love gladiolus. But I wanted nothing to grow on my hilltop but natural or nearly natural flowers that could survive if I couldn't water them at all. For years I have been digging up yucca, Indian turnip, bluebells, mariposa lilies, and similar wild plants, and transferring them to my hill. The recent drought years have helped in some ways; the big prickly pear cacti with their rich, silky yellow blooms centered in red have spread naturally. Ball cacti, which we call pincushion or nipple cactus—think about that—have appeared everywhere, with cone-shaped blooms of fluorescent pink. Yucca has appeared where I did not put it; the stalks covered with bell-like white blooms shoot so high that they are visible for a half-mile. Rush skeletonplant, also called prairie pink, is nearly invisible to most folks, because it has almost no leaves, only stems that appear to be swollen joints. Innocuous above ground, skeletonplant may have roots more than twenty feet in depth, long enough to withstand many dry years.

Spring brought waves of hairy beardtongue, which is a lot prettier than it sounds. The stalks stand as much as a foot tall in this area; the flowers are shaped like a throat, sometimes as large as my thumb, with a tufted stamen that results in the name, and shaded from white through lavender to a deep amethyst. Purple cone-flower, also called black sampson and, by a limber-tongued few, *Echinacea angustifolia*, is more abundant this year than I've ever seen it, which will please my cousin who gathers the roots for relief of pain, especially toothache, and uses the plant juices for burns. Before you dismiss my cousin as either an old-fashioned crank or New Age fanatic, you should know that extracts from the plant's root are used in the cough medicine that's probably in your medicine chest, and in other healing compounds. Salsify is also called goatsbeard; it most resembles a large dandelion when it goes to seed, with each seed carrying a white umbrella for wind transport. Some folks say the cooked roots taste like oysters, but I find the resemblance shaky; they remind me of parsnips: tasty when smothered in butter and spices, but watch out for the bitter, milky sap in the stems.

Unfortunately, these have been good years for Canada thistles, one of several that have proliferated. I pull these whenever I can, but it's a struggle because the roots go deep. Even if I wear gloves, I pay for my destruction, because tiny barbs work out of my fingers for several days, painful and infected. I'm probably being wasteful, because some authorities say the peeled stems may be eaten as greens, but my experience in eating thistles has taught me the labor and pain aren't justified by the flavor. I encourage a few mullein plants, as the leaves are supposed to give relief to bee stings; dried leaves were once smoked for bronchitis. The yellow flowers are supposed to make a fine hair dye; I may try it on my graying locks one day soon. I regularly gather yarrow and wrap it in scraps of cloth; its sharp, spicy smell repels moths from wool clothes. Indians used it in various tonics, and as a mild laxative, though the prairie variety may contain some alkaloidal poison.

So even most of the species I encourage because they are hardy natives also have a use, discovered by people who couldn't run to the corner drugstore for a pill suited to each ailment. Some day we may need to gather our food and medicine from hillsides like this one, and I'll be ready. I enjoy spreading these bits of knowledge, and one of my favorite recent experiences was watching a well-known Colorado newswoman and her camerawoman munching freshly peeled snakeroot. Their tongues and lips were numb within seconds; fortunately, they'd already interviewed me.

In this day of specialization, many people look with scorn upon anyone without a degree in something; and yet, ironically, scientific degrees have become so specialized that a worker may have no concept of the whole of a thing, but know only a tiny pigeon-holed fragment of it. People nurtured by test tubes in sterile labs can have little respect for the generalist, the person who has specialized in learning a lot about many aspects of life. In the same way, people used to eating in fast food joints that all look the same and serve up the same processed cardboard masquerading as meat have no respect for mere "countryside." It is just land, empty and therefore useless. Only in recent years have botanists begun to explain to the public that every piece of nature's puzzle may have a specific and vital part to play in making the world function. A synthetic is not the same as real leather; a condor raised in a cage is not a wild condor; a human who has never been in the country may not be capable of appreciating it as anything but an economic resource. But our survival may depend on knowledge that we destroy in a thoughtless quest to go faster, have more fun, make more money. Nature is precise, as well as demanding.

In 1948, before digital clocks beeped at us all day long to remind us of the passage of time, Aldo Leopold wrote about the mating dance of the woodcock:

> The show begins on the first warm evening in April at exactly 6:50 p.m. The curtain goes up one minute later each day until 1 June, when the time is 7:50. This sliding scale is dictated by vanity, the dancer demanding a

romantic light intensity of exactly 0.05 foot candles. ...
At daybreak the whole show is repeated. In early April
the final curtain falls at 5:15 a.m.; the time advances
two minutes a day until June, when the performance
closes for the year at 3:15. Why the disparity in sliding
scale? Alas, I fear that even romance tires, for it takes
only a fifth as much light to stop the sky dance at dawn
as suffices to start it at sunset.[85]

Few humans could distinguish between light ranges as subtly as the
woodcock, nor would they see the need to; no doubt a technician
could build a machine to make the distinction. But nature has
created the woodcock with such precision that he times his dance to
exact specifications registered in his tiny brain. How dare humans so
casually manipulate a system that can create such phenomena? How
can a state issue a *permit* to pollute an environment created with such
exactness? If we weren't so arrogant, we would never consider it.

Aldo Leopold lived in two worlds, teaching at a university and
living on a poor farm, land "wheated out" by the greed of previous
owners, forced to produce beyond its capabilities until it was sterile
and comparatively lifeless. Yet when he compared the diversity of
plant species on his farm to that within the urban area where he
worked, he discovered that the country was still far more varied than
the city. For ten years he kept track of plants which bloomed in both
areas, the "total visual diet," he called it. For example, in April,
fourteen species of plants bloomed in the suburbs and on the
campus where he worked, whereas twenty-six species bloomed on
his "backward farm." When he had surveyed both areas throughout
the spring and summer months for ten years, he concluded that "the
backward farmer's eye is nearly twice as well fed as the eye of the
university student or businessman." He had recorded a total of 120
species blooming in the urban setting, and 226 on the farm. He was
further discouraged by the "blindness of the populace" in failing to
see as he did in both areas, and the failure of citizens to consider
whether we can have both progress and plants.[86] In the forty-five
years since he wrote, despite the growth of environmental awareness

from an important social force to an industry, many citizens have become even more blind to the worth of the natural world. Or perhaps it would be more correct to say that as a nation we have continued to define "value" in terms of money, rather than in a philosophical sense. The motto of development today might be, "If you can't put a price on it, it's worthless."

I had tea with my neighbor Margaret one day while I was trying to clarify my thinking on these questions. She summed up all my philosophical and botanical meandering in a few words, as she is distressingly prone to do. She handed me a bag of Romaine lettuce she'd picked from her garden; the roots were still attached. "It keeps better with its roots in a jar of water," she said, smiling.

So now I have a lettuce bouquet on the counter. The upright leaves are fresh and attractive in varying shades of green; as I wash dishes I break one off now and then to nibble. I've been eying my pampered, inedible house plants. They're pretty, but I can't eat them. I have a feeling they are doomed to be replaced, just like the rest of us.

Butchering the Crippled Heifer

First:

> aim the pistol at her ear. Stand close.
> She chews slowly, eyes closed. Fire.
> She drops. Kicks. Sighs.
> Cut her throat and stand back.
> Blood bubbles and steams.

Then:

> wrap chain around each ankle,
> spread the back legs with a singletree.
> The tractor growls, lifting;
> the carcass sways.

Next:

> drive the knife point in,
> open the belly like tearing cloth,
> > the blade just under the skin.
> Cut around the empty udder.
> Don't puncture the stomach.
> Sheathe the knife and reach in.
> Wrap your bare arms around the slick guts.
> Press your face against warm flesh.
> Find the ridge of backbone; tear the
> membranes loose. Hold the anus shut;
> pull hard until the great blue stomach bag
> spills into the tub at your feet.
> Jerk the windpipe loose with a sucking moan,
> her last sound.

Straighten.
>Breathe blood-scent, clean digested grass.
>Plunge one arm into the tub, cut loose the heart,
>and squeeze the last clots out; slice the liver
>away from the green gall, put it all in cool water.
>Eat fresh liver and onions for supper,
>baked heart tomorrow.

Finally:
>Cut off the head and feet,
>haul them and the guts to the pasture:
>coyotes will feast tonight.

Then:
>pull the skin taut with one hand,
>slice the spider web of tissue with care.
>Save the tail for soup.
>Drape the hide on the fence.

Let her hang:
>sheet-wrapped, through three cool October days,
>while leaves yellow and
>coyotes howl thanksgiving.

Cut her up:
>bring one quarter at a time to the kitchen table.
>Toss bones into the big soup kettle
>to simmer, the marrow sliding out. Chunk
>scraps, pack them in canning jars.
>Cut thick red steaks, wrap them in white paper,
>labeled for the freezer.

Make meat:
>worship at a bloody altar, knives singing praises
>for the heifer's health, for flesh she made
>of hay pitched at forty below zero last winter.

Your hands are red with her blood,
slick with her fat.

You know
      where your next meal is coming from.

The Cow versus the Animal Rights Activist

I'm a rancher; beef cattle provide most of my money and food. I *like* cows; I've had a warm partnership with them for thirty-five years. I admire a cow's instincts, and suspect her of having a sense of humor, as well as of knowing more than we think. I envy her adaptation to the arid plains, and her apparent serenity in emergencies.

I also love to cut into a tender sirloin steak with a hint of pink in the center, and dip each bite into the luscious brown juice surrounding the potatoes on my plate. I relish each mouthful, thinking dreamily of the cow whose flesh I'm eating; I remember when she was born, how she became crippled so that her destiny became the dark freezer in my basement rather than the meat department of a brightly lighted supermarket. I have always considered that the relationship between me and my cattle was a little like a good marriage, with good days and bad days, but considerable satisfaction on both sides.

Suddenly my personal paradox has frightening possibilities, because animal rights activists are declaring in sizeable headlines that it is not possible to love animals and also kill them. Anyone who says so, they declare, is vicious, sadistic, and untrustworthy. Some extremists declare that doing anything at all with an animal but letting it follow its normal patterns is immoral, and others declare that we have no right to experiment with animals even to save human lives. Ranchers are targets because we confine cattle in pastures, brand them with hot irons, and cut sections out of their ears to show ownership. Those, say the activists, are the actions of exploiters, unfit to be environmentalists or associate with your daughter. Activists have destroyed research labs to free the animals, sometimes loosing dangerous bacteria. Some deer and bison lovers follow hunters into the woods, shouting to frighten the game. One screaming activist repeatedly whacked and poked a bison hunter with the point of a ski pole; the hunter, a model of nonviolence, neither screamed back nor made threatening gestures with his Rolling Block .45-70, capable of decimating an activist with one shot.[87] In a middle-sized town near our ranch, activists scream obscenities and spit on women in fur coats. At a National Cattlemen's Association meeting, a speaker warned ranchers that new employees may work undercover for animal rights groups. An auction yard in Dixon, California, and a meatpacking plant in San Jose were torched by arsonists, and an unlit Molotov cocktail lobbed into the offices of the California Cattlemen's Association.[88] A popular country singer, k.d. lang, was part of a "Meat Stinks" campaign supported by People for the Ethical Treatment of Animals, a group that opposes using animals "other than for companionship."[89] Radio and television stations in beef-producing areas, including South Dakota, promptly stopped playing all of lang's records.[90] I was disappointed; watching lang croon sweet nothings into the ear of a dairy cow—in no danger of being eaten because she is too valuable as a milk factory, and tough as guitar strings—was the highlight of my television watching.

Her problem, and the difficulty of the ski pole–wielding activist confronting the bison hunter, is lack of information. The beef cattle industry has three major phases. First, farmers and ranchers own basic herds and produce breeding cattle, or yearlings sold as feeders. They keep the breeding cattle, and sell the yearlings at a sale market where the price is determined by supply and demand, and by bidders. When the ranchers sell, they have no opportunity to add costs of materials to the product, passing expenses on to the consumer as most businesses do. Ranchers take the price offered on sale day, or take the cattle home—where they will require more care, more expense.

The second phase of the beef cattle industry consists of stocker operators whose pastures put additional weight on feeder cattle before they enter feedlots, the third phase. Confined in muddy, stinking feedlots, cattle consume huge quantities of pesticide-laced grain designed to make the meat fat enough for consumer preference, and produce immense amounts of polluted runoff. The dangers posed to humans by the chemicals in both the meat and runoff have drawn environmentalists' attention to the cattle industry—but they are attacking the wrong end of production. Feedlots are generally operated by corporations that control feeding, butchering, and in some cases supermarket sales of meat, grain, and associated products. In 1988, three companies—Iowa Beef Packing (IBP, owned by Occidental Petroleum), ConAgra, and Excel (Cargill)—accounted for 70 percent of all fed cattle slaughtered in the United States. These monopolies, which also control a considerable amount of the nation's grain, flour, pork, egg, and poultry production, do pass costs to the consumers, hiking prices far above what ranchers get for their labor.[91] But enormous corporations are tough to find and difficult to move; it's easier to attack individual hunters and ranchers.

I'm afraid that one day I'll be sweating and swearing in the corral, struggling to brand calves twice my weight, and suddenly find I'm surrounded by people with no sense of humor who have come to "liberate" my cows.

I'd like to discourage that kind of behavior, partly because some ranchers are impatient and armed, and partly because it's based on lack of information. Unchecked ignorance and paranoia can escalate misunderstandings to bloodshed. And some of my cows, unaccustomed to noise and rudeness, might kick the strangers, who would sue me, not the cows.

I recognize the difficulty many people face in reconciling their love of animals with their love of meat, but I believe the problem is increasing because we are getting further from the realities of human existence. As we developed our large brain, we also built a complicated set of desires that seems to imply that enough wealth will allow us to sit still. We want our food to be easily obtainable; now that we no longer have to run it down and beat it to death, many of us buy it precooked. When someone markets predigested dinners, there will be buyers. But many of us will continue to wear leather shoes, lust after leather skirts and jackets and leather upholstery on our car seats, and relish a good steak or hamburger. As long as humans have such desires but remain unwilling or unable to slaughter and skin the animals that can satisfy them, ranchers will be needed.

In defense, beef industry representatives say a pregnant woman produces four hundred thousand times as much estrogen every day as she would get from the average serving of beef injected with growth-inducing hormones.[92] I've spent my life doing hard physical labor while eating organically raised cattle, so I understand the healthy properties of red meat, and I despair at the perception among many Americans that this tasty stuff isn't good for them. I am part of an industry that requires me to donate one dollar from each animal sold to the Beef Check-Off plan, which promotes the facts about eating beef and health—a group defense instituted, reluctantly, by cattle ranchers in response to misinformation spread by antibeef activists. In part, this idea comes from paranoia about cholesterol and growth hormones; in part, it's a result of government-subsidized campaigns by producers of other foods. In many countries, the beef I eat in a year would make a family wealthy, but I am frustrated by being unable to sell directly to consumers beef raised on grass that is the natural product of my land.

Like most ranchers, I work more closely with cows than any animal rights activist I've ever met. I kneel in steaming cow manure and hot urine while talking kindly to a cow and urging a calf from her birth canal. I must brand calves so they won't stray or be stolen; castrate bulls to make them edible steers and protect bloodlines. I've cut cows' throats, helped gut and skin them, and canned every edible part of them for my family's use; in the process I've gained a deep appreciation for what killing our own meat can mean to humans. Because of this close involvement with the lives of cows, I feel I have worked hard for the right to eat their flesh. My relationship with cows is intimate, balanced—the cow is capable of killing or injuring me—and demands the most complete responsibility from the human half of the equation. The relationship is reviewed by both parties almost daily, and its implications carefully considered at least by the human half. Who knows what the cows are thinking?

Animal rights activists seem to me guilty of simplistic thinking and tunnel vision, although I envy people who forswear *all* killing and eating of flesh; I believe they have an easier road than those of us who try to strike a balance between exploitation and love. Similarly, I don't consider strolling along behind a fur-wearing woman screaming epithets, or shooting a cow, or burning a packing plant, to be meaningful activism; such actions are too simplistic, and too close to terrorism. During the easy environmentalism of the 1960s, one could lie on the lawn smoking grass on "Gentle Thursdays," sing "We Shall Overcome" and shout "No More War," and go back to class, one's pacifist duty done for the week. During that period, a few hard-working environmentalists passed strict laws which gave us a sense of power, but were sometimes as narrow and poorly thought out as the actions behind the corporate greed that made them necessary.

All of us—ranchers, environmentalists, and animal rights activists—if we expect to be taken seriously, should put as much work into defining and achieving realistic, fair goals as ranchers spend trying to keep cows alive. Few of us are born with that kind of dedication; we have to develop an interest in detail, a respect for our fellow animals—even Democrats, feminists, and snail darters—and an understanding of our responsibilities to the whole spectrum of life on the planet. What E. B. White wrote nearly sixty years ago is still true:

> Before you can be an internationalist you have first to be a naturalist and feel the ground under you making a whole circle. It is easier for a man to be loyal to his club than to his planet; the by-laws are shorter, and he is personally acquainted with the other members.

> The effect of any organization of a social and
> brotherly nature is to strengthen rather than to dimin-
> ish the lines which divide people into classes; the effect
> of states and nations is the same, and eventually these
> lines will have to be softened, these powers will have to
> be generalized. It is written on the wall that this is so.
> I'm not inventing it, I'm just copying it off the wall.[93]

Statistics from a few years ago declared that the average
American ate fourteen cows in a lifetime, but consumption will drop
to a twenty-five-year low in 1990 as hysterical and ill-informed folks
screech about the dangers of beef.[94] I've eaten more than my share
in an effort to make up for vegetarian relatives and friends. When I
calculated this my own family consisted of my parents, and my
husband and me; we would butcher two animals, usually heifers, per
year. Assuming each of us ate about one-fourth of each animal, I was
eating an entire cow every four years, which means I've gobbled
upwards of ten so far. If I live to be eighty, as I hope to do, I'll have
eaten at least twenty of my own herd, not to mention the beef I eat
in restaurants when I'm upholding the honor and economy of
ranchers while surrounded by midwesterners lying about how good
the frozen fish tastes. I am willing to take responsibility for the
deaths of those twenty bovines, because I've saved the lives of many
more than that.

Vegetarians may whittle the number of beefeaters down, but
I'm confident beef will remain part of the American diet. Ranchers
are learning to produce lean meat; I believe we will soon begin to
move away from the dangerous chemicals and growth hormones
we've been talked into using in order to raise productivity above
sensible limits. At the same time, we are becoming aware of growing
criticism of the damage cattle do to public lands by poorly controlled
grazing. Little has been done, however, to control the meat and
grain monopolies which will eventually control our food supplies
and determine grocery prices.

It's a popular pastime now to debunk the myth of the
independent cowboy and the cattle baron, and rightly so in many

ways. Although there's truth to the legends, they were popularized and distorted by dime novels and bad movies; and some cow folk even bought their own advertising campaign or fantasy, and played their roles more eagerly than pulp heroes. They deserve to be reminded of reality.

But simply pronouncing the death of the age of the cattle baron and cowboy is too simple. Sure, those men—and their womenfolk—treated the West as if it was their kingdom. They battled its hardships, "civilized" it as they thought best—because they were given a challenge to do so by the wisest spirits of their age. Where I live was "the Great American Desert," shunned by all but the hardiest explorers. Later, the thinkers in their comfy New England offices decided that "rain follows the plow," and all that was needed to make the desert bloom were a few hardy souls to build claim shanties and plow to the horizon. The New England philosophers had no idea what difficult conditions westerners faced, but the westerners went right on working until they controlled everything but the weather.

We now see their errors, but we might have been guilty of the same actions, now seen as abuse, had we been cattle barons in those days. And some changes have been made not out of lack of concern, but through economic necessity. Cowboys, paid "forty a month and found," used to ride the range constantly, moving cattle around so that grazing was spread evenly over a wide area. Today workers who might once have become cowboys and cowgirls are instead making big wages in a city, and many ranchers operate alone, or assisted only by their smaller number of children or seasonal help. They have tried to adapt the advice given to farmers by agricultural experts within the government to invest more money, get big, and become efficient, but it didn't work as well on mobile cattle as on rows of corn; it didn't work on corn either, but that's another story, and Wes Jackson is telling it in his sustainable agriculture research at The Land Institute.[95]

This generation's heroes are people who work to save our environment: the dead Saint Ed Abbey, Wendell Berry, Wes Jackson, Annie Dillard, Ann Zwinger, Gary Snyder, Barry Lopez, Gretel

Ehrlich, Bil Gilbert, Kim Stafford, and other writers who contemplate humanity and nature. Some have attained almost mythical stature themselves, and we all try to learn from and imitate them. We believe, fervently, that they are right; those old ranchers believed in Manifest Destiny and the American Way just as passionately. What if we're wrong again?

Instead of blaming ranchers and farmers for doing what they were told to do, environmentalists need to show us what's wrong with the way we graze cattle, if they know. Most of the complainers have never been personally introduced to a cow, have no clear idea what's wrong with her grazing habits, and wouldn't know a good stand of native grass if they were lying in it reciting poetry or reading Abbey. They're willing to take someone else's word—just as the ranchers took the government's word for how to use the land. Too many environmentalists condemn without knowledge. None of the rhetoric changes the fact that the grasslands are in trouble, and only the people who own the land are likely to resolve the problems.

When I left the ranch, bound for a life of comfortable academic superiority in some ivory tower, I cared considerably less about cows than I do now, though I already knew more than the average American about the brutal facts of bovine life. Living beside a packing plant for a few months made a temporary vegetarian out of me. I saw cows unloaded daily, heard the thud as the knacker's maul struck their foreheads, the bawl of pain as they were swung, only stunned, off their hooves by a hook thrust into an ankle. Sometimes, I could hear the bubbling, choking screech cut short as a worker finally opened a steer's throat. My cat grew sleek dragging home fleshy bones larger than he was, and I watched smugly when a steer escaped and ran through the streets, ineffectually pursued by a police force with little experience in cattle management. But as soon as I moved back to South Dakota, where I look out on my walking larder through every window, I went back to eating meat without hesitation. I earn every mouthful. The outmoded butchering practices used in packing plants have been changed; animals are killed with a gun, rather than stunned, before butchering begins. Other changes in the beef industry show increased awareness of public scrutiny.

When I returned to the ranch, I had shed some of the narrow attitudes with which I grew up, and I became involved in the complicated process of keeping a cow alive. I've learned, but I've remained a part of a wider world. Critics think ranch men read only *Farm Journal* and their wives do nothing but cook and raise children, but many are college graduates, and even those who aren't read more widely than their ancestors did. They also watch television; the rest of the world is no longer distant and inaccessible to them. They are informed about conditions in the "outer" world, and aware that most consumers know little about ranching or the food processing industry. For example, while farmers and ranchers know a good deal about what happens to their products—meat, grains, hay—when these leave the land, many folks who buy those products or by-products neatly wrapped in polyethylene haven't a clue about their production, and don't want to. Knowing the origins of our food and frivolities helps us make sensible choices about what we really want; in some cases, the sacrifice is not worth the benefit. When I shop for groceries, I carry a booklet that categorizes products by how socially responsible the producer is.[96] I avoid products if the Council on Economic Priorities reports no reductions in animal testing by those companies, and no company contributions toward alternative research. On the other hand, I wouldn't hesitate to use any compatible animal heart to save the life of a child. But if the child was cocaine-addicted in the womb, and the operation was at taxpayers' expense, I could not support it.

Cattle have been domesticated for centuries, and belong in a separate category from animals bred for laboratory tests, and from wildlife; we are not likely to stop eating and managing cattle herds, nor should we. Wild cattle herds would be hardly more aesthetically satisfying than tame ones, as Indians have discovered while dodging sacred cows. A poorly managed herd of cattle can be as repugnant as Edward Abbey insisted, but that's the fault of the human manager, not the cows. With adequate feed and water and space to move while grazing selectively, a herd of cattle can be at least as acceptable in polite society as the average dog or child. Cattle do attract flies; before poisonous sprays and other costly forms of fly control existed, we built "oilers," slinging old feed sacks on a wire between two posts. We poured used crankcase oil on the cloth (recycling!) and cows rubbed oil on their bodies to discourage flies and lice. When the chemical companies noticed us using a product we didn't buy, they developed spray, injections, and fly-killing ear tags.

But most folks don't know this, because they spend more time with domesticated cats and dogs, and half-savage children, than with cows; and it is the activities that result from ignorance that bother me. Since I have become moderately well known as an articulate ranch woman, I've been questioned several times about animal rights.

What do I think of proposed laws to make branding illegal, for example? My reply: the folks who pass that law can find and return or replace the stolen cattle, catch and prosecute the thieves, and pay the costs of the confusion and crime. Branding does hurt, but it places a permanent mark on a cow, so even if she's illegally butchered, an owner has some chance of proving it. No other method is as useful, and I'll consider another method of marking my cattle when we stop licensing cars to identify them and prevent their theft. Every few years, someone suggests that acid brands are more merciful; I'd like that idea tested on the folks who suggest it: which hurts most, a burn with a hot iron, or an acid burn? Even if they are less painful, acid brands might not be enough; local old-timers talk about the days when government agencies used them. Enterprising cowboys sometimes roped the cows, smeared axle grease on the brands to neutralize the acid, turned the cows out until the hair grew back, and a few months later branded cows that appeared ownerless. Speaking of pain, what about breeds of dogs—Boxers, Doberman Pinschers, Schnauzers—not considered attractive unless their ears and tails are chopped off? Poodles, among the most widely popular dog breeds, just have their tails trimmed, though dogs with extremities intact are now allowed in some shows. What about the thousands of pets killed each year because owners couldn't be bothered with them any longer? Is it more merciful to keep a wild predator like a cat confined to an apartment for its entire life than to brand a cow once? So-called "pet" cats slaughter wild songbirds by the millions in most cities, but few animal rights activists picket pet owners. Why do suburbanites let their dogs run loose to chase and kill wildlife and calves?

Today's cattle live very well compared to their ancestors, perhaps too well for the health of the species; some old breeds are dying out. We may need their genetic diversity in coming years, if we continue to breed cattle for beef and milk production instead of their ability to survive, coddling them with medications until they can no longer resist disease. The average calf is observed and protected from predators at birth, and quickly vaccinated against many diseases. When necessary operations like branding, ear-marking, castration, and dehorning occur, they are done with sterile equipment, supplemented with healing sprays to keep flies and maggots from the wounds. In the wild, only the fittest animals would survive a tough winter; modern cattle operators carefully control herd feed throughout the year for maximum gain, and maximum protection of pasture. Sick, weak, crippled, or otherwise unfit animals are culled from the herd, instead of being allowed to suffer and pass on their genes and illnesses. Ranchers who habitually abuse their cattle damage their own income and endanger them-selves, both indirectly—by hurting their own profits—and directly; an abused or frightened cow can be a dangerous proposition.

As the rancher's awareness of chemical dangers increases, and as costs climb, some of us are realizing that we could raise organic, lean beef with less effort and expense, with the help of a real demand in the market from an informed public. Some ranchers already nervous about growth hormone implants would give them up if the steers didn't gain; heavier steers mean more income. As I write this, several tuna-packing companies have finally instituted policies that will make the killing of dolphins unprofitable. If the public demands chemical-free beef, it will be produced; ideally, South Dakota could encourage the sale of cattle straight from the organic grass of our pastures to the hungry cus-tomer—rather than selling the land for garbage dumps. I have heard of no state-sponsored efforts to keep native grass unplowed and grazed by cows for organic beef. If state officials put half the energy and cash spent on tourism into promoting the state's ranchers—whose product can keep the land relatively undamaged—we might discover a strong demand for grass-fed beef. And why not give tourists the chance to visit real, working ranches?

So if you like beef but don't like chemicals, cholesterol, or high food prices, get acquainted with a rancher who raises cattle on grass. Get a few friends together, buy a fat young "beef," and butcher it yourself—or ask a hunter to help. If one person does it, you'll just be a well-fed oddity. If two people do it, or five, it might become a movement. Think of it! Ranchers and beef eaters, joining together to beat chemical companies and monopolies; why, it's the stuff democracy is made of.

I'll say it again: I love cows, and consider my care and understanding of them superior to the treatment they'd get at the hands of the average animal rights activist.

Bridges

—*for Jerry, and for Thomas Telfor,*
builders of bridges

The first time you swerved to the roadside,
I thought you'd forgotten that in Scotland,
we had to drive on the left side of the road.
You were looking at a stone bridge,
double arches spanning the end of a loch,
aiming your camera at its stone curves.
I was more interested in the rainbow,
one multicolored vault over two in aged gray stone.

Your work is linking steel and concrete
to span wild rivers and dry washes
on Wyoming prairies;
mine is fitting words into stories.
I hadn't known you'd marvel at ancient bridges
just as I study poems by the masters.
My eye was tuned to standing stones,
the shape of poems waiting in the landscape,
yours to bridges,
but we began to see each other's dreams.

Once, you walked without pause onto a thin stone curve
hung two hundred years ago across a river
that howled for blood and bone.
After one cry, I held my breath;

you knew how true those men of your trade and art
fit key stones together, suspending granite
to carry coaches racing north and south
between kingdoms at war.

Suddenly I saw bridges everywhere.
I'd never noticed them before,
though one kind or another
upholds everything we do.
When my road swept across a bridge,
my eye was on a distant mountain;
when I walked trusting over creeks,
or the sea's mouth, I felt its teeth;
its fetid tongue left salt on my lips.
But I never looked down.
I never paused at the brink to study what
would hold me up, make my road smooth,
give me the illusion it was all one level path.

As quick as the chasm is bridged,
we forget how hard it was to toil
down one side and up the other,
clutching desperately at slick rock.
On the last day, we paused by a stream
to admire, together, an eight-arched viaduct.
Once it carried railroad cars
to the lead mines in the mountains,
a worker's job, requiring granite bones, steel muscles;
strength, not loveliness. Still,
the weight flew in graceful curves
from one pier to the next,
like a ball tossed by children,
or the metaphor that sometimes bounces
into the middle of a poem.

This causeway of words connects us,

builders of bridges;
ospreys fly beneath it,
a river churns and boils.

Work Boots and
the Sustainable Universe

In April of 1989, I bought a new pair of Red Wing boots to wear for ranch work. I paid $135, and gulped a little as I wrote the check. It seemed like a lot of money, but I know it is important to keep my feet comfortable and healthy; they are my primary form of transportation around the ranch. They don't depend on foreign oil; they start even in the coldest weather.

I've been thinking about those boots. When I returned to the ranch after my divorce, I was concerned about saving money, and bought work boots at a discount store. Before long my feet hurt, and the boots were run over and full of holes; I walked with a halting gait. My husband George, who always had hard-to-fit feet, insisted I buy good boots, and introduced me to Red Wings. (This is the only commercial message which will appear, and no one could pay me enough to say this if it weren't true.)

With George's help, I bought a pair of boots identical to the ones I wrote the check for a few days ago. They had a relatively smooth sole, so I wouldn't collect too much manure and mud. They laced in front, and the ankles were high, both as protection from rattlesnake bites, and because my ankles are weak from repeated injury. In 1974, that pair of boots cost me sixty-five dollars.

By 1981, the leather was getting so thin over my bunions that cactus spines penetrated my foot. I went to the Red Wing store, where my measurements were on file, and bought an identical pair for eighty-three dollars. That pair lasted until I bought the most recent ones, in 1989.

That's a total of $282 for boots in fifteen years. I wear those boots most days of the year, doing every kind of labor except horseback riding; my riding boots are of mule hide, cost $110, and are a different story entirely. This means that the boots I wear for work have cost me an average of $18.80 a year. Rattlesnakes have struck at me, cacti have stabbed me, but my feet are in pretty good health, and much of the credit is due to those boots. My feet are, excuse me, the foundation of my work on the ranch; if they cause me pain, everything I do is more difficult. It pleases me that they are made of cowhide, and treated with natural oils, so the cows I do my work for are repaying me with every step I take.

I would be even happier if I could skin a cow that had died naturally and make my boots from her hide, but I haven't the necessary skills, nor do I wish to devote to this the time required to learn them. Instead, I barter money earned from the sale of those cows. My boots sustain my feet; the cows sustain me; I sustain the cows; the circle of responsibility is complete.

Responsibility means, at the very least, sustainability. No functioning system in the natural world can spend more than it makes, can use more than it creates. Not without cheating someone, and ultimately itself. When a natural system goes temporarily consumption mad, it soon dies, or readjusts itself. This nation's trillion-dollar debt is the most visible symbol of nearly two centuries of malfunctioning. The fact that the system has struggled along for so many human generations—an eyeblink in the real time of the world, the time by which other organisms are judged—only means we had a huge reservoir of resources. We have wasted more of them than any other nation in history. Everyone has a favorite statistic on fuel efficiency, garbage, or water.

Now we have an immense and growing deficit in cash and in resources, but our history of abundance blinds us to the chasm of starvation ahead. If we instantly and unanimously begin to be responsible, to adhere to the moral and economic true path, making each endeavor prove its sustainability, we may save most of our pathetic human lives. But no matter what we do, I believe many of us will die—are dying now—because of our irresponsibility.

Some of us are trying; some of us recycle our aluminum, bicycle to work, grow some of our own food. When we hear news of multimillion-gallon oil spills, we're understandably discouraged because we know many individuals, as well as governments and multinational corporations blinded by greed, will go on spoiling and spending until the crisis occurs. Then we will all have to sacrifice to survive.

It's convenient and popular to blame governments and big companies, and certainly both are guilty of behavior toward the environment ranging from insensitive to downright criminal. We need stronger laws to force pollution control. Activists have already forced a lot of changes on the corporate culprits; individuals can be harder to convince or control. Many toxic wastes don't come from factories and big business, and we shouldn't be blaming them entirely, any more than we should expect them to clean up the whole mess for us. Household products may actually produce more toxic waste than industrial pollution; though each of us may contribute only a small amount, the accumulation in a landfill may result in major pollution. For example, fingernail polish often contains several chemicals the Environmental Protection Agency (EPA) calls potentially harmful; "if you bought your fingernail polish in a 55-gallon drum, you could not legally throw the empty drum into a landfill . . . as many as 350,000 nail-polish bottles find their way into Tucson [Arizona] landfills every year. Along with these are other potent chemicals contained in such items as nail-polish remover, batteries, and oven cleaner."[97] Mercury, contained in batteries, paints, dyes, electric and electronic devices like silent light switches, fluorescent lights, plastics, pharmaceuticals, pesticides, pastes, glues, and adhesives, can damage the human central nervous system, impair mental development, and damage kidneys, even at low exposure. When items containing it are landfilled, mercury escapes slowly into the soil and groundwater.[98] Our landfills are in trouble not so much because of nonbiodegradable products as from the huge amounts of waste we throw away—sixty-nine pounds per person more than we threw away in 1980, according to the U.S. Environmental Protection Agency. The automobiles Americans drive everywhere contribute more to global warming than hard-to-spell newsmakers like chlorofluorocarbons (CFCs); 180 million of the 500 million vehicles on earth are right here in the United States. More than 65 percent of water pollution comes not from industrial giants but from individual use: chemicals washed off lawns and fields, gunk that runs down sinks.[99] Each one of us is contributing to global pollution, and each of us needs to behave more responsibly to control it, to make our lives part of sustaining the earth instead of destroying it.

It is ironic that the poor and weak, many of them living so close to starvation that they can't waste resources, will suffer most when the effects of pollution begin cutting into food and water supplies, while the rich, who have encouraged and mandated waste, will be able to observe the massacre from the high windows of the palaces built on the bones of the dying. The deadly barb in the irony is that people closer to the earth, who have scratched out a bare living on naked soil, have learned to survive on very little indeed. When the greedy and rich are cut off from the things they call "necessary," when their machines do not work, when water does not flow at the twist of a handle, when their food must be killed with their bare hands or dug from the unyielding earth, then they will begin to suffer, and to die very quickly, because they do not know how to function without their gadgets. The poor will not have time to laugh.

Forgive me if this sounds like the plot of a science fiction novel you've read several times. That does not mean it is not true.

Sustainability is the only long-term answer, in major developments as in minor ones. The government can't do it all, even if it were the most uncorrupt, ideal, and environmentally sensitive government imaginable, which of course it isn't. Pretend this is a war, and we are losing; this is, in fact, the case.[100] As a beginning, as a strategy simply to ensure your survival until tomorrow morning, take responsibility for what is yours.

First, take stock. What do you really need to survive? Water, food, shelter, clothing; we probably need love, too, but we can last longer without it than we can without water. Where does your water come from? How much is there? Where would you get it if it didn't run out of the kitchen faucet? Is the nearest lake or creek clean enough to drink? Why not? What is in it? How did it get there? How much of the water pollution did your household provide? How much water do you use a day? Can you use less? Even these questions, if you live in a water-wasting city, can be complex and require hours of study. Demand the answers of the officials who have been elected on their promise to be responsible; make them truly responsible.

You might choose to plant a garden instead of a wasteful lawn, to dig clams, eat fried ants, or kill and butcher a deer. Providing one's own food makes clearer the process required. Taking charge on shelter is a tough demand; most of us aren't carpenters. But there is burgeoning literature on determining how efficient your home is, and making it more so. Clothing also raises difficulties in this appearance-conscious society. Cotton is popular among environmentalists, but what are the consequences of raising cotton? Do government subsidies, herbicides, and pesticides mean growing cotton is worse than making polyester? Where does your clothing originate? Do you own more than you really need?

Challenge yourself, your church members, your sewing circle, bingo club, Rotary, children, or any other group to have waste-free days, to get through a day without using anything that isn't biodegradable. Alternatively, collect the trash you generate in a single day and look it over; how much is recyclable? Get the message to elected officials. Rate eating establishments and other businesses by the amount of trash they generate, don't patronize the ones that waste, and let them know why they are losing your business. Write letters to the editor. Urge your town or county to charge for trash by amount and weight; expense is always a great deterrent. Buy products with a minimum of packaging, or give unnecessary packaging back to the store manager and request products that aren't overpackaged. Some activists have been known to collect an entire cart full of merchandise that is wastefully packaged and wheel it to the manager's office, where they explain their objections, and leave the cart for senior personnel to contemplate. Use humor, not anger, wherever possible.

We've wasted time and billions of words talking, debating,

lobbying; we know what to do, and we know the cost if we don't. No more conferences, no more seminars, no more fact-finding commissions, no more easing out of our libidinous ways with gas and styrofoam, no quarter. Demand laws that will stop pollution, with real punishment for those who ignore them. Maybe the presidents of oil companies which fail to provide double-hulled tankers and responsible captains should have to lick the oil off the beaches. We're all to blame for buying gas hog cars, but we know enough about how economical a car can be to mandate good mileage and safe design by law. When our sons and daughters come home in body bags because we are wasting oil, perhaps we will realize how much it is really costing us. For too long we have taken refuge in the lie of individual powerlessness. If we vote, we can do a great deal. Congressmen assume that each letter they receive represents the thinking of ten thousand people. Elected officials respond when enough citizens scream loudly enough; vote them out of office if they don't respond.

My point is not to tell you *how* to be responsible, but to urge you to think, think out each step in the process of providing your necessities, and be inventive and tough on yourself and others to reach sustainability. How much do your work boots—your "necessities"—cost you? How much do they cost the earth?

Beef Eater

I have been eating beef hearts
all my life.
I split the smooth maroon shape
lengthwise,
open it like a diagram, chambers exposed.
I cut tough white membranes off valves,
slice onions over the heart,
float it in water,
boil it tender.
I chop prunes, apricots, mushrooms
to mix with dry bread,
sage from the hillside.
I pack the crevices full,
nail the heart together,
weave string around the nails.

Gently,
I lift the full heart
between my hands,
place it in the pan
with its own blood, fat, juices.
I roast that heart
at three hundred fifty degrees
for an hour or two.
Often I dip pan juices,
pour them lovingly over the meat.

When I open the oven,
the heart throbs
in its own golden fat.

I thicken the gravy with flour,
place the heart with love
on my Grandmother's ironstone platter,
slice it evenly from the small end;
pour gravy over it all,
smile as I carry it to the table.

My friends have begun to notice my placid air,
which they mistake for serenity.
Yesterday a man remarked on my large brown eyes,
my long eyelashes,
my easy walk.

I switched my tail at him
as if he were a fly,
paced
deliberately
away.

Endnotes

1. Gina Bellafonte, "Toxic Emissions," *Garbage*, September/October 1989, p. 15.
2. Patricia Summerside, "Education Money Can't Buy," *Reader's Digest*, July 1990, pp. 79–81; condensed from *Policy Review*, Winter 1990 (214 Massachusetts Ave., N.E., Washington, DC, 20002).
3. Reginald and Gladys Laubin, *The Indian Tipi: Its History, Construction and Use* (New York: Ballantine Books, 1957), p. 25. This is the best source of information about tipi life, referred to by most buckskinners, who keep it hidden in the lodge, as "the book."
4. The best way to become educated to buckskinning is by reading one of several magazines published by muzzle-loading enthusiasts, and to find a local group to help you learn. Ask about them at gun shops.
5. Phenylbutazone, an anti-inflammatory, usually referred to as "bute" or "horse bute" by those familiar with it. Not recommended for humans.
6. Stan Steiner, *The Ranchers: A Book of Generations* (New York: Alfred A. Knopf, 1980), p. 97.
7. Aldo Leopold, *A Sand County Almanac and Sketches Here and There* (New York: Oxford University Press, 1949), p. 158. First published 1949.
8. James Willwerth, "Not Your Average Dude Ranch," *Time*, June 11, 1990, p. 67.
9. Steiner, *The Ranchers*, p. 227.
10. *Congressional Record—Senate*, May 4, 1989, p. S 4932.
11. *Rapid City Journal*, April 10, 1991, p. A1. Elmer Kelton, *The Good Old Boys* (Garden City, N.Y.: Doubleday & Co., 1978), p. 24.
12. Mike Royko, "Yuppie dudes favor workingman's duds," *Rapid City Journal*, February 13, 1991.
13. John P. Wiley, Jr., "Phenomena, comment, and notes," *Smithsonian*, October 1988, pp. 23–28.
14. S. Boyd Eaton, Marjorie Shostak, Melvin Konner, *The Paleolithic Prescription* (New York: Harper & Row, 1988).
15. Wendell Berry, "Six Agricultural Fallacies," in *Home Economics* (San Francisco: North Point Press, 1987), p. 124.
16. *Ibid.*
17. Stephen Strauss, *Technology Review*, April 1987, pp. 11–12.

18. Frederick Manfred, *Lord Grizzly* (New York: New American Library, 1964), p. 60.
19. *Ibid.*
20. *Ibid.*, p. 160.
21. *Ibid.*, p. 143.
22. John G. Neihardt, *A Cycle of the West* (Lincoln: University of Nebraska Press, 1961), p. 182. First published 1949, Macmillan.
23. Frederick Manfred, *Conquering Horse* (New York: New American Library, 1959), p. 94.
24. *Ibid.*
25. *Ibid.*, p. 99.
26. Manfred, *Lord Grizzly*, p. 162.
27. Neihardt, *A Cycle of the West*, p. 179.
28. Stephen P. Maran, "When all hell breaks loose on the Sun, astronomers scramble to understand," *Smithsonian*, March 1990, p. 33, also discussed the effects of these flares.
29. Reinhold Niebuhr, "The Serenity Prayer," *Familiar Quotations*, John Bartlett, Fifteenth and 125th Anniversary edition, Emily Morison Beck, ed. (Boston: Little, Brown and Co., 1980), p. 823.
30. Gary Paul Nabhan, "The Evolution of a Naturalist: Finding the Wild Thread," *Petroglyph*, vol. 2, no. 1, Spring 1990, pp. 5–7.
31. Henry David Thoreau, "January 3, 1853," *H. D. Thoreau: A Writer's Journal*, ed. Laurence Stapleton (New York: Dover, 1960), p. 152; reprinted in *Of Discovery and Destiny*, ed. Robert C. Baron and Elizabeth Darby Junkin (Golden, Colo.: Fulcrum, Inc., 1986), p. 149.
32. *The Militant*, February 10, 1989, quoted in *Utne Reader*, March/April 1990, p. 26.
33. Wendell Berry, "Higher Education and Home Defense," *Home Economics*, p. 50.
34. Andrè Voisin, *Grass Productivity*, trans. by Catherine T. M. Herriot (Washington, D.C.: Island Press, 1988), pp. 123–8, 226–7.
35. All contributions to The Land Institute, 2440 E. Water Well Rd., Salina, KS 67401, are tax deductible, the newsletter is free, and stipends are available to help students of sustainable agriculture. Jackson's work was the subject of "Back to Eden," Evan Eisenberg, *The Atlantic Monthly*, November 1989, pp. 57–89; a *Smithsonian* Earth Day profile in April 1990, an article in *Audubon*, November 1989, and he was included in *Life* magazine's September 1990 issue on the one hundred most important people of the past century. The Land Institute's symposium "The Marriage of Ecology and Agriculture" in October of 1989 generated follow-up articles in the *Washington Post*, the *Los Angeles Times*, the *New York Times*, and numerous regional publications.
36. Wendell Berry, *Farming: A Handbook* (New York: Harcourt Brace Jovanovich, Inc., 1970).
37. Barry Commoner, *Greenpeace*, September/October 1989; reprinted in "Why Environmentalism Failed," *Utne Reader*, March/April 1990, p. 104 (italics mine).

38. John O'Connor, "Toxic Logic," *Mother Jones,* April/May 1990, p. 49. O'Connor is executive director and founder of the National Toxics Campaign.
39. *Ibid.*
40. Lisa Jones, "Grand Canyon Beach Erosion Stirs Debate," *The Christian Science Monitor,* July 10, 1990, p. 12.
41. J. D. Marston, quoted by Diane Sylvain, "This land is sacred," *High Country News,* May 20, 1991, p. 8.
42. Private letter to author.
43. Bob Ostertag, "Greenpeace Takes Over the World," *Mother Jones,* March/April 1991, p. 33.
44. David Beers and Catherine Capellaro, "Greenwash!" *Mother Jones,* March/April 1991, pp. 38–41, 88.
45. Lynn White, Jr., "The Historic Roots of Our Ecologic Crisis," *Science,* vol. 155 (March 10, 1967), 1203–07. Widely quoted, including Margot Adler, *Drawing Down the Moon: Witches, Druids, Goddess-Worshippers, and Other Pagans in America Today* (Boston: Beacon Press, 1986), p. 19.
46. *Omni,* June 1990, pp. 22, 96.
47. Don Olsen, "Anyone for biodiversity and Tarahumara garbanzo beans?" *High Country News,* June 3, 1991, p. 8; Olsen was also the source for the preceding sentence.
48. Gene Logsdon, "Putting Farmers Out to Pasture," *Oahe Facts & News,* United Family Farmers, July 1987, p. 3. Logsdon is a contributing editor to *New Farm* and *Ohio* magazines, writes a weekly newspaper column, and works a small farm in Ohio.
49. Gore Vidal, "Sex Is Politics," *The Second American Revolution and Other Essays, 1976–1982* (New York: Random House, 1983), p. 151.
50. Edward O. Wilson, Harvard University, cited in *Harper's* Index, January 1990.
51. Rev. Larry Rice, director of the New Life Evangelistic Center, St. Louis, Missouri, quoted in "Preacher counters Easter Bunny with meals of rabbit," *Rapid City Journal,* April 17, 1991, p. A2.
52. Barbara G. Walker, *Women's Rituals: A Sourcebook* (San Francisco: Harper & Row, 1990), pp. 26, 102, 159–60.
53. "U.S. mostly Christian," *Rapid City Journal,* April 13, 1991, p. A7; survey of 113,000 adults done by ICR Survey Research Group of Media, PA, for City University of New York Graduate School and University Center. Error "should not cause overall results to vary from what all Americans would say by more than a fraction of a percentage point." Figures for Buddhism, Hinduism, and Islam are from *The New York Public Library Desk Reference* (New York: Webster's New World, 1989), pp. 189–90.
54. Bulletin, United Church of Christ of Benzonia, Michigan, May 26, 1991; published by UCC Photo Series Sunday Bulletin Service.
55. Adler, *Drawing Down the Moon,* p. 42. Adler's revised edition provides the clearest and most objective analysis and definition of paganism I've seen; I am deeply indebted to her for the formation of my thoughts on this subject.
56. *Ibid.,* p. 7.

57. *Ibid.*, p. 52.
58. Vidal, "Sex Is Politics," p. 156.
59. Adler, *Drawing Down the Moon*, p. 12.
60. Winona LaDuke, Ontario activist, "Greenpeace Takes Over the World," *Mother Jones*, March/April, 1991, p. 37.
61. Vidal, "Sex Is Politics," p. 156.
62. *Ibid.*, pp. 150–1.
63. *Ibid.*, p. 153.
64. Beers and Capellaro, "Greenwash!" p. 88.
65. Merlin Stone, *When God Was a Woman* (New York: Harcourt Brace Jovanovich, 1976), p. 3.
66. Riane Eisler, *The Chalice & The Blade* (San Francisco: Harper and Row, 1988), who credits James Melaart, *Catal Huyuk* (New York: McGraw-Hill, 1967) and Ester Boserup, *Women's Role in Economic Development* (London: Allen & Unwin, 1970); *The State of the World's Women 1985* (compiled for the United Nations by New Internationalist Publications, Oxford, U.K.), and Barbara Rogers, *The Domestication of Women: Discrimination and Developing Societies* (New York: St. Martin's, 1979).
67. James Melaart, formerly assistant director of the British Institute of Archaeology at Ankara, and in 1976 teaching at the Institute of Archaeology in London, quoted in Stone, *When God Was a Woman*, p. 17.
68. Adler, *Drawing Down the Moon*, p. 9.
69. Private letter to author.
70. Wendell Berry, "God and Country," *Christian Ecology: Building an Environmental Ethic for the Twenty-first Century*, The Proceedings of the First North American Conference on Christianity and Ecology (P. O. Box 14305, San Francisco, CA 94114), ed. by Frederick W. Krueger, pp. 15–17.
71. Adler, *Drawing Down the Moon*, p. viii.
72. Steiner, *The Ranchers*, pp. 120, 227. Rendering as a responsive reading is mine.
73. Space does not allow a thorough discussion of the conflict here; see the special ranching issue published by *High Country News*, March 12, 1990, in which the grazing slogan appeared, p. 16.
74. Gallup poll commissioned by gunmaker Smith & Wesson; *Time*, April 11, 1988, p. 63.
75. Paxton Quigley, *Armed and Female* (New York: St. Martin's Paperbacks, 1989) for statistics, p. 4; for statements by police, p. 66 and chapter 4. For equipment adapted to women, chapter 9. Formerly active on behalf of handgun control, Quigley presents the fairest analysis I've seen of this complex question, including antigun arguments, methods for choosing the appropriate handgun, child safety ideas, and gun laws, along with appraisals of alternate methods of self-defense. She rates each handgun from personal experience, commenting on performance, fit, and brand. Her resource list includes gun ownership laws in each state, lists of shooting schools, defense courses, gunsmiths, accessory suppliers, shooting organizations, videotapes, and a comprehensive bibliography.

76. *Time*, May 8, 1989, p. 104.
77. George Will, Washington Post Writers Group, *Rapid City Journal*, March 22, 1989.
78. Bill Tammeus, *Kansas City Times*, Scripps Howard News Service, in "Knave of a year produces great quotes," *Rapid City Journal*, December 28, 1989.
79. Dick Willis, "Studies portend major drought due for state," *Rapid City Journal*, February 18, 1990, pp. A1–A2.
80. *Ibid.*
81. Leopold, *A Sand County Almanac*, p. 83.
82. *Ibid.*, p. 49.
83. *Ibid.*, p. 50.
84. Frank J. Popper and Deborah Epstein Popper, "As population dwindles, bring back buffalo to save Great Plains," *Rapid City Journal*, August 12, 1989, p. A4.
85. Leopold, *A Sand County Almanac*, pp. 30–32.
86. *Ibid.*, p. 47.
87. Craig Vetter, "The Buffalo Wars," *Outside*, May 1991, p. 142. Comments mine; the author's view differs.
88. Jon Christensen, "Call 1-800-SABOTAGE," *High Country News*, March 12, 1990, p. 16.
89. "Big Stink in The Beef Belt," *Time*, July 16, 1990. lang does not use capitals in her name.
90. "Mitchell radio station bans lang," *Rapid City Journal*, July 2, 1990.
91. "Facing Up to Monopoly: Antitrust Policy and the Meat Industry," factsheet produced by the Western Organization of Resource Councils, Billings, MT 59101, p. 3. WORC's other factsheets include "Monopoly Power in the Beef Industry," "The Meat Trust," "Corporate Profiles: The Big Three," "Monopoly Power in the Pork Industry," and "Monopoly Power in the Lamb Industry."
92. John Howard, chief executive officer of the Black Hills Packing Co., Rapid City, S.D., quoted by Shirley Safgren in "Meat Ban 'Not a Health Issue,'" *Tri-State Neighbor*, February 10, 1989, p. 1B.
93. E. B. White, selections from monthly department "One Man's Meat," *A Treasury of American Writers from Harper's Magazine*, ed. by Horace Knowles (New York: Bonanza Books, 1985), p. 16.
94. Knight-Ridder News Service, *Agweek*, January 1, 1990, p. 15.
95. See note 35 and Suggested Further Reading.
96. *Shopping for a Better World: A Quick and Easy Guide to Socially Responsible Supermarket Shopping*, Council on Economic Priorities, 30 Irving Place, New York, NY 10003.
97. William J. Rathje, "Once and Future Landfills," *National Geographic*, May 1991, pp. 130–131.
98. "Scientists Suspect Poisoning of Fish by Mercury Emissions from Incinerators," *Rachel's Hazardous Waste News*, September 12, 1990, Environmental Research Foundation, P.O. Box 3541, Princeton, NJ 08543-3541, p. 1.

99. Monte Paulsen, "Ten Myths About Our Environment Crisis," *Utne Reader*, May/June 1990, p. 108, reprinted from *Casco Bay [Maine] Weekly*, January 4, 1990.

100. I believed this to be my original thought until I saw it in reviewing one of the best summaries of worldwide pollution I've seen: Thomas A. Sancton, "What on Earth Are We Doing?" *Time*, January 2, 1989, p. 30. Sancton says, "Yet humanity is in a war right now, and it is not too Draconian to call it a war for survival. It is a war in which all nations must be allies." In this issue, *Time* named the earth "planet of the year," to call attention to key problems; several excellent articles summarize our dilemma and suggest strong solutions; for example, *Time* recommends for garbage control: "1. Raise the price of garbage collection and toxic-waste removal and the penalties for improper disposal. ... 2. To encourage recycling, sharply increase the variety of containers that can be returned. ... 3. Increase funding for the testing of chemicals. ... 4. Ban ocean dumping. 5. Ban the export of waste."

Suggested Further Reading

Barnaby, Dr. Frank, gen. ed. *The Gaia Peace Atlas: Survival into the Third Millennium*. New York: Doubleday, 1988.

Baron, Robert C., and Elizabeth Darby Junkin, eds. *Of Discovery & Destiny: An Anthology of American Writers and the American Land*. Golden, Colo.: Fulcrum, 1986.

Berry, Wendell. *The Gift of Good Land: Further Essays Cultural and Agricultural*. San Francisco: North Point, 1981.

———. *The Long-Legged House*. New York: Ballantine, 1971.

Brown, Lester, project director. *State of the World*. Worldwatch Institute. A report on progress toward a sustainable society, 1989. Worldwatch, P.O. Box 6991, Syracuse, NY 13217-6991.

Cohen, Gary, and John O'Connor, ed., *Fighting Toxics: A Manual for Protecting Your Family, Community, and Workplace*. Washington, DC: Island Press, 1990.

De Bell, Garrett, ed. *The Environmental Handbook*. New York: Ballantine, 1970.

Garreau, Joel. *The Nine Nations of North America*. New York: Avon, 1981.

Gimbutas, Marija. *The Language of the Goddess*. New York: Harper and Row, 1989.

Graves, Robert. *The White Goddess*. New York: Farrar, Straus and Giroux, 1966.

The Great Law of Peace of the People of the Longhouse. Iroquois League of Six Nations. Mohawk Nation at Akwesasne via Rooseveltown, NY: White Roots of Peace, n.d.

Hubbell, Sue. *A Country Year: Living the Questions*. New York: Harper and Row, 1987.

Jackson, Wes, Wendell Berry, Bruce Colman, eds. *Meeting the Expectations of the Land: Essays in Sustainable Agriculture and Stewardship*. San Francisco: North Point, 1984.

Jackson, Wes. *Altars of Unhewn Stone: Science and the Earth*. San Francisco: North Point, 1987.

Junkin, Elizabeth Darby. *Lands of Brighter Destiny: The Public Lands of the American West*. Golden, Colo.: Fulcrum, 1986.

Kumin, Maxine. *To Make a Prairie: Essays on Poets, Poetry and Country Living*. Ann Arbor: University of Michigan Press, 1979.

Macfadyen, J. Tevere. *Gaining Ground: The Renewal of America's Small Farms*. New York: Ballantine, 1984.

Meeker-Lowry, Susan. *Economics as if the Earth Really Mattered*. Philadelphia, Penn.: New Society Publishers, 1988.

Merchant, Carolyn. *The Death of Nature: Women, Ecology and the Scientific Revolution*. San Francisco: Harper and Row, 1990.

Meyer, Marvin W., ed. *The Ancient Mysteries: A Sourcebook, Sacred Texts of the Mystery Religions of the Ancient Mediterranean World*. San Francisco: Harper and Row, 1987.

Reisner, Marc. *Cadillac Desert: The American West and Its Disappearing Water*. New York: Penguin, 1987.

Robinson, James M., ed. *The Nag Hammadi Library in English*. San Francisco: Harper and Row, 1988.

Sale, Kirkpatrick. *Dwellers in the Land: The Bioregional Vision*. New York: Coward, McCann and Geoghegan, 1980.

Walker, Barbara G. *The Woman's Dictionary of Symbols & Sacred Objects*. San Francisco: Harper and Row, 1988.

———. *Women's Rituals: A Sourcebook*. San Francisco: Harper and Row, 1990.

Periodicals

Center for Rural Affairs Newsletter, free subscriptions, P.O. Box 405, Walthill, NE 68067.

Environmental Action, 1525 New Hampshire Ave. N.W., Washington, DC 20036.

Environmental Periodicals Bibliography, International Academy at Santa Barbara, 2060 Alameda Padre Sierra, Santa Barbara, CA 93103.

Garbage: The Practical Journal for the Environment, P.O. Box 56519, Boulder, CO 80322-6519.

High Country News, P.O. Box 1090, Paonia, CO 81428.

Northern Lights, P.O. Box 8084, Missoula, MT 59807-8084.

Rain: Journal of Appropriate Technology, 1135 S. E. Salmon, Portland, OR 97214.

Shopping for a Better World, Council on Economic Priorities, 30 Irving Place, New York, NY 10003; $4.95. Call 1-800-U-CAN-HELP for bulk prices.

Whole Earth Review, P.O. Box 15187, Sausalito, CA 94965

Catalogs

An Environmental Sourcebook, conservation sources, Center for Resource Economics/Island Press, 1718 Connecticut Ave. N.W., Suite 300, Washington, DC 20009; 1-800-628-2828, ext. 416.

New Society Publishers, New Society Educational Foundation, P. O. Box 582, Santa Cruz, CA 95061-0582.

Real Goods, 966 Mazzoni St., Ukiah, CA 95482.

Seventh Generation, Colchester, VT 05446-1672; 1-800-456-1177.

Regional Organizations

Dakota Resource Council, R. R. 2 Box 19C, Dickinson, ND 59601; (701) 227-1851.

Environmental Research Foundation, P.O. Box 3541, Princeton, NJ 08543-3541.

International Alliance for Sustainable Agriculture, 1701 University Ave. S.E., #202, Minneapolis, MN 55414.

The Land Institute, 2440 E. Water Well Rd., Salina, KS 67401.

Land Stewardship Project, 512 Elm St., Stillwater, MN 55082.

League of Rural Voters Education Project, 3255 Hennepin Ave. S., #255B, Minneapolis, MN 55408.

National Toxics Campaign, 37 Temple Place, 4th Floor, Boston, MA 02111.

Northern Plains Resource Council, 419 Stapleton Bldg., Billings, MT 59101; (406) 248-1154.

Powder River Basin Resource Council, P.O. Box 1178, Douglas, WY 82633; (307) 358-5002.

Technical Information Project, Inc., P.O. Box 1371, Rapid City, SD 57709; (605) 343-0439.

Western Colorado Congress, P.O. Box 472, Montrose, CO 81402; (303) 249-1978.

Western Organization of Resource Councils, 412 Stapleton Bldg., Billings, MT 59101; (406) 252-9672.

Safe in the Sun

Safe in the Sun

Mary-Ellen Siegel, M.S.W.

Foreword by Albert M. Lefkovits, M.D.

Walker and Company *New York*

To those who provide the sunshine in my life:
my husband, Walter,
and each of our children
and
grandchildren—
Ephram, Eli, Matthew, David, Jonathan, Joshua,
Tzippy, Samantha, Ilana, Hannah, and Elizabeth

A note to the reader: The author and the publishers have exerted every effort to ensure that information set forth in this book is in accord with common practices. However, in view of ongoing research and findings and inevitable differences of opinion among authorities, some practices may vary and others may change in the future.

No part of this book is intended to provide personal medical care to any individual, and we urge you to consult your own physician on all matters relating to your health.

Copyright © 1990, 1995 by Mary-Ellen Siegel

All rights reserved. No part of this book may be reproduced or transmitted in any form or by any means, electronic or mechanical, including photocopying, recording, or by any information storage and retrieval system, without permission in writing from the Publisher.

First published in the United States of America in 1990
by Walker Publishing Company, Inc.; revised edition published in paperback in 1995.

Published simultaneously in Canada by Thomas Allen & Son
Canada, Limited, Markham, Ontario

Library of Congress Cataloging-in-Publication Data
Siegel, Mary-Ellen.
    Safe in the sun / Mary-Ellen Siegel ; foreword by Albert M.
Lefkovits. — Rev. ed.
        p.   cm.
    Includes bibliographical references and index.
    ISBN 0-8027-7459-8 (pbk.)
    1. Skin—Care and hygiene.   2. Skin—Cancer—Popular works.
3. Eye—Diseases—Popular works.   I. Title.
RL87.S55   1995
616.5—dc20   95-9685
                                                            CIP

Printed in the United States of America

10   9   8   7   6   5   4   3   2   1

Contents

Chapter 6

Part III
Coping with the Effects of the Sun

Chapter 7

Chapter 8

Chapter 9

Foreword

Until relatively recent times, people of fashion protected their skin from the sun. Only those who had to work outdoors, such as field workers, exhibited signs of chronic sun exposure. In the early 1920s, the famous designer Coco Chanel, returning from a vacation in the sun, created a new fashion, making the suntan a desirable end in itself. The bronzed, tanned look soon became identified with the leisure class who could afford to follow the sun year-round.

After World War II, travel became accessible to the less affluent, who then sought to vacation in the Mediterranean, Caribbean, and other places where a suntan was assured. Dermatologists became alarmed as impressive evidence accumulated over the past thirty years linking sun exposure to premature aging of the skin and to the increase in skin cancer throughout the world.

In this comprehensive book, Mary-Ellen Siegel presents information culled from the findings of leading dermatologists and ophthalmologists that demonstrate the link between sun exposure and damage to the skin and eyes. In addition, she explains how people can enjoy the outdoors but still protect themselves, and what can be done to repair any damage that has already occurred. This information is presented in a clear fashion, making it of great value to the general public. I commend this as a means of helping people cope with our changing environment.

Albert M. Lefkovits, M.D.
Assistant Clinical Professor of Dermatology
Mount Sinai School of Medicine, New York
Member, Skin Cancer Foundation Medical Council

Acknowledgments

A number of people are always available to give of their time and expertise when I am writing a book. Some read portions of the manuscript; others tell me of their experiences; still others just stand by and listen while I try to work out details; and countless others, by word and deed, give their support. I am most grateful to all of them.

They include members of the faculty of the Division of Social Work, Department of Community Medicine; the staff of the Levy Library at the Mount Sinai School of Medicine; the staff of the Hillcrest Branch of the Queensborough Public Library, and Dr. Steven Rozenberg of 10/10 Optics.

Ezra M. Greenspan, M.D., Lyn Ratner, M.D., Bernard Simon, M.D., and Michael Wartels, M.D., answered questions and made helpful suggestions.

Beth Walker's patience, enthusiasm, and suggestions are enormously appreciated. Steven Gray's contributions were extremely helpful, as were Helen Driller's.

Mitzi Moulds and her staff of the Skin Cancer Foundation were enormously helpful. Joyce Weisbach-Ayoub, Public Information Director, was far more than an important resource: she was always right there when I needed her, providing encouragement and suggestions as well as information.

My family, as always, encourages and sustains me. All of them are very important to me, but in the preparation of this book I owe a special debt of gratitude to my husband's daughter, Jacqueline S. Lustgarten, M.D., associate clinical professor of ophthalmology at the Mount Sinai School of Medicine in New York. Drafted—rather than politely asked—to look over the sections on eyes, she took on the assignment with characteristic good nature and the same high level of care she extends to her patients, making suggestions and changes.

Albert M. Lefkovits, M.D., assistant clinical professor of dermatology at the Mount Sinai School of Medicine in New York, gave enormously of his time and expertise, for which I am most appreciative.

People often wonder how we choose our careers. As a psychotherapist, medical social worker, and health writer, I was inspired by my father, Monroe E. Greenberger, M.D., a caring urologist and excellent communicator, and by my mother, a natural and trained health care giver who also had the ability to tell a good story.

Introduction

My father began taking home movies long before it was fashionable, and my sister and I have since transferred these to videotape. Now it is possible, in just a few short hours, to watch ourselves grow from infancy to maturity. Summers found us basking on the beach or ducking the waves on Long Island, and winters appeared to be spent on the snow-covered hills of New York's Central Park. Our sun-kissed faces were a clear indication—so it seemed in those days—of robust health and the advantages of the good life.

Now we know better. Those days of sun worshiping have put us at risk for skin cancers and melanoma. How could anything that made us look so attractive and feel so good be bad for us?

The evidence is in. The sun causes premature aging and wrinkles, and at the worst may contribute to the development of melanoma, a form of skin cancer that can spread throughout the body. Back in the 1930s, the risk of developing malignant melanoma was 1 in 1,500. Now the lifetime risk is 1 in 105. According to the Skin Cancer Foundation, the risk will become 1 in 75 by the year 2000.

Skin cancer *can* be prevented, and although the effects of the sun are cumulative, you can still reduce the risks by starting to take proper precautions now. Careful and frequent screenings on your own and by a dermatologist greatly increase the likelihood of detection and treatment, with the higher probability of a complete cure.

You can still delight in summer and winter sports. There are ways to be safe in the sun without giving up the many pleasures to be derived from it. The following chapters describe the benefits of sunshine, the risks of exposure, and how damage that has already occurred can be treated or reversed. But most important, we will discuss how you can protect yourself from the sun's damage.

Mary-Ellen Siegel, M.S.W.

I

Effects of the Sun

1   *What's All the Fuss About?*

You may think, "Sure, the sun can give me skin cancer, and it can age my skin, but not for a while; and besides, skin cancer is curable. With all those new methods of turning back the clock, it will be a long time before I *look* old."

Not so, the experts tell us. People are incurring skin cancer at younger and younger ages. Even teens and young adults are getting it. The average age of people who have developed melanoma, a life-threatening form of cancer, has been dropping. And those wonderful "laugh lines" that appear at twenty are beginning to look like serious wrinkles by the time sun worshipers reach their thirties.

All the attention to and warnings about sun exposure have arisen because of clear-cut evidence that ultraviolet radiation—from the sun or from artificial sources—is virtually the sole cause of skin cancers. And although most skin cancers are not life-threatening, treatment for them can be disfiguring. Such eye conditions as cataracts, macular degeneration, skin cancers on the eyelid requiring surgery, and melanomas (the deadlier form of skin cancer) can result from unprotected indulgence in the sun.

This risk has always existed, but with the depletion of the ozone layer it has increased. And because fewer people in the past were able to afford vacations under the sun, public and professional awareness then was at a far lower level than it is now.

Ultraviolet Radiation

Although it lies some 93 million miles away from the earth, the sun is the source of all energy on our planet. Life as we know it couldn't have evolved or been sustained without this energy. No wonder many societies have worshiped the sun; they recognized their debt to the sun even before they understood the scientific principles of photosynthesis and the chains of development through which our natural fuels can be traced to the sun.

The energy that comes to earth from the sun is emitted as radiation of various wavelengths, referred to as the *electromagnetic spectrum*. Included in this spectrum are radio waves, X rays, infrared rays, visible light, and ultraviolet radiation (UVR).

Infrared radiation, which we experience as heat, represents 45 percent of the total energy; another 49 percent of the total energy reaching the earth falls into the visible light spectrum, which we perceive as colors. Ultraviolet radiation represents 6 percent of the total energy reaching the earth, and although we don't see it directly, it is strong enough to induce photochemical reactions and to penetrate the skin. Responsible for both immediate and long-term damage to the skin, UVR eventually causes the skin to sag and wrinkle. In short, it can give us anything from an attractive tan to a fiery sunburn, can cause wrinkles and "sun spots," and ultimately can give us cancer. Ultraviolet radiation stimulates certain cells called *melanocytes* to produce a brown pigment called *melanin*. Melanin acts as a natural defense mechanism to UVR exposure and gives skin the tanned look sought by so many. If for some reason we are especially photosensitive (naturally, from an illness, or because of medication), ultraviolet radiation can cause immediate serious damage.

Most of us are aware that the sun is hottest at midday and that, the nearer to the equator we are, the stronger it is. This has to do with the position of the sun in the sky; when the sun is directly overhead, its rays reach us vertically rather than at an angle, minimizing the distance they must travel through the earth's protective atmosphere before striking us. Seasonal changes also affect the ozone layer: where and when it is thinnest, the sun's rays are strongest. Altitude and surrounding terrain also influence the amount of UVR we receive. Snow reflects the sun even more effectively than sand and water. The potential for damage is greater at high altitudes than near sea level, because less atmospheric filtration occurs. Clouds and pollution may obstruct some UVR, but they do not prevent dangerous levels of it from reaching us. Moreover, the ultraviolet radiation from even the newest, most modern tanning parlors is unsafe, too, as will be discussed fully in Part II.

Three types of UVR are emitted from the sun. The two with which we are concerned are UV-A and UV-B. UV-C is highly toxic to human, plant, and animal life, but fortunately it is absorbed by the ozone layer and by the rest of the earth's atmosphere before it can reach the earth. UV-B, which represents 0.5 percent of the total energy that reaches the earth, can penetrate the top two regions of the skin. It is responsible for redness and burning and can cause immediate damage to the skin. It is more dangerous than UV-A and is recognized as a direct cause of major skin and eye problems, as well as sunburning and tanning. Although UV-A is a much lower intensity than UV-B, it can penetrate the third region of the skin, the dermis. And since UV-A represents 5.5 percent of the total energy reaching us, its potential for damage is great.

Scientists have found that UV-B wavelengths are quite sensitive to small changes in atmospheric ozone concentrations. Consequently, increased levels of UV-B (as well as UV-A) are now reaching the earth as a result of ongoing depletion of the ozone layer high up in the stratosphere. For this reason, even if you spend no more unprotected time in the sun than your parents did, your chances of developing age-damaged skin or cancer are far greater than theirs were when they were your age.

The Earth's Fragile Ozone Layer

Ozone is a form of pure oxygen. A layer of ozone blankets the upper atmosphere, where the atmospheric density is extremely low. Over 99 percent of the atmosphere lies beneath the ozone layer. The layer is quite fragile; if all the ozone molecules were compacted into a continuous thin layer, it would be less than one inch thick.

Ozone also forms in the lower atmosphere. Exhaust from

cars and factories reacts with radiation from the sun to make ozone. Breathing too much ozone can be dangerous, as joggers and others may find if they inhale too much ozone-polluted air on hot smoggy days.

Until this century, the ozone layer in the stratosphere had remained balanced for billions of years. And because the amount of UV radiation present in the sunlight striking the earth depends on the concentration of ozone, this too remained constant. Plants and animals (including humans) have evolved and lived under that stable amount of untraviolet radiation. Now all of this is changing.

Back in the 1920s, chlorofluorocarbons (CFCs) were first synthesized. These chemicals, composed of chlorine, fluorine, and carbon atoms, do not combine easily with other substances. Because they vaporize at low temperatures, they work well as coolants in refrigerators and air conditioners and as aerosol propellants in various types of spray cans. They are also good insulators and are widely used in plastic foam materials. They are simple and inexpensive to manufacture.

But in the mid-1970s it was discovered that CFCs float upward a great distance, ultimately reaching ozone molecules in the upper atmosphere. Solar radiation releases the chlorine in the CFCs, which in turn breaks apart the ozone molecules, which then re-form as regular molecules of oxygen gas (O_2). In response to scientific concern about the ozone layer, the use of CFCs in spray cans was reduced 60 percent between 1974 and 1978. In 1978, nonessential aerosols of CFCs were banned in the United States, Canada, and Scandinavia. However, the chemicals continued to be produced and used in other ways; and in the rest of the world, CFCs continued to be used in aerosol cans. Overall, production of CFCs increased.

In 1985, a shocking discovery was announced. British scientists had found a hole in the ozone layer, centered over Antarctica. This hole appears every spring, but when the winds change for the rest of the year, the hole seems to reclose. Still, in 1987, ozone levels across the Southern Hemisphere were noted to be down 5 percent over the levels at which they had previously remained stable. Scientists have increased their warnings that the continued manufacture and use of products that contain CFCs pose a major threat to life on the planet, but a total worldwide ban has not yet gone into effect.

What does this mean for us? Even if no more CFCs are released, those already released are likely to remain in the atmosphere for another 100 years. Adverse effects on plant and animal life are almost certain to occur.

The sun's rays are now and will remain stronger and more dangerous than they were in previous generations. According to the Skin Cancer Foundation, for each 1 percent drop in stratospheric ozone, there is a 3 to 6 percent increase in nonmelanoma skin cancers and in all likelihood a significant increase in malignant melanoma, too. Increased ultraviolet radiation (particularly UV-B) also suppresses the immune system in a number of ways. It can influence the onset of herpes simplex virus type 1 (better known as cold sores) and some immune diseases such as systemic and discoid lupus erythematosus. Clearly, the sun actually *does* present greater risks today than it did in the past.

2 How Skin Reacts to the Sun

The skin is the body's largest organ. It protects the internal organs, helps prevent dehydration, and aids in disposing of bodily wastes. The skin differs from other body organs in that worn-out and dead cells are continually (and automatically) shed and regenerated. But don't be misled. Even though your suntan fades as older cells are shed, damage still occurs because the ultraviolet rays of the sun penetrate beyond your skin's visible portion or epidermis.

Tough but supple tissue, the skin is composed of several discrete layers of cells. The topmost of these is called the *stratum corneum* or *horny layer*. The end product of the maturing cells in this horny layer is keratin, a fibrous protein whose concentration is greatest in parts of the body that are subject to abrasion, such as the palms of the hands and the soles of the feet. It is thinnest in areas such as behind the ear.

Under the stratum corneum lies the *stratum spinosum*, sometimes called the *prickle cell layer*. Here can be found the fast-growing squamous cells that have matured and moved upward from the lowest layer, the *stratum germinativum*, better known as the *basal layer*. Approximately one out of every six cells in the basal layer is a melanocyte, which produces melanin. The amount and the compactness of the arrangement of melanin normally produced are genetically determined: darker-skinned people produce and thus have more melanin than fair-skinned people, and their melanin is distributed more densely. Ultraviolet radiation, from the sun or from tanning devices (as described in chapter 6), stimulates production of melanin, resulting in suntan. Melanin also offers some protection against ultraviolet radiation, which is why fair-skinned people exposed to the sun burn faster and with more damaging results.

Concealed from view beneath the epidermis is the dermis. It contains blood vessels, glands, nerve endings, and connective tissue consisting of elastic and collagen fibers. Also situated in this layer are the Langerhans cells, part of the immune system, whose function is to fight off invasions of foreign substances such as bacteria, viruses, and allergens. The elastic tissues of the dermis are altered with age, as they begin to break down and lose elasticity. The fibers then stiffen, and the skin begins to wrinkle and sag. Genetics play a role in susceptibility, but even the best hereditary support is no match for excessive exposure to ultraviolet radiation.

Beneath the dermis lies the *subcutis,* also known as the *subcutaneous fatty tissue.* Hair follicles, oil glands, and sweat glands pass through this fatty layer and all the way to the epidermis. These glands aid in maintaining body temperature and in holding moisture in the skin, and this in turn makes skin soft and supple.

Benefits of the Sun

Notwithstanding all the dangers posed by the sun, some (but not too many) benefits may be derived from sun exposure. The warmth feels good: it can actually lift your mood. I'm writing this on the first sunny day in almost a week, and I find my spirits rising as I look out of the window and see the sun glistening on the treetops.

The Sun and Vitamin D

Sunlight manufactures vitamin D in the skin, and the vitamin is then absorbed by the body. The main function of vitamin D, which is also found in dairy products and in other fortified foods, is to bring about absorption of calcium from the intestinal tract; it is thus essential for the healthy development and growth of bones. Children who do not receive any vitamin D from the sun or in their foods are at risk of developing rickets—a condition in which bones soften and bow, and normal growth is impaired.

In the absence of any unusual medical condition, brief exposure to sunlight on a regular basis anywhere on the body is sufficient to produce an adequate amount of dietary vitamin D. When this is not possible, a vitamin D supplement (available in many multivitamins) can be used to obtain the same protection.

Seasonal Affective Disorder

Sunlight is a morale booster for us all, but for people who suffer from seasonal affective disorder (SAD), it seems to be essential. SAD is a disturbance of mood and behavior that actually resembles certain seasonal changes seen in some lower mammals. People who suffer from this condition experience a depression in the winter, usually starting in early fall and continuing to worsen as the winter progresses. The depressed feelings begin to decrease when the days get longer and warmer in the spring. Symptoms include sadness, anxiety, irritability, decreased physical activity, increased (or sometimes decreased) appetite, carbohydrate craving, weight gain (or sometimes loss), extreme tiredness and need for more sleep, decreased sexual energy, premenstrual symptoms, and difficulties trying to work. Almost all SAD sufferers experience problems with interpersonal relationships during the winter months. Although it is much more common in women than in men, SAD also afflicts men and children. Most often, SAD begins in a person's twenties or thirties.

Specific treatments for this condition exist for people whose doctors have ruled out other psychiatric problems, for whom nothing else is occurring in their lives that could be responsible for the depression, and who have had the problem for at least two fall-winters *and* are fine during the summers. Antidepressant medications may work for some sufferers, but it may not be physiologically desirable for some individuals, and others may simply not want to use them. For these sufferers of SAD, a therapy that makes use of all the wave frequencies present in sunlight is very successful.

The treatment involves regular exposure to full-spectrum bright artificial light of a higher intensity than is usually present in either the home or the workplace. A light fixture that can hold four 40-watt tubes of full-spectrum bright artificial light produces an intensity of light that is anywhere from five to ten times brighter than typical room light. Depending on when the person with SAD experiences his or her symptoms, the physician may recommend using this light therapy in the morning or in the evening, usually for about two hours. This kind of lighting system can be used at home, and those for whom the therapy is successful usually experience a mood change in a matter of days.

SAD isn't treated by exposure to the sun, but it is treated with light that mimics sunlight's effects on a person's visual system, without the danger posed by ultraviolet radiation. It must be noted, however, that this therapy should not be undertaken by a do-it-yourselfer in the absence of professional guidance. If you believe you suffer from SAD, see your family physician, who will probably recommend a specialist familiar with this treatment.

Treatment of Psoriasis and Alopecia Areata

Some skin disorders are actually treated with artificial "sunshine"—that is, ultraviolet light. Psoriasis is such a disorder. A chronic, noncontagious skin condition that tends to run in some families, it is characterized by red scaly patches covered by thick, silver-gray scales. The cause of the condition is not known, and although psoriasis may sometimes look a little like eczema, it is not a related condition. While stress or physical illness can generate outbreaks, this is not the cause. Psoriasis results from a rapid turnover of epidermal cells that do not mature properly. The immature cells pile up, causing lesions or patches. Since skin usually takes a month to renew itself, most of us aren't aware of this shedding, but in someone with psoriasis the renewal of the top layer of skin occurs so quickly that layers of dead skin just accumulate, prompting itchiness or even painful cracklike sores. Psoriasis can affect any area on the body, but generally it appears on the hands, elbows, knees, legs, nails, genital areas, or scalp. It can occur at any time in life from infancy to old age. A number of people report that their symptoms improve in the summer and get worse during the winter, when there is little exposure to sunlight. Interestingly, psoriasis seldom occurs on the face, where sunlight exposure is likely to occur throughout the year.

Most people who have psoriasis can be treated by a variety

of effective drugs. But these medications are sometimes ineffective in treating severe and very disfiguring cases of psoriasis.

One therapy that works well for many psoriasis sufferers is exposure to artificial ultraviolet-B (UV-B) light, sometimes in combination with applications of coal tar. Generally, a dermatologist (a physician who treats diseases of the skin, hair, and nails) recommends twenty-five treatments under a special therapeutic UV-B light considerably stronger than sunlight.

Are psoriasis sufferers who have been treated with this UV-B treatment at greater risk of skin cancer? Studies are inconclusive, although some indications suggest that such patients are far more likely to develop skin cancers than are patients with psoriasis who were not treated with UV-B therapy. The Skin Cancer Foundation states that the risk may be considerably higher than is reflected in some studies, given that it may take many years of exposure to UVR before skin cancer develops. The foundation recommends that patients being treated with UV-B place a lightweight shield, such as a pillowcase, over their head if arms or legs are being treated, and that they even wear gloves to protect hands. The foundation also emphasizes that tanning salons are no substitute for therapeutic ultraviolet treatment. Tanning salons are discussed in chapter 6.

Some patients are treated with PUVA, which makes use of a light-sensitizing medication called Psoralen that is applied topically (on the surface of the affected area), taken internally, or in some cases put into bathwater. Then the patient is placed under a therapeutic dose of ultraviolet-A (UV-A) light. According to the Skin Cancer Foundation, the skin cancer risk for patients who receive PUVA treatments is in the range of 10 to 15 percent, so the foundation recommends that, unless the psoriasis is very extensive, UV-B be tried first. PUVA treatment, like the UV-B treatment discussed earlier, is not to be confused with tanning salons, or home sunlamps. It must be administered under meticulous medical supervision, and care must be taken during the treatment to protect the eyes. PUVA is used both for stubborn cases of psoriasis and for alopecia areata, a disease in which the body forms antibodies against some of the hair follicles. Small, smooth, round, or oval patches of baldness appear on the scalp or beard of individuals with this condition. Sometimes alopecia areata clears up spontaneously. But when it doesn't, PUVA may be utilized.

At one time people thought that many health benefits could be derived from the sun, and although we know better now, at some unconscious level we do tend to think that the sun is good for us. Yet in just these few pages we have covered all the known health benefits of the sun and/or ultraviolet radiation. Still, we ought not minimize the pleasure to be obtained from basking in the warmth of the sun. So, in order to enjoy it but still protect ourselves, let us investigate exactly what the sun can do to our skin.

Skin Type as a Predictor of Damage from the Sun

Researchers today are able to confirm that people with fair skin, red or light hair color, light eye color, and freckles are likely to burn severely and, even if they do eventually tan, suffer cumulative damage.

The concept of skin typing came into being in the mid-1970s, when studies were done under careful laboratory conditions to categorize and measure a person's skin response to sunlight. The extent of a person's sensitivity to ultraviolet radiation is measured as the minimal erythema (sunburn) dose of UVR that provokes even the slightest perceptible sunburn in that person's skin. Referred to as an *MED value,* this measurement bears a strong (though not absolute) relationship to skin type.

Why is it that some types of skin seem to burn more easily than others? Quite simply, it has to do with the amount of melanin in the skin: the more melanin, the more protection against UVR damage. As was mentioned earlier, melanin, a brown pigment, is produced by epidermal cells called *melanocytes.* Everyone, from fair-skinned people to black-skinned people, has the same number of melanocytes. However, the rate of production of melanin in your skin is determined by the stimulation it receives, as well as by your genes. Thus, fair-skinned people, who have less melanin in place from the start, also have melanocytes that don't respond to the sun by producing a nice all-over tan; they burn. If they foolishly persist in sunning themselves, they may develop a tan by the end of the summer, but the damage to their skin is accumulating. Some people almost as fair may be able to tan more easily, and some people with much darker skin tones may burn easily; generally, however, the darker the skin, the greater the protection from ultraviolet radiation.

Dermatologists recommend that you learn your skin type, because you can use this guide as a way of safeguarding yourself from the effects of the sun. Although the accompanying chart does not discuss ethnic groups, generally those with Type 1 or 2 skin are of Celtic, Scandinavian, or North European descent. Type 3, 4, and 5 typically include descendents of Italians, Spaniards, and Greeks; Type 5 descendents of Asians and many Hispanics; and Type 6 descendents of black Africans. But since ethnic groups have merged over the years, many Africans (and Asian-Americans) have light skin, and some North Europeans are quite dark.

People who are least sensitive to the sun (skin types of the higher numbers) have the greatest concentration of melanin in their dermis. These pigments, which are formed in the basal layer of the skin, move up to the stratum corneum in response to ultraviolet radiation, and this results in a tanned appearance. People with the greatest sensitivity to the sun (skin types of the lower numbers) have a lower concentration of melanin in their dermis, which is why they burn rather than tan.

Some dermatologists believe that relying on this chart may give you a false sense of security. They note that striking individual differences occur, and they point out that someone with dark skin and hair may still be very vulnerable. They suggest that you try to recall whether some time in the past you tanned or burned after a forty-five-minute exposure at noon on a hot summer day—without sunscreens. Don't try it now, but think back to those days before you were cautious and sensible.

If you are one of the lucky people who tans but doesn't burn, you do have more protection than your fair-skinned friends from that noonday sun. But *only* about as much as if

Skin Types and Skin Reactions to Ultraviolet Radiation

Skin Type	Reaction to Sun	Examples
Type 1	Always burns, sometimes painfully; seldom or never tans; peels; extremely sensitive to UVR	People with fair skin, blue or sometimes brown eyes, freckles, blonde or red hair
Type 2	Usually burns, sometimes painfully; sometimes tans, but not very much; may peel; very sensitive to UVR	People with fair skin, red, blonde, or brown hair, and blue, hazel, or brown eyes
Type 3	Burns moderately; tans gradually; sensitive to UVR	Average Caucasian
Type 4	Seldom burns; tans easily and reacts with almost immediate darkening of skin (IPD: Immediate Pigment Darkening); moderately sensitive to UVR	People with white, olive, or light brown skin, dark brown hair, and dark eyes
Type 5	Almost never burns; tans easily and considerably; IPD reaction; minimally sensitive to UVR	Brown-skinned people, often of Asian or Indian descent
Type 6	Never burns, but tans greatly; IPD reaction; not sensitive to UVR	African-Americans

you were wearing a Sun Protection Factor (SPF) sunscreen of 2 or 3. And if you have developed a gradual deep tan, that offers you at most the equivalent of an SPF of 4. That's not very much, considering that the Skin Cancer Foundation recommends that everyone use a sunscreen with an SPF of 15 or higher.

Extreme Reactions to Ultraviolet Radiation

Certain people are at special risk of damage from UVR. They were born with partial or total lack of melanin pigment in their body (a condition called *albinism*), and they are prone to severe sunburn, skin inflammations or rash, and skin cancer—all resulting from *any* exposure to ultraviolet radiation. Total albinos have pale skin, white hair, and pink eyes, and their skin and eyes have an abnormal sensitivity to light. Albinism is represented in all ethnic groups.

People suffering from vitiligo, a skin disease that can develop at any age, have irregular patches of various sizes that are totally lacking in pigment. Often these patches have unusually dark borders. The cause of vitiligo is not known, but it may be related to other autoimmune diseases in which the body acts against some of its own cells (in this case, against melanocytes responsible for producing melanin). These unpigmented patches may burn after only brief exposure to the sun; thus, extreme care must be taken by those who have vitiligo.

A number of other conditions are often activated, prompted, or exacerbated by sunlight. Among them are most types of acne, herpes simplex, psoriasis, and viral infections of the skin. Contrary to the popular belief that "a little suntan" is good for these conditions, people who have them are likely to find that their skin troubles increase after exposure to sun. Eczema may be an exception: some people say that the sun actually improves it, but others find that the sun aggravates the condition. True, a nice tan will mask skin imperfections, but products are available that cover imperfections—whether an innocuous rash or a deep and large scar—similarly, with no health risk.

People who have discoid lupus erythematosus (DLE) or systemic lupus erythematosus (SLE) react very poorly to the sun. The former is a chronic, recurrent disease, primarily of the skin, with a characteristic red, scaly, butterflylike pattern covering the cheeks and bridge of the nose; it can also occur on other parts of the body. The latter is also a chronic disease, but it is inflammatory and can affect many systems of the body. One-third to one-half of all people with lupus are photosensitive, which means that they are extremely sensitive to sunlight or any form of ultraviolet radiation. In these people, severe sunburn is only one possible consequence of sun exposure: they may experience anything from a minor flare-up of symptoms to a serious exacerbation of their disease requiring intensive medical attention.

Almost 10 percent of otherwise healthy people are affected by a disorder called polymorphous light eruption (PMLE). Usually before the age of thirty, these individuals exhibit an abnormal response to the light from UV-A and UV-B. Those affected are most often fair-skinned women, and their symptoms include recurrent sunburns, raised skin lesions, tiny blisters, and other skin eruptions.

A number of people suffer solar urticaria, a photosensitive reaction that develops within minutes of exposure to sunlight or even artificial light sources. Although rare, it can be severe in its eruptions and frequency.

Also known to cause photosensitivity in some people are various inherited disorders in which the body abnormally produces certain parts of the hemoglobin molecule located in the red blood cells. Such disorders, known under the general term of *porphyrias,* range from mild to rather serious. Sufferers are extremely sensitive to UVR because these substances affect their bodies much as do the photosensitive drugs discussed in the next section.

Xeroderma pigmentosum is an extremely rare genetic disorder characterized by sun sensitivity and an inability to repair ultraviolet-damaged DNA. Individuals who have it develop skin cancer at a frequency more than 1,000 times that of the general population.

Chemical Photosensitivity

The term *chemical photosensitivity* refers to adverse skin reactions resulting from exposure to both UVR and any of various chemicals. Some people will suffer skin rashes, severe sunburn, or hives if they go out in sunlight following contact with insecticides or the coal tar extracts used in asphalt and roofing materials. In some instances, the adverse response to the sun may occur almost immediately; in others, no symptoms appear until hours or even days after exposure. Certain medications taken internally or applied topically to the skin can cause similar reactions. Some common plants are similarly implicated: limes, lemons, garden-variety parsnip, celery, fennel, dill, garden carrots, and buttercups, among others.

Photosensitive reactions vary not only with the contributing chemicals but also to some extent among people. For instance, assorted perfumes, colognes, shaving products, and deodorants contain ingredients that absorb light into the skin of some individuals, causing a bad sunburn or rash where the substance has been applied. Meanwhile, someone else using the same product may have no problem at all.

Warnings are printed on the labels of numerous medications that are known photosensitizers. Look for words to the following effect: "This product may cause adverse reaction to ultraviolet rays." Always read any inserts in the medication you take, and consider obtaining a consumer-oriented guide to both prescription and nonprescription drugs that you can consult before taking any medication. If you have any doubt about the safety of a medication, or if you know you will be going out in the sun after taking it, discuss the situation with your physician or pharmacist.

Photosensitizers include a number of antibiotics, oral medications taken by diabetics, antidepressants, Psoralen, which was discussed earlier as a treatment for psoriasis, and birth control pills.

Medications that contain ingredients from the coal tar group and used for treating eczema and psoriasis, nalalidixic acid prescribed for certain urinary tract infections, and a number of antihistamines are also on the compendium of chemicals that cause photosensitivity. Obviously, the medications you take internally may cause an adverse skin reaction wherever you are exposed to UVR, but cosmetics or medications applied to the skin are likely to cause problems only in that area.

Many of the drugs involved in chemotherapy to treat cancer are photosensitizers. Discuss this subject with your doctor or nurse if you are receiving chemotherapy.

Ouch! A Sunburn Hurts

Who is likely to get sunburned? Anyone exposed to intense UVR may, but people with the sensitive Type 1 or 2 skin are at the greatest risk because their skin has the lowest concentration of protective melanin in the dermis. And the very young and the elderly are particularly prone to sunburn.

Anyone who has been exposed to the sun on a gradual basis and built up a tan is less likely to burn. This is because the sun's rays speed up mitosis of the epidermal cells, causing thickening of the stratum corneum in four to seven days, which in turn renders the skin less penetrable to UVR. But dermatologists remind us that just because you don't burn doesn't mean the sun is not doing damage. It is.

If you have ever had a severe or even moderately uncomfortable sunburn, you probably remember just what it felt like. Your skin turned pink or even scarlet, and there may have been some mild swelling. Later in the evening—perhaps just as you were trying to get to sleep, or maybe the next day—your skin may have turned even brighter red, with considerable attendant swelling or blistering. Anything (including water) touching the skin made you want to scream in pain. Perhaps you had strap marks where a bathing suit's covering ended, but if you were wearing a lightweight cotton covering, some of the sunlight may have penetrated to render the line between the unburned and sunburned areas almost unidentifiable. Some areas of the skin are more sensitive than others, and naturally any sunburned area that you had to cover before going out in public bothered you the most. Your skin may have felt tender, warm, and tight, and the sunburn probably itched. It may have been painful, but the worst was probably over within twenty-four hours. If you suffered an extremely severe sunburn (sometimes called *sun poisoning*), however, you might have become nauseated, sustained chills and fever, and even suffered from tachycardia (accelerated heart rate) in addition to experiencing blistering and peeling.

The explanation for this sunburn process is still not fully understood, but experts believe that, when the epidermis is damaged by UVR, the dead epidermal cells become unevenly distributed, and the body responds by releasing various chemical substances that precipitate skin inflammation. Among these substances are prostaglandins, which may widen the small blood vessels of the skin, causing the redness. As the blood supply to the burnt area increases, tissue fluid and white blood cells collect there and cause swelling. Water is lost through the skin, and you may actually become dehydrated.

Sunburn on lips can be especially painful. Lifeguards know this, so they cover their lips with a total sunblock like thick zinc oxide. People who are fair-skinned, have protruding lips, or breathe through their mouths and habitually keep their lips parted are especially vulnerable to severe sunburn there, sometimes resulting in dreadful sores.

Sunburns eventually heal without any scars, unless an infection develops because damage prevented tissue from protecting itself against bacteria. Mild sunburns can usually be treated with an assortment of nonprescription remedies that are applied to the skin; some are in lotion form, and others are sprays. If symptoms persist, medical attention should be sought.

The best way to avoid sunburn and the accompanying discomfort and damage to skin is to prevent it by using sunscreen and wearing protective clothing whenever you are exposed to ultraviolet radiation.

Sunstroke

Sunstroke or heatstroke can happen to anyone—a child, an old person, an athlete, or anyone else who has allowed his or her body temperature to rise to a dangerously high level. Unlike heat exhaustion, which usually responds to rest and replacement of body fluids and salts, heatstroke is a medical emergency that can be fatal.

Heatstroke can happen in the shade or in an overheated house, but frequently it is the result of too much sun. The symptoms are very hot, dry skin and no sweating, along with a body temperature of 104° F or higher, weakness, dizziness, rapid breathing, nausea, and sometimes mental confusion or unconsciousness that may occur suddenly and dramatically.

First aid for heatstroke consists of cooling the person quickly by applying an ice bag or crushed ice, by wrapping the person in wet sheets, or even by hosing the person down with cold water. Then get the victim to an emergency room, or call the local medics!

Actinic or Solar Keratoses

Actinic keratoses—also called *solar keratoses* because they appear almost exclusively on individuals who spend a great deal of time in the sun—begin as pink spots that are smooth and flat or slightly raised above the skin surface, but they eventually become irregular, scaly, and wartlike and turn red or brownish in color. They almost always occur in sun-exposed areas such as the forehead, nose, tips of the ears, upper cheeks, and backs of the hands. People with Type 1 or 2 skin are especially vulnerable to actinic keratoses.

They can be quite unsightly, but of far greater importance is their strong potential for progressing to become squamous cell cancers. For this reason actinic keratoses need to be carefully observed and treated to prevent their further growth. Several effective treatments, all of which offer a cure, are discussed in Part III.

The Sun's Effect on the Immune System

It's amazing how many myths most of us grew up believing. I always thought that sunlight was a healing force and that a good vacation in the sun, summer or winter, would help fortify me for the school year ahead. But was I ever wrong!

Scientific evidence indicates an association between exposure to ultraviolet radiation and suppression of the immune system. Cancer—and skin cancer in particular—has been closely linked with immunosuppression in a number of situations. For instance, people treated with immunosuppressive chemotherapy drugs for lymphomas appear to be at increased risk for the development of skin cancers. And organ transplant patients, who take medications that suppress their immune system so that they won't reject the new organ, have an increased incidence of cancer development. Stephen E. Ullrich and Margaret L. Kripke of the Department of Immunology at the University of Texas's M. D. Anderson Cancer Center published data on this subject in the 1989 *Journal of the Skin Cancer Foundation*. In discussing kidney transplant patients they say, "There is a preponderance of skin cancers in these patients and most are found on sun-exposed sites of the body. These data suggest that like murine [mouse] skin cancer, the development of human skin cancer may be associated with suppression of the immune response."

How does ultraviolet radiation suppress the immune system? First, let's review how the immune system works. Under normal circumstances, the body recognizes and destroys foreign invaders before they endanger its health. If the body didn't have this ability, minor cuts, infections, and illnesses could be fatal. The foreign invaders, called *antigens,* are recognized by the body, which then mobilizes to attack them. White blood cells attack the bacteria (or other antigens) and stimulate the production of antibodies in the blood plasma. These antibodies then circulate through the bloodstream and attack the antigens. The antibodies continue to circulate after the original invasion has been defeated, and they are able to recognize the same antigens if they ever try to reenter the body. This explains why some childhood illnesses give us lifelong immunity and why vaccination (which makes use of weak antigens to stimulate antibody production) can give your body the same antibody protection as if you had already had the disease in its more virulent form.

Three kinds of cells are important in the immune system: B cells, T cells, and natural killer (NK) cells. *B cells,* manufactured in the bone marrow, produce antibodies that help defend the body against infection or toxic substances. *T cells* are stimulated by antigens to circulate throughout the body. These cells, produced in the thymus gland, are among the larger number of lymphocytes—colorless cells produced in lymphoid organs such as lymph nodes, the spleen, and the thymus.

Natural killer (NK) cells are stimulated by viral infections, possibly through production of interferon—a chemical substance that is itself naturally released by the body in response to viral infections. The natural resistance conferred by NK cells differs from the immunity acquired through previous exposure and is not caused by B or T cells.

Scientists now recognize that anyone with a suppressed or deficient immune system is susceptible to a number of diseases, including cancer. Individuals who already have cancer have low immunity and are especially vulnerable to infections and other illnesses. Although researchers are hard at work trying to find ways to strengthen existing immune systems, it is essential that we avoid anything likely to weaken our immune system.

If (as more and more evidence suggests) excessive exposure to ultraviolet radiation lowers the body's immunity, that in itself should be a good reason to be wary of the sun.

As was noted earlier in this chapter, the skin serves as the main barrier between our body and our environment. All kinds of things brush up against and try to enter our skin: viruses, fungi, bacteria, and chemical and physical carcinogens. The skin is protective not just because it is the body's outer covering but because it possesses a number of properties that collectively permit it to be called an immune organ. The Langerhans cells of the dermis and epidermis are antigen-presenting cells that are capable of communication with T and some non-T lymphocytes.

Although the relationship between skin cancer and exposure to sunlight was noted almost 100 years ago, and although it was demonstrated in the 1920s that ultraviolet radiation can cause skin cancer in mice, understanding of the relationship between ultraviolet radiation and the immune system is far more recent. Basically, transformation of cells by UVR is thought to occur as a result of changes in the nuclear DNA.

Studies in mice indicate that those treated with UVR show an increased incidence of leukemia, lymphoma, and skin cancer, suggesting that UV-induced immunological changes may have great significance for humans. Ullrich and Kripke posed the question "Does UV also suppress the human immune response?" They then described a study in which healthy volunteers were exposed to the radiation generated by a commercial tanning bed. After the volunteers underwent twelve 30-minute exposures, a blood sample was taken from each and an immune profile was done. Sure enough, the immune system's reactivity to certain allergens was depressed, and T cell and NK cell functions were adversely affected. Similar results were reported after volunteers were exposed to natural sunlight.

Do sun worshipers, like the mice that were exposed to UVR, have an increased risk of developing such nonskin cancers as leukemia and lymphoma? Is their immune system harmed in such a way that they are vulnerable to numerous minor or serious disorders? The jury is still out, but it is certainly worth considering these possibilities before you take off unprotected for a vacation under the sun.

Photoallergies

A *photoallergy* is defined as a bodily response to some chemical that involves participation of the immune system after exposure to ultraviolet radiation. Photoallergies differ from the phototoxic reactions to chemicals discussed earlier in that, with photoallergic reactions, each time an exposure occurs, the reaction is more severe. Some ingredients in cosmetics (such as fragrances, antibiotic agents, and antifungal agents) and in sunscreens (particularly PABA—para-aminobenzoic acid) have been reported to cause photoallergenic reactions in a number of people. Such reactions can be as simple as a skin rash or as severe as a very uncomfortable eczema-like rash that may scale or crust. Ceasing to use the offending allergen usually eliminates the problem, although often the rash must be treated by a dermatologist with medications that include antihistamines or steroids.

Distinguishing between photosensitivity and photoallergy may be difficult, but it helps determine the most effective treatment. Thus, any rash or skin eruption that occurs and worsens or that fails to clear up when you have removed what you suspect might be the offending cause should be checked by a physician, preferably a dermatologist.

3 Sun and the Eyes

Back in the days when I considered a suntan glamorous and thought that it was even healthful to stretch out in the sun, I avoided sunglasses. Wearing them resulted in "panda marks," as we teenagers called those white circles surrounding our eyes where the sunglasses had successfully screened out the sun.

Then when I got a little older I noticed that, if I didn't wear sunglasses for reading outdoors, I would squint and get crinkly little lines all around my eyes—lines that were beginning to look like wrinkles. So on went the sunglasses, at least for reading in the sun.

I learned a few more important lessons when I married a man whose daughter is an ophthalmologist. She's Jacqueline Lustgarten, M.D., an associate clinical professor of ophthalmology at the Mount Sinai School of Medicine in New York. As a member of the American Academy of Ophthalmology, she is a medical doctor, educated, trained, and licensed to provide complete medical eye care. She's very strict about matters relating to eyes, both with patients and with her own family. When her family skis, her sons don't dare go up on the slopes without sunscreen and sunglasses.

Structures and Function of Eyes

Sight is one of our most important senses; many people feel that it is the one they would most regret losing. And yet many of us don't take proper care of our eyes, perhaps because we don't really understand their structure or how they work.

Eyes need light in order to fulfill their function as the sensory organ of vision. Many of us see better in daylight than in artificial light, but ironically the visible portion of ultraviolet radiation also represents a threat to the well-being of the tissues of the eye.

Our eyes work harder than most of us realize. Like a

camera, the eye also has a lens through which light passes before focusing on the retina, the thin light-sensitive film that lines the inside of the eye. A chemical reaction takes place there in which, as on the film in a camera, an image is briefly recorded.

The region of the eye, or ocular area, consists of many parts. Eyebrows help to protect eyes by preventing rain and sweat from running down into them. Eyelids are also protective. They work like shutters, allowing the eyes to rest; and they blink quickly (this is called the blink reflex) if anything comes too close. Glands in the eyelids produce tears, washing the eye every few seconds during the blink reflex. Eyelashes trap dust, dirt, raindrops, and snowflakes that might otherwise fall into the eye.

The structure of the eye itself is complex and intricate. The eyeball (globe) fits into the socket (orbit), a skeletal pocket in the skull. Covering most of the eyeball and the inside of the eyelid is the conjunctiva, a transparent lining. This membrane sometimes gets infected, causing conjunctivitis, which some people refer to as pink eye. The conjunctiva manufactures oily secretions that prevent friction from occurring when the eye moves. It can also become red and irritated from allergies.

The eye is composed of elaborate layers, each of which serves a specific purpose. The outer layer consists of the tough but sensitive cornea and sclera. The sclera is the white of the eye, which protects it from injury and irritation. The cornea, an extension of the sclera at the front of the eye, acts as a transparent window through which light can pass. The cornea covers and protects the iris, the colored part of the eye, but is extremely sensitive itself, as you know if you have ever felt a particle of sand or an eyelash scratch against it. The iris expands and contracts to widen or narrow the pupil, the opening at its center, thus controlling the amount of light that passes through to the layers behind it. When too much light is directed toward the eye, the pupil gets smaller, allowing a narrower stream of light in. When there is insufficient light, the pupil opens wide, permitting as much available light as possible to enter.

Behind the pupil is a natural lens that, in a person's normal state, is so clear that light can pass right through it. This flexible structure focuses light by altering its shape. The lens is held in place by muscles and ligaments that help it focus. The lens is flat and thin when you look at things in the distance, but it becomes short and fat when you look at something close to you.

In front of the lens is an area termed the anterior chamber; it is filled with a watery fluid that helps maintain the proper pressure inside the eye. Attached to the innermost lining of the eyeball is the retina, which receives the image that the lens has refracted or bent. The retina is made up of many nerve endings that act as light receptors. Cells called cones and rods (approximately 6 million and 120 million of each, respectively) transmit the images to the optic nerve at the back of the eye. The cones work in bright light and pick up colors; the rods work in dim light and cannot register color but are important for peripheral vision and in seeing light, shape, and movement. The area behind the lens and in front of the retina is filled with a jellylike substance called the vitreous humor, which is colorless and clear.

When the optic nerve receives the images from the cones and rods, it transmits the messages to the visual centers of the brain. Interestingly, the retina, like a camera, receives these pictures "upside-down," but the brain turns them around.

Ultraviolet Radiation

In order for the eye to fulfill its main function as the sensory organ of vision, light must penetrate the tissues of the eye and reach the retina, where absorption takes place. But ultraviolet radiation, whether incurred from the sun or in tanning salons, can have very deleterious effects upon the eyes.

What are some of the specific hazards? Most people have noticed a feeling of discomfort and fatigue from driving, fishing, skiing, reading, or even just casually sitting in glaring sunshine. There are two kinds of glare that you may have experienced. When the sun is extremely bright and the overall level of light is very high, you may experience direct glare. Reflected glare occurs when concentrated light bounces off a white or shiny surface, such as water or snow.

As chapter 1 noted, the types of energy that are emitted from the sun include radio waves, X rays, infrared rays, visible light, and ultraviolet radiation. Infrared rays, which provide much of the heat on our planet, are not considered harmful, but in combination with wind they can cause the natural moisture in the eyes to dry out. Most of our concern in this book, however, focuses on ultraviolet radiation—especially UV-A and UV-B. UV-C is absorbed in the upper atmosphere, but UV-A and UV-B reach the surface of the earth, where UV-A represents 5.5 percent of total solar energy and UV-B represents only 0.5 percent. UV-A can induce sunburn, but not nearly as intensely as UV-B; however, it penetrates through three layers of skin and causes long-term damage, including wrinkles and cancer of the skin. UV-B penetrates only the first two layers, but its intensity enables it to cause both immediate and long-term damage. The depletion of the fragile and protective ozone layer, a consequence of artificially prepared chemicals that have been released into the atmosphere, permits much more ultraviolet radiation to reach the earth than in previous times, thus increasing our risk of damage from the sun.

Does ultraviolet radiation affect the eyes? It certainly does. Sometimes eyes are already contaminated with a virus that hasn't yet evidenced itself. Some studies indicate that there is a higher rate of such infections—including conjunctivitis—requiring treatment after exposure to sunlight.

Sunburn of the eyelids doesn't usually occur, because the eyelids normally move, but a person who falls asleep in the sun may discover that the lids have become seriously sunburned, with accompanying pain and swelling. And individuals with a history of prolonged sun exposure are at risk of basal cell and squamous cell cancers and malignant melanoma of the eyelid.

Reflexes make people blink and squint in strong sunlight, and these reactions offer some protection to the eyes. The cornea also reflects and absorbs some UVR; and although some damage to it may occur, the cornea repairs itself quickly. Moreover, its action serves to prevent some permanent damage to the eye. There is speculation that the present-day increase in exposure attributable to the thinning of the protective ozone layer may result in long-range permanent damage to the cornea. The lens of the eye also absorbs some of the light, and because it yellows with age, its capacity to absorb light increases with age. But while it absorbs the UVR not already intercepted by the cornea, it also places itself at risk of developing cataracts. People who have had all or part of a lens removed (for treatment of cataracts) no longer have this protection and must take special precautions to guard their eyes against ultraviolet radiation. However, some intraocular lenses (placed after cataract surgery) contain compounds that absorb UV light. Currently, most lenses offer this protection, but some ophthalmologists prefer not to use such lenses. If you are planning cataract surgery, discuss this with the ophthalmologist who is doing the procedure. If you have already had cataract surgery, ask the surgeon if a UV-absorbent lens was implanted; they are a fairly recent development.

UVR and the Conjunctiva

Exposure to considerable ultraviolet radiation can cause benign growths on or a thickening of the conjunctiva, the protective membrane that lines the eyelids and covers the eyeball. This, in turn, can result in the appearance of a yellow spot on either side of the cornea—a condition called *pinguecula* that can be unsightly. Finally, pinguecula can lead to pterygia—the formation of a thick, triangular bit of pale tissue that extends from the border of the cornea near the nose toward the middle of the eye. Pterygia can also result directly from ultraviolet radiation; it is fairly common in some equatorial climates, as the physiological result of a hot, dry climate and nearly vertical rays of sunlight.

Cancer of the conjunctiva, although rare, has been associated with prolonged sun exposure. According to the Skin Cancer Foundation, such problems are more likely to occur in people who live close to the equator, where the sun is strongest, or who pursue outdoor occupations, such as farmers, fishermen, and construction workers.

The cornea blocks much of the ultraviolet radiation that reaches the eye, and the crystalline lens inside the eye prevents almost all of the remaining UVR from reaching the retina. But the effects of UVR—and in particular, UV-B—on the cornea can be very dramatic.

Snow Blindness

The American Academy of Ophthalmology has 20,000 members and is the world's largest organization of eye physicians and surgeons. Members like to advise people on taking care of their eyes, and in the spring of each year they send out warnings about some of the dangers that lurk on the ski slopes. Many skiers believe that spring is the best time of all for skiing, because snow and sun coexist. But this is also the most likely time to develop a severe case of sunburn of the eyes, called *snow blindness*—a temporary but aptly named condition. Surfers too are at great risk of incurring this condition, because the concentrated reflected light from the water has the same effect as does the light from the snow.

Symptoms can be quite frightening: a gritty sensation and conjunctival redness progressing to pain, inability to tolerate any kind of light, and uncontrollable lid closure. Upon examination, the center of the surface of the cornea seems to be denuded of cells, the cause of the intense pain. Generally the condition clears up on its own in a few days, although sometimes lubricants, pain relievers, antibiotics, or patching of the eye is prescribed by an ophthalmologist. Excessive exposure of the delicate tissues in the eye to ultraviolet radiation causes this painful, albeit temporary condition. As one victim said, "I felt as if someone had taken sandpaper and stroked it back and forth against my eye." Anyone who experiences persistent symptoms or a great deal of pain should consult an ophthalmologist.

Snow blindness, medically known as *ultraviolet keratoconjunctivitis*, can easily be prevented by wearing goggles or sunglasses that filter out the ultraviolet radiation produced by the sun. In Part II we will discuss the best types of sunglasses to use for various activities, including skiing.

Painful though snow blindness may be, there is little evidence that the damage to the cornea is permanent. But damage to the lens of the eye from chronic exposure to the sun is another story.

UVR and Cataract Formation

For many years, ophthalmologists have suspected an association between long exposure to ultraviolet radiation and the formation of cataracts. It had long been noted that people living in areas where there was a great deal of sunshine had a relatively high rate of cataracts. Furthermore, studies in laboratory animals had demonstrated that ultraviolet radiation damaged the animals' lenses.

A major study published in the December 1, 1988, *New England Journal of Medicine* and conducted by Hugh R. Taylor, M.D., and his colleagues at the Johns Hopkins School of Medicine in Baltimore indicated that extensive exposure to sunlight can triple a person's risk of developing a cortical cataract, the type of cataract that forms in the outer layer of the lens.

The study involved a survey of 838 Chesapeake Bay watermen, ranging in age and in the number of years they had worked on the bay. Dr. Taylor and his staff chose this group because they formed a stable occupational group with a varied amount of total sun exposure. The study combined a very detailed occupational history of each man from the age of sixteen, laboratory and field measurements that revealed how much sun each man had been exposed to, and ophthalmological examinations to determine the type and extent of any cataracts.

Using sophisticated mathematical measures, Dr. Taylor and his group were able to demonstrate conclusively that the men who had developed cortical cataracts had been exposed to much more UV-B from the age of sixteen onward than had those who hadn't developed this type of cataract. UV-B, you will recall, is the type of radiation that causes severe sunburns, and it is more clearly implicated in skin cancers than UV-A is. Although far less UV-B than UV-A reaches the earth (it is highest in summer and in the tropics between 10 A.M. and 2 P.M.), many scientists believe that the amounts of it penetrating the earth's atmosphere are increasing because of the deterioration of the protective ozone layer. Dr. Taylor estimates that, for every 10 percent increase in UV-B, there will be a 6 percent increase in cortical cataracts.

Unlike epidermal skin color, which has a significant effect on how a person's skin reacts to the sun, iris color does not seem to make any difference in a person's level of protection from UV-related eye problems. So whether your eyes are light blue or dark brown, excessive exposure to UV-B puts you in the same high-risk category for developing cataracts. Individuals who have had a cataract removed need to be mindful that their eyes are especially vulnerable to damage by the sun, unless an intraocular lens containing UV-absorbent compounds was implanted.

UVR and the Retina

According to many researchers, years of exposure to ultraviolet radiation may seriously damage the retina, resulting in age-related macular degeneration. Some studies have found no connection between exposure to ultraviolet radiation and the later development of macular degeneration, but other research suggests that a link exists. And related studies have indicated that intense light can cause retinal damage in monkeys.

Paul Sternberg, Jr., M.D., assistant professor of ophthalmology at Emory University in Atlanta, and other investigators concerned about the potential danger of ultraviolet radiation to the retina have searched for ways to protect it from injury. Their work is based on the theory that the retina is jeopardized by oxidative damage to the retinal pigment epithelium (one of its layers). But until some way of medically protecting the retina from damage is perfected, it is perhaps wisest to rely on UV-protective sunglasses and a brimmed hat. Given that macular degeneration affects 28 percent of people seventy-five to eighty-five years of age and that over

100,000 Americans are legally blind as a result of it, you should certainly be cautious about spending much time in the sun without protecting your eyes.

Photosensitivity

In earlier chapters we discussed photosensitivity—the occurrence of adverse skin reactions following exposure to both UVR and certain medications or chemicals. People who are taking medication internally or who suffer from a disease that causes photosensitivity need to be especially protective of their eyes in the sun, since ocular damage has also been associated with photosensitivity. Anyone undergoing PUVA treatment (in which a photosensitive drug called Psoralen is administered to the patient, and then a particular area of the body is exposed under medical care to ultraviolet radiation) for psoriasis or some other condition must take special care to protect eyes and skin when sun exposure cannot be avoided.

Tanning Devices

In the spring of 1989, the Centers for Disease Control of the U.S. Department of Health and Human Services reported on a study done in Wisconsin, where dermatologists, ophthalmologists, and emergency room personnel were surveyed about injuries caused by tanning devices. The 48 ophthalmologists who completed the questionnaire had treated a total of 162 patients during the preceding year for eye injuries related to tanning devices. Of these patients, 129 had suffered corneal injuries, 4 had suffered both corneal and retinal injuries, and 19 had suffered unspecified eye injuries.

Why didn't these tanning enthusiasts wear safety goggles? Many of them did: 24 percent of those who sustained eye injuries from suntanning devices were wearing safety goggles during the tanning session. In these cases, either some radiation seeped through or around the goggles or the goggles themselves did not totally block out the rays.

Brandford L. Walters, M.D., and Ted Martin Kelley, M.D.,

from Michigan State University commented in an article in the *American Journal of Emergency Medicine* that it used to be rare for emergency room physicians to see instances of burns to the cornea, and when they did the burns were usually the result of accidental exposure to chemical or physical agents. For example, people involved in heavy industrial manufacturing might be burned by arc welders. Occasionally the burn might be caused by a home sunlamp or by direct exposure to the sun while sunbathing or boating.

The study conducted by Dr. Walters and Dr. Kelley found that the incidence of corneal burns had increased greatly in the mid-1980s. Of the patients treated at two different emergency rooms for UV-light-induced corneal burns, 40 percent had been exposed at a commercial tanning facility. The researchers noted that the number of corneal burns increased as more commercial tanning facilities began sprouting up around Michigan State University. Many of the people who turned up in emergency rooms for treatment of corneal burns had completed a session under the UV lights just a few hours earlier. Most of the burns were not serious and healed with little or no treatment. But not everyone was so lucky. After exposure to tanning devices, two people noticed blind spots that didn't go away. When they saw an ophthalmologist a few days later, they were informed that severe burns had occurred on their retinas; both individuals were left with substantial permanent loss of vision.

Dermatologists are in agreement that even tanning devices promoted by their manufacturers as "safe UVA" units are *not* safe. Ophthalmologists concur: the wise policy is to stay away from them. But if you insist on using any type of sunlamp or tanning bed, be sure to protect your eyes with goggles that are sanitized (otherwise they can transmit eye infections from the previous user) and that fit tightly. Closing your eyes will not protect them; both solar UVR and artificially produced UVR can sear right through your eyelids.

Cancer and Eyes

The cumulative effect of exposure to the sun has been linked conclusively to skin cancer, and most people associate these cancers with lesions on the face, hands, or other frequently exposed areas of the body. Malignant melanoma, which may occur on exposed or unexposed areas of the body, is usually found in individuals who have had intermittent sun exposure or a history of searing sunburns during childhood. These life-threatening cancers can also occur on the eyelid, and if detected early can be treated very successfully. Unfortunately, when they are allowed to progress to an advanced stage before diagnosis, extensive surgery may be necessary. Melanoma can also develop inside the eye.

Protecting Yourself

Sunglasses are a must on any day that is sunny enough to give you a sunburn. A brimmed hat or billed baseball-type cap can cut sun exposure of the eyes by one-quarter to one-half and thus is a wise investment. Dr. Jacqueline Lustgarten of the Mount Sinai School of Medicine is as careful about summer sun as she is about the ski slopes. She urges her patients to take sensible precautions, and sends her sons off to camp each day with sunscreen, sunglasses, and a baseball cap. In chapter 5 we will discuss how to choose appropriate sunglasses.

II

UVR and Sun Safety

4

Sunscreens: Protecting Your Skin from the Sun

The sun feels great, doesn't it? But good as it may be for the spirit, it certainly is not good for the skin. So today's smart look is a paler one, indicating that you have the good sense to guard your health by protecting your skin from the sun. In this chapter, we will discuss how you can achieve this protection successfully with the least effort.

As you will remember from chapter 1, ultraviolet radiation is emitted from the sun in three different wavelengths: ultraviolet A (UV-A), ultraviolet B (UV-B), and ultraviolet C (UV-C). UV-C is toxic to human, plant, and animal life, but it is filtered out by the atmosphere and never reaches Earth. UV-B rays are the short, burning ones that worry most people because they penetrate the top two regions of the skin and are responsible for red, burning, and immediately damaged skin. UV-B rays are at their most intense between 10 A.M. and 2 P.M. (11 A.M. and 3 P.M. Daylight Savings Time).

UV-A rays are of lower intensity than UV-B, but they can penetrate the third region of the skin, the dermis. UV-A's potential for long-term damage is great—even though it may not appear to burn the skin—because it is present all day long, year-round, whether the sky is cloudy or sunny, and sometimes even through window glass. It is especially concentrated during the early morning and late afternoon, when the sun is at an oblique angle overhead. Most people think of UV-A as the tanning rays and of UV-B as the burning rays, but all ultraviolet radiation causes both premature aging of the skin and skin cancer.

Often, people concern themselves with immediate health or beauty effects and forget about long-term effects. Thus, more effort has been expended on protection from the burning rays of UV-B than on protection from the equally damaging UV-A. One way to accomplish this is with the newer sunscreens, used reliably and correctly.

Back in 1987, a study indicated that fewer than half of all Americans used sunscreen products at all, and most of those who did failed to use them properly. Others thought that if they stayed under a beach umbrella they would be protected, forgetting that sand reflects a considerable amount of ultraviolet radiation. This reflected sunlight jeopardizes areas of the skin not generally exposed to the sun, such as areas under the chin and nose, or even the bottoms of the feet.

Most people are surprised to learn that sunscreens have been around for a long time. A chemical sunscreen containing a mixture of benzyl salicylate and benzyl cinnamate was introduced in 1928. Then in the 1940s, a Miami Beach pharmacist concocted a product (probably to protect his own bald head), using cocoa butter; he marketed it as Coppertone Suntan Creme.

Today's sunscreens are far more sophisticated and offer protection not available years ago. All dermatologists, the Skin Cancer Foundation, and the Food and Drug Administration recommend that you use one. Taking precautions in the sun should become automatic, like placing small children in car seats and buckling the seat belts on everyone else, even for a short trip.

Once it becomes a habit, you hardly even think about it. For instance, I use sun protection every day from May through October in New York, even if I'm just dashing out to mail a manuscript from the local post office. My husband, who once was an airline pilot for Uncle Sam, went on sun protection "automatic pilot" after I began researching this book. His hair is thinning, so he protects both his face and head by wearing a cap with a visor. We have learned by experience that sometimes one of us runs into an acquaintance with whom we stand chatting on the corner, finally going for a bagel or muffin and a cup of coffee. Then we decide to "walk it off," resulting in more than a half-hour of unanticipated sun exposure just when UV-A is at its strongest.

Questions and Answers about Sunscreens

How do you decide which sunscreen to use? If you go to a drugstore, variety store, or the cosmetic counter of a department store, you can easily be overwhelmed by the array of products displayed. However, the following question-and-answer format should help you decide what is best for you.

What are sunscreens?

Unlike the once-popular "suntan lotions," which encouraged a tan, sunscreens are substances applied to the skin that either absorb or reflect the sun's rays in order to prevent UVR from reaching the skin.

Are there different types of sunscreens?

All sunscreens work by blocking—to various extents—the harmful rays of the sun from penetrating the layers of your skin. Most of them only block UV-B, but some also protect you from UV-A. Sunscreens can be grouped into two categories: chemical and physical.

The chemical screens contain absorbing chemicals that act as a filter, absorbing solar energy before it can penetrate the skin. The absorbed energy excites the sunscreen temporarily, but then as the chemical relaxes back to its original state it transforms that energy into something harmless such as heat. This process of energy conversion is continuously repeated. Chemical sunscreens are usually colorless or white, and form an invisible film on the skin, without altering appearance or staining clothing. Examples of active chemical agents are PABA (para-aminobenzoic acid), PABA esters, benzophenones, cinnamates, salicylates, and anthranilates.

Physical screens are usually opaque and contain ingredients that do not absorb UVR, instead reflecting and scattering the rays away from the skin. Examples of physical screens are those that contain titanium dioxide and zinc oxide. Physical screens are manufactured in bright, neon colors, as well as in the traditional white.

Because physical screens stain clothes, have a gritty consistency, and are messy to use, most people choose to use them only for very vulnerable spots such as the lips, the nose, and the helix of the ear.

Some physical agents are available in skin-tone colors for use by people with particular vulnerability, such as those with vitiligo (see chapter 2).

Do sunscreens protect against both UV-A and UV-B?

Physical sunscreens reflect both UV-A and UV-B, thus protecting against both kinds of rays. Until recently, most chemical screens only absorbed the burning UV-B rays. Because they blocked out these rays, they often gave users a false sense of security and thus could actually promote a tan. Sunburn didn't occur, so people remained in the sun for longer periods of time, allowing UV-A rays to be absorbed into the deeper layers of the skin, with resulting long-term skin damage. But now most sunscreens do absorb both UV-A and UV-B; look for labels that say so.

Known as *full-spectrum* sunscreen agents, dibenzoylmethanes can protect against the entire UV-A waveband. These agents have been available in Europe and Australia for some time but were introduced into American products only in the late 1980s. One of these compounds, Parsol 1789, has been found to block much more of the UV-A rays than oxybenzone (which has been available for a longer period of time). Combined with other chemicals such as Padimate-O, it provides excellent protection.

A number of cosmetic companies manufacture opaque makeup that performs as both a physical and chemical sunblock, offering broad protection.

What is meant by SPF?

SPF (or sun protective factor) is the ratio of the amount of energy required to produce a minimal sunburn through a sunscreen product to the amount of energy required to produce the same minimal sunburn without any sunscreen protection. For example, if you usually get slightly sunburned after

20 minutes in the sun without any protection, when you use a sunscreen with an SPF of 15 you theoretically will get the same sunburn only after staying out in the sun for 20 × 15 = 300 minutes, or 5 hours. However, SPF and tanning can be affected by your skin type, by the formulation of the sunscreen, and by the intensity of UV exposure. For instance, if you get sunburned at the pool or lake in Maine in 20 minutes, you might be badly burned in only 10 minutes at a high altitude relatively near the equator in New Mexico.

The Skin Cancer Foundation recommends that everyone use a sunscreen with an SPF of 15 or more. Little is known about the effectiveness of sunscreens with higher SPFs, although they most likely last longer and offer more protection during shorter periods.

Has the FDA made a statement about sunscreens?

Yes. Back in 1978, the Food and Drug Administration issued proposed rules that "would establish conditions for the safety, effectiveness and labeling of over-the-counter drug products." Sunscreens are considered drugs in the United States because their use can affect the structure or function of the skin; thus, they fall under FDA jurisdiction. The FDA allows sunscreen manufacturers to print the following notice on their labels: "Liberal and regular use of sunscreen products may help reduce the chance of premature aging of the skin and skin cancer."

Every sunscreen seems to say "contains PABA" or "PABA-free." What is PABA?

PABA (para-aminobenzoic acid) is one of the earliest-developed sunscreen chemicals. It is not used much today, because it causes an adverse skin reaction in a number of people (especially on skin that has been sunburned or windburned, and in areas around the eyes), and it tends to stain clothing. PABA has been around since the 1920s and was extremely popular until the introduction of PABA esters. These esters are strong yet nonreactive with the skin and far less likely to cause irritation.

Sunscreens described as "PABA-free" usually contain PABA esters.

Can sunscreens cause skin sensitivity in some people?

Unfortunately, they can. This is perhaps the main reason that PABA has declined so much in popularity and use. A number of users suffer redness and itching about twenty-four hours after applying sunscreens that contain PABA. The allergy may be caused by the PABA ingredient itself or by the combination of sunscreen plus ultraviolet light, resulting in a photocontact dermatitis. It is possible to be allergic to one form of PABA and not to others.

Allergies can sometimes arise from other ingredients in the sunscreen, such as fragrances, preservatives, or the base used in formulating the product. Switching to another brand can make a big difference.

Reactions are usually temporary, but they can easily be misunderstood by people who think that their allergy is to the sun; instead of changing suncreens, these people may use more of it or may switch to a version of the same product that has a higher SPF. The greater concentration of chemicals in the product may simply increase the sensitivity.

Individuals who have a history of allergies—especially to hair dyes, sulfonamines, or procaine—or who are taking anti-hypertensive or diuretic drugs may be sensitive to PABA and PABA esters. Discuss your situation with your doctor before using sunscreens that contain these ingredients, or ask if it would be safe for you to do your own patch test. Apply the sunscreen to a small patch of skin (preferably on the underside of the forearm) and then cover the area with a small adhesive bandage. Then after twenty-four hours, remove the bandage. If there is any redness or swelling of the covered area, don't use that sunscreen. But even if there is no reaction, expose the area to fifteen minutes of sunlight and then wait another twenty-four hours. If a reaction appears the next day in the form of redness or swelling, your test is positive and you should avoid this product.

Cinnamates are used in a number of sunscreens. Some people who are allergic to them are also sensitive to cinnamon-flavored products such as mouthwashes, chewing gum, and toothpastes.

Some of the new broad-spectrum sunscreens can cause

allergic reactions in some individuals—especially those who are sensitive to benzocane, sulfonamides, or PABA.

If you are unable to stay out of the sun, and can only tolerate chemical sunscreens with a low SPF, your druggist may be able to combine it with a titanium dioxide paste, to afford you a safe and nonallergenic sunblock.

Don't become unduly alarmed by this discussion, because the overwhelming majority of people have little or no sensitivity to sunscreens.

Are some sunscreens genuinely waterproof?

Yes. The vehicle or base containing the UVR-absorbing chemical determines the sunscreen's effectiveness under various conditions, such as immersion in water. A sunscreen's ability to adhere to your skin while you are sunbathing, sweating, or swimming is called its *substantivity*.

Sunscreens that contain PABA esters such as Padimate-O are considered very substantive. Sunscreens that use an oil or cream base are more water-resistant than those that use an alcohol base.

If a sunscreen is labeled *waterproof*, it must maintain its rated SPF for 80 minutes in water. Sunscreens that are *water-resistant* are supposed to maintain their SPF for 40 minutes in water. Interestingly, some products actually have a higher SPF than is labeled on the product so that, even if some of it is washed away, the sunscreen will still offer the advertised protection.

Waterproof sunscreens are an excellent choice if you plan to be swimming or dodging ocean waves, and the water-resistant ones are good if you are active and anticipate perspiring.

After swimming in a chlorine-filled pool and drying yourself vigorously with a towel, don't expect your sunscreen to continue to be effective. Play it safe—even if you dry naturally—and reapply sunscreen.

Do sunscreens come in different formulas?

Most sunscreens are sold in bottles and tubes as lotions or creams. The clear lotions seem more like liquids; their advantage is that they're not greasy, so sand doesn't stick to the skin. Clear lotions usually have an alcohol base, and are especially good for people who have oily skin. Some people complain that they find it difficult to determine whether they have covered all of their skin when using a clear lotion.

Most cream formulas are not especially greasy; and although they go on creamy white, they disappear when rubbed in. It is easier with cream formulas to see if you have missed any spots.

Various under-makeup moisturizers have an SPF of 15. They offer a good way to protect your face, with or without makeup. If you are planning to be out in strong sun or for a long period of time, however, you will want to add additional sunscreen.

Sunscreens may be packaged in tubes (like ointments), in spray containers, in stick form, or in plastic bottles. Some are lightweight gels that absorb into the skin instantly. Individually wrapped sunscreen towelettes are perfect to put into your bag or pocket or to leave in your desk drawer for unexpected outings. Hair sprays often have an SPF built into them. This feature helps protect hair color from oxidizing, and it may give some protection to scalp, but a low-SPF hairspray will not sufficiently protect scalp if the hair itself doesn't provide a good barrier.

How do you choose a sunscreen?
Wisely, we hope. Don't just grab the first bottle or tube that you see on the counter. Think about how you will be using it. Will you just be wearing it while walking through the shopping area of your city, sightseeing on a vacation in a foreign city, or sitting quietly on your front porch reading the paper? If so, you will not need a sunscreen that is waterproof or water-resistant.

If the weather is hot, or if you plan to be running after the kids in the park, participating in any sports, or encountering some water, you will certainly want a water-resistant sunscreen. If you will be swimming, a waterproof sunscreen is essential.

The Skin Cancer Foundation recommends that everyone use a sunscreen with an SPF of 15 or more. Remember, a sunscreen with an SPF of 15 or more costs only pennies more than one with less protection. If you still feel you want a bit of a tan, start by using sunscreen with an SPF of 15 or more, and then later in the season use sunscreen with a lower number. A sensible tan like this shouldn't get you into any major health trouble; but remember, it certainly will accelerate skin aging. There is no way around this simple rule: tan now, pay later.

Is an expensive sunscreen better than a moderately priced one?

Better is a tricky word. Will an expensive sunscreen protect you more? No. Will it appeal to you more because of its texture, fragrance, packaging, or dispensing qualities? Perhaps. An SPF is an SPF, and whether you buy your sunscreen at a large discount chain store, or at a fancy cosmetics counter in a department or speciality store, you should be getting the same protection. Stay with a brand-name company, if you feel more confident about its products, and remember that good turnover assures you of a fresher product. The appendix tells you how to receive a listing of sunscreens recommended by the Skin Cancer Foundation.

Is there a special way to apply sunscreens?

Naturally, you should follow directions on the bottle. But many manufacturers neglect to tell you how important it is to apply a sunscreen *before* going out in the sun. Experts say that it takes at least thirty minutes for a sunscreen to sink into the skin. Sunscreens with PABA should be applied two hours before exposure.

Sunscreen binds best to cool dry skin, and you'll miss far fewer spots if you remember this and use some common sense. Always put the sunscreen on before you put on your bathing suit or clothes. That way you won't miss areas of demarcation, where the clothes end and you begin! Be generous with sunscreen; and if you use a cream formula, leave a film that you can feel. Some oil-free screens are designed to disappear, so they will not leave a film. Apply the sunscreen over all exposed areas of your body, and consider using an additional thick dab of physical screen on "hot spots."

How much sunscreen should I use?

More than you probably think. The average adult wearing a bathing suit should plan to use half a teaspoon on *each* of the following parts of the body: the face and neck; each arm and shoulder; the front and back of the torso; and each leg and top of the foot.

Most people are rather stingy with their sunscreen and don't use enough for proper coverage. It is better to use plenty of a lower-SPF sunscreen than not enough of a higher-SPF sunscreen.

How often does sunscreen need to be applied?

The Skin Cancer Foundation suggests that you apply sunscreen before every exposure to the sun and that you reapply it frequently and liberally. They suggest doing this every two hours, as long as you stay in the sun, and reapplying it after swimming or perspiring heavily.

Just because an SPF seems to give you the protection you need for a few hours (according to the mathematical equation given earlier) does not mean that you are fully protected for that amount of time. Rather than playing the numbers game, use an SPF of 15 or more, and apply it frequently.

Is there a way to protect the head if you are bald or hair is thinning?

Bald men must protect their head in the sun, since this skin is very vulnerable. Wearing a sunscreen and a cap while sitting in the sun is essential. But people with thinning hair face a difficult dilemma. Hairsprays with an SPF built into them are useful for people with thick hair, but the SPF is usually too low to provide protection for exposed parts of the scalp, so wearing a hat or cap is probably the only way to get complete protection. But most men prefer not to wear a bathing cap while they are swimming or to wear a hat when they are dressed in a business suit. Aerosols that spray through thinning hair directly onto the scalp are available.

When should you use sunscreen?

You should use sunscreen whenever you are going to be exposed to sun for any period of time. If you are just going to spend lunch hour (when the sun is strongest in UV-B radiation) sitting in the park across the street from your office, you need protection. If you are going to the beach for the day, even if the weather report is for hazy, overcast weather, you need sunscreen, because UV-A comes right through those clouds.

Protect your hands, arms, and other exposed areas with sunscreen (or appropriate clothing) when you fish, jog, ski, or play golf, tennis, or other outdoor sports. Protect your lips with a balm that has maximum sunscreen; women can use a lipstick that offers protection. Any time you are out in mid-summer or at high noon, are surrounded by sand or snow, or are in the tropics, use maximum protection.

You need sunscreen even when you are going to be sitting in the car, unless you are sure that you will be keeping the windows closed. I learned this quite graphically last summer. The air-conditioning in my car was giving me trouble, so I drove with the window open. My face was well protected because I apply a moisturizer with an SPF of 15 under any makeup or, more often, wear makeup that provides a total sunblock; but I hadn't bothered to protect my arms because I wasn't planning to be outside for more than a few minutes at a time. Within a week I had a "watch strap mark," indicating that the sun had gotten to me after all! Even if I had remembered to use a sunscreen on my hands and arms, if it weren't a broad-spectrum one that blocked out much of the UV-A as well as the UV-B, I would probably have tanned. Moreover, a car's side windows do not usually block out UV-A.

Many women use a good-quality broad-spectrum sunscreen as a moisturizer under makeup (allowing a half-hour for it to set before applying makeup) and also put some on their hands and arms to avoid acquiring age spots. Men should apply sunscreen after shaving each morning.

A surprising statistic tells us that 80 percent of sun exposure is incidental. Your skin absorbs those rays when you do errands, walk the dog, push the baby carriage or shopping cart, or simply walk to and from lunch. That adds up to a lot of cumulative exposure, and although you are not likely to get a sunburn from these errands, the damage is accruing in the third layer of your skin, the dermis. Eventually you will pay the penalty with prematurely sun-damaged and aged skin and perhaps with an increased risk of cancer.

Wouldn't an overall even tan offer some protection against sunburn?

It may offer you protection against the searing sunburn you would have gotten without the tan; that's precisely the selling point that tanning salons try to use. But the truth is that a tan is not healthful; instead, it is the recorded evidence of damage that the skin has suffered. A suntan offers no more protection than a sunscreen with a 2 or 3 SPF, which is minimal. Thus, even with a tan, damage will accumulate.

How long can you store sunscreen?

This is a tough question. First check the bottle to see if there is an expiration date on it. Some sunscreens require this, but others have ingredients that don't lose their potency, so there may be no date.

Oil can separate from the solids in some products, downgrading the SPF, and the SPF can also deteriorate from exposure to heat. A good idea is to mark the date you purchased the sunscreen, so you will know later how long you have had it. Avoid storing opened or closed sunscreens in warm places such as medicine cabinets in bathrooms. Try to buy the product at a store that has a high turnover; look at boxes and bottles and notice whether they seem free of dust and dents.

Children need sunscreens, too, don't they?

They certainly do, although sunscreen companies instruct you not to use these products on babies before the age of six months. Consult your pediatrician if some sun exposure seems unavoidable. Whenever possible, keep baby out of the sun altogether.

By the age of one year, children should be using sunscreen. If you have any questions about starting to use it earlier or waiting longer, discuss these with the baby's doctor. You can purchase sunscreens that are clearly targeted for children, or you can buy any non-PABA milky lotion or cream. Avoid clear lotions, which may contain alcohol and can sting.

When applying a sunscreen, avoid covering the eyelids (kids love to rub their eyes), because the ingredients can irritate the eyes. Apply it generously to all uncovered areas; putting little dabs on the face and shoulders is not enough. Reapply the sunscreen frequently—every sixty to ninety minutes is not too often. Be sure to apply sunscreen under sheer fabrics such as thin T-shirts or light, lacy bathing suits, since the sun can penetrate thin wet fabrics.

If you screen out all the sun, will you develop a vitamin D deficiency?

Probably not, if you are eating a normal diet—particularly one that includes milk and milk products fortified with fat-soluble vitamin D. Foods rich in vitamin D are egg yolk, liver, tuna, salmon, and cod liver oil. Dark-skinned people in cold climates and people who habitually wear a total sunblock and clothing that doesn't permit any UVR to penetrate should, for added protection, take a high-potency multivitamin formula containing 400 IU of vitamin D. This will supply the United States required daily allowance (RDA). Vitamin D, sometimes called the "sunshine vitamin," is transformed by kidney action into a more potent form, in which it assumes the role of a hormone. It is secreted into the bloodstream, where it helps to control the absorption of calcium from the digestive system, maintaining healthy bones. It is needed by adults as well as by children. Bodies make their own vitamin D, but the energy from ultraviolet light helps to activate its production. Most experts say that about fifteen minutes of exposure to sunlight two to three times a week by any area of the body is sufficient.

Individuals who don't go out at all (such as nursing-home residents) or who work a schedule that allows them little fresh air (except perhaps in a heavily polluted area) and who may not be getting enough fortified foods (this can include vegetarians who don't eat any meat by-products, including homogenized milk or eggs) require a vitamin D supplement.

But you should avoid megadoses. Excess vitamin D is stored in the liver, and a surplus of it can cause serious problems. From too much vitamin D, adults can develop deposits of calcium throughout their body, deafness, nausea, loss of appetite, kidney stones, fragile bones, high blood pressure, high blood cholesterol, or increased lead absorption.

Babies need vitamin D in order to avoid rickets. Doctors

no longer advocate the old-fashioned "sun bath." Instead, they advise keeping the baby out of direct sun. Nursing mothers are advised to give their babies a vitamin D supplement, frequently contained in a multivitamin preparation. Formula-fed babies get vitamin D in the formula. These supplements are particularly important in relatively cold climates, in the winter, and in severely polluted areas, when many babies are rarely taken outdoors. Use only the amount recommended by your pediatrician, because megadoses of vitamin D in infants are extremely harmful; risks associated with megadoses in infants include calcium deposits in the kidneys and an excess of calcium in the blood. As with so many good things—medication, vitamins, or even healthful food—more is not always better.

Should elderly people use sunscreens, too?

Absolutely. They don't want to develop skin cancer, and because their lifetime exposure to the sun began in the days before the dangers were recognized, their cumulative exposure is already great. Many older people have already had one or more skin cancers, so they must be extremely cautious.

Studies have indicated, however, that older people who use sunscreens with an SPF of 15 daily may have less than half the vitamin D level of those who don't use it. Rather than cutting down on SPF, take a multivitamin that includes vitamin D, or take an additional vitamin D supplement. Don't overdo it, though, or you risk incurring vitamin D toxicity. Very little sun exposure is needed to spur the skin to manufacture vitamin D—far less than the amount needed to cause sunburn or tanning. Solar radiation may also penetrate light clothing sufficiently to help manufacture the vitamin.

After years and years of sun exposure, is there any value in starting to use a sunscreen now?

Yes. It's not like closing the barn door after the cow gets out: it is never too late to begin protecting your skin from further assault. One exciting development is the news that dermatologists now believe that protection from the sun—either through use of a sunscreen or as a result of staying out of the sun altogether—may allow the skin to regenerate collagen and elastin, the tissues responsible for keeping skin smooth.

Is there a way to know how much ultraviolet radiation is reaching us?

Unfortunately, such information is not readily accessible to most of us. But one company—Solar Light Co. of Philadelphia—has produced a weatherproof sunburn UV meter for continuous recording of ambient levels of sunburning ultraviolet radiation. This meter consists of an outside sensor cabled to an indoor data acquisition system; it provides information for meteorological records and for local radio stations to broadcast warnings.

Wouldn't it be wonderful if all weather reports included information about the amount of ultraviolet radiation likely to affect us? Then we would know whether we needed to pack sunscreen in our bag or briefcase along with (or instead of) our umbrella, and frequent updates would help us plan protection all day.

Why is it that some people just won't use sunscreen—even though they know better?

Good sense tells most of us to take precautions against aging skin and cancer, and the same good sense makes us wonder why some people refuse to heed warnings.

Psychologists at the University of California at Riverside wondered, too; so Howard S. Friedman and Barbara Kessling conducted a study, published in *Health Psychology* in 1987. For this study they interviewed sunbathing and nonsunbathing beachgoers about their health practices, kowledge about skin cancer, moods, and thoughts about the social rewards to be obtained through sunbathing. One finding was a partial confirmation of a stereotype of sunbathers as individuals who are relaxed but very concerned with their appearance. But another portrait also emerged: an action-oriented, risk-taking person who values the appearance (as opposed to the careful nurturing) of health and who associates with like-minded individuals. Sunbathers, Friedman and Kessling found, were far less concerned with actual health than with the appearance of health, and although many of them exercised and maintained the right weight, they tended to be risk takers as far as other health behaviors are concerned. As regards the dangers of UVR exposure, many professed ignorance; others just paid no attention to warnings.

Some people simply avoid listening to the odds or hear them but think that they won't be "unlucky." Perhaps that's why Las Vegas is full of people—some at the gaming tables, and others sitting around the pool, basking in the hot sun!

Other Ways to Protect the Skin

Sunscreens are an excellent way to protect your skin from the sun. Invisible, easy to use, and always available, sunscreens can afford you safety while enjoying the great outdoors anytime and anywhere.

For additional safety, or when frequent application of sunscreens is not desirable, you can adopt other ways to protect your skin.

Clothing

Whenever possible when sun exposure is inevitable, wear long-sleeved shirts and long pants made of lightweight but tightly woven fabrics. Hold an article of clothing up against the light. The less you can see through it, the more protection it will give you. Fibers that are sheer enough to see through seldom provide much protection; the sun simply goes through them. Tighter weaves—preferably dyed—allow less sun to penetrate to the skin. The darker the fabric is, the more light and heat it will absorb; and so on a hot day it may be quite uncomfortable.

Clothes made of natural or man-made fabrics with a tight weave that cover most of your body can absorb and reflect a good deal of the sun's radiation. Mesh fabrics or weaves with large gaps, and wet clothes of *any* fabric permit more UVR penetration. Remember this, especially after you have been swimming or perspiring. Some studies indicate that a typical white cotton T-shirt may offer an SPF of under 10, which is inadequate for anyone who needs high-level sun protection, or who is remaining outdoors for a lengthy period of time. Such individuals should also use sunscreen under their clothes, especially to cover sensitive areas.

In response to a growing need for more protection and people's resistance to the cumbersome task of frequently reapplying sunscreen to the entire body, fabrics and especially prepared clothing have been developed in the last few years offering protection of 30 and more SPF. Those companies that have received or applied for FDA clearance for their products are also able to claim that the protection will last through many washings. Attractive and stylish clothing for infants, children, men, and women offer head-to-toe coverage but remain comfortable and cool in even hot weather. Generally such clothing is available only through mail order. For a catalog and further information try the following: Sun Precautions, Inc. (Solumbro 30+ SPF Ultra Sun Protective Clothing) 1-800-882-7960; Frogskin (Frogwear) 1-800-845-9531; Solar Protective Factory, Inc. (Solarweave fabric) 1-800-786-2562.

Hats

A hat with a wide brim or a baseball-type cap offers good protection for the head and forehead and supplemental protection for the eyes. A visor alone can protect the forehead and eyes. For optimum protection—either because you will be out in the sun for hours on end (while fishing, perhaps) or because you are at particular high risk—a hat that offers more extensive coverage is useful.

Look for hats with large brims and flaps that can protect the face, ears, and neck. Find one that is light, durable, and made of cotton or a combination of cotton and polyester. Better yet, get a hat that is made with the newer SPF protective fabrics.

Umbrellas, Parasols, Awnings, and Such

Such items are useful indeed, but don't count on them for total protection. If possible, select ones made with the SPF protective fabrics. Staying under a beach umbrella or other covering outdoors only gives you partial protection, because the sun's rays scatter and can get to you even under an umbrella. Cover-up clothing, sunscreen, and shade are all vital elements of your defense against the effects of the sun.

Windows and Glass

Most windows and glass screen out UV-B, and some of the newer ones block out some UV-A. If you are putting new windows into your home, ask if they block out a lot of the sun's ultraviolet rays and also keep furniture and fabrics from fading.

Glass generally does not serve as a complete barrier between you and ultraviolet radiation. So if your desk is right next to a window and you have been enjoying that beautiful sunlight and view, remember to put a broad-spectrum sunscreen on each day before going to work. However, as long as you don't sit right at the window "soaking in the sunshine," you probably won't need this protection unless you are going to be outdoors.

The windshield of your car, because of its slant, screens out a great deal of the sun's UV-A, but the side windows don't do a very good job of it. Therefore, if you are planning a long car ride, or if you spend a great deal of time each day in the car (even with the windows closed and the air-conditioning on) take precautions: use sunscreen and wear cover-up clothes.

Protecting Babies and Children

Unless your pediatrician suggests otherwise, you should not apply sunscreen to babies under six months of age. But there are a number of ways of protecting babies and young children without keeping them indoors all summer (or year-round in the Sunbelt).

A number of excellent products are available to help shield babies from reflected sunlight. Some playpens come with their own canopy or shade; or separate canopies and shades can be purchased to attach to the playpen you already have. Baby hats with Foreign Legion–style flaps offer more protection than do conventional hats. Washable shades attach by an elastic hem to carseats or infant carriers, for partial or complete shade; fiber mesh shades attach with Velcro to standard carseats; and a number of shades are made to attach to carriages. Car shades that attach to car windows with suction cups work just the way home window shades do and will afford added protection to small children sitting in the backseat of the car.

Protective products of the types listed above are available in many stores. If you can't find them where you live, various mail-order companies often gather unique and useful products to list in their catalogs. One company committed to sun protection for small children is The Right Start. Call them at 1-800-LITTLE-1 for a catalog or for more information.

5

Sunglasses: Protecting Your Eyes from the Sun

The world certainly looks brighter on a sunny day; the grass and pavements glitter, and the skies are the bluest blue. Why dim it all with sunglasses?

As a matter of fact, there are several good reasons. Glare from the sun can give you a headache and make you squint (helping to set those fine lines and wrinkles), and large amounts of visible and invisible ultraviolet (both UV-A and UV-B) light can be harmful to the eyes. In addition, bright sunlight can damage the cornea, the lens, and the retina of your eye.

As we saw in chapter 3, studies have established that people whose eyes have had a great deal of exposure to UV-B are at greater risk for cataract development, and some studies also indicate that exposure can lead to serious damage to the retina, resulting in age-related macular degeneration. Snow blindness, a reversible condition, is not uncommon among skiers who fail to wear protective eye coverings.

Long before scientific studies confirmed the adverse effects of sunlight on the eyes, different people created ways of shielding the eyes. Natives of the arctic region and Native Americans carved goggles of walrus ivory or wood with narrow slits in them to limit the amount of light that entered their eyes and to protect themselves from snow blindness. At one time the Chinese ground lenses from colored pieces of crystal for the same purpose.

Everyone needs sunglasses. The color of your eyes has no bearing on your vulnerability to the sun. The stronger the sun is and the more you are out in it, the greater is your need for protection. Skiers and boaters undergo a great deal of UVR exposure over a long period of time, as do people who spend time on tropical beaches, so they require especially good eye protection. Surfers should wear goggles that screen out ultraviolet radiation. Sunglasses should also be worn when driving in bright sun, because the glare is likely to make you squint, limiting your vision and increasing your risk of having an accident. A typical clear windshield does block a good deal of ultraviolet radiation, however, and a tinted one blocks still more.

People who have had their natural lens removed for treatment of cataracts no longer have the natural protection the lens provides, so they must be especially careful to guard their eyes from ultraviolet radiation. Beginning in the early 1980s, many people who were operated on for cataracts have had an intraocular lens containing compounds that absorb UV light placed in the eye. Anyone who has had cataract surgery or is contemplating it should discuss this option with an ophthalmologist.

Individuals who are undergoing PUVA treatment (which makes use of the photosensitive medication Psoralen), as described in chapter 2, should wear sunglasses for at least twenty-four hours after treatment, because of the increased risk of developing cataracts. People being treated with other photosensitizing drugs should take similar precautions.

For your health and comfort and for greater safety when driving or performing any task that requires accurate vision in the sun, you should wear sunglasses. A hat with a brim also provides good protection against ultraviolet radiation.

Questions and Answers About Sunglasses

To help you choose appropriate sunglasses, I have turned to a number of experts: the American Academy of Ophthalmology; the Sunglass Association of America; the American National Standards Institute; the Food and Drug Administration; the Skin Cancer Foundation; Jacqueline Lustgarten, M.D., associate clinical professor of ophthalmology at the Mount Sinai School of Medicine; and Dr. Stephen Rozenberg, optometrist at 10/10 Optics. *Consumer Reports* has also provided much of the information in written form. The question-and-answer section that follows is a synthesis of these sources.

What do sunglasses do?

They make you much more comfortable in bright sunlight. Sunglasses enhance the eye's normal filtering effects, as well as freeing you from squinting and grimacing. Most important, properly selected sunglasses protect your eyes from the short- and long-range adverse effects of ultraviolet radiation upon your eyes.

What are the different types of light?

Ultraviolet radiation (invisible light) represents only 6 percent of the total quantity of solar energy reaching the earth. The remainder of the energy is composed of infrared rays and visible light rays.

Infrared rays are experienced as heat, and there is no evidence that this energy does the eyes any harm. Visible light, which is perceived by us as colors, is important because it enables us to see objects; however, as we all know, when too much of it strikes our eyes we become uncomfortable. The visible spectrum of light consists of the rainbow of individual hues that combine to form white light. The first wavelength in this visible spectrum is blue-violet light, which many scientists believe can be damaging to the eyes.

What are the effects of blue light?

A number of experts believe that cumulative exposure to blue light may affect the retina and be a factor in developing macular degeneration, a condition in which the functioning of the macula (the high-resolution or fine-tuning part of the retina, needed for close work) grows progressively worse. This condition can eventually result in blindness. Other experts, however, feel that the relationship of blue light to macular degeneration has not yet been satisfactorily established.

Some eyeglass makers promote their products with claims that the lenses block all blue light. But sunglasses that block out all blue light can distort colors, not letting you identify reds as red, greens as green, and blues as blue. Most experts believe that just limiting the blue light is sufficient. General-purpose sunglasses that meet the American National Standards Institute (ANSI) guidelines block at least 75 percent of visible light, thereby providing adequate protection from blue light.

What types of sunglasses offer the best general protection?
Routine protection for the eyes on a sunny day is provided by a lens that lowers the brightness of all wavelengths of light and filters out most invisible ultraviolet radiation and visible blue light.

Until recently, it was difficult for a consumer to evaluate sunglasses in terms of their protection, so many people felt more confident in purchasing an expensive brand or shopping for them at an optical store that also made prescription glasses.

But now, at long last, the Sunglass Association of America (SAA), an industry group, working together with the United States Food and Drug Administration (FDA) has developed and adopted a UV labeling program for rating nonprescription sunglasses and providing consumers with uniform, sound, and useful UV labeling. Because sunglasses are medical devices, they are regulated by the FDA; and both that agency and the SAA were becoming increasingly concerned about the seeming use of scare tactics in the marketplace and, on the other hand, the public's need for eye protection. In 1985 the two groups began preliminary discussions on the issues involved, culminating in a series of meetings in 1988 on the subjects of solar energy and the eye, the role of sunglasses, and sunglass standards.

The voluntary labeling program to be carried out by the SAA is based on the UV categories specified by the American National Standards Institute and was developed by consensus agreement among representatives from the eyecare profession, educators, researchers, the military, other government agencies, and industry; as such, it constitutes the only authoritative document covering the properties and performance of sunglasses. Known as the ANSI Z80.3-1986 Sunglass Standard, it specifies precise standard wording for labels to be placed on a tag or sticker included with each pair of sunglasses.

What are the specifics of the SAA labeling program?
The SAA labeling program specifies standard wording on labels as follows:

1. "Meets ANSI Z80.3 cosmetic UV requirements. Blocks at least 70% UVB and 20% UVA."
2. "Meets ANSI Z80.3 general purpose UV requirements. Blocks at least 95% UVB and 60% UVA."
3. "Meets ANSI Z80.3 special purpose UV requirements. Blocks at least 99% UVB and 60% UVA."

Further, the program also allows the manufacturer or importer-distributor to specify the actual percentage of UV-B and UV-A blocked by the product, beneath the basic policy statement. This additional information, if used, is to be stated in the following form:

"These lenses block XX% UVB and YY% UVA."

To help consumers understand what the labeling means in terms of personal selection and use, the following information on types of sunglasses is also available to consumers:

* *Cosmetic sunglasses* are lightly tinted and are recommended for nonharsh sunlight activities, such as shopping or other around-town uses, out of the direct sun. They block less than 60 percent of visible light, but they block at least 70 percent of UV-B radiation and at least 20 percent of UV-A radiation. These are the least protective sunglasses.
* *General-purpose sunglasses* are recommended for any sunlight activity, such as for beach, boating, driving, flying, hiking, picnicking, and snow use. They are adequate for most uses for most people. General-purpose sunglasses block from 60 percent to 92 percent of visible light, and they block at least 95 percent of UV-B radiation and at least 60 percent of UV-A radiation.
* *Special-purpose sunglasses*, as their label implies, are recommended for special purposes. They may block from as much as 97 percent to as little as 20 percent of visible light. Darker shades are recommended for people who often engage in activities in very bright environments, such as skiing, mountain climbing, or vacationing at a tropical beach. Lighter shades may be preferred in dim-

mer situations, such as for skiing on overcast days. Special-purpose sunglasses block at least 99 percent of UV-B and 60 percent of UV-A.

Do all sunglasses meet or exceed these guidelines?

Not all sunglasses meet the ANSI guidelines. Remember that these guidelines are voluntary; consequently, you may see nonprescription sunglasses that do not display a label at all. If you do, don't buy them.

On the other hand, some sunglasses may exceed the guidelines. For instance, widely recognized brands such as Bolle, Bausch & Lomb, and Corning, as well as some very moderately priced but less well-known brands, make lenses that claim 100 percent UV-A and UV-B protection. Light transmission varies, depending on the color of the lens, but a given pair of sunglasses should meet or exceed the guidelines for its type, whether cosmetic, general-purpose, or special-purpose. Generally, eyecare professionals feel that the ANSI Z80.3-1986 establishes sufficient protection and does not need to be exceeded, although some experts have suggested that the standards should be more stringent.

Is any special style of sunglass frames better than others?

Sunglasses that wrap around or fit closely offer the most protection. Sunglasses with small lenses that sit down about ½ inch from the nose allow roughly 20 percent of the light to reach the eye by seeping in around the lenses, as do larger sunglasses that do not fit close to the face.

In one study it was noted that if sunglasses do not fit closely, almost three times as much UV radiation reaches the eye as would if they fit correctly. One way to keep light from reaching the eyes around the frames is by using side shields, which are attached to some models.

Sunglasses should be comfortable. When you try them on, make sure they fit with snug, comfortable pressure behind your ears and that the frame distributes the weight evenly on your nose. Frames range widely in style and construction, so it is wise to check them carefully before you buy. Hinges should look sturdy, and the ear pieces (temples) should not have too much play, to ensure continued good fit and service.

Do ordinary eyeglasses block ultraviolet radiation?

Most people are surprised to learn that plastic lenses do block a great deal of UV light. Glass lenses do not block it unless there is a sunglass coating applied to them. A clear dye coating can be applied to plastic lenses to give additional protection.

What color should sunglasses be?

The color of the lens and the darkness of the tint are unrelated to their ability to block UVR. Thus, in choosing a color, personal preference may win out; still, experts agree on certain guidelines, as follows.

Trust your eyes to see if the lenses seem too dark or not dark enough. If you are particularly light-sensitive, you may prefer darker lenses or medium ones even in the winter. If you know you will be wearing the glasses at the beach or while skiing, you may want dark lenses; if you just plan to be walking along city streets on sunny summer days, a medium shade is probably just fine. Naturally you won't want your glasses to be so dark that you can't see clearly, but you will want them to be dark enough to save you from squinting, especially if you are driving or engaging in some other activity that requires keen sight.

Some colors can distort reality. Amber glasses, for instance, are excellent for blocking blue light, but they can also make differentiating red from green difficult. If you are considering buying a pair, arrange to go outside the store and look at traffic lights. If you have trouble distinguishing red, green, and yellow, don't buy them. Many people find that brown and brown-amber lenses improve contrast, and they have no problems with them in traffic. Try this out for yourself.

Blue lenses look attractive, but they allow too much blue light to penetrate, so they are not recommended.

Gray lenses are neutral and transmit all colors evenly. Lenses of a brownish or greenish hue are least likely to distort colors, and the light they pass is natural and comfortable. Generally, dark gray or dark green tints permit the most normal color vision. Sunglasses should not make the world look different; rather, they should just block the bright rays of the sun and eliminate glare. And of course, they should block UVR.

Remember, however, that the color of the lenses and the

lightness or darkness of that color do not affect their UVR-blocking qualities. For this information, you must depend on the labels.

Is it true that very darkly tinted sunglasses that do not block UVR are worse than no glasses?

Various experts have asserted that dark glasses can make the pupils dilate (open up more), allowing more UVR to reach deeper eye structures. Other experts counter that even very dark sunglasses cause pupils to dilate only slightly. Regardless of this controversy, if you are careful to purchase sunglasses that meet ANSI standards for the purpose for which you plan to wear them, you need not be concerned since little or no UVR will be transmitted. It is also worthy of note that the experts who sounded the alarm did so before the industry began to advise consumers of the amount of UVR protection in each pair of sunglasses.

Are there different types of lenses?

There certainly are, and choosing among them can become confusing. Thus, the following primer on lenses may be helpful:

* *Plain lenses*: Just as the name indicates, these are plain lenses in plastic or high-impact glass, tinted uniformly.
* *Gradient lenses*: These lenses are relatively light at the bottom of the lens and get progressively darker toward the top. Lightly tinted versions are used for fashion glasses, meant to be worn indoors or when there is no sun. Single-gradient sunglasses are good for driving because they cut overhead glare and still give good vision for the dashboard. Outdoors in bright sun, however, they can be bothersome; as you move your head around, the light seems to change continually.
* *Double-gradient lenses*: These lenses are darker at the top and bottom and lighter in the middle. Many people like them for sports. However, *Consumer Reports* found that they were not good for driving because they dimmed the dashboard more than the view of the road. And as in single-gradient lenses, the differences in shading they

create can be annoying when you move your head up and down.

* *Polarizing lenses*: These lenses are especially good for eliminating direct glare and glare reflected from shiny surfaces. Consequently, they are favorites with fishermen, who must constantly look into the water, and with drivers, who must cope with glare that bounces off the road or passing cars.

* *Mirror lenses*: Ideal for unusually intense glare, these lenses feature a thin metallic coating over a regular sunglass lens, creating a mirrored look (usually orange or blue) that adds an extra barrier against glare. Silver-coated mirror lenses are made with very thin metallic coatings and can be applied to plain or gradient-type lenses. They reflect rather than absorb light, thereby effectively reducing glare. Most coatings are vulnerable to scratching, but some can have a scratch-resistant coating applied.

* *Photochromic lenses*: These lenses are very light-sensitive, automatically lightening or darkening in response to the sun's brightness. All-weather photochromic lenses change density and color, depending on both light and temperature, so they are good for all kinds of conditions. They are especially suitable if you are going to be switching from the bright outdoors to shady or indoor areas. However, some may take up to five minutes to lighten (they darken in about half a minute), which can be annoying if you have just come in from outside and are now depending on your prescription lenses in order to see what you are doing! Photochromic lenses are usually acceptable for driving, because they never get extremely dark in the car—since the roof and windows block out much of the outside light. They are especially convenient for people who don't want to carry extra glasses with them.

How can you tell if sunglasses are distortion-free?

Holding the glasses in your hand, look through one lens at a time at a vertical line; then move the glasses back and forth. Next look at a horizontal line, and move the glasses up and down. If the lines either bend or seem distorted, don't buy the glasses.

Vision can also be distorted by frames with wide temples that obstruct peripheral vision. Many sunglasses that have wide sides are just fine for relaxing at the beach but pose a real hazard if you are driving or even walking in busy traffic.

Do lenses come in different materials?

Most sunglasses today are made of plastic, because plastic sunglasses are lighter than glass ones and are more resistant to impact. The FDA requires that all eyeglass lenses, including those for sunglasses, be made of impact-resistant glass or plastic. They are not shatterproof, but they can withstand moderately sharp blows and so are reasonably safe for general use.

Plastic sunglasses require more care than glass ones, because they can easily become scratched. Clean them by rinsing them off with water and then wiping them with a very soft tissue. Be sure not to use a coated tissue; it will add new smudges.

What is the safest, most impact-resistant lens material available?

Polycarbonate is an impact-resistant plastic first introduced in the 1960s for use in bulletproof windows. It is extremely strong and a sensible choice in industrial, hobby, or leisure settings that are likely to involve exposure to flying objects such as materials or a ball. Polycarbonate lenses are tougher and 50 percent lighter than glass lenses; tougher and 10 percent lighter than conventional plastic lenses. Safe as they are, they may not offer you total protection in sports such as racquetball, but they are far less likely to shatter on impact than ordinary plastic glasses. For extra protection, they should be made with material 3 mm thick.

Since polycarbonate lenses block almost all UVR rays, they offer excellent protection, but they are not suitable for every prescription. Even more than regular plastic, they are prone to becoming scratched or pitted, which may distort vision and lessen some of their protective qualities.

Skiers should wear goggles to protect themselves from

wind, and it would be wise to get the safe polycarbonate ones, which provide near total protection from UVR.

Are there special coatings for glasses?

Yes. As was stated earlier, clear UV-absorbing coatings are available for everyday prescription glasses. If for some reason you do not want a tint or want to have year-round UVR protection, this is a good idea. If you wear a hat, you may not be bothered by visible light; yet UVR protection is still important. Discuss this with your eye-care professional.

Are tinted glasses good for night driving?

No! Never wear sunglasses at dusk or at night. Many people have the mistaken idea that a yellow tint in their glasses helps brighten things, but it simply cuts down on the light that enters your eyes. Many cars and trucks have tinted windshields, cutting out some light and providing all the reduction you need. Headlights may bother you, which is why there is a temptation to wear glasses with yellow lenses or a light tint at night. But in cutting back on the light that enters your eyes, you are also reducing the amount of light available to permit you to see vehicles, people, or anything else with which you might collide.

If you are bothered by a reflection off the inside of your regular prescription glasses, you may be tempted to get a tinted pair for night driving. An antireflective coating is a better solution, according to Dr. Stephen Rozenberg, optometrist at New York's 10/10 Optics. This actually increases the amount of light that passes through, thus reducing or eliminating "ghost images."

Do good sunglasses have to be expensive?

Absolutely not. *Consumer Reports* noted only minor differences in UV-reducing qualities between the least expensive and the most expensive ones. The frames, the overall appearance, and the lenses' degree of freedom from distortion may be of superior quality in moderate- or higher-priced glasses, but it is quite possible to find excellent sunglasses for under $15. If you don't need prescription lenses, you may want to have a few pairs of sunglasses on hand—either for different purposes or just to make a fashion statement. Be sure that any sunglasses you buy meet the ANSI requirements for their intended purpose and that a tag or sticker to this effect is included with the glasses.

What's the best approach if you need prescription glasses?

There is really no best approach, because there are so many individual needs. Your regular prescription glasses block a certain amount of UVR, and they can be treated with chemicals that block still more. This will give you protection but may not meet your needs for comfort, since visible light will still be causing some glare and making you squint, unless you wear a wide-brimmed hat or visor. For this reason, many people choose to have a pair of sunglasses made up with their prescription.

If you have antireflective coatings (the same kind used on good camera lenses and binoculars to improve clarity and reduce glare) added to your regular prescription lenses, you will find that glare is minimized but that the glasses still do not substitute for sunglasses. These coated lenses are most useful if you have poor night vision or if you work in an environment with low light. Such coatings, despite their glare-reducing qualities, can increase the amount of light transmitted through lenses from 92 percent to almost 100 percent, yet they do not transmit any additional ultraviolet radiation.

If you generally stay out of the sun or wear eyeglasses only for reading, you may prefer to have one pair of nonprescription sunglasses and one pair of clip-on lenses that you slip over your prescription glasses. Far less expensive than buying a second pair of glasses, these clip-ons should meet the appropriate ANSI standards and should be so labeled.

If you wear eyeglasses for driving, you may prefer the clip-ons for occasions when the sun suddenly dims or when you go through a tunnel; in these instances, rather than having to change glasses, you can simply flip up the clip-ons. Before buying them, discuss this option with your optician, because some plastic lenses (especially those with antireflective coatings) are easily scratched and so may not be compatible with clip-ons.

Do contact lenses block UVR?

Some do, but not all of them block a sufficient quantity of it. Discuss this with your eyecare professional. Generally speaking, you are better off wearing sunglasses over your contacts: it will give you more protection and will save you from having to squint when the visible light hits your eyes.

Should children wear sunglasses?

It's a good idea, but the sunglasses must be made of a totally safe material if children are going to be running and playing in them. Many experts believe that children's glasses should, whenever possible, be made of polycarbonate.

The natural lens in a young child's eye is somewhat transparent to UVR, so the eye needs extra protection. But unless sunlight is very strong—for example, if the child is fishing, skiing, or traveling in the tropics—a baseball hat with a brim may provide sufficient sun protection.

Because the potential for cumulative damage to a child's eyes is so great from exposure to UVR, numerous experts have stated that eye protection is an essential part of preventive care, on a par with immunization and early dental care.

Do I need to wear sunglasses every time I venture out into the sun?

No, not unless you feel especially sensitive to the sun. When braving the midday summer sun, when driving in a great deal of glare, while skiing, and certainly when exposed to the sun for extended periods of time, you need this protection. Use good sense: if you are squinting, you need them; if you are wearing a hat that protects your eyes and you are not engaging in an activity that involves much sun exposure, you may be able to leave them in your pocket or bag. But don't leave your sunglasses home, since weather (like your schedule of activities) has a way of changing after you go out.

Can I depend on sunglasses to protect me at all times?

Even sunglasses that claim to eliminate 100 percent of ultraviolet radiation will not protect you if you continue to stare directly at the sun or at an eclipse. Similarly, they will not protect you against artificial light sources such as ultraviolet lamps or lamps in tanning booths. For these purposes, you need totally opaque goggles.

What are the best sunglasses to get?
The best sunglasses are those that protect you from ultraviolet radiation and visible light. Beyond that, you need to decide which kind best suits your lifestyle; and only you know the specific uses to which you will put them.

Do they need to be attractive? Not unless that's important to you.

Should they be comfortable? Of course.

Ruth Domber, owner of 10/10 Optics, says it best: "If you are comfortable in glasses, and you like how you look in them, you'll wear them. Glasses that are in your dresser drawer or lying in a case on your desk won't do you any good, no matter what stringent guidelines they meet."

Other Kinds of Protection

According to Hugh R. Taylor, M.D., associate professor of ophthalmology at the Wilmer Eye Institute of the Johns Hopkins School of Medicine, and his colleagues, another good source of eye protection against the sun is a simple brimmed cap. These researchers found that such a cap can cut ocular exposure to UV-B by half, and that the wearing of ordinary glasses with plastic lenses may reduce it to about 5 percent. To minimize ocular exposure to UV-B, people should wear a brimmed hat and close-fitting sunglasses with UV-B-absorbing lenses.

6 Sunless Tanning: Tanning Salons, Tanning Accelerators, and Self-tanners

You've heard the claims: "Indoor tanning: safer than the sun, with absolutely no harmful side effects." Entrepreneurs and devotees of this kind of artificial ultraviolet radiation contend that it is safer than a day at the beach or on the ski slopes, and can actually protect you from the damaging rays to which you will be exposed outdoors. According to the Skin Cancer Foundation, close to 2 million Americans regularly visit tanning parlors. About 80 percent of the people who use these facilities are women, mainly under thirty years of age.

Questions and Answers About Sunless Tanning

If you've been thinking of getting a tan without spending the time and money on an island vacation, you will want to know more about the safety of these devices. To clear up the confusion, I consulted members of the American Academy of Dermatology, the Skin Cancer Foundation, and the FDA. The question-and-answer section that follows is a synthesis of the reports provided by these experts.

What are sunless tanning devices, and how do they work?
For many years, various artificial sources of ultraviolet radiation have been widely used for tanning in the United States. People could buy single- or double-lamp devices at drugstores and variety stores. Resorts sometimes had a sunroom with

overhead sunlamps or other devices that emitted UVR. The ones currently available are usually referred to as tanning beds or booths. They are clamshell-like Plexiglas units on which the would-be tanner lies; lights from above and below reach the body. At one time these units emitted shortwave ultraviolet radiation (UV-B), but it soon became evident that UV-B was implicated in an increased risk of skin cancer, so these devices now use long-wave ultraviolet light sources (UV-A), which advertisers claim are safe. However, although these devices may be advertised as producing only UV-A, many of them also emit some UV-B as well.

Where are these tanning devices available?
They are available just about everywhere. Health clubs, beauty salons, barber shops, gas stations, and videotape outlets may have one or more tanning beds; tanning salons can be found in malls and in neighborhood shopping centers across the nation. Home units are also available.

Tanning salons have become especially popular near college campuses, where students like to get a head start on spring break. One enterprising young man opened a one-stop business near a large city university where students can drop off dry cleaning, do laundry, get a tan while waiting, and pick up a video and the snacks to go with it.

Who uses tanning beds?
In 1993, the Skin Cancer Foundation's *Sun & Skin News* reported almost 21,000 tanning salons listed in the United States. During peak season (from winter through spring), 2 million people a day use them. Half of these frequent salons on a regular basis.

Many users say they get a nice even tan, rather than the red burn they used to get when they tried to cram in too much sun on a short vacation. In a late-1980s study conducted by health educators examining factors that motivated people to use artificial tanning facilities, several common opinions were revealed: tanning is accomplished in less time, a tan is attractive and appealing, the salons have a pleasant atmosphere, and burning is avoided. Many users also believed that tanning beds cure or palliate acne, arthritis, and sinus problems.

Others said that they found the salons to be relaxing places where they met friendly people; the ambiance in itself was very appealing. In my own interviews with people who have patronized tanning salons, I noted the same findings but also met a number of people who commented that they wanted to prolong a suntan they had acquired while on vacation; a few admitted that they thought that a tan could camouflage some signs of abusing alcohol or drugs.

Quite a few sun-sensitive people (Type 1 or 2) who otherwise never sunbathe use tanning beds. Why? They know that they have difficulty tanning in the sun, because whenever they try they get a sunburn. But even though they accomplish their goal of tanning without visible burning when they use artificial ultraviolet radiation, they still remain in the category of high risk for skin cancer.

Is UV-A safer than UV-B?

In some ways UV-A is safer, and in other ways it is far more dangerous. You will remember from our discussion in chapter 1 that UV-B can burn the outer layer of the skin more severely but that UV-A penetrates more deeply. These long waves are so intense that about half of them can penetrate to the dermis, which is where the long-term damage occurs. Collagen is lost, your blood vessels decrease in number, and the connective tissue of the dermis is altered. Photoaging is only one hazard, however; skin cancer is a far more serious risk. One reason the tanning bed is appealing is that you probably won't get the blistering kind of sunburn from it that you might get on an island vacation where you are exposed to UV-B as well as UV-A. With artificial tanning, your melanin is stimulated by the penetration of UV-A, so you *may* get a beautiful golden tan.

But while the short-term risks of UV-A are less than those of UV-B, the long-range risks are greater. There is usually a twenty-year lag between exposure to ultraviolet radiation and development of skin cancer—considerably longer than the period since the inception of these devices.

But aren't tanning devices safer than the sun?

The 1989 report of the National Institutes of Health warns, "Some UV-A lamps generate more than five times more

UV-A per unit time than solar UV-A radiation reaching the earth's surface at the equator. At these doses, even pure UV-A is likely to have adverse biological effects."

And even prior to that report, the Food and Drug Administration had agreed with the American Medical Association and the American Academy of Dermatology when they stated that the claim that these UV-A sunlamps are safer than the sun is very misleading.

People who use tanning booths seem convinced that a good "base tan," gradually achieved, will protect them from sunburn. Some specific research findings, rather than the researchers themselves, have supported that impression. Data derived from studies done with hairless mice indicate that mice first exposed to UV-A radiation similar in wavelength to the UV-A emitted by most tanning salon units, and then exposed to the sun (which emits UV-B as well as UV-A), enjoyed significant protection against the development of skin tumors.

So what does this mean? According to Robert S. Stern, M.D., dermatologist at Beth Israel Hospital in Boston, in an editorial in the *Journal of the American Medical Association,* entitled "Beauty Today and Youth Tomorrow?" such data suggest that "at least in the hairless mouse, a brief visit to a tanning parlor before exposure to the sun . . . might help reduce the risk of sun-induced nonmelanoma skin cancer." But then he goes on to explain why the experience of mice in a controlled study like this differs from the way humans experience ultraviolet radiation exposure. The mice had never been exposed to UV-B or sunlight before their exposure to UV-A, whereas humans are. Dr. Stern concludes, "For humans, it is most likely that no matter how acquired, an equal tan results in equal damage to the skin." He concedes that intermittent use of tanning salons may carry a very small risk, but as you know if you have ever used a tanning salon, an occasional session does not produce the cosmetic appearance that most users are seeking.

It is also important to understand that radiation effects are cumulative. Having a tan is equivalent to applying a sunscreen with an SPF (sun protecting factor) of 2 to 4; this simply means that it will take two to four times longer to burn than it would without any protection. But many people, especially those with Type I skin, may *never* be able to build up a protective base. And in any case the UVR protection afforded by a tan is minimal. For this reason, Dr. Stern further states, "Therefore, even if it looks good, a UV-A induced tan does not provide substantial protection from sunburn due to subsequent sun exposure, an often-stated goal of tanning salon users."

Claims that tanning can improve a person's mental state, circulation, or anything else are totally unsubstantiated. There is no known health benefit to be derived from a tan or from exposure to artificial UVR.

Are there any immediate risks of exposure to tanning salons?

The Consumer Product Safety Commission estimates that in a single year there were almost 1,800 hospital emergency room visits for treatment of injuries sustained as a result of time spent at tanning parlors. Most of these accidents were to the eyes—particularly to the cornea. Although consumers are told to wear goggles, many do not heed the instruction, and the UV-A can pass right through the eyelid.

Contrary to some common beliefs, a UV-A tan doesn't protect people from a UV-B sunburn outdoors. Instead, it can augment it and cause a worse burn. One physician reported seeing a man with second-degree burns all over his body; the man had visited a tanning salon, and then followed this exposure with outdoor sunbathing.

Some UV-B may be emitted by tanning beds, and this can cause immediate and painful sunburn even if the tanner doesn't go out in the sun later. Photosensitivity following tanning sessions is often more intense than photosensitivity following outdoor sun exposure. For people taking photosensitive medications or suffering from a photosensitive condition such as lupus, the results can be disastrous.

How can you tell when you've had enough?

You can't tell; that's one of the problems with tanning salons. Unlike skin exposed to sunshine, skin exposed to indoor ultraviolet radiation remains cool to the touch, and since you probably won't get an immediate red sunburn (which you might get on the beach), you can't rely on that warning signal.

What are the positions of federal agencies on these devices?
The Food and Drug Administration (FDA) and the Federal Trade Commission (FTC) share responsibility for regulating sunlamps and tanning devices.

The FDA requires manufacturers to place a warning label on all such machines. This label warns consumers that eye and skin injuries, allergic reactions, and long-term risks of skin cancer and premature aging of the skin may result from ultraviolet radiation emitted during exposure. The statement also instructs the user to "wear protective eyewear: failure to do so may result in severe burns or long-term injury to the eyes. Consult physician before using sunlamp if you are using medications or have a history of skin problems or believe yourself especially sensitive to sunlight. If you do not tan in the sun, you are unlikely to tan from the use of this product."

It sounds like fair warning, doesn't it? But in reality, these signs are not always posted where users can see them. If goggles are not provided, if users are unable to control the unit, and if each unit is not equipped with a working timer, the FDA can recommend that the units be seized—as indeed the U.S. district attorney's office in various jurisdictions can do and often has done. When the problems are corrected, the units may be returned under FDA supervision. As of 1995, the FDA has not banned the sale of tanning devices or sunlamps, but such a ban appears to be on the horizon.

The FTC, on the other hand, assumes responsibility for investigating false, misleading, and deceptive advertising claims. If, along with the FDA, the FTC determines that labels or advertisements are not based on valid scientific facts, it has the authority to take corrective action.

The FTC has on many occasions issued orders prohibiting tanning parlors and other companies that have artificial tanning devices from claiming that they do not pose a risk of skin damage to the user. What kind of misleading claims are you likely to see in an advertisement? The FTC distributes a fact sheet that warns against some typical false claims: "You can achieve a deep year-round tan with gentle, comfortable, and safe UV-A light"; "No harsh glare, so no goggles or eye shades are necessary"; "Tan year-round without the harmful side effects often associated with natural sunlight"; and "No danger in exposure or burning."

The FTC has responded to instances in which firms have made such misleading or false claims by ordering the firms to include the following statement in all or certain ads and promotional materials: "NOTICE–Read the mandatory FDA warning label found on every tanning machine for important information on potential eye injury, skin cancer, skin aging and photosensitive reactions." If this statement appears in the ad, the FTC may (under certain circumstances) permit an ad to claim that its tanning equipment is safe, that it is safer than other devices or other methods of tanning, or that it has health benefits.

If I choose to use these devices, how can I minimize the risks?

Dermatologists hope that you won't ever place yourself under one of these artificial ultraviolet radiation lights. If you do, however, you should make every effort to minimize your risks. Schedule no more than thirty to fifty half-hour sessions per year.

Using an overall sunscreen isn't very sensible under these circumstances, because you will just have to prolong the tanning sessions to achieve the tan you are seeking. However, if there is some part of your body (such as your nose or lips) that you don't want to tan, cover it with a sunscreen that has an SPF of 15 or higher or with a total block such as zinc oxide. Use of a tightly woven dry fabric covering in addition to a sunscreen will provide still greater protection. In addition, observe the following safety guidelines:

* Be sure that instructions are posted or photocopied and handed to you, and that they specify the recommended exposure limits for your skin type. And abide by these instructions and recommendations.
* Confirm that there is a manually set timer on the tanning device that will either automatically shut off the lights or

somehow signal you (loudly, in the event that you fall asleep) at the end of your predetermined exposure time.

* Safety goggles should be provided. In addition, the operator should require that you use the goggles. Laxity on this score should be taken as a warning signal that the business may not be observing other safety measures. The goggles should fit snugly and should not be cracked. Sunglasses or cotton wads are not acceptable substitutes. The goggles should be sterilized between uses to prevent the spread of any eye infections.

* Check with your physician to ensure that neither the treatment for any condition from which you suffer nor the disease itself is likely to be provoked or exacerbated by ultraviolet radiation.

* Consider any medications you may be taking: Antihistamines, tranquilizers, birth control pills, and antihypertensives can cause photosensitivity.

* If you have ever suffered from photosensitivity in the sun, whether as a consequence of chemicals or of allergies, discuss this with your physician. Artificial ultraviolet radiation may trigger the reaction again, this time faster and more intensely. Sunscreens cannot be relied upon to prevent allergic-type reactions in people who are photosensitive.

Operators of tanning salons do not need to obtain an operating license beforehand, and they may be totally ignorant of the risks. In compliance with the FDA, they may post the warning sign, without recognizing the long-range or immediate dangers of UVR. Be sure that a qualified attendant is there, or bring a friend with you who can help in an emergency.

Keep in mind that standards for electrical safety and ultraviolet output are not always adhered to. Poor sanitation can result in acquiring infectious diseases, head lice, and skin infections.

What are the warning signs of injuries, and what should I do about them?

If you have a severe skin burn, an eye burn, or any kind of allergic reaction, seek professional medical attention immediately. Report a new lesion or any change in an existing lesion, mole, or sore to a physician.

If you have followed instructions and still have incurred a serious injury, it is possible that the device may be malfunctioning. Report it to the manufacturer of the device and to the FDA through your local FDA office. Look in the phone book under "U.S. Government, Health and Human Services, Food and Drug Administration."

Tanning Pills

Some tanning pills are promoted as a safe means of tanning; others are meant to bolster resistance to sun damage. Neither should be taken without close medical supervision.

The FDA does not approve of pills that contain beta-carotene and/or canthaxanthin (although beta-carotene is available by prescription), both of which are chemical relatives of vitamin A. Sometimes called French bronzing pills, they are available outside the United States and occasionally by mail order or through health food stores here. Advertisements sometimes promise "a handsome natural-looking tan without the sun."

According to both the FDA and the Skin Cancer Foundation, some of the ingredients in these pills have been found to have toxic side effects. Beta-carotene is a natural component of a number of fruits and vegetables, including oranges, carrots, and tomatoes. It is sometimes used as a food additive in butter and cheese to add color and in chicken feed to make egg yolks a brighter yellow. The pills may do the same thing to you: instead of giving you the handsome melanin-colored tan you are seeking, they are likely to turn your skin a jaundicelike yellow or orange.

How does this occur? In combination with the canthaxanthin, beta-carotene accumulates in the skin, thereby coloring it; but at the same time it forms deposits in the blood, in fatty tissue, in the liver, and in other organs, sometimes causing toxicity.

Another kind of pill contains a form of Psoralen, which is used to treat psoriasis and alopecia areata. Physicians have sometimes prescribed this particular chemical, called 8-methoxypsoralen, for some people with Type 1 skin to help increase their resistance to sun damage. It is theorized that the chemical may thicken the skin and accelerate melanin production, thus affording the user greater safety in the sun. It has been recommended by some physicians for certain individuals who are allergic to sunscreens and cannot avoid the sun. However, it should only be used under scrupulous medical supervision. Perhaps in the future this treatment will prove to be a satisfactory way to be safe in the sun, with a suntan. But in the meantime, unless an experienced dermatologist suggests it, trust the FDA and stay away from these pills.

Tanning Accelerators

You don't swallow these "guarantees" of a safe tan, at least not literally. But if you swallow the advertising claims made about tanning accelerators and don't take proper precautions, you will be encouraging the same sun damage that you would get if you went out in the sun to burn rather than to tan.

Introduced by a number of major cosmetic companies in the mid-1980s, they continue to be touted as promoters of a fast and deep tan if used once daily for at least three days before sun exposure. The chief ingredient in these products is tyrosine, an amino acid that plays a role in the production of melanin.

Studies done at the prestigious Cleveland Clinic and by *Consumer Reports* magazine of two of these products indicated that the accelerators didn't encourage tanning, with or without sunlight. Reliable and responsible cosmetic and drug companies are continuing to test the products, and they dispute these earlier findings. While the accelerators don't work for everyone, they acknowledge, they purportedly are successful for others. On another front, the FDA is considering whether the claims made for these products are such as to remove them from the category of cosmetics and place them in the category of drugs.

If you do decide to use one of these accelerators (most of the dermatologists I consulted take a wait-and-see attitude toward them), be sure to use a sunscreen, too. Look carefully at labels: some accelerators may combine both in one product. But you need to check the SPF factor in the sunscreen and determine whether it needs to be reapplied regularly.

Sun-free Self-tanners

So-called bronzers have been around for many years, and earlier generations of them worked fairly well on men's skin, if carefully applied. But skin with uneven pigmentation or blemishes didn't take kindly to these bronzers, and it was difficult to get them on smoothly, so they didn't work for everyone.

Newer products are far more effective. They look natural, are relatively easy to apply, and are formulated for both men's and women's skin. Some of these products are actually self-tanners that are applied to the skin to give it the color and glow of a tan. These products contain dihydroxyacetone (DHA), an ingredient that safely oxidizes on the skin's surface upon reacting with the protein in the upper layers of the epidermis. In just a few hours, the DHA produces a natural-looking tan that lasts at least three days and won't wash or rub off. As the skin cells renew themselves, the tan fades. Some products of this type incorporate a sunscreen in their formula, but whether they do or not you should be aware that this artificial tan in itself does not give you any more protection from the sun than you would have had without it. If you plan to rely on the built-in sunscreen protection, check to see whether the protection is designed to last as long as the tan. In all likelihood, additional sunscreen must be applied regularly.

Self-tanning products are harmless, but they must be applied with care. They tend to yield less than desirable results for people with uneven skin conditions or facial hair. Keep it away from your hairline, eyebrows, and eyelashes, lest your hair become discolored. It can stain clothing, too, so you must wait for it to dry (about a half-hour) before allowing clothes to come into contact with any part of the skin to which you have applied the product. Wait at least an hour before you shave, bathe, or swim, because these activities can stop the color-developing process.

Transparent gels that you apply to the skin to simulate a tan work in much the same way as the old bronzers, but they have been greatly improved. They are easier to apply, are formulated for men and women, and look very natural. If your skin has many irregularities or you don't want to wait a few hours or you wish to be able to wash the tan away rather than waiting for it to fade, you will like these gels. Other bronzers are brushed in the same manner as blush is and can also give the appearance of a suntan.

According to dermatologists, these products are safe (unless you happen to be allergic to one or more of the ingredients) and offer a healthful alternative to soaking up the sun to achieve a tan.

III

Coping with the Effects of the Sun

7

Treating Sun-damaged Skin

Most of us grew up under the influence of a number of health warnings: Don't go out in the rain without your raingear; if someone on the bus or in the movies is coughing, move away; stay out of the ocean when the waves are too rough. The list is endless, with some strictures having more validity than others. Unfortunately, we were also told to "get some sun," in order to avoid contracting rickets or simply to be suffused in those seemingly beneficent rays. Few people ever heard that the sun could damage their skin, prematurely aging it or causing cancer.

During our growing-up years, most of us didn't listen to any advice. Later, when I would regret this inattention, my mother, in her infinite wisdom, would say, "Don't cry over spilt milk. Just mop it up."

There is nothing to be gained from rehashing old behaviors. By now you know all about the effects of the sun on your body, and you know how to be safe in the sun; still, you will want to know what can be done to treat and (in some instances) to reverse the damage already done.

It is easy to confuse natural aging with *photoaging*—skin changes that occur only in skin exposed to significant amounts of sun or other sources of ultraviolet radiation. There are a number of differences, however, and the two kinds of skin changes are biologically separate events. Natural aging is a condition in which there is a deepening of normal expression lines and a loss of elasticity and thickness of skin. In photoaging, the skin may have deep wrinkles; be coarse, parched looking, thickened, and leathery; and lack elasticity. Telangiectasia (fishnetlike display of "broken" blood vessels); mottled, irregular pigmentation; brown "age spots," solar lentigines (flat brown spots on the backs of hands and on the face); actinic or solar keratoses (smooth, flat or slightly raised pink spots that become irregular, scaly, and wartlike and turn darker—and have a strong potential for moving on to become squamous cell carcinomas) may all be present.

All of the above are treatable and in some instances reversible.

Heatstroke and Sunburn

In heatstroke and sunstroke, body temperature can rise to a dangerously high level. This is an emergency that can be fatal. First aid for heatstroke consists of quick cooling. Application of an ice bag or crushed ice, or even wrapping in a wet sheet or hosing down with cold water will help while someone calls the local medics or arranges to get the victim to an emergency room.

Sunburns may happen—if not to you (since you are careful!), then to someone you know. Mild sunburns can usually be treated with an assortment of nonprescription sunburn preparations. These often contain a local anesthetic and are available in various forms: liquid, cream, ointment, aerosol, and pump spray. The alcohol included in some of these products cools the skin but may cause further irritation on sunburned skin. Read directions carefully. Generally these nonprescription medications work well on small areas, but if applied to most of the exposed area (such as 50 percent of the body surface) or if applied more than four times daily, they can be absorbed into the body, causing toxicity. Most sunburn remedies should be kept away from the eyes and should not be used if the skin is broken, raw, or blistered. In the event of a severe sunburn or symptoms that worsen or persist more than a few days, or if any sign of infection or increased swelling appears, medical attention should be sought.

When a sunburn begins to heal, the skin tends to feel dry and rough. A good moisturizing lotion or petroleum jelly applied to it will help keep the skin moist and will minimize or even prevent peeling. Other treatments for sunburn include soaking in either a cool plain bath or one to which Burrow's solution or oatmeal has been added. Sunburn raises the temperature of the skin, increasing the damage already done by the sun. Cooling the skin minimizes the damage. In addition, cool water works as an anesthetic, quelling the pain, and it subdues swelling and inflammation. Pat rather than rub the skin dry, using a clean towel.

Aspirin, ibuprofen, and acetaminophen are all useful in alleviating pain from sunburn. Many doctors suggest taking two aspirin or ibuprofen after sun exposure, repeating the dose every two hours for the next twelve hours to avoid the discomfort of a severe sunburn.

Photoaging Treatments

Many of the results of photoaging do not pose health threats, but they can have an adverse *emotional* effect. In a society that values good looks and youth, no one wants to have unnecessary acquired cosmetic flaws or to look old prematurely. There is no reason to endure unsightly photoaging, if it is making you unhappy. Fortunately, much can be done about this. When sun exposure is completely avoided for a number of years, a layer of new collagen (a protein that, along with elastin, is responsible for the support and elasticity of the skin) appears in the dermis, causing the skin to begin to appear younger and more attractive. A number of safe and efficacious methods can contribute significantly to making your skin look the way it should.

Techniques and medical methods to treat photoaging vary; options include dermabrasion, cryosurgery, electrosurgery, chemical peels, 5-fluorouracil (5-FU) treatments, collagen injections, plastic surgery, and (newest of all) the use of tretinoin, also known as Retin-A®. *All of these procedures should be performed or supervised by an experienced physician, preferably a board-certified dermatologist or plastic surgeon.*

Dermabrasion

Dermabrasion is a technique of skin abrasion or burning that is performed with a motor-driven, high-speed tool. It has come a long way since it was first introduced in the 1950s. Today, the abrading device looks a bit like a miniature sanding tool, and indeed it does sand or plane the skin.

Prior to the procedure, patients are usually given an intravenous painkiller and a mild sedative to help them relax and avoid pain. Then, section by section, the skin is frozen by application of an aerosol freeze spray. This simultaneously firms up the skin, facilitating the planing, and numbs the skin. Then the physician takes the rapidly rotating brush and strokes it across the face to remove the upper layers of the skin. Some patients say that the procedure is painful, and for this reason general anesthesia may be used. Others say that only the spray of blood and skin bothered them. The face is bandaged afterward, but the patient usually removes the bandages at home.

To reduce swelling, patients are advised to keep their heads elevated the first few nights. Painkillers and antibiotics are prescribed for the period of convalescence. Crusting, intense redness, and swelling develop in the abraded skin within twenty-four to forty-eight hours. Within two weeks, the crusts shed, leaving the skin thinner but still pinkish red, with the color gradually diminishing within a few months. People usually need to take two weeks off from work or social activities following dermabrasion. Sun exposure must be avoided during this time, so a sunscreen or other protection should be worn even for brief outings in the sun.

Dermabrasion is most often used to treat acne scars, but it has also been successfully used to treat other scars and actinic keratoses of the face and scalp. It is more successful on fair-skinned individuals than on those with dark or olive complexions, because the latter are at greater risk of developing hyperpigmentation (areas of darkened skin). Advocates of this treatment say that skin texture is improved, wrinkling is reduced, and mottled skin is replaced by more supple skin of nearly uniform color. They also say that it helps prevent recurrence of actinic keratoses for at least four years; and with careful protection from the sun, this time can be extended. Authorities who are less enthusiastic about this technique for actinic keratoses state that the lesions may recur within eight months of dermabrasion.

Dermabrasion carries some risk for infections, scarring, and permanent skin discoloration. Because it is a slow, painstaking procedure that requires much skill, it should be performed only by a physician specially trained and experienced in the technique.

Chemical Peels

Sometimes referred to as chemabrasion, a chemical peel involves application of a caustic chemical material to the face. This material destroys the top layer (or layers) of the skin, causing it (or them) to slough off and permitting the growth of new, fresh skin. Chemical peels, unlike other treatments for photoaged skin, are only done on the face, because the procedure might scar other areas such as the arms or hands.

There are two kinds of chemical peels: trichloracetic acid (TCA), often referred to as a superficial or light peel; and phenol. TCA is used to treat light wrinkling, sun damage, and irregular pigmentation. The greater the amount of sun damage, the stronger the solution used. The procedure takes about an hour to perform if the entire face is done, and it causes little or no pain. An anti-anxiety medication may be given prior to the procedure, but usually only a mild pain medication is needed. The physician applies the TCA solution with cotton-tipped applicators. When application is completed, a white frost develops on the face, and is then rinsed off with cold water or alcohol. Some physicians tape the face, in a process called occlusion, which keeps air from reaching the treated area, thus prolonging the activity of the ingredients and increasing the depth of the peel.

A TCA chemical peel doesn't remove deep wrinkles or those near the mouth, but it may reduce moderate wrinkles, and it often fades solar lentigines and freckles. The effect on pigmentation is unpredictable, however, and nevi often get darker.

Phenol peels are stronger than TCA peels and are more likely to be used for actinic keratoses. They may be used over the entire face or just in small areas such as around the mouth. Because phenol peels can cause some systemic side effects, they are not appropriate for individuals with chronic kidney disease or liver disease. Cardiac arrhythmias occasionally occur during a full phenol peel, so for this reason physicians should monitor the patient's heart with a continuous EKG during the procedure.

Sedation and painkillers are administered prior to a phenol peel, and the procedure follows much the same steps as are used for the lighter TCA peel. The chemical formula most often used includes phenol, cotton oil, liquid soap, and distilled water.

Following either kind of peel, there is some swelling and a feeling of tightness, warmth, and pain. Later, the skin itches. A hard crust and scabs eventually form, although some physicians may recommend the use of antibiotic creams immediately after the peel, in order to reduce or avoid the hard crusts. The scabs loosen after seven to ten days and fall off, leaving a layer of very pink skin that heals and forms new skin.

Following a chemical peel, it is essential to avoid the sun. On occasions when it is impossible to stay out of the sun during the next few months, a total sunblock must be used.

Sometimes hyperpigmentation occurs in the treated area, particularly in dark-skinned people, so many physicians feel this technique is best suited to patients with light skin. It is always possible that skin color may differ between treated and surrounding skin. Occasionally, scarring occurs, particularly if the solution penetrates too deeply.

Chemical peels should never be administered by nonmedical personnel; only an experienced physician should perform them.

Cryosurgery

Cryosurgery—whose prefix, *cryo*, means "icy cold" or "frost" in Greek—is a form of surgery that makes use of subzero temperatures to destroy tissue. In one form of cryosurgery, solid carbon dioxide or liquid nitrogen is applied to a growth with a sterile cotton-tipped applicator or is sprayed directly onto the skin. A blister then forms, which is followed by necrosis (death) of the tissue. The procedure can be repeated if necessary, either at this time or at a later session.

In other forms of cryosurgery, a freezing chemical is circulated through a metal probe, which is then applied to the unwanted growth. The tissues freeze when they adhere to the cold metal of the probe, and the cell membranes burst, killing the cells, which are then sloughed off. Underlying structures are not affected. Stitches or bandaging is not needed, and healing is usually uneventful. Scarring seldom occurs, but sometimes hyperpigmentation surrounds the lesion, and depigmentation can occur at the lesion site. The hyperpigmentation is usually temporary, but the depigmentation can be permanent.

Cryosurgery can be used to treat various sun-induced conditions such as solar lentigines, actinic keratoses, and skin cancers. It can be used on any part of the face (including the eyelids), on the hands, and on any other part of the body. Often, lentigines and actinic keratoses are treated by contact with cryoprobes cooled by nitrous oxide gas or with cotton-tipped wooden applicators dipped in liquid nitrogen. Many physicians prefer to spray the liquid nitrogen evenly over the surface of the lesion until it turns completely white, with the whiteness extending beyond the margins of the lesion.

There is no pain during the procedure, but discomfort or pain may develop later. After the problem areas are frozen, hivelike skin eruptions may occur nearby, and later a brown crust forms that may exude some fluid. The lesions separate and fall off in seven to ten days.

Complications or postoperative infections are rare, and cryosurgery is safe even for people with other medical problems.

Surgery: Excision, Curettage, Electrosurgery, and Plastic Surgery

Some small precancerous growths, such as actinic keratoses, benign nevi, and dysplastic nevi may be removed surgically, usually in the dermatologist's office. This may be done for the purpose of biopsy (as described in chapter 8) as a form of treatment, or for cosmetic reasons. The physician uses a scalpel blade or a curette (a spoon- or scoop-shaped instrument) to remove the growth. The edges of the skin may or may not be sutured (stitched). Local anesthesia is usually all that is necessary for the procedure; occasionally a pain reliever may be prescribed for postoperative discomfort or pain.

Electrosurgery makes use of surgical instruments that operate on a high-frequency current. In electrocoagulation, the physician uses a needle or snare to destroy tissue. This technique is sometimes referred to as electric cautery or galvano-cautery. It is used to remove moles, growths, brown spots, and discolorations, as well as actinic keratoses and skin cancers.

Electrodesiccation, also called fulguration, is another form of electrosugery. Here, tissue is destroyed by being burned with an electric spark. This technique is suitable for eliminating small superficial growths and for aiding in curettage. The procedure helps to destroy and dry up unwanted growths. The wounds heal well by themselves without any stitches. It may be used for various sun-related growths, particularly telangiectasia on the face. Occasionally, tiny scars may remain where the needle was placed; but if a minimum amount of current is used, such scarring is less likely to occur. This is another reason for choosing an experienced physician.

Although there are various ways to minimize wrinkles, a surgical face-lift is the only way to eliminate sagging skin. This surgery consists of trimming away excess skin and pulling the rest of the facial skin slightly tighter. Deep furrows on the brow can be eliminated similarly, by trimming away and tightening the skin. The procedure is performed by a plastic surgeon.

A blepharoplasty, which works in much the same way as a face-lift, eliminates sagging eyelids that may be impeding vision and causing distress about appearance. It is performed by a plastic surgeon or by an ophthalmologist who has special training in plastic surgery.

Many people choose to have various defects—congenital or acquired, sun-related or not—surgically corrected. Either dermatologists or plastic surgeons can remove unsightly growths, but changes in contours of chins, jaws, and noses, as well as face-lifts and blepharoplasties, fall within the realm of plastic surgery.

Collagen Replacement

Collagen is a protein in the body that helps to support the skin and other soft tissues. As was explained in chapter 2, elastin and collagen fibers are part of the connective and elastic tissue in the dermis, the layer beneath the epidermis. Age and sun damage break down this tissue, causing sagging and wrinkles. Most people have heard about collagen, perhaps because so many expensive cosmetics include it in their ingredients. But collegen cannot be absorbed through the skin in cream or ointment form. On the other hand, it *can* be implanted.

The collagen used in implantation is a natural animal protein made from the skin of cattle. It is injected through a small hypodermic needle, filling in skin depressions such as those caused by wrinkles.

Approved by the FDA in 1981, Zyderm® collagen implants have been demonstrated to be safe and effective. They are available in three forms: Zyderm® I, the original product; Zyderm® II, introduced in 1983; and Zyplast, introduced in 1985. Acne, surgical and trauma scars, and wrinkles (whether age-related or sun-induced) generally are greatly improved by these purified bovine collagen injections, performed by a dermatologist or plastic surgeon.

Generally, a person's state of health is not a limiting factor in considering this procedure. However, anyone with a history of autoimmune disease, such as lupus or rheumatoid arthritis, or severe allergic reactions should not undergo the procedure. The physician will test for allergies to the material by injecting a small amount of collagen into the forearm twenty-eight days before the planned procedure. The test site is then observed seventy-two hours later and again four weeks later. For added safety, the doctor may test the patient again, this time using the forearm or forehead as the test site. The double testing technique reduces the chance of causing a serious adverse treatment reaction.

If all goes well in the testing, an appointment is made for the collagen injections. It takes only a few moments to perform the procedure; injections are done at one time, but depending on the extent of the wrinkling, several sessions may be necessary. There is little or no discomfort associated with the injections, and people can return to their usual activities immediately afterward.

The benefits of collagen injections are temporary, because the protein eventually dissolves, so it may be necessary to repeat the procedure six months to several years later, depending on the body chemistry of the individual and on the form of collagen used. Generally, Zyplast® lasts longer than Zyderm®. Long-lasting results also depend on factors such as stress at the treatment site. For instance, laughing, crying, smoking, and sun exposure will speed up rewrinkling! Anyone undergoing this treatment must recognize that the collagen injections will not last forever; and protection from the sun is essential.

Fat Injections

The idea of transferring fat from one part of the body to another in order to correct various defects is not new, but the procedure was rarely performed until the introduction of fat suctioning. Fat suctioning or liposuction may be familiar to you as a way of getting rid of unwanted fat that causes bulged, diet-and-exercise-don't-help-much hips, buttocks, and thighs. In liposuction, incisions are made into an area where there is an excess of this fat, and it is suctioned out by a high-pressure vacuum system.

For the purpose of reducing or eliminating facial wrinkles, fat tissue is obtained in semiliquid form from an area adjacent to the stomach; this tissue is then injected into the wrinkled area of the face. The relatively simple procedure involved was first introduced in the mid-1980s, but the jury is still out on whether it is successful. At question are the viability of the fat that is removed and the length of time before the wrinkles return. Because they constitute an autologous procedure—a procedure in which something is taken from the body and then reintroduced to it—fat injections do not fit the definition of a product or a medication, and therefore they do not require FDA approval.

Fibril Injections

Fibril is a synthetic substance that offers a new alternative to collagen and fat injections. Researchers who have been studying fibril gel since 1984 say that it may be a very effective treatment for patients who are allergic to collagen. It is thought that fibril may stimulate the production of replacement collagen in the injection location. Approved by the FDA in 1988, fibril injections have provided longer-lasting results than collagen in clinical studies. But as with collagen injections, stress at the location of the implant contributes to the wrinkles' return. Since the procedure is still somewhat new, patients considering it should determine whether the physician is experienced with the particular material.

Silicone Injections

You don't hear too much anymore about this method of treating wrinkles, perhaps because it never received FDA approval for that purpose. Silicone is a synthetic plastic that can be injected into the body. When injected into wrinkles or deeper furrows it can smooth them out. Unlike collagen, it is nonallergenic and doesn't have the disadvantage of eventually dissolving. However, it can cause a permanent unsightly bulge, either because the injection wasn't placed perfectly or because it shifted. Sometimes impurities slip into the silicone during the manufacturing process that can cause chronic (and sometimes severe) skin reactions. Additionally, there are no well-recognized standard procedures for ensuring the purity of silicone.

Topical Chemotherapy

Chemotherapy is defined as treatment by means of drugs. It has become most widely known as a treatment for cancer. When an anticancer drug in cream or lotion form is applied to the skin surface, the procedure is described as topical chemotherapy. Precancerous actinic keratoses are successfully treated with the drug fluorouracil, known variously as 5-fluorouracil, 5-FU, Adrucil, Fluoroplex, and Efudex. 5-FU is an antimetabolite cancer drug that is given internally to patients suffering from internal cancers, to inhibit cancer cell growth. These patients often experience gastrointestinal side effects and lowered blood counts. But since only about 6 percent of a dose applied to the skin is absorbed, none of these systemic side effects occurs when 5-FU is used in topical chemotherapy.

For widespread actinic keratoses—especially of the face and scalp—and for some basal cell carcinomas (see chapter 8), 5-FU is very successful. It is also safe, easy to administer, and produces excellent cosmetic results: skin often looks smoother and younger. 5-FU not only can eradicate visible precancerous lesions but actually can seek out and destroy those that remain hidden below the surface of the skin. Occasionally, 5-FU is used to treat just a few actinic keratoses, if they are in a place of cosmetic importance. This is because the scarring or change in pigmentation that may result from cryotherapy or electro-desiccation is unlikely to occur with 5-FU.

Topical 5-FU is available from the manufacturer as a solution or cream formulated at different strengths, ranging from 1 to 5 percent. Fairer-skinned people frequently are given lower strengths of the drug. Depending on the type of lesion to be treated and the skin type of the individual, a physician may decide to use a stronger concentration, which can be made up by a pharmacist.

The patient usually applies the 5-FU sparingly and carefully twice daily to the affected areas of skin, using the fingertips and carefully avoiding the eyes, nose, and mouth. The use of cosmetics or other creams during treatment is usually discouraged. The sun must be avoided, too, because it can greatly intensify the expected inflammatory response. Tretinoin (Retin-A®) is sometimes added to enhance the penetration of 5-FU. Patients are seen regularly by the physician, who will decide whether treatment should be discontinued or changed in some way.

By the end of the second week or early in the third week, the skin begins to look dreadful! It is red and dry and may be accompanied by blisters, oozing, and discomfort such as might be encountered after sunburn. Occasionally, an allergic reaction or severe irritation may arise soon after treatment is begun. This usually responds to anti-inflammatory corticosteroid creams; painkillers may be used if necessary. The inflammation usually affects only areas where there are lesions, leaving the adjacent skin unaffected.

Usually the patient applies the 5-FU for three to four weeks. At the end of that time, if all of the keratoses have not disappeared or been destroyed, another treatment regimen of 5-FU may be recommended.

Actinic keratoses on the scalp, neck, back, chest, and backs of the hands usually require longer treatment than those on the face. Healing begins to take place as soon as the treatment is discontinued, and within a few weeks the skin looks far better than it did before treatment began. At times, 5-FU may be combined with other chemicals to eradicate various lesions associated with photodamage. 5-FU does not prevent the development of new keratoses in the future.

Tretinoin (Trade Name: Retin-A®)

By now most people have heard of Retin-A®. It's the so-called fountain-of-youth drug that can actually make wrinkles disappear. Unlike various high-priced cosmetics that have been touted to do this but never really smoothed anything out but your wallet, tretinoin has been proved to reduce fine wrinkling, pore size, and mottled pigmentation; it can also stimulate blood flow to give a youthful rosy glow to the skin. Clinical evidence shows that it increases collagen formation and skin cell turnover, resulting in a thicker epidermis and distributing melanin pigment evenly throughout the epidermis. At the same time, the stratum corneum (the lowest layer of skin) is thinned, which helps rough, sun-damaged skin become smoother and younger looking. Tretinoin can fade solar lentigines and telangiectasia and can even reduce actinic keratoses.

This doesn't happen overnight, of course, but after four to six months of regular use, people look as if they have had a dermabrasion or chemical peel. It's not a substitute for a face-lift for sagging skin, but it is an effective way to turn back the clock just a bit and to improve photoaged skin. Although many people who have used tretinoin are very pleased with it, others have been disappointed. They could not or would not tolerate some of the irritating effects of the treatment that may occur such as dryness, peeling, redness, and swelling. Nevertheless, individuals who stay with the initial treatment plan for eight to twelve months, followed by a maintenance schedule, are usually very satisfied with the results.

Tretinoin-treated skin is supersensitive to the sun, so a

sunscreen is an absolute necessity! If you opt for this treatment, do everything you can to minimize your sun exposure, as described in Part II. Women may find it useful on a general year-round basis to use a moisturizer with an SPF of 15 under or in place of makeup; alternatively, they may prefer to use an emollient sunscreen. Men can use a sunscreen as an after-shave lotion. Sunscreens that have an SPF higher than 15 are usually unnecessary and may indeed have too high a concentration of potentially irritating chemicals. If you get sunburned despite your best intentions, your doctor will probably tell you to discontinue the treatment temporarily. Likewise, your doctor may recommend that you suspend treatment if you are going to be vacationing in a sunny climate or taking a ski trip.

Treatment Combinations

There are several ways to treat sun-damaged skin, and combinations of treatments are often successful. For instance, facelifts may be combined with topical tretinoin treatments.

If you are considering a treatment strictly for cosmetic purposes, you may wish to meet with a dermatologist and a plastic surgeon, and even get a second or third opinion. Listen carefully to the options outlined for you, and then decide if you want to choose one of them. Such treatment is considered elective—meaning that it's not urgent—and it is really up to you!

If you have a precancerous condition such as actinic keratoses or nevi, heed the advice of a dermatologist, perhaps getting a second opinion. But don't reject treatment altogether, since some treatment, while usually not urgent, is ultimately necessary. Waiting too long can mean developing cancer and having to undergo far more extensive treatment than would have been required if you had begun it earlier.

Is Treatment Expensive?

Private physicians' fees vary from one community to another, but most physicians are willing to adjust fees or to work out a special schedule of payments with you. Insurance companies that pay or reimburse in part or in whole for treatment of medical conditions may not pay for strictly cosmetic treatments. But sometimes they will pay or reimburse if scarring or serious photodamage has significantly affected your self-image and self-esteem. Treatment is often available on a sliding fee scale at a local hospital that has a clinic or is involved in research.

Is Treatment Necessary?

If you have developed precancerous actinic keratoses or dysplastic nevi, it is important that you be evaluated by a dermatologist. But if you have thus far only developed wrinkles as the result of photodamage, you may choose not to do anything to reduce or reverse them. But, please, protect yourself from the sun now to avoid any greater cumulative damage, which might lead to skin cancer. And remember that evidence now exists that sun protection can not only stop ongoing damage but also allow some natural regeneration (read: rejuvenation) to occur.

Wrinkles aren't so bad: the wonderful actress, Helen Hayes, likes to refer to them as her "service stripes." A favorite child I know once said, "I like people with crinkly skin. They like to read stories and buy presents, and they let you stay up late."

If you don't want to try tretinoin, but you're dissatisfied with your photoaged skin, remember that a sunny disposition and becoming clothes and hairstyle can go a long way toward making you an attractive person. There are also a number of excellent ways to camouflage discolorations and other cosmetic defects.

Camouflage

Pigmentation problems, scars from treatments, telangiectasia (a condition characterized by prominent blood vessels), and various sun-induced damage cannot always be successfully reversed. In addition, some procedures to correct problems may themselves result in unsightly pigmentation problems or scars. Thus, additional surgery or treatment may not be the answer.

At one time, various nonprescription bleach products containing ammoniated mercury were popular, although they were not very effective. Unfortunately, they caused many allergic reactions and could be absorbed by the body, causing other adverse reactions. Consequently, these products were banned by the FDA in 1974. Today, some lightening agents containing the safer hydroquinone are available; but they, too, are often ineffective, and they can cause irritation that may increase pigmentation or cause complete loss of it.

Fortunately, marvelous products are made that disguise even the most unsightly scars. A number of companies make long-lasting, greaseless, waterproof concealers that offer good coverage and match or blend into any color of skin—from the palest Celtic to the darkest African. Generally these products do not contain perfumes or irritating ingredients, and they can be worn without any makeup or under your usual makeup. If they aren't available at your local pharmacy or department store, ask your dermatologist for advice and suggestions.

8

Cancer of the Skin

"It's only skin cancer." How many times have you heard people say that? Whether they are breathing a sigh of relief that they don't have a life-threatening form of cancer or they are trying to console a friend who has been given a recent diagnosis, the average person tends to perceive skin cancer as a minor problem. It's true that most skin cancers are curable, but they can still be serious and sometimes disfiguring. The American Cancer Society estimates that 50 percent of all people who live to the age of sixty-five will have at least one. And over 2,000 people die each year of nonmelanoma skin cancers. Even malignant melanoma—if caught early—is curable.

What Is Cancer?

Cancer is a general term used to describe various groups of diseases characterized by abnormal cell growth in the body. Cancer cells do not usually stay in any one place; instead they move around, crowding between normal cells and even penetrating them. Unchecked by medical intervention, these cells tend to spread to distant body sites.

Cancer cells differ from normal cells in many ways. They have an irregular, disordered appearance when viewed under a microscope; they serve no useful function in the body; and they do not wear out and die. Instead, these malignant cells continually divide and multiply, reproducing themselves as they invade and destroy surrounding tissues.

Cancer is not just one disease but many related diseases. It can arise in any organ or tissue of the body. In this book we will concern ourselves only with cancers that arise on the skin and whose cell growth begins in one or more layers of the skin. The major types of skin cancers are basal cell and squamous cell carcinomas (a carcinoma is a type of cancer that grows in tissue that covers or lines the body or internal organs), and malignant melanoma. Malignant melanoma is a life-threatening illness because the melanoma cancer cells can metastasize (spread) throughout the body.

You will remember from our discussion in chapter 2 that the skin is the body's largest organ. The visible portion of the skin, the *epidermis,* consists of several different cell types and layers of cells. The bottom row of cells is composed of basal cells; the middle layer consists of squamous cells. Melanin-producing melanocytes are interspersed between them. Squamous cells are fast-growing cells that have matured and moved upward from the basal layer. If basal cells become cancerous, the growth or lesion is called a *basal cell carcinoma;* if squamous cells become cancerous, the condition is called *squamous cell carcinoma.* When melanocytes become malignant, the result is *melanoma.*

Is Skin Cancer Common?

More than 700,000 new cases of skin cancer are diagnosed in the United States each year. That represents one-third of all new cancers. It is predicted that one in six Americans will develop skin cancer in his or her lifetime. The rates in other parts of the world are comparable.

As evidence that skin cancer is caused by sun exposure, 90 percent of all skin cancers occur on parts of the body that have been exposed to the sun, among people who spend long hours in the sun. According to the Skin Cancer Foundation, skin cancer takes decades to develop, and the effects of ultraviolet radiation are cumulative. Thus, even a few weeks of sunbathing each summer will, after twenty or more years, amount to considerable exposure, which in vulnerable people could lead to skin cancer.

Who Is at Greatest Risk of Getting Skin Cancer?

People with the least melanin in their skin—those with Type 1 or Type 2 skin (fair skin and blue or green eyes), as described in the chart on page 15—are especially susceptible to developing skin cancer. In addition, people who have been exposed to radiation from X rays, chemicals such as coal tars and arsenic (at one time used to treat various diseases, including asthma), thermal burns, and chronic draining of the sinuses have an unusually high vulnerability.

Since skin cancer takes years to develop, people with the largest amount of cumulative exposure to UVR are the ones at greatest risk. Melanoma, which we will discuss in the next chapter, is related to episodes of burning and to short intensive exposures. Exhaustive studies have shown that the people most likely to get skin cancer belong to one or more of the following groups:

* Those who have fair skin and sunburn easily (Type 1 or 2 skin)
* Those who are photosensitive
* Those who live in the south or southwest United States or in other areas of the world relatively near the equator (the number of cases doubles with every 8 degrees latitude nearer the equator)
* Those who live at high altitudes (more UVB light penetrates the thinner atmosphere; the city with the highest rate of skin cancer in the United States is Albuquerque, New Mexico, where the altitude is high and the latitude is low)
* Those who experience prolonged exposure to the sun, such as:
  construction workers
  farmers
  athletes (professional and amateur)
  sailors and others who work on the water
  lifeguards
  ski instructors
  sun worshipers
* Those with genetic conditions predisposing them to skin cancer (such as Gorlin's syndrome, xeroderma pigmentosum, or albinism)
* Those with excessive exposure to X rays
* Relatives of people who have had basal cell carcinomas

* Men, more than women, in the over-forty age range
* Women, more than men, in the under-forty age range
* Those who have a number of unusual moles
* Those who have had severe childhood or adolescent sunburns
* Those whose families have a history of melanoma

People who fall into one or more of the above categories are at highest risk, but everyone—with the exception of most dark-skinned African-Americans—is at risk of developing skin cancer as a result of continued, unprotected exposure to the sun.

The Skin Cancer Foundation states that 80 percent of an individual's lifetime sun exposure is received by the age of twenty; thus, for many adults, protection from the sun may not be enough. They must be aware of the warning signs of skin cancer so that it can be diagnosed and treated early, when a cure is easily obtained.

Who Actually Develops Skin Cancer?

Individuals in the highest risk categories are the most likely to develop cancer, but anyone can get it. Twice as many men as women get skin cancer, but the difference in rates may be related to the greater numbers of men who have traditionally worked in outdoor occupations.

Some diseases and genetic conditions predispose people to develop skin cancer. These include xeroderma pigmentosum, xeroderma, Gorlin's syndrome, and albinism.

Xeroderma pigmentosum: This rare, inherited skin disease is characterized by sensitivity to UVR; exposure to UVR results in freckles, keratoses, and skin cancers. The condition usually starts in childhood, and most people who have it are unable to repair skin normally following exposure to UVR. The skin of affected people shows early aging (even before age five). Frequently, skin cancer develops in these individuals.

Xeroderma: This chronic inherited skin condition is characterized by irregularly pigmented skin that first appears extremely dry and rough and later becomes thin, ulcerated, and scarred. Even brief exposure to the sun exacerbates these conditions and can lead to cancer.

Gorlin's syndrome: This rare genetic condition renders people susceptible to various skin disorders and multiple basal cell carcinomas.

Albinism: This genetic condition places people at special risk of damage from UVR. Born with partial or total lack of melanin pigment, albinos are prone to serious sunburns and to skin cancer. People with total albinism have pale skin, white hair, and pink eyes; they are represented in all ethnic groups.

Where on the Body Does Skin Cancer Usually Occur?

About 80 percent of skin cancers occur on the face, head, or neck; another 10 percent occur on other exposed areas of the body, such as the backs of hands. According to Perry Robbins, M.D., associate professor of dermatology at the New York University School of Medicine and founder of the Skin Cancer Foundation, over 80 percent of skin cancers occur on the face, head, neck, and back of the hands. Skin cancer may develop anywhere on the face (including the lips), on the tips of the ears (especially in men and women whose hair doesn't cover their ears), on the top of the heads of bald or balding men, and on or around the nose. Men's shoulders, backs, and chests and women's lower legs have become more common sites in recent years, a result of the last several decades of sun exposure to these locations.

People who drive cars in the United States are more likely to develop a skin cancer lesion on their left arm or the left side of their face than on the right side, because when they drive with open windows their left side is more exposed to the sun. In Great Britain there is a higher incidence of skin cancer on the right side of the face and on the right arm, reflecting the opposite driving sides in the two countries.

What are Premalignant Lesions?

Even before cancer actually occurs on the skin, a premalignant lesion (growth) may appear. In chapter 2 we discussed some of such growths that have the potential to become malignant. Actinic keratoses, sometimes called solar keratoses, are appropriately named because they appear almost exclusively on people who have had a great deal of sun exposure. They consist of smooth, flat, or slightly raised pink spots that later become irregular, scaly, and wartlike (actual warts do not become cancerous) and are red or brownish in color. Like skin cancers themselves, they usually develop in exposed areas such as the face or the backs of hands.

These scaly, hyperpigmented lesions were once called farmer's skin or seaman's skin because they were generally found on people who pursued outdoor occupations. In the past they were most often seen in older people, and since there was a time lag between the development of these lesions and subsequent actual skin cancer, many physicians did not recommend treatment. Today people live longer, and these premalignant lesions are showing up on younger people, so treatment is recommended for almost everyone who develops actinic keratoses.

Some of these premalignant keratoses are known as senile keratoses, and they may be found in older people on parts of the body that have not been exposed to sunlight.

Keratoacanthoma is a fast-growing, uncommon skin lesion that most often occurs on sun-exposed areas of the body. Although it invades the skin, it does not spread and can clear up without treatment. It usually appears as a smooth, red nodule, often with an umbilical spot in the center. It can be aggressive and locally destructive of skin tissue.

Leukoplakia is a precancerous condition that generally appears in mucous membranes on the lips or on the inside of the mouth. The symptomatic smooth, opaque white patches are associated with pipe smoking.

Is It Cancer?

Only a physician can tell for sure whether a particular growth is cancerous or not. But you can check a number of things yourself. Perhaps a good simple rule to remember is this:

If a new growth or discoloration appears and doesn't go away after a few weeks, or if a change (in color, size, shape, or thickness) occurs in an existing mole, growth, or discoloration, see a doctor.

The American Cancer Society, the American Academy of Dermatology, and the Skin Cancer Foundation all urge you to perform regular self-examinations of your skin. This will enable you to detect the beginnings of any skin cancer—including the most serious one, malignant melanoma.

The best course, whenever you are in doubt, is to see your personal physician first and then, if symptoms persist, to see a dermatologist.

The Dermatologist's Examination

If you're lucky, the suspected skin cancer you bring to the attention of a dermatologist will be diagnosed as a temporary or even self-limiting condition (something that goes away on its own), and you will be relieved to know that you don't have cancer.

When you first visit the dermatologist, you will be asked some relevant questions about your own personal and family medical history. The dermatologist will then examine the area. His or her trained eye—aided by nothing more than a magnifying glass—can sometimes determine that a growth is completely harmless. But before sending you on your way, reassured, praised for your caution, and reminded to return if any changes in the growth occur or any new ones appear, the dermatologist is likely to do a total body skin exam.

A total body skin examination involves a thorough inspection of your skin by a physician who is a trained skin specialist. This procedure is performed to determine whether any abnormality exists in your skin, hair, or nails. In a well-lighted examining room, the physician will carefully examine all areas of your skin, including not-so-visible parts such as your scalp and the backs of your ears.

The Skin Cancer Foundation, the American Academy of Dermatology, and the American Cancer Society recommend that *everyone* have a total body skin examination (TBSE) once a year. If you fall into a high-risk category because of skin type, history of sun-exposure, *and* either a tendency toward unusual or numerous moles or a family history of skin cancer, you may even arrange to have such examinations more frequently. If you have had any precancerous lesions as described in chapter 2, you should be examined by a dermatologist regularly and frequently. Your physician can also aid you in learning more about self-examination.

Why should everyone have a TBSE annually? Dr. Deborah S. Sarnoff offers three good reasons:

* You may have an abnormal mole where you can't easily see it, such as on your back.
* You may not recognize a premalignant growth as significant.
* Skin sometimes serves as a window for diagnosing other diseases, such as thyroid conditions, internal cancers, or diabetes. A thorough examination of the skin may aid in early detection of these conditions.

Although many dermatologists and family doctors routinely advise patients to have a TBSE, others only recommend this for patients who have a personal history of skin cancer. Dr. Sarnoff suggests that you ask your dermatologist (or make an appointment with one especially for this purpose) to perform this examination. It takes only a few minutes, and the examination is usually included in the cost of a regular office visit.

Suspect Growths

Even the most experienced dermatologist can't always be certain that a benign (noncancerous) growth really is benign. Sometimes the most highly trained eye and most powerful magnifying glass cannot, with absolute certainty, determine a diagnosis. In such an instance, the dermatologist may recommend a biopsy—the removal and microscopic examination of suspect tissue or body fluid.

Biopsies are not all the same. An incisional biopsy, in which a small piece (rather than the entire growth) is removed, is often performed on a suspected growth of skin cancer. The method used to achieve this varies according to the type of growth. Among the possibilities are the following:

* *Shave biopsy:* Tissue is thinly sliced off with a scalpel.
* *Curette or scrape biopsy:* Tissue is superficially scraped off.
* *Scissor biopsy:* A growth that protrudes above the surface of skin is removed.
* *Sponge biopsy:* A lesion is abraded with a cellulose sponge.
* *Wedge biopsy:* A preshaped portion is excised.
* *Punch biopsy:* A small piece of tissue is removed, using a special instrument (something like a cookie cutter) or a scalpel that pierces through the skin to remove a deeper part of growth. This method is used when growth itself is too large to remove merely for diagnostic purposes. Generally, stitches are required to close the skin following this kind of biopsy.

In many instances, the entire growth is removed in a procedure termed an *excisional biopsy.* This is done when the growth is small or when it is essential to know the extent and depth of the suspected cancer.

If the pathologist finds the sample noncancerous, you will have a good reason to celebrate but not to relax, since you will want to remain vigilant for any subsequent growths.

If the biopsy report is positive for cancer, your doctor will identify what kind of cancer it is, tell whether it has spread to the outer borders of the sample, and outline any treatment recommendations. Before proceeding with treatment, you may wish to seek a second opinion, if you have not yet done so; your insurance company may even insist upon this.

Because at least 10 percent of all individuals with newly diagnosed skin cancers have more than one skin cancer at the same time, the dermatologist will be especially careful to examine your entire body, even if you only consulted the doctor for only one growth. Your lymph nodes near the suspected malignancy will also be examined to determine whether they are enlarged.

Basal Cell Carcinoma

Slow growing but potentially destructive, basal cell carcinoma is the most common of all cancers, including skin cancers. Sometimes referred to as *basal cell epitheliomas,* these cancerous growths affect more than 560,000 people yearly. They grow out of the cells in the deep basal layer of the epidermis and are seen most often on individuals with white skin—particularly people of northern European extraction. Basal cell carcinoma (BCC) does not metastasize (spread), as internal cancers do, but if left untreated it can badly damage and destroy underlying tissues and structures. If neglected, BCC around the eyes or ears can lead to disfigurement and even loss of function of these organs.

BCC usually begins on a sun-exposed area of the body: the face, ears, neck, scalp, shoulders, or back. The tumors may also begin on nonexposed areas.

At one time, BCC usually struck older people, especially men who had worked outdoors; it was seldom seen in children, teenagers, or people in their twenties. Today, however, the incidence has increased markedly among males and females in these age groups, as well as among those in midlife. No one is immune to it.

In almost every instance, the onset of BCC is directly related to sun exposure. Exceptions involve exposure to arsenic or radiation and complications resulting from burns, scars, vaccinations, or tattoos. Of course, these factors can also contribute to the onset of BCC that is primarily sun related.

A number of warning signs are specific for BCC. Appearance of the cancer usually can be felt as well as seen, and the growth may have pearly or shiny edges. The color may be reddish or purplish and may even have small red dots around it. In dark-skinned people, the bump can be so dark that it looks like a mole.

An open sore that is at first mistaken for an insect bite or scratch that doesn't heal and/or begins to bleed, ooze, or crust can often be a sign of BCC. Basal cell carcinomas are still sometimes referred to as *rodent ulcers*, because of their resemblance to a rat bite—a once-common phenomenon.

Sometimes a reddish patch or irritated area on the chest, shoulders, arms, or legs may persist, itch, hurt, or crust. The growth may be smooth with an indentation in the center that may slowly enlarge, with tiny blood vessels developing on the surface. Less often, BCC may first appear as a pale or waxy area on taut skin, resembling a scar without sharp borders.

If you find these symptoms a bit confusing, you are not alone. BCC has many variations in size, shape, and color, and it can mask itself as anything from a cyst to a scar to a sore to a bite; thus, it is quite difficult, if not impossible, for a nonphysician to self-diagnose.

Squamous Cell Carcinoma

The second most common type of skin cancer, squamous cell carcinoma affects over 140,000 people each year. These cancers not only grow faster than BCC but they have far greater potential to invade and destroy underlying structures and to metastasize to lymph glands and other parts of the body.

SCC most often arises on the rim of the ear, the face, the lips or mouth, or the back of the hand. Usually SCC begins as a slightly raised pink opaque papule or as a red scaly patch or wartlike growth, later ulcerating in the center. The affected area may increase in size, even to the extent of becoming mushroomlike in appearance, crusting and ulcerating in the center.

As with BCC, a high proportion of SCC arises on sun-exposed areas of skin. The cancers may also develop in scar tissue, in areas of chronic irritation, in nonhealing wounds or trauma, in ulcerations, in infections, and in areas of prior radiation treatment. Cases of SCC that arise from causes other than sun exposure are more likely to involve metastasis.

Good sense dictates that anyone who has scars on sun-exposed areas of the body—for instance, on the chest from cardiac surgery—or who has had radiation treatments to the head and neck area, should be especially careful in the sun.

Like BCC, SCC is difficult (particularly in the early stages) for a nonphysician to self-diagnose. Frequent skin self-examinations of all sun-exposed areas, with special attention to areas that have suffered trauma or been exposed to X rays, are a wise investment of time in skin health and the prevention of cancer growth. Squamous cell carcinoma can be treated successfully, especially at an early stage. Report any changes in skin growths or appearance to a physician, who can make a definitive diagnosis and outline a treatment plan.

In all, there are approximately 2,300 deaths each year from basal cell and squamous cell carcinoma, most from squamous cell carcinoma, but the overall five-year survival rate is 95 percent. It could be higher still if detected and treated early.

Bowen's Disease

Bowen's disease is sometimes described as a precancerous condition, but other experts consider it a rare form of cancer. It appears as a scaling, reddish pink, raised growth, usually on unexposed areas of the skin. Many people with Bowen's disease have taken patent medicines that contain arsenic, such as tonics or appetite stimulants. Skin affected by Bowen's disease may look like a solar keratosis, but the growth becomes large and thick and generally remains within the confines of the epidermis. Also called *intraepidermal epitheliomas,* these growths can become very unsightly and can break out from the epidermis to invade deeper layers of skin, becoming SCC.

Eyelid Cancers

Any cancer that can appear on the rest of the skin can also develop on the eyelid. This sensitive part of the skin is very vulnerable to the sun, and unless you have had a lifetime of protection via sunglasses and a brimmed hat or visor you are vulnerable to it. You need both a hat and glasses, because a hat alone will not protect you from solar radiation that is reflected up from the ground, particularly ground covered by snow or water.

As elsewhere on the body, the most common cancer of the eyelid is BCC, which represents about 80 percent of all eyelid cancers. Most often it appears on the lower lid, but it also occurs on the upper lid, especially among people who have had a long history of sun exposure. SCC accounts for 7 to 9 percent of eyelid tumors, and these too are closely associated with prolonged exposure to UVR. Malignant melanoma, which will be discussed in chapter 9, is also found on eyelids.

Regular ophthalmological examinations provide a good opportunity to detect eyelid cancers. Unlike the rest of your skin, both sides of an eyelid lesion can be examined. Reported cancers of the eyelid in the United States have doubled since 1977. People who live in sunny areas are most at risk.

Eyelid cancers do not always begin, as one might expect, with a lesion. Instead, the earliest sign may be loss of eyelashes, a persistent eye infection, a bump that could be mistaken for a sty, or a bump that goes away and then returns in the same location. Thus, individuals suffering from any of these symptoms should not ignore it or try to treat it themselves but should see an ophthalmologist, who may perform an office biopsy through the eyelid to examine all layers.

Generally eyelid cancers don't invade the eye, but if a cancerous basal cell hits the globe of the eye, vision is affected and the eye may even have to be removed. Some cancers of the eye can spread to distant areas.

Squamous cell carcinomas of the eyelid can start out as primary lesions or develop from precancerous actinic keratoses. Malignant melanomas can also arise on the outer lining of the eye. The most common eyelid cancers are those of the sebaceous or tear glands, which can recur, invade, and damage the eye itself, and even spread to distant areas. This type of cancer tends to be recognized late because it initially resembles a sty. It should be made clear that most people with sties don't have cancer; but if a sty stubbornly recurs after healing, it should be investigated carefully. Cancer of the eyelids, like most cancers, responds best to treatment when detected early.

Does One Skin Cancer Mean Increased Risk of Getting Another?

Once a person is diagnosed with skin cancer their risk of developing another one rises dramatically. The most important risk factors were those that initially placed people at risk: a skin complexion that burns instead of tanning (Type 1 or 2 skin), and frequent sun exposure.

Every dermatologist with whom I have spoken agrees that all people, regardless of age or sex, should protect themselves from the sun, but most add that those who have already had one cancer, especially if they are old, need to be especially vigilant because their chances of developing another one are so great; some authorities say their chances of a recurrence are as high as 50 to 60 percent. Most dermatologists recommend that anyone who has had skin cancer be professionally examined two to four times a year.

9

Malignant Melanoma: Life-threatening Skin Cancer

Throughout the world, and especially in areas where people have had intense exposure to the sun, the incidence of malignant melanoma is rising at an alarming rate. In the United States, one-third of all new cancers diagnosed each year are skin cancers. One-fifth of these skin cancers are malignant melanomas. Half the melanoma cases occur in people under fifty-five years of age, 30 percent among those forty-five or younger.

In 1991, about 6,900 melanoma-related deaths occurred, making melanoma the fourth leading cause of death from cancer among people between the ages of twenty and fifty. Despite this grim statistic, melanoma is almost always curable if detected early and treated promptly. Early detection is easily accomplished, since melanoma is visible, in contrast to cancers that begin internally and are difficult to diagnose or even to suspect until they have already spread. For this reason, survival rates are steadily improving, but there remains a pressing need to prevent future cases of melanoma and to teach more people to recognize the early warning signs of the disease so that they can be diagnosed when it is at an early stage.

What Is Malignant Melanoma?

Malignant melanoma is a cancer that originates in skin cells called *melanocytes* that are found in the basal layer of the skin. Interestingly, these cells, which produce the dark pigment, melanin, are also found in the respiratory tract and in surrounding nerve cells.

Malignant melanoma develops when melanocytes are transformed into cancer cells—cells that grow abnormally and (in the case of malignant melanoma) migrate to parts of the body far from the original site where they appeared. This movement, called metastasis, occurs through the bloodstream or the lymphatic system. Then the cancer cells crowd out other cells, at their new locations, continuing to spread and multiply, reproducing themselves by cell division, invading and destroying surrounding tissues. They may form additional tumors and, by depriving normal cells of nourishment, may cause weight loss and obstruct normal functioning. Malignant melanoma, unlike the skin cancers discussed in the previous chapter, can metastasize if not detected and treated early; for this reason, it is a potentially life-threatening form of cancer and should never be viewed as "just a little skin cancer."

Types of Melanoma

Many doctors divide malignant melanoma into four classifications: superficial spreading melanoma, nodular melanoma, lentigo maligna melanoma, and acral lentiginous melanoma. However, some authorities now consider these all to be variants of the same basic melanoma.

Superficial spreading melanoma is the commonest type, constituting 60 to 70 percent of melanomas in both men and women. It is an irregular brown, black, or bluish black growth, sometimes inflamed, with a tendency to ulcerate and bleed. Uncommonly, it may start from a preexisting growth, but more usually it appears as a new growth. If ignored or unrecognized, it may either metastasize or develop into a nodular melanoma (which may itself metastasize).

Nodular melanoma tends to be very fast growing. It can arise on skin that had appeared normal or in a preexisting mole; it frequently ulcerates. Because it has a rich blood supply, it may resemble a blood blister.

Lentigo maligna melanoma (sometimes called *Hutchinson's melanotic freckle*) often arises on the face or some other sun-exposed area, often in older people. It is usually dull brown or black, with a very irregular lateral margin. It may remain in place (in which case the correct term for it is *lentigo maligna*) for years without metastasizing or invading neighboring tissues. The appearance of raised nodules within it signals that it has begun to invade the dermis; at this stage, it is termed *lentigo maligna melanoma*. Although it can metastasize to the lymph glands, this form of melanoma is less likely to do so than either superficial spreading melanoma or nodular melanoma.

Acral lentiginous melanoma most often arises on the sole of the foot and sometimes occurs on the palm of the hand. It has a raised dark area, surrounded by a lighter area that may extend several centimeters around the raised area. A variety of this type of melanoma, called *periungual melanoma*, often arises in the region of the nail bed of hands or toes; it can easily be mistaken for warts or ingrowing toenails.

Melanomas can arise anywhere on the skin, under nails, and in hidden areas such as the genitals, the rectum, and membranes of the nervous system and the respiratory tract. Some melanomas arise in the eye, as will be discussed later in this chapter.

What Causes Malignant Melanoma?

Like other skin cancers, melanoma seems chiefly to be caused by exposure to ultraviolet radiation. Numerous studies indicate that, whether this UVR is obtained from sunlight or from artificial sources such as tanning salons, exposure increases a person's risk of developing melanoma later. Unlike other skin cancers, which usually develop from a lifetime of cumulative exposure, melanoma tends to be more common in Caucasians who have experienced intermittent and intense exposures—often in the form of a history of searing sunburns in childhood or adolescence. Research indicates that people who vacation in the sun, thus incurring a series of isolated bouts of sunburn, are more likely to develop malignant melanoma than those who actually work in the sun.

You have probably noticed that moles often run in families.

Melanoma is linked to different types of moles—congenital (those present from birth or early childhood), acquired (those that develop later), or dysplastic (those that are unusual or atypical). Melanoma can develop even in people who have avoided the sun, especially if they have moles.

Other possible causes currently being investigated are immune system deficiencies, tumor-causing viruses, and chemical carcinogens. As discussed in chapter 2, exposure to ultraviolet radiation can bring about changes in the immune system. Moreover, the effects of UVR can be cumulative; and although it has not been established how exposing the skin at one site changes the immune response at a distant site, this effect has been demonstrated to occur. Margaret L. Kripke, professor and head of the Department of Immunology at the University of Texas's M. D. Anderson Cancer Center in Houston, says, "It is possible that local effects of ultraviolet radiation on immune cells in the skin might also play a role in the growth and spread of melanoma cells."

Types of Moles

Moles serve no function but in themselves are not dangerous; indeed, most of us have a number of these small colored spots, which are sometimes characterized as freckles or birthmarks. The average person's body has about twenty-five moles by adulthood. Some of these spots are present at birth, but most develop through life.

Unlike freckles, which lie flat on the skin, moles are elevated. The scientific name for a mole is *nevus*. Moles are usually brown, but they can range in color from pink to very dark brown, because they contain cells similar to melanocytes, the pigment-producing cells found in the basal layer of the skin.

Congenital Nevi

These moles are either seen at birth or develop by the time a baby is six months old; however, they may be so light as to be barely noticeable. About 1 percent of babies are born with them. Generally, these moles run in families, and one or both parents may carry the trait. In some families you can see three generations of a family, all with a number of moles. People with congenital nevi are now thought to be at a higher risk of developing melanoma in later life.

Congenital nevi may never become troublesome, but some do develop into melanoma. Arthur Rhodes, M.D., chief of the Division of Dermatology of the Children's Hospital in Boston, suggests that, if a pigmented mark is present on your child at birth, you should consult your physician. "Not all pigmented marks are moles," he says. "Congenital moles usually elevate the skin surface at least a bit when viewed from the side using a flashlight in a darkened room." Some flat brown marks may be café-au-lait spots, which are present in 1 out of every 100 white babies and 12 out of every 100 black babies. Mongolian spots may also appear. These are blue-gray and most often appear on the buttocks or back; they usually disappear by age twelve. Your child's pediatrician should be able to differentiate among these various marks.

Congenital nevi have been subdivided into three groups, according to their size in the person's infancy: small (less than 1.4 cm in diameter), medium (1.5 to 20 cm in diameter), or large (greater than 20 cm in diameter). Naturally these nevi will occupy different amounts of the body surface as the child grows.

Some physicians believe that medium and large moles should be removed, because of the high risk of developing melanoma in a large congenital nevi. If the mole looks normal, the physican may simply watch it carefully and consider removing it later in an office procedure. Many dermatologists photograph the moles to aid in maintaining careful observation of them over a period of time. Medium and large moles should be examined by the patient at home for any changes and every six to twelve months by a physician. If any changes develop in small or medium congenital nevi, the doctor will probably suggest either that it be removed or that a biopsy of it be performed. People with large congenital nevi have a 5 to 20 percent lifetime risk of developing melanoma, and for that reason some dermatologists prefer to remove them if doing so would not be cosmetically undesirable.

Anyone with nevi should watch out for and report the following danger signs:

* changes in color (lightening or darkening)
* changes in surface (a bump, a sore, or bleeding)
* change in size (enlargement greater than can be explained by normal body growth)
* pain or itching that lasts more than a few days

These changes do not necessarily indicate cancer. But if cancer has developed, early detection and treatment are essential. Since people with congenital nevi are at a higher risk of developing melanoma than the general population, they should be especially careful to protect themselves against ultraviolet radiation.

Acquired Normal Moles

Some moles develop during the first thirty years of life, and these are termed normal moles. Most of them stay that way, but melanoma can develop in a normal mole. Thus, if one changes it should be seen by a dermatologist to assess whether the change signifies anything abnormal. Ordinary moles usually have the following characteristics:

* *Shape*: Round or oval; symmetrical with sharp, well-defined borders between the mole and the surrounding skin; may be flat, bumpy, or elevated
* *Color*: Uniformly tan, brown, or skin color; most look like others on the body
* *Size*: Usually less than 5 or 6 mm in diameter (slightly smaller than a pencil eraser)
* *Number*: In adults, usually ten to forty, generally scattered over the body
* *Location*: Concentrated on sun-exposed areas above the waist, such as the face, trunk, arms, and legs; seldom found on scalp, female breasts, or buttocks
* *Onset*: Usually appear during early childhood through mid-twenties; seldom after age thirty-five

Dysplastic Nevi

Some unusual moles are known as *dysplastic nevi*. The word *dysplastic* means abnormally developing. Such moles may develop at any time, but they are most likely to appear in adulthood. These moles are important to diagnose because studies indicate that people who have them are born with a tendency to develop malignant melanocytes. About 8 percent of Caucasians have dysplastic moles. The dysplastic mole itself may become malignant, or another mole or lesion may appear that is malignant.

It is possible (and indeed quite likely) for a person to have a combination of normal moles and dysplastic nevi. The latter may appear on both sun-exposed and sun-protected areas. Considerable evidence suggests that dysplastic nevi are related to sun exposure early in life, and that they tend to be larger in diameter and more numerous in sun-exposed areas than in sun-protected ones. Furthermore, research has substantiated that people with dysplastic nevi have cells that may be more likely to change when exposed to ultraviolet radiation than are normal cells. Studies also indicate that people with dysplastic nevi tend to be more susceptible to sunburn than people without these moles.

The tendency to develop dysplastic nevi may be inherited, or such nevi may simply develop randomly without any known family tendency to form them. Where dysplastic nevi exist in two or more family members, the condition is sometimes called *dysplastic nevus syndrome*. In families in which one or more members have developed melanoma, the risk of other members' developing the disease is extremely high.

If you have or suspect you have a dysplastic nevus, you should see your personal physician or a dermatologist. Dysplastic nevi look different from normal moles, but even an experienced dermatologist may have difficulty differentiating one from melanoma just by looking at it. Thus the physician may suggest a biopsy—the removal and microscopic examination of some or all of the suspected tissue.

If you have any question about whether your mole is a normal acquired one or a dysplastic one, err on the side of caution and see a doctor. Dysplastic nevi usually have the following characteristics:

* *Shape*: Irregular and often asymmetrical; the border may be irregular and seem to fade into surrounding skin.
* *Surface*: Often pebbly or cobblestoned.
* *Color*: Mixed and irregular, with speckles of tan, brown, dark brown, black, and red/pink within a single mole; moles may not look alike.
* *Size*: Usually (but not necessarily) larger than a pencil eraser; some may be unusually large, even 8 mm or more in diameter.
* *Number*: As many as 100, but there may only be a few.
* *Location*: Usually found on the back, chest, abdomen, arms, and legs; also occur on areas not normally exposed such as scalp, buttocks, groin, or female breasts.
* *Onset*: Many appear before age twenty-five, and appearance of new ones may continue through life; relatively stable once developed; new ones or growth in existing ones should be brought to a physician's attention.

Dermatologists today are very careful to examine the skin of anyone who has dysplastic nevi, taking a family history and doing a biopsy on nevi that may look most suspiciously like melanoma. Allan C. Halpern, M.D., Assistant Professor of Dermatology at the University of Pennsylvania, emphasizes the importance of diagnosing dysplastic nevi because people who get them have a high chance of developing melanoma by age fifty. He recommends frequent professional examinations (some specialists suggest follow-up examinations every three to six months) and what he describes as "aggressive observation." He also suggests taking photographs to maintain a record of any growths or changes. Thus, anything suspect can be removed; and if it is melanoma, it is caught when it is recently emerged and usually curable. Dr. Halpern, like all dermatologists, stresses that it is crucial for such individuals to avoid sun exposure.

Warning Signs of Melanoma

Malignant melanoma should be suspected if a new, pigmented mole develops in anyone over age forty; actually, any new growth or lesion, especially after adulthood, should be looked at by a dermatologist. Research shows that a number of people are not aware of the warning signs, do not realize that malignant melanoma can develop in a mole that has been present for a long time, or think that it can only begin in an existing one. The reality is that it can begin in either a preexisting mole or on "normal" skin.

Normal moles are usually:

* smaller than a pencil eraser
* of one shade or color, rather than a mixture

Normal moles should not:

* itch
* have ragged outlines
* continue to grow in adult
* be inflamed, bleed, ooze, or crust

A mole that deviates from the norm is not necessarily malignant, but it does warrant attention and should be checked out by a physician.

Melanoma may appear in a fingernail or toenail as a widening brownish or blackish band running up and down the nail. When such a band develops in a single nail, particularly in a person of middle age or older, a doctor's diagnosis should always be sought.

The American Cancer Society, the American Academy of Dermatology, and the Skin Cancer Foundation have devised a simple ABCD rule to help people remember some of the signs of melanoma:

A. ASYMMETRY: One half of the mole or growth does not match the other half.

B. BORDER IRREGULARITY: The edges are ragged, notched, or blurred.

C. COLOR: The pigmentation is not uniform. Shades of tan, brown, and black may be present. Red, white, and blue may add to the mottled appearance.

D. DIAMETER: Any mole larger than 6 mm (the size of a

pencil eraser) or exhibiting a sudden or continuing increase in size should be of special concern.

Here is a fuller description of the warning signs of malignant melanoma, as summarized in a brochure entitled *The Many Faces of Melanoma*, © by the Skin Cancer Foundation New York, NY (and reprinted here with permission):

* change in size: especially sudden or continuous enlargement
* change in color: especially multiple shades of tan, brown, dark brown, and black; the mixing of red, white, and blue; or the spreading of color from the edge into the surrounding skin
* change in shape: especially the developing of an irregular, notched border that used to be regular
* change in elevation: especially the raising of a part of a pigmented area that used to be flat or only slightly elevated
* change in surface: especially scaliness, erosion, oozing, crusting, ulceration, or bleeding
* change in surrounding skin: especially redness; swelling; or the developing of colored blemishes next to, but not a part of, the pigmented area
* changes in sensation: especially itchiness, tenderness, or pain
* change in consistency: especially softening or hardening

Who Is at Greatest Risk of Developing Malignant Melanoma?

For many years authorities thought that those at highest risk of developing malignant melanoma were people with red hair and freckles. True, the incidence is 7 to 10 times greater among people with fair skin, and it is 15 times more common in whites than in non-Caucasians, but now it is known that a number of other variables affect a person's level of risk for this disease.

"Generally," says Allan Halpern, M.D., of the University of Pennsylvania, "people at risk of developing malignant melanoma fall into one of two groups. The first is sun-sensitive Caucasians who blister easily from the sun, burn readily, tan poorly, or live close to the equator. The second group includes people who have a family history of malignant melanomas and have inherited the gene that places them at increased risk. They tend to develop a number of moles."

Dr. Halpern suggests that you be particularly on the look-out for changing moles that do not appear in obvious places like the forearms and face. Pigmented birthmarks are also at risk of turning into malignant melanoma.

People who have a number of dysplastic nevi are 22 to 30 times more likely to develop malignant melanoma than is the average person. Besides the fact that these moles develop into melanoma, they are considered markers, identifying people who are also at an increased risk of developing malignant melanoma elsewhere on their bodies. Studies show that dys-plastic nevi are larger and more prevalent in areas that have been exposed to the sun (especially during the person's first years of life) than in areas that have been protected. And a greater number of moles, in turn, increases the person's risk of eventually developing malignant melanoma.

Researchers have noted that the cells of individuals with dysplastic nevi show greater sensitivity and greater propensity to mutation (changes) from ultraviolet radiation than do normal cells. A person who has dysplastic nevi and a personal or family history of melanoma is thought to have almost a 100 percent risk of developing melanoma. But this circumstance should not unduly alarm you; remember that melanoma in its earliest stage is usually curable. Consequently, the Skin Cancer Foundation recommends that individuals in this very high-risk category personally check themselves and have regular checkups (total body skin examinations) at least once a year from a phsyician who specializes in skin diseases.

Approximately 15 out of every 100 melanomas of the skin develop in a congenital mole. Most congenital moles are small (less than 1.5 cm in diameter), but the lifetime risk of developing melanoma increases in individuals with large moles. It has been estimated that 5 out of every 100 people with congenital moles will develop melanoma by the time they reach age sixty. Melanoma occurs in young children only very rarely; but it may develop anytime after age twelve.

About 1 in 50 people who have been cured of a malignant melanoma are at extremely high risk of developing another melanoma within three years. This frequency is greatly increased (to 15 in 50) if the person has a relative with melanoma, because it tends to run in families.

Even if you conscientiously apply sunscreen or have little opportunity to be out in the sun now, you may be at risk. According to Arthur Sober, M.D., dermatologist and melanoma specialist at Massachusetts General Hospital in Boston, "Even a single blistering sunburn in adolescence would double the risk of developing malignant melanoma later in life."

Some experts believe that if you have had a painful sunburn during the first ten to fifteen years of your life, your chances of developing malignant melanoma are tripled. Sidney Hurwitz, M.D., clinical professor of pediatrics and dermatology at Yale University School of Medicine, states that if all children used a sunscreen whenever they were out in the sun, from infancy until age eighteen, 81 percent of accumulated lifetime sun exposure would be eliminated. That would certainly lower the rate of melanoma for the next generation.

A number of studies have demonstrated that early intense exposure is responsible for the onset of melanoma. Careful investigation of the sun-exposure habits of patients who develop melanoma reveals that such patients frequently have, in addition to genetic risks (family history, moles, skin types, and so on) a history of a blistering sunburn in childhood or adolescence. These studies indicate that youngsters who were "poor tanners" (such as those with Type 1 or Type 2 skin) *and* had a blistering sunburn in childhood or adolescence were at greatest risk. But even "good tanners" were at serious risk if they spent long vacations in sunny areas during childhood, had a painful sunburn in childhood, and were often encouraged to be outdoors. Data show that individuals who are born in or who migrate to hot, sunny areas (southern United States, Australia, Israel) during childhood rather than during young adulthood are at very high risk. The time of arrival, rather than the length of time a person lived there, was a key risk variable. For instance, people who were born in western Australia or who arrived there before age ten had four times the risk of those who immigrated there after age fifteen; those who arrived before the age of ten also developed more moles on their arms than those who arrived later. Similar findings exist for Israel and New Zealand.

Children's personal schedules (no school in the summer; opportunities to be outdoors after school, on weekends, and even during recess at school) allow them to spend considerably more time outdoors than adults do, so it is easy to see how extensive their exposure to the sun can be. Unfortunately, this exposure can lead to melanoma twenty, thirty, or more years later.

Indoor workers have a higher risk for melanoma than outdoor workers, indicating that repeated, widely separated incidents of intense sun exposure in adulthood may be more likely to cause melanoma than daily, cumulative sun exposure. The reason is still undetermined, but among the various theories under consideration are several related to the effects of such bursts of exposure on the immune system.

The different types of melanoma are associated with different risks. Lentigo maligna melanoma usually arises on the sun-exposed skin of the elderly, strongly suggesting that years of sun exposure is a major cause. Superficial spreading melanoma, the most common type, places blonds, individuals with light or medium skin color, those with many freckles, and those who burn rather than tan or burn before tanning (Types 1 and 2 skin) at highest risk. People who have blond, light brown, or red hair and light skin, but who can tan are at risk for nodular melanoma.

Although the incidence of malignant melanoma is considerably higher in Caucasians than in other racial groups, having dark brown or black skin is not a guarantee against melanoma. Black people, for example, may develop acral lentiginous melanoma, especially on the palms of the hand, the soles of the feet, under the nails, or in the mouth.

Four factors have emerged for placing people in the highest risk category of all: having spent more than two hours per day in the sun for ten to twenty years prior to diagnosis of melanoma; pursuing an indoor occupation in tandem with outdoor recreational habits; having light eye color; and evidencing poor tanning ability. Still, this list of special risk factors doesn't mean that the rest of the population is home free.

In some studies it has been shown that malignant melanomas most often do not develop from preexisting moles. Furthermore, those that do arise from moles are not always from dysplastic or congenital ones. But evidence indicates that, when melanomas do arise from moles, the moles usually were larger than 6 mm in diameter. This does not contradict the fact that people with dysplastic nevi are at great risk of developing the disease; rather it means that dysplastic nevi are markers for the development of melanoma *somewhere* on the body. For this reason, such individuals need to be especially careful to inspect their bodies for changes in the skin and to have frequent professional skin examinations.

Predicting the Course of Melanoma

Although melanoma that is recognized and diagnosed early stands the best chance of being cured, a number of people delay seeking diagnosis and treatment. Why?

Some lesions may begin in an area that is not easily visible (the back, for instance), and as a result it is overlooked until it enlarges or is brought to a person's attention by someone else.

Many people who have little or no knowledge of the disease wait until the lesion is large, thick, and already invasive before consulting a physician about it. The American Cancer Society, the Skin Cancer Foundation, and hospitals and health groups throughout the country provide an important service in conducting screenings and in disseminating educational materials that help alert people to the signs of melanoma, in hopes of removing lack of knowledge from the roster of reasons for delaying diagnosis.

Still other people choose to ignore the warning signs,

minimizing the seriousness because hiding their head in the sand reduces their fear and anxiety of cancer.

In a study conducted by Dr. Barrie Cassileth of the University of Pennsylvania Cancer Center in Philadelphia, it was found that patients waited an average of six months from the time they noticed changes in a mole until the time they decided those changes warranted professional examination. The study also established that people are more likely to be diagnosed early if they go to a dermatologist rather than to a phsyician for whom skin diseases are not a specialty. Experts cite this as a good reason to have regular examinations (at least when you recognize a warning sign or if you are in a high-risk category) conducted by a dermatologist. Anything suspect will then be removed (in whole or in part) and submitted for biopsy. The resulting reading of the extent of disease is closely linked to the prognosis (forecast of the disease's progress and probable outcome).

Melanomas observed in the earliest stage of development are thinner than those in later stages. When melanoma is diagnosed in its earliest and thinnest state, 99 percent of patients thus afflicted will survive for five years or more.

Still, no matter how alert you are to changes in your skin, it is possible that the diagnosis of melanoma may be made after it has begun to spread or invade beyond the site of its earliest stage.

The level (depth in skin) and thickness of melanoma, among other criteria, are referred to by pathologists as its *microstage*. Tumors with a low-risk microstage account for a growing number of the melanoma cases now seen by physicians. Such melanomas tend to be somewhat flat, but later they may develop a nodule.

Recent findings suggest that tumor volume, rather than just size, may be a critical factor in the prognosis of the melanoma. Reporting on a study of patients with malignant melanoma, Robert J. Friedman, M.D., dermatologist at New York University School of Medicine, says that patients with tumors measuring less than 200 mm had a nearly 90 percent five-year disease-free survival rate. In contrast, patients whose tumors measured more than 200 cubic millimeters had only a 10 percent survival rate for the same period. "Measurement of tumor volume [the portion within the dermis] may prove to be of significance in the prediction of survival rates," he says. Dr. Friedman explained that measuring a tumor's volume may more accurately reflect the three-dimensional nature of tumors, in comparison with more common measurements that rely on a single dimension such as the level or thickness of the tumor. But until further studies are completed, the thickness of the original tumor will probably still be used as a major predictor of outcome.

Melanoma does its most severe damage (ultimately ending in death) by metastasizing (spreading) to the lungs, the liver, the neurological system, or other body structures and organs. How fast and where it will spread is not always predictable; there may be some association between where the melanoma initially appeared and where it goes next.

If metastasis has begun before diagnosis, surgery alone cannot cure the melanoma, but control of the disease is certainly possible.

Melanomas of the Eye and the Eye Area

Lentigo maligna, described earlier in this chapter, is a premalignant lesion that can develop on the eyelid. Malignant melanoma can occur on any portion of the skin, including the eyelids; however, melanoma accounts for less than 2 percent of all eyelid cancers. The growth may be tan or brown with irregular borders, and like other eyelid cancers this tumor requires surgical removal and (possibly) radiation for large lesions.

Melanoma of the eye is the most common cancer of that organ, but it is still rare. Some eye tissues contain pigment-producing cells in which melanoma can develop. As in the case of malignant melanoma of the skin, dark-skinned populations are at a lower risk than fair-skinned ones. The relationship between ultraviolet radiation and intraocular (within the eye) malignant melanoma has not been proved. However, one important study reported in the September 26, 1985, issue of the *New England Journal of Medicine* demonstrated that people who developed melanoma in the eye were more likely than the general population to have spent time outdoors in their gardens, to have sunbathed, or to have used artificial tanning devices. In addition, those who rarely wore hats, visors, or sunglasses while in the sun had a higher risk for developing the disease. All of this evidence certainly suggests that sunlight exposure is closely related to the development of intraocular malignant melanoma. Overall, the study's authors, who were associated with the National Cancer Institute and a number of prestigious medical centers, concluded that the risk factors involved in developing intraocular malignant melanoma are the same as those involved in developing it on the skin.

Melanomas can arise in the iris, in the ciliary body (which contains the muscles that control the shape of the lens), or in the choroid (the middle layer of tissue in the wall of the eyeball, consisting of blood vessels and dense pigment). Unfortunately, few signs or symptoms appear until the tumor reaches a relatively large size. Sometimes loss of vision, a sensation of floating spots, or protrusion of the eyeball may occur. It is also possible for tumor growth to cause secondary changes such as cataracts, glaucoma, or retinal detachment. The average age for developing this cancer is fifty, and there are no differences in rates of incidence between men and women. Intraocular melanoma is rarely associated with melanomas of the skin, since skin cancers do not commonly metastasize to the eye; however, it can spread from the eye to almost any organ of the body. Frequently it spreads to the liver, and sometimes melanoma of the eye is only diagnosed after it has already spread and appeared elsewhere.

Regular examinations by an eye-care specialist can help to diagnose this cancer before it spreads. Other diagnostic tests available are CT scans (the use of computers and X rays to obtain a highly detailed image) and ultrasound, which can help to locate the tumor. Blood tests, radioactive scans, and other X rays are used to determine whether the cancer has metastasized. Some tests may make use of a dye injected into a vein in the arm to highlight the blood vessels of the eye prior to taking an X ray that may identify a tumor.

Early Detection Is Crucial

"If you catch a melanoma before it invades the dermis [the layer beneath the epidermis, where the mole is first noticeable], it is easily cured by outpatient surgery," says Dr. Allan Halpern. In this very early stage of malignant melanoma before invasion—called the *radial growth phase*—almost 100 percent of people will survive eight years if they have had the growth surgically removed. However, the deeper the melanoma grows into the skin, the more dangerous it becomes. If malignant melanoma spreads to the lymph glands, cure is extremely difficult to achieve; only 30 pecent of patients whose melanoma has reached this stage survive the disease. Sometimes micrometastisis occurs and cannot be detected at the time of diagnosis.

Early detection can result in surgical removal and cure. Later detection often involves combating a disease that is stubbornly resistant to treatment.

Reducing Risks of Malignant Melanoma

Stay out of the sun, avoid tanning salons, and see a dermatologist regularly if you have congenital moles, any unusual moles, or a large number of moles. Such preventive action may help you avoid developing melanoma at all, because any suspect lesion can be removed before it progresses to become malignant melanoma. If you have atypical moles, make sure that other family members are carefully checked too. And if someone in your family (a parent, grandparent, aunt, uncle, brother, sister, or child) has ever had melanoma, you should be examined for the presence of atypical moles or melanoma. If there is a tendency toward congenital moles in your family or if a child in your family has one, a thorough professional examination of your child should be conducted at puberty, when moles sometimes first assume the atypical appearance. Prevention and surveillance are the best defenses against malignant melanoma. Be sure to conduct self-examinations of your skin regularly, especially in hard-to-see areas.

Remember that even individuals at high risk can reduce their life-threatening risk substantially. Melanoma that is recognized early and removed through simple in-office surgery can result in total cure.

Afterword

An interesting thing happened to me as I began to research and write this book. I became very aware—my husband says "hypervigilant" is more like it—of the effects of the decrease in the ozone layer and of ultraviolet radiation on myself and on everyone else. Not content to wear sunscreen every day, I badgered all those I care about to do the same.

And while I worked on this book, I remembered all the wonderful days I spent in the sunshine as a child, and then again as a parent of young children. Would I do it over again? I wouldn't spend summer days indoors, but I would certainly be more careful. I would know how to protect my skin and eyes, and I would stay out of the sun while it is at its strongest.

Sometimes when I look in the mirror and see a few more wrinkles than necessary, I ask myself if those glorious days on the beach were worth them. The answer is no. I could have enjoyed the warmth and glow of the sun and still protected myself. But I remember more of my mother's good advice: "Don't look back too often or you'll trip over your feet as you walk forward."

So when summer comes around and our eleven grandchildren join us in the backyard for fun and sun, there will be sunscreen, hats, and shade to go around.

I now feel completely safe in the sun. You should too.

Mary-Ellen Siegel

Appendix: Guide to Further Information

To Find a Dermatologist, Plastic Surgeon, or Ophthalmologist

Your personal physician or local hospital should be able to recommend a dermatologist, plastic surgeon, or ophthalmologist. Alternatively, you can call your local medical society and ask for a referral. Most medical societies give three names in response to such requests. The *Directory of Medical Specialists* lists all physicians who are American Board Certified Specialists. A new directory, or a supplement to the existing one, is issued every two years. Many local libraries have the book, or the librarian can suggest where to find it. Dermatologists, ophthalmologists, and plastic surgeons are listed (by community) as such. The credentials or affiliations of any American Board Certified Specialists can be checked by consulting the alphabetical index of the directory.

Most states maintain a medical directory of all state-licensed physicians; this directory is usually available in local libraries. The American Medical Association (AMA) also publishes a directory of physicians in the United States. These books are good sources of information about physicians.

You can also contact the professional organization to which most board-certified dermatologists belong:

American Academy of Dermatology
P.O. Box 4014
Schaumburg, IL 60168-4014
(708)330-0230

Similarly, you can contact the professional organization to which most physicians certified by the American Board of Plastic Surgery belong:

American Society of Plastic and Reconstructive Surgeons
444 East Algonquin Road
Arlington Heights, IL 60005
(708)228-9900

To find an ophthalmologist, you can contact the professional organization to which most board-certified ophthalmologists belong:

American Academy of Ophthalmology
655 Beach
San Francisco, CA 94109
(415)561-8500

Information for Those Concerned About Skin Cancer

Perhaps the best single source of specific materials on skin cancer is the Skin Cancer Foundation:

Skin Cancer Foundation
245 Fifth Avenue
New York, NY 10016
(212)725-5176

This nonprofit organization offers a wide variety of publications on the prevention, diagnosis, and treatment of skin cancer. People are asked to send a stamped, self-addressed envelope for published materials. They also will provide you with their ever-changing current list of sunscreen products that have been approved by the foundation's photobiology committee and thus have received the Skin Cancer Foundation's Seal of Recommendation.

Information for Cancer Patients and Their Families

Cancer Information Service

The National Cancer Institute supports cancer research throughout the country and also conducts their own research. Of special interest and extreme usefulness to cancer patients and their families is the NCI's information and referral service, called the Cancer Information Service (CIS) of the National Cancer Institute. The CIS can be reached toll-free. In the continental United States, call 1-(800)-4-CANCER. In Hawaii (on Oahu), call 524-1234; call this number collect from neighboring islands.

This nationwide telephone service answers questions from cancer patients and their families. When you call the CIS number you are connected with the regional office serving your area. Counselors there can give you accurate, personalized answers to your cancer-related questions, tell you about various community agencies and services available, and identify the medical library nearest to your home. Upon request, they will give you the name of the closest Comprehensive Cancer Center and tell you where any experimental programs for skin cancer (including melanoma) are being conducted. If you wish, they will guide you in finding a private physician, and in some instances they can give you the names of specific physicians.

Spanish-speaking staff members are available to callers from most parts of the country.

PDQ

The NCI computerized system known as PDQ (Physician Data Query) gives doctors quick and easy access to the latest treatment information for most types of cancer, to descriptions of clinical trials that are open for patient entry, and to names of organizations and physicians involved in cancer care. Many physicians are able to access PDQ from their office computers, but others use a medical library. Ask your local librarian if a medical library in your community has this service and if it is available to you.

Another NCI resource is the Office of Cancer Communications:

Office of Cancer Communications
National Cancer Institute (NCI)
National Institutes of Health
Building 31, room 10A24
Bethesda, MD 20892

Write to it for a list of available written materials on cancer in general, on skin cancers or melanoma, or on any other specific cancer.

The American Cancer Society (ACS) offers many services as well:

American Cancer Society
1599 Clifton Road, N.E.
Atlanta, GA 30329
(510)465-2345
1-800-ACS-2345

In addition to funding research, the American Cancer Society sponsors several patient-support programs. Many local ACS divisions and units can help with transportation to radiation or other medical appointments, and some can help you find and finance care in the home.

Look in your local telephone directory for the nearest American Cancer Society division or unit. Counselors can give you information about locally available services and can provide you with various written materials. If you are unable to find the local division, contact the national office.

If you live in Canada, consult the Canadian Cancer Society:

The Canadian Cancer Society
10 Alcorn Avenue
Toronto, Ontario, Canada M4V3B1
(416)961-7223

It offers many of the same services as the American Cancer

Society and maintains divisions in every province. Check the telephone directory for the division nearest you, or call the national office.

To Find Help in Coping with Diagnosis and Treatment for Skin Cancer

Your physician may be able to refer you to a social worker, psychologist, or psychiatrist experienced in helping people cope with diagnosis and treatment of cancer, and with their changing or changed appearance. Self-help groups, sometimes professionally led, may also be available in your community. If your physician can't give you a recommendation, call the social work or psychiatry department of your local hospital or the American or Canadian Cancer Society nearest you for a referral.

Index

Note: Organizations listed in the appendix are not covered in the index.